WITHDRAWN

PULITZER'S
POST-DISPATCH
1 8 7 8 - 1 8 8 3

PULITZER'S

POST-DISPATCH

1878-1883

BY JULIAN S. RAMMELKAMP

PRINCETON, NEW JERSEY

PRINCETON UNIVERSITY PRESS

1967

T O   M A B E L

Preface

In December 1890 the nation's most fabulously successful newspaper dedicated an imposing building on New York's Park Row—a monument to the new age of mass circulation metropolitan journalism. To commemorate the event it issued a pamphlet which said that "the foundation of the New York World was laid in St. Louis. . . . The battle of new ideas and new theories of journalism was fought there under the banner of the Post-Dispatch."[1] Thus did Joseph Pulitzer, whom modern journalists account America's greatest editor,[2] acknowledge the importance of his four and a half years as publisher of the Post-Dispatch where he developed the basic outlines of the style of journalism with which on the World he was to revolutionize the American newspaper scene.

Pulitzer's debt to his St. Louis experience has always been known and often alluded to. Yet, because it was a prologue to his editorship of the more important World, biographers and newspaper historians have never examined very closely the Post-Dispatch between 1878 and 1883, the years of his St. Louis apprenticeship. It is one purpose of this study to fill this gap, to examine the origins of Pulitzer's "sensational" journalism for which he has been so lavishly praised and damned.

A second purpose emerged during the course of my investigation. It relates to a more general significance of Pulitzer's journalism. The publisher is famous for having been a crusader for public causes, a reputation the New York World long enjoyed, and which is still a hallmark of the St. Louis Post-Dispatch. Of course, to a large degree, crusading was simply good newspaper business—it attracted circulation—and it became a part of Pulitzer's sensationalism. For, although he preferred not to think of himself that way, Pulitzer was preeminently a businessman who happened to be in the business of journalism.[3] But beyond this, this Hungarian immigrant was imbued with an idealism about democratic self-government and individual opportunity which prompted him, once he sloughed off his ambitions for a political career, to dedicate his journals to reform, to making

---

[1] *The World, Its History and Its New Home* (pamphlet, New York, 1890), p. 94.

[2] *Editor & Publisher*, LXVIII (July 21, 1934), 60.

[3] Pulitzer claimed that he "never spent an hour at any one time in the business office," and one historian declares Pulitzer was "indifferent" to the "details" of newspaper publishing. (Willard Grosvenor Bleyer, *Main Currents in the History of American Journalism* [Boston, 1927], p. 332.) This legend, sedulously cultivated by Pulitzer, is grossly inaccurate.

democracy work in the new industrial–urban milieu which arose in the post-Civil War era. As such, he was representative of a breed becoming increasingly important, for the years when Pulitzer inaugurated the *Post-Dispatch* were also years when a middle class movement of reform was germinating in St. Louis as elsewhere in the burgeoning cities of the nation. This movement, which has been neglected in the past by historians preoccupied with the farm revolt boiling up at the same time,[4] has been particularly obscured in the case of cities like St. Louis, located in the midst of the rural ferment. It was a movement reacting against what James Bryce called "the one conspicuous failure of the United States."[5] To clean up and render efficient municipal government, to improve urban living and facilitate trade, and to curb the growth of monopoly that was threatening economic freedom for the small businessman, the *Post-Dispatch* devoted its energies—and fashioned a highly effective brand of crusading journalism. It became the spokesman for middle class reformism in St. Louis.

In using such terms as "middle class," "urban middle class," and "middle class reformism" I realize I am treading on treacherous ground. The terms are at best imprecise in a society such as ours. Certainly, however, at its core an urban middle class contained small merchants—such as Pulitzer was in these years—shopkeepers, professional men, and an increasing body of salaried employees in new large businesses. At its further limits it could also include more substantial businessmen and, on the other end, even salesmen and clerks. Above all, it embraced the mass of property-owning residents of a large city.[6] Pulitzer's *Post-Dispatch* had them in mind when it referred, as it frequently did, to "the honest merchant and quiet citizen." It was to and for them that it principally spoke in conducting its crusades for the public good, voicing their preconceptions, their morality, their resentments and frustrations, and in so doing often clashing with rural dissidents outstate.

The significance of singling out this element in the movements of reform which took root in the late 1870s and 1880s is that this class, amorphous as it was, was a potent force in the growing urban communities. Moreover, as the cities grew, so did this class. Thus, its

---

[4] This neglect is in the process of being corrected. See, for example, Arthur Mann, *Yankee Reformers in the Urban Age* (Cambridge, Mass., 1954).

[5] James Bryce, *The American Commonwealth*, 3rd ed. (New York, 1901), I, 637.

[6] Richard Hofstadter, *The Age of Reform: From Bryan to F. D. R.* (New York, 1955), pp. 99, 215-17, 222-24, discusses the rise and characteristics of the middle class. See also, Christopher Lasch, *The New Radicalism in America, 1889-1963: The Intellectual as a Social Type* (New York, 1965), pp. xii-xiii, for additional comments.

voice began to be heard in national politics. To be sure, like all classes it was inclined to view the ills of the new age in terms of its own needs and predilections, and basically at first its concern for other segments of society, particularly their growing economic problems, was not great. Also, it was confused. Sometimes, as is evident in the *Post-Dispatch,* it hankered for the good old days of the primacy of small economic and political units, and some of its ideas of reform harked back to the past. But almost in spite of itself, if Pulitzer's paper was any indication, it began to come to terms with an increasingly interdependent society and gradually to advocate reforms calling for community and governmental action, in the process tending to modify the absoluteness of old-style individualism. It even began to express concern for the plight of the poor. These developments also came to interest me in this study of the *Post-Dispatch.*

During the course of my investigation I have had the support of many persons whose patience has been as remarkable as their generosity. I launched upon this project at the suggestion of the late Professor Arthur M. Schlesinger, Sr., who blended exactness in scholarship with warm and tolerant encouragement. I completed it with the help and direction of Professor Arthur M. Schlesinger, Jr., who, in spite of a multitude of scholarly and public activities, was generous with his time and advice. Louis M. Starr of the Columbia School of Journalism also read my manuscript, giving me the benefit of detailed advice and saving me from many errors. I hasten to add that these men did not necessarily agree with my conclusions nor are they responsible for whatever deficiences still remain.

In St. Louis, too, I owe many debts of gratitude. In particular, I wish to thank Irving Dilliard, for several years editor of the editorial page of the *Post-Dispatch* and presently at Princeton University. He is a rare combination of journalist and historian, and spent many hours with me discussing the history of the newspaper. Chief among many others then or earlier on the *Post-Dispatch* whom I plagued with questions were Frank A. Behymer, Richard J. Collins, Byron J. Dietrich, Harry M. Duhring, Albert G. Lincoln, Mrs. Frances Cabanne Saportas, and Daniel R. Fitzpatrick. The publisher, Joseph Pulitzer, III, saw to it I had the freedom of the newspaper's facilities, and has graciously given me permission to quote from the correspondence in the Pulitzer Papers at Columbia University and the Library of Congress. Miss Gertrude McDonald, granddaughter of John A. Dillon, co-founder of the *Post-Dispatch,* was generous with her time and information, as were others conversant with the history of St. Louis and its newspapers, including especially the late Lee

Meriwether and Daniel J. W. McAuliffe, onetime managing editor of the St. Louis *Republic*. Because we were engaged in similar projects, Professor James W. Markham, now at the University of Iowa, and I exchanged much useful information.

I have had the stimulus of reading a manuscript, soon to be published, by Professor George Juergens of Amherst College. It is an excellent analysis of the style and policies of the New York *World* in the middle 1880s. His ideas and mine as to the factors influencing Pulitzer's journalism do not always jibe—in part, I think, because Pulitzer, so sensitive to the public, realized he must play to a larger, lower class audience in New York to win a mass circulation. In any event, there was a continuing evolution in his style beyond the foundations laid in St. Louis.

In a more general way I wish to mention Professors Joe Patterson Smith of Illinois College, James B. Hedges of Brown University, both deceased, Frederick Merk of Harvard University, and Carl Bridenbaugh of Brown University. Their high standards of scholarship and inspirational qualities produced a greater impact upon me than they perhaps knew. For a practical knowledge of the newspaper world, acquired as a reporter on the Jacksonville, Illinois, *Journal-Courier*, I am grateful to the publishers, William A. and Robert A. Fay. Cecil Tendick, the managing editor, taught me about reporting, an occupation which on smaller papers is still much the same as it was in the early 1880s on the *Post-Dispatch*.

I availed myself of the facilities of a number of libraries and the generous help of numerous librarians. In the St. Louis area I used the Public Library, the library of the *Post-Dispatch,* the Mercantile Library, the Washington University libraries, and the library of the Missouri Historical Society. At Columbia, Missouri were the State Historical Library and the library of the University of Missouri School of Journalism. I also used extensively the Columbia University Library, the library of the Columbia School of Journalism, Widener Library at Harvard University, the Library of Congress, and the Albion College Library, Albion, Michigan. I wish in particular to thank Edward MacConomy, Assistant Chief of the Research and Bibliography Division, Library of Congress; Miss Elizabeth Tindall, St. Louis Public Library; Roy King of the *Post-Dispatch;* the interlibrary loan staff of the Washington University libraries; Charles Van Ravenswaay, formerly director of the Missouri Historical Society; and Miss Elizabeth Hance, Albion College Library. Roy A. Grisham, Jr., of the Princeton University Press reduced my manuscript to order and offered many valuable suggestions.

Above all, my wife, Mabel Tippitt Rammelkamp, deserves mention. Her multiple role of chief critic, co-researcher, typist, and encourager, made this book possible.

Julian S. Rammelkamp

Albion College, Michigan
April 1966

Contents

PULITZER'S
POST-DISPATCH
1878-1883

CHAPTER I

A Newspaper is Born

"Gentlemen," cried the good-natured auctioneer from his perch on a borrowed chair. "I now propose to sell to you the *Evening Dispatch,* a paper that will live when all the other evening papers are dead."

Laughter greeted this bit of hyperbole, common to public auctions of bankrupt property. A score of newspapermen, local politicians, and idlers were clustered at the Fourth Street entrance to the great-domed courthouse to witness the sale of the latest casualty of St. Louis's rough-and-tumble journalism. It was an uncomfortable day, chilly and damp, typical of St. Louis in mid-December, but the crowd had gathered early to speculate on who might bid for the property and what it would bring.[1]

After sixteen years of uncertain existence, the *Evening Dispatch* had finally succumbed in the fall of 1878. Since the paper's founding in 1862 its history had been "a long record of failure and loss"; all told, more than $250,000 had been sunk into the enterprise, $100,000 in the past four years alone, but to no purpose. In 1877, in a desperate effort to keep it alive, the owners, Wolcott and Hume, had secured a $15,000 mortgage on the property. In addition, there were accumulated debts of $12,000 for supplies. The paper's old flatbed press was battered and worn, and its type and office equipment were broken down. For a month before its final crisis the paper had been perfunctorily issued to protect a contract with the city for legal advertising, an arrangement which provided its only steady income. It was so poorly edited that in the days preceding the November elections the names of candidates who had withdrawn from local contests were not even deleted from its columns, and much of its scanty news was stolen from outraged competitors who complained that such practices "would bring a blush to the cheek of the heathen Chinee." Worst of all, fewer than one thousand subscribers remained, a handful of hardy souls who did not object to stale news and atrocious editing. In short, the *Evening Dispatch* was a hopeless wreck.[2] In view of

---

[1] St. Louis *Evening Post,* Dec. 9, 1878; St. Louis *Globe-Democrat,* Dec. 10, 1878.

[2] St. Louis *Post-Dispatch,* Jan. 12, 1882; *Globe-Democrat,* Dec. 10, 1878; *Evening Post,* Aug. 29, 1878, Oct. 3, 1878, Oct. 25, 1878, Nov. 18, 1878, Dec. 7, 1878; George S. Johns, *Joseph Pulitzer: Early Life in St. Louis and His Founding and Conduct of the Post-Dispatch up to 1883* (reprinted from the *Missouri Historical Review* [1932], St. Louis, p. 49.)

1

this, the Circuit Court of St. Louis declared the paper bankrupt and ordered it sold at public auction at noon, December 9, 1878, to satisfy the creditors.[3]

The bantering newspapermen in front of the courthouse differed over what the *Dispatch* might bring. John A. Dillon, the dignified editor of the *Evening Post*, thought bidding might go as high as $9,000, although he considered the paper's debts too great to justify a bid from him. His estimate was based on the *Dispatch's* only two assets, the contract to publish the city's printing and, more important, an exclusive, afternoon Western Associated Press franchise, almost indispensable if a journal hoped to flourish. His own *Evening Post* lacked both.[4] But gruff William Hyde, longtime editor of the powerful *Missouri Republican,* voiced a common opinion when he growled, "I would not give a damn for it." [5]

Just before the sale began a "tall, graceful figure" with a "pale, Mephistophelian face" arrived on the edge of the crowd, where he was greeted with good-natured sallies from numerous old friends. Joseph Pulitzer had returned to St. Louis a bridegroom only a few weeks before, apparently to establish himself in law practice after pursuing a restless, somewhat rootless existence for a decade as a reporter, editor, and politician. St. Louis had seen little of him for three years, however, as he had paid only flying visits to the town between extended voyages to Europe, a fling as Washington correspondent for Charles A. Dana's New York *Sun,* and a brief try at law practice in the national capital. Ostensibly, the youngish Mr. Pulitzer—he was thirty-one—had casually wandered over from a nearby attorney's office to witness the auction of the *Dispatch.*[6]

Conversation ceased as all eyes turned towards the auctioneer. Following a description of the property under the hammer and announcements concerning the mortgages burdening it, the *Dispatch*

---

[3] Disposed of at the same time was the *Morning Journal*, a similarly bankrupt sheet owned by Wolcott & Hume. *Globe-Democrat*, Dec. 10, 1878.

[4] *Globe-Democrat*, Dec. 10, 1878; *Evening Post*, Aug. 29, 1878; Victor Rosewater, *History of Co-operative News-gathering in the United States* (New York, 1930), pp. 147-56, describes the unsuccessful attempts by competitors to break the monopolistic grip of the Western Associated Press on American journalism west of the Appalachians in the 1870s. The *Evening Post* was affiliated with the weak and ephemeral National Associated Press.

[5] *Evening Post*, Dec. 9, 1878.

[6] Don C. Seitz, *Joseph Pulitzer: His Life and Letters* (New York, 1924), pp. 87-97. This is the standard biography. See also, James Wyman Barrett, *Joseph Pulitzer and His World* (New York, 1941), pp. 48-49, which is more vivid, but less satisfactory. Oswald Garrison Villard, "Joseph Pulitzer," *Dictionary of American Biography* (New York, 1933), XV, 260-63, is an informed sketch. *Globe-Democrat*, Dec. 10, 1878; *Evening Post*, Dec. 9, 1878.

was placed on the block. "How much?" called the auctioneer. "Who will make the first offer?"

Simon J. Arnold, a clerk in the municipal tax collector's office, bid $1,000. There was whispered speculation that he was representing City Collector Rosenblatt and Chauncey I. Filley, important figures in local Republican politics. Arnold countered offers from one or two others until he reached a bid of $2,500. Then, from the shadows of the hallway behind the auctioneer a voice called "2,600." This set off a new flurry of bidding until the unseen stranger topped by $100 Arnold's final offer of $3,000. The tax clerk retired from the scene, and the paper was declared sold.

But when the auctioneer turned to obtain the high bidder's name, he had vanished. After an angry expostulation at this violation of auction ethics, Arnold was summoned and awarded the *Dispatch* for $2,500, his last offer before the bogus bids from the hallway.[7]

Who had actually bought the paper? When questioned, Arnold said he had served as the agent of Joseph Pulitzer, the real purchaser. But when the interested spectators turned to ask him, Pulitzer had disappeared. It was not until evening, in the dining room of the Lindell, St. Louis's leading hotel, that a reporter from the *Globe-Democrat* at last cornered him. Delighting in the role of mystery man, Pulitzer blandly denied that he had had anything to do with the transaction at the courthouse. The reporter persisted, pointing out that Arnold "told me distinctly that he had purchased the paper for you." "Did he?" was the soft-spoken reply. "Generous man."

Exasperated, the reporter told his editor that "no one better understands the use of language—to conceal one's thoughts—than Mr. Pulitzer. He parries the question like a skillful fencer, and it is as hard to pin him to a point as it is an eel."[8]

The editor of the *Globe-Democrat,* laconic and formidable Joseph B. McCullagh, must have allowed himself an inward smile. Dismissing the frustrated reporter, he turned to his desk and wrote an editorial paragraph for the next morning's edition.

The fine Pulitzerian diplomacy which has so often shrouded coming events in the dim twilight of uncertainty, is now brought into requisition to hide from mortal vision the fate of our evening contemporary, the *Dispatch.* But we think we detect the coming journalist behind the evasive interviewee, and behold in Mr. Pulitzer the future wielder of the destinies of that newspaper.[9]

[7] *Evening Post,* Dec. 9, 1878; *Globe-Democrat,* Dec. 10, 1878.
[8] *Globe-Democrat,* Dec. 10, 1878.
[9] *Ibid.*

McCullagh was not merely speculating; he had definite information. Although it was true that the scraggly-bearded Pulitzer had indeed come back to St. Louis with the thought of hanging out a lawyer's shingle, he had been persuaded by Charles P. Johnson, a brilliant criminal attorney in St. Louis, to abandon the plan and reestablish himself in journalism, a field he knew better. Probably Pulitzer was already half persuaded, because more than once during the past three years he had made inquiries about purchasing papers, both in St. Louis and New York. In any case, when he heard the *Evening Dispatch* was for sale, Pulitzer had sought the advice of an old friend in the St. Louis newspaper field, Daniel M. Houser, part owner and business manager of the highly successful *Globe-Democrat*. For "several evenings" prior to the sale Pulitzer had been closeted with Houser, figuring how he might purchase the *Dispatch* and nurse it back to life. He informed Houser that he had only $5,000, a slender amount for an aspiring publisher. But Houser, who knew his man, encouraged him, and Pulitzer decided to make the plunge. He was well aware of the risks, but no one then or later ever had reason to accuse Joseph Pulitzer of faint-heartedness.[10]

It is little wonder that this young man had faith in himself. Motivated by intense ambition, guided by an alert intelligence, and driven by a violent, almost neurotic energy, Joseph Pulitzer had by 1878 come a long way from the day early in October 1865, when, as a penniless and friendless German-speaking immigrant, he had arrived in St. Louis. Yet Pulitzer was not a typical newcomer. Born the son of a Jewish merchant of refinement and substantial means in Mako, Hungary, in 1847, he had received an excellent education before coming to America. At the age of seventeen, seized by wanderlust, he had left home to seek a career in the military forces of the Austrian Empire, just then embroiled over the Schleswig-Holstein question. He was rejected by the army because of weak eyes and a seemingly frail constitution, but was persuaded in Hamburg by one of a swarm of Union Army agents on the Continent to come to America to enlist in the struggle to put down the Slave Power. Perhaps a love of freedom, which became so much a part of his outlook in later years, had something to do with his decision, though more likely the youthful spirit of adventure determined his course.[11]

At the end of the war, following a year's service with the Army of

---

[10] John Norris to Joseph Pulitzer, March 10, 1900, Pulitzer Papers, Columbia University. The Papers are deposited in two places, Columbia University and the Library of Congress; hereafter they will be identified (UC) and (LC). Johns, *Pulitzer*, pp. 47-49; Seitz, *Pulitzer*, pp. 87-97, 99.

[11] Seitz, pp. 40-43. William Robinson Reynolds, "Joseph Pulitzer," unpubl. diss (Columbia, 1950), pp. 1-3. This is the most reliable study of Pulitzer.

the Potomac, Pulitzer was discharged in New York. He spoke no English and could find no work in the teeming metropolis, so he turned westward towards St. Louis where he had heard there was a large German population. There he hoped to find the congenial surroundings he needed to make a start in his adopted land.[12] Probably by catching rides aboard freights as so many unemployed ex-soldiers were doing in the fall of 1865, he reached the left bank of the unbridged Mississippi at East St. Louis, the railhead for roads from the east. In his own words, "I had not a cent. I was hungry and shivering with cold. I had no dinner, no overcoat. The lights of St. Louis looked like a promised land to me." Hailing two German-speaking deckhands aboard a ferryboat coming into the slip, the wanderer was given a job firing the ferry's boiler the remainder of the night to pay his passage to the Missouri shore. "I don't remember how many trips back and forth across the river I made that night, but the next day I went ashore and walked the streets of St. Louis." [13]

At first Pulitzer existed on odd jobs. He was a mule hostler at a military post, a stevedore on the riverfront, and a waiter in a German beer garden.[14] But his driving ambition soon asserted itself. Taught by his European training to value the importance of a disciplined intellect, he sought out the Mercantile Library where he spent his spare time reading omniverously, both in German and, much more painfully, in English. His approach to knowledge was practical. "What can you get from that?" he once inquired of an instructor in philosophy at the local high school.[15]

Pulitzer's energy and intelligence, combined with determination and resourcefulness, brought him in a few months' time to the notice of a pair of prominent lawyers, Charles P. Johnson and William Patrick, who hired him as a messenger boy.[16] Through them he was assigned the difficult task of plunging into the Ozark wilderness southwest of St. Louis in the dead of winter to register a new rail-

---

12 Although Johns and Seitz claimed that he came to St. Louis to learn English because he thought no Germans lived there, Pulitzer had served in a German-speaking regiment during the war and must have heard about the well-known Teutonic community there. Reynolds, "Pulitzer," pp. 3-4, indicates Pulitzer may have even visited St. Louis before he enlisted in the army.

13 Seitz, *Pulitzer*, pp. 50-51.

14 *Post-Dispatch*, May 12, 1881.

15 Denton J. Snider, *The St. Louis Movement in Philosophy, Literature, Education, Psychology, with Chapters of Autobiography* (St. Louis, 1920), p. 163; Reynolds, "Pulitzer," pp. 7-11; Johns, *Pulitzer*, pp. 9-11.

16 Johnson was a former circuit attorney of St. Louis and lieutenant governor of Missouri. Patrick had once been United States district attorney. Both men were well known and afterwards Pulitzer's fast friends. Seitz, *Pulitzer*, p. 53; William A. Kelsoe, *St. Louis Reference Record* (St. Louis [1927]), p. 64.

road charter in each of the county courthouses along the proposed right-of-way. Impressed with the efficiency with which he carried out the assignment, Patrick offered Pulitzer the opportunity to read law in his office. In the spring of 1867, after only a few weeks of industrious study, he satisfied the lax requirements of the time and was admitted to the bar. His practice never went beyond serving papers and acting as a notary public, but this was a long step forward; Pulitzer was acquiring friends in the English-speaking community.[17]

It was in the flourishing German-speaking society of St. Louis, however, that he at last found the avenue that led to success. The Mercantile Library's chess room was a favorite rendezvous for the group of German-American intellectuals who were the leaders of the city's Teutonic element. Two of these were Carl Schurz, well-known politician and soldier and now a publisher of the high-minded *Westliche Post,* and his associate, the gentle Dr. Emil Preetorius. Pulitzer was drawn to them, and they, in turn, looked with favor upon the newcomer. One day in 1868 when the *Westliche Post* needed a local reporter, Schurz and Preetorius offered the job to their young friend, who, though utterly inexperienced, possessed the necessary qualities.[18]

From the start he was "exasperatingly inquisitive" and "so industrious . . . that he became a positive annoyance to others who felt less inclined to work. . . ." His competitors attempted to cure him by sending him on wild chases to remote parts of the city, but "Joey" only smiled and never relaxed his efforts. "He was quick, intelligent and enthusiastic, but of all his qualities the most notable was his determination to accomplish whatever he set out to do." He was a "tall, gaunt looking specimen," quite evidently in want on his meager pay. But his pale, angular features were seen everywhere, and newsworthy St. Louisans became accustomed to close questioning by the solemn reporter with the cheap pair of glasses perched on an over-prominent nose. Playful rivals loved to twist his nose while saying mockingly, "pull-it-sir." [19]

Pulitzer quickly became invaluable to his office. Within two years, with Schurz in Washington as a United States Senator and Preetorius ailing, he was in practical charge of what had been a slow-moving *Westliche Post.* He made it a live-wire newspaper from which the English-language press translated many a scoop. This experience,

---

[17] Johns, *Pulitzer,* pp. 11-14.
[18] *Ibid.,* pp. 14-15.
[19] *Ibid.,* pp. 15-19.

showing what resourceful energy could do, remained a bright memory, strongly influencing Pulitzer's later career.[20]

His association with the *Westliche Post* was significant in another way: it introduced Pulitzer to American politics, especially reform politics. A plunge into the political arena was almost inevitable, since journalism in St. Louis still was little more than an adjunct to partisanship. Like most of his German friends, Pulitzer became a Republican, but, following the lead of the *Westliche Post,* he was far from the thick-and-thin party server that most editors were in that day. Carl Schurz and Emil Preetorius had been "Forty-Eighters," members of that high-minded band of revolutionaries who had fled from tyranny in Germany imbued with ideals of freedom and self-government, and in America had joined the new Republican Party during the upheaval over slavery because it was dedicated to liberty. But by 1870 they had become disillusioned with the party's policies on both state and national levels. To them, the excesses of reconstruction in Washington and Jefferson City were trampling on individual liberty and making a mockery of self-government.[21] Therefore, as co-publishers of the *Westliche Post,* Schurz and Preetorius campaigned against "Grantism" and condemned Missouri's Drake Constitution which had been framed by the Radicals to exclude ex-Confederates from the franchise.[22] In St. Louis a corrupt Radical municipal administration also damaged the ideals of local self-government which the editors of the *Westliche Post* held so dear. In emulating his employers Pulitzer conceived a fidelity to the principles of a free society outweighing mere party loyalty.[23]

Nevertheless, young Pulitzer early developed political ambitions which were to remain with him for a long time. Late in 1869 a special election was held to fill a vacancy in the lower house of the state legislature from a strongly Democratic district in St. Louis. Although he was given little chance to win, the Republicans nominated Pulitzer, and after a campaign conducted with characteristic energy he scored an unexpected triumph. In January 1870 he took his seat at Jefferson City and immediately threw himself into the

---

[20] *Ibid.,* pp. 17, 21; Reynolds, "Pulitzer," pp. 15-16.

[21] Carl Wittke, *We Who Built America* (New York, 1939), pp. 255-56.

[22] Schurz came to St. Louis in 1867 to join forces with Preetorius as co-owner of the *Westliche Post.* See Claude Fuess, *Carl Schurz: Reformer* (American Political Leaders) (New York, 1932), p. 142.

[23] Walter Williams and Floyd C. Shoemaker, *Missouri: Mother of the West,* 2 vols. (Chicago, 1930), II, 209, 569. Thomas S. Barclay, "Emil Preetorius," *Dictionary of American Biography,* 21 vols. (New York, 1935), XV, 185; J. Thomas Scharf, *History of St. Louis City and County,* 2 vols. (Philadelphia, 1883), I, 941-42; Fuess, *Schurz,* p. 171; Catherine Virginia Soraghan, "The History of St. Louis, 1865-1876," unpub. M.A. diss. (Washington University, 1936), p. 50.

turbulent debates of a western legislature. His greatest efforts were spent in seeking to reform St. Louis's municipal administration. To Pulitzer's mind, St. Louisans were the victims of a travesty upon self-government. Their local government was dominated by a county court, several of whose members were chosen by the voters outside the city. This division of powers not only violated the spirit of self-government but invited corruption. Grafting officials escaped punishment in the labyrinth of divided responsibility, and a ring of boodlers fastened itself on the city. Under the leadership of the *Westliche Post,* Pulitzer and several other German-American legislators introduced a bill to bring the county court under the control of the city. But opposing lobbyists blocked its passage. Frustrated and angry, the excitable Pulitzer became involved in a noisy shooting scrape with one of the lobbyists, a member of the local boodling ring. Already the politician-journalist's brand of reform was acquiring an enduring characteristic—the amelioration of urban problems—and in the process he conceived a lasting dislike for rural legislators who refused to give St. Louis her freedom.[24]

As one of Carl Schurz's lieutenants, Pulitzer in 1870 participated in the Liberal Republican revolt in Missouri which overthrew the Radicals by combining with the Union Democrats to elect B. Gratz Brown governor. As editor he conducted a vigorous campaign in the *Westliche Post,* lining up the German vote for Brown. The campaign imbedded even more deeply in the young man's maturing outlook the principles of Liberal Republicanism: an end to vindictive policies of reconstruction and devotion to local self-government.[25]

After the election, the Liberal Republicans completed the destruction of the Radicals in Missouri by repealing the reconstruction laws. Following this success, the Liberal movement spread to the national arena in 1872. As Schurz's protégé Pulitzer took an active part in the effort to destroy "Grantism." Although only twenty-five, he had by now become a member of the coterie of German-American and native politicians who were chosen delegates from Missouri to the national Liberal convention in Cincinnati where he took an active— if minor—role in the proceedings, loyally supporting the candidacy

24 Johns, *Pulitzer,* pp. 21-28; Reynolds, "Pulitzer," pp. 20-23; Soraghan, "History of St. Louis," pp. 30-31, 41-43, 46; Thomas S. Barclay, *The Movement for Municipal Home Rule in St. Louis* (Columbia, Mo., 1943), pp. 59-60, 63.

25 Reynolds, "Pulitzer," pp. 24-25; Johns, *Pulitzer,* pp. 28-29; Williams and Shoemaker, *Missouri,* pp. 192-225, gives a general account of the Radical era and its downfall in Missouri. See also Thomas S. Barclay, *The Liberal Republican Movement in Missouri* (Columbia, Mo., 1926), p. 282; and a detailed account of the overthrow of the Radicals and the election of Brown in Norma L. Peterson, *Freedom and Franchise: The Political Career of B. Gratz Brown* (Columbia, Mo., 1965), ch. 13.

8

of B. Gratz Brown for the presidential nomination.[26] Following the convention, whose choice was Horace Greeley, Pulitzer loyally stumped the German-American communities of Missouri, Ohio, and Indiana for the ticket. He spoke in his native tongue since he did not yet have command of English. In this campaign he embraced the Liberal Republican ticket and principles with a fervor typical of his nature and acquired a reputation as an effective orator. He was becoming an ambitious politician.[27]

The election was a debacle for the Liberal Republicans, especially in Missouri. Not only was Greeley beaten, but in Missouri, where the ex-Confederates were reenfranchised, the Democrats captured the governorship. Discouraged, Schurz and Preetorius were fearful lest the catastrophe engulf the *Westliche Post*. To fortify it they offered their vigorous young editor a part interest in the concern. But proprietorship was brief. The senior partners soon discovered that Pulitzer was difficult to work with. Determined to dominate the establishment, he was headstrong and independent, a poor partner. The will to dominate whatever he undertook was characteristic of Pulitzer. Schurz and Preetorius soon repented of their earlier decision and made him the handsome offer of $30,000 for his holdings. Always canny, the young man accepted.[28]

Financially independent for the first time and well known in St. Louis as a journalist-politician, Pulitzer by 1873 had come a long way in a remarkably few years. He was now self assured and somewhat formal, but with close acquaintances still unaffectedly friendly. At work he remained the immigrant boy struggling to make his mark: humorlessly ambitious, eager, persistent, full of nervous energy.[29] A practical idealist, Pulitzer generalized from his experiences: anybody with energy and determination could succeed in America. The only necessity, he believed, was to keep opportunity open to all comers.

After 1873 there was an uncertain interlude. He went to Europe for a rest. But soon he was back looking for an occupation to contain

---

[26] Schurz himself supported Charles Francis Adams. Fuess, *Schurz*, pp. 185-86. Brown was selected for Vice President. Peterson, *Freedom and Franchise*, ch. 15.

[27] Reynolds, "Pulitzer," pp. 26-27; Johns, *Pulitzer*, pp. 29-30.

[28] Seitz, *Pulitzer*, pp. 74-76; Johns, *op. cit.* pp. 31-32. Neither author, surprisingly, places much emphasis on Pulitzer's will to dominate as a cause for his departure, though this early became a striking part of his nature. Schurz wryly remarked later that if Pulitzer had remained in partnership much longer, he would have owned the whole paper—a prophetic statement. Bleyer, *Main Currents* (Boston, 1927), p. 324.

[29] Johns, *Pulitzer*, pp. 31-34; *Globe-Democrat*, Dec. 10, 1878; James Creelman, "Joseph Pulitzer—Master Journalist," *Pearson's Magazine*, XXI (March 1909), 238-39.

his energies and ambitions. Politics remained his primary interest, but now and again he took a fling at journalism. Slowly mastering English, he began to write for the St. Louis *Times* and other papers of the English-language press. As it developed, his literary style was shrill, repetitive, hurried and humorless—harsh to the ear. But it made up in vigor what it lacked in grace. Despite his deficiencies Pulitzer was becoming an effective writer.[30]

During these years, too, occurred a further evolution in Pulitzer's political ideas. After the reenfranchisement of the ex-Confederates in Missouri in 1871 the Democratic Party achieved complete domination of the state, reducing Liberal and Radical Republicans to hopeless minorities. At the same time, postwar rural depression gave rise to the Granger revolt which, in the election of 1874, produced an independent People's Party. The new party framed a platform that called for economic measures to ameliorate the farmer's plight. It demanded a reduction in governmental expenditures, reduced taxes, easing of currency restrictions, and above all, regulation of railroads. Nothing was said about "Grantism" which the Liberals had fought against. A new day in politics was dawning, one involving economic issues brought on by industrialization; but the Liberals had difficulty comprehending it.[31]

Indeed, the frustrated Liberal Republicans broke up. Some returned to the ranks of the regulars, while others like Carl Schurz flirted with the Granger independents. Pulitzer rejected both alternatives. The demise of the Liberals left him, a politician, without a party, but because he was a reformer he could not return to the Republicans who stood for all he was against, nor could he ally himself with the agrarian rebels whom he accused of neglecting the vital issues, which he continued to define as the "alarming centralization of power at Washington," corruption and reconstruction. To him, the farmers' party was a Republican Trojan horse built to trap unsuspecting liberals, for its only result would be to assure the permanence of Grantism by splitting the opposition. In any case, Pulitzer was a product of the urban middle class; and he never trusted the rural radicals. He was suspicious of their attacks on property and contemptuous of their affinity for an inflated currency.

[30] Kelsoe, *St. Louis Reference Record*, p. 39; St. Louis *Times*, Apr. 15, 1908. See characterization of Pulitzer's style by Barrett, *Pulitzer*, p. 76.

[31] Reynolds, "Pulitzer," p. 30; Williams and Shoemaker, *Missouri*, II, 264-78; Edwin C. McReynolds, *Missouri: A History of the Crossroads State* (Norman, Okla., 1962), pp. 287-88. See also, Solon Justus Buck, *The Granger Movement: A Study of Agricultural Organization and Its Political, Economic and Social Manifestations, 1870-1880* (Cambridge, 1933); and Solon J. Buck, *The Agrarian Crusade (The Chronicles of America Series)* (New Haven, 1920), for general accounts.

Above all, farmers led an existence alien to his experience, and he rarely was to understand or sympathize with their complaints. It is true that, like them, he in time came to fear corporate wealth, but more because of its effect on small urban enterprise than agriculture.

In 1874, however, it was the old Liberal issues which were uppermost in Pulitzer's mind, and in support of them he turned to the Democratic Party, which now seemed most hospitable to the principles of decentralization, local self-government and opposition to privilege. In the seventies the Democracy had fallen under the control of Samuel Tilden and his genteel reformers, men whose detestation of "Grantism" made the party similar in view to the now dead Liberal Republican movement. It was logical, therefore, that Pulitzer should have announced during the campaign a change in party allegiance. Like other ex-Liberals, he joined the Democratic Party, whose principles he upheld for the rest of his life.[32]

The next year, as a delegate to the state convention which rewrote Missouri's constitution, Pulitzer returned to the right of St. Louisans to govern themselves against the encroachments of county voters and a rural legislature. Together with a number of other delegates from St. Louis, he supported proposals to separate the city from the county and to allow St. Louis to be governed by a charter giving it a large measure of self-determination. For the most part, these proposals were accepted, although the legislature still retained controls which would cause trouble in the future. In the convention debates Pulitzer displayed hostility towards the rural delegates, making extreme claims for the independence of St. Louis which received no serious consideration.[33]

Now a Democratic politician, Pulitzer was drawn into the national campaign of 1876. Having a better command of English than in 1872 and an increasing prestige among reformers, he addressed large audiences throughout the Middle West in behalf of Samuel Tilden. His itinerary wound up in Cooper Union in New York, where he castigated the evils of the Republican administration. In the bitter dispute over the election which followed, Pulitzer returned to journalism, reporting the deliberations of the Election Commission in Wash-

---

[32] Reynolds, "Pulitzer," pp. 30-32; Johns, *Pulitzer*, pp. 35-37. Eric F. Goldman, *Rendezvous with Destiny* (New York, 1952), pp. 10-28, discusses the views of the Tilden-type Democrats. Sidney Fine, *Laissez Faire and the General-Welfare State: A Study of Conflict in American Thought*, (*University of Michigan History and Political Science Series*, XXIX) (Ann Arbor, Mich., 1956), p. 51, mentions the similarity of thought between the Liberal Republicans and the Tilden Democrats.
[33] Reynolds, "Pulitzer," pp. 32-41; Barclay, *Movement for Municipal Home Rule*, chs. 4-5.

ington for Dana's New York *Sun*. He wrote verbose stories filled with personal observations and biases in the style of the time.[34]

The attractions of Washington became more than political. In the summer of 1878 he was married to Kate Davis, a distant relative of the President of the Confederacy and a beautiful brunette "of the clear gypsy type, with a rich color and great melting eyes." [35] After a honeymoon abroad, where he observed once more the inequalities of European society, Pulitzer brought his gracious bride to St. Louis in the autumn, determined to establish himself in some steady occupation befitting a family man with responsibilities. Still nursing political ambitions, his solution was to enter the highly competitive business of journalism by purchasing the broken-down *Evening Dispatch*.[36]

That he was no unknown when he launched himself in a second try as a newspaper proprietor is obvious from the wide notice his purchase received from the Democratic press of the Middle West. The Paducah, Kentucky *News* declared, "Mr. Pulitzer is one of the ablest men in the country, and will be remembered as the gentleman who made such magnificent speeches in Indiana and Ohio during the last Presidential campaign"; the Kansas City *Times* observed that Pulitzer "is a man of original genius. He does not follow routines and beaten ways. His thoughts and methods are peculiar to himself. . . . He has a strong *penchant* for journalism, and to have a paper of his own. Under his management, the *Dispatch* will not be a commonplace paper." [37]

At noon on the day following the sale the new publisher visited his dilapidated property at 111 North Fifth street and took formal possession. But he was preoccupied. After inspecting the premises and introducing himself to the one or two reporters in the editorial room and to the female compositors upstairs, Pulitzer ordered that the afternoon's two editions were to be printed as usual—if only to prevent forfeiture of the press franchise and the city printing contract. Then Pulitzer disappeared. The mail edition that afternoon numbered 978 copies, which were trundled to the post office nearby in a wheelbarrow by Anthony Brown, a Negro porter who was to remain with the paper for many years. The first copy of the edition hawked on the streets, according to one recollection, was

---

[34] Reynolds, *op.cit.*, pp. 42-54; Paducah (Ky.) *News*, as reprinted in the *Post and Dispatch*, Dec. 31, 1878.

[35] St. Louis *Life*, May 6, 1893.

[36] Johns, *Pulitzer*, pp. 42-47; Reynolds, "Pulitzer," pp. 57-60.

[37] *Post and Dispatch*, Dec. 31, 1878.

bought by Isaac Mason, a steamboat captain, and was sold by a newsboy named "Reddy" Galvin.[38]

The *Dispatch's* two competitors in the English-language field were the *Evening Star* and the *Evening Post*. Both were of recent origin. The *Star* had been founded only two days before Pulitzer bought the *Dispatch,* and its first issues were bright, well edited, promising.[39] The *Evening Post* had been established January 10, 1878, by John Alvarez Dillon, a dignified and cultured man of thirty-four. Like Pulitzer, Dillon was a veteran journalist imbued with liberal sympathies but in almost no other respect did he resemble his more energetic, self-made rival. He was a native of St. Louis and belonged to its most select society. He was the son of Colonel Patrick Dillon, an ambitious Irish immigrant who had parlayed a respectable living as a merchant into a considerable fortune from real estate investments in the growing city.[40] Anxious to establish his children among St. Louis's first families, the elder Dillon raised John carefully. In 1861, instead of enlisting in the army John went east to Harvard College to acquire education and polish.[41] Being talented and serious-minded, he applied himself to his studies, particularly the classics, and acquired a taste for literary and cultural subjects. He returned to St. Louis in 1864 and fulfilled his father's ambitions by marrying into its oldest society. Dillon's bride was Blanche Valle, daughter of one of the handful of French families who were the creme de la creme of St. Louis; her great-grandfather was Jean Baptiste Valle, last French and Spanish commandant at the historic river port of Ste. Genevieve below St. Louis, and her grandfather was Pierre Chouteau, a founder of the trading post of St. Louis. The couple embarked on a honeymoon in Italy where they took up residence in Rome and lived in aristocratic leisure for two years.[42]

---

[38] *Evening Post,* Dec. 10, 1878; *Post-Dispatch,* Dec. 9, 1928, Dec. 18, 1953. Galvin later became famous as a nearly illiterate but ingenious police reporter on several St. Louis journals. (Theodore Dreiser, *A Book About Myself* [New York, 1922], pp. 280-85.) Dreiser's jaundiced opinion of Galvin is considerably watered down by Max Putzel, *The Man in the Mirror: William Marion Reedy and His Magazine* (Cambridge, Mass., 1963), pp. 49, 51.

[39] Scharf, *History of St. Louis,* I, 943; *Evening Post,* Dec. 10, 1878; *Post-Dispatch,* May 10, 1879.

[40] Florence Dorsey, *The Road to the Sea: The Story of James B. Eads and the Mississippi River* (New York, 1947), see esp. pp. 1-38; Scharf, *History of St. Louis,* I, 162. Interview with Gertrude McDonald, Jan. 16, 1951; Miss McDonald is John Dillon's granddaughter.

[41] *Ibid.* St. Louis *Spectator,* Feb. 27, 1892. It was at Harvard, apparently, that Dillon became acquainted with Robert Lincoln, son of the President, whom he referred to later as "my friend." Dillon to Joseph Pulitzer, April 15, 1888, Pulitzer Papers (CU).

[42] Interview with Gertrude McDonald, Jan. 16, 1951; personal letter from

In 1867, however, the life of ease had to be abandoned. Old Patrick Dillon had died, making James Eads, a relative by marriage, the executor of his estate and his son's guardian. Just at this time, Eads, whose engineering exploits on the Mississippi River were destined to make him famous, was launching the project of the great bridge which today bears his name, and, according to family tradition, he drew heavily upon the Dillon estate, greatly depleting it. Finding himself in straitened circumstances, John returned with his young family (there were two children now) to St. Louis where he was made secretary-treasurer of the Illinois–St. Louis Bridge Company, formed to construct Eads' span. He had no apparent qualifications for the job other than his family—and financial—ties with Eads.[43]

Dillon remained with the company five years, but was not happy in business. At last he found an opportunity to escape into a profession where he could pursue his literary bent. In 1872 he secured a position on the recently founded *Morning Globe*,[44] whose moving spirit was Joseph B. McCullagh, just then beginning to build a reputation as one of the great editors in the Middle West. In 1875, McCullagh forced a consolidation with the rival *Democrat*, merging the two papers into a single powerful organ, the *Globe-Democrat*.

Under McCullagh's tutelage John Dillon developed into "one of the best editorial writers St. Louis journalism has produced."[45] His urbane style reflected his former unhurried life, intellectual tastes, and aristocratic background. It was characterized by an effortless grace and fluency, a thoughtful, intellectual approach to events of the day, an easy but unostentatious familiarity with history, the classics, and literature, and a refined, somewhat rueful sense of humor. In time Dillon became schooled in the rough and tumble of journalism, but he was sensitive, easily discouraged, and sometimes apologetic— an oddity in a day of personal journalism when editors habitually composed libelous attacks upon their enemies. But Dillon was also a man of integrity, with a deep sense of justice. Altogether, he was a respected figure in St. Louis journalism.[46]

Mrs. H. L. Beadel, Feb. 9, 1951. Mrs. Beadel was Dillon's last surviving daughter. *The Harvard Graduates Magazine*, XI (1902-1903), 277; Scharf, *History of St. Louis*, II, 1,268-2,169; *St. Louis Directory*, 1865, p. 302.

[43] C. M. Woodward, *A History of the St. Louis Bridge* (St. Louis, 1881), pp. 15, 59; *St. Louis Directory*, 1868, p. 264; 1869, p. 273; 1870, p. 271; 1871, p. 199; 1872, p. 144; interview with Gertrude McDonald, Jan. 16, 1951. Soraghan, "History of St. Louis," pp. 178-80.

[44] Interview with Gertrude McDonald, Jan. 16, 1951; *St. Louis Directory*, 1873, p. 227.

[45] St. Louis *Times*, April 15, 1908.

[46] All his life Dillon showed a deep interest in education and travel. Each of his sons was sent to Harvard and his daughters to Harvard Annex. Indeed, the latter were among the first girls of upper class families in St. Louis who went beyond

14

By 1878 Dillon had resolved to leave the *Globe-Democrat*—a morning paper—and try his hand at publishing an evening paper of his own. On January 10, 1878, the first issue of the *Evening Post* appeared, a four-page sheet rolled from the presses of the *Globe-Democrat*.[47] The paper was a blend of his own somewhat rarefied tastes and the methods of McCullagh's vigorous journalism. It was "bright looking, carefully written, well printed but academic in style and substance."[48] Its pages were characterized by such features of limited appeal as a series of articles describing and analyzing examples of architecture in the city.[49] The paper also emphasized society news. "Society in St. Louis, which has long wanted an 'organ', may congratulate itself that it at last possesses one," it said, promising that "no improper matter of any kind will be admitted to its columns," such as scandals which occasionally titillated conversations among the select in the West End.[50] On the editorial page good-tempered essays such as one entitled "Socialism" reasonably discussed controversial questions of the day. Clearly, as the editor himself was frank to admit, the *Evening Post* was designed to circulate "principally among the wealthy classes." Consequently, it never attained a circulation much beyond 3,000 copies.[51]

There were other factors limiting the growth of the *Evening Post*. Its wire news was inadequate, its two daily editions were published on the presses of the *Globe-Democrat,* and its office was a cubbyhole at 321 Pine Street in the rear of a building belonging to its powerful neighbor. The *Republican* accused the *Post* of being an "illegitimate offspring" of the *Globe-Democrat,* a charge Dillon refuted with characteristic mildness. Actually, the *Post* was thoroughly independent, although in appearance and content it resembled the morning paper.[52]

Despite the drawbacks, by December 1878 the *Evening Post* had become the leading afternoon paper. Borrowing from McCullagh's maxims, Dillon "grasped the idea of the true mission of a daily journal." Its "chief aim will be to give the news of the day. . . . Spe-

---

finishing school. Following college, each child was sent on a tour of the Continent. St. Louis *Life*, Dec. 14, 1889; interview with Gertrude McDonald, Feb. 5, 1951.

47 *Evening* Post, Oct. 5, 1878.

48 Frank R. O'Neil to Joseph Pulitzer, April 25, 1907, Pulitzer Papers (CU).

49 *Spectator*, Dec. 9, 1882; *Evening Post*, Sept. 7, 1878, Oct. 15, 1878.

50 *Evening Post*, Aug. 30, 1878, Oct. 26, 1878.

51 *Ibid.*, Oct. 14, 1878; personal letter from R. Bruce Jones, Editor of *N. W. Ayer & Sons American Newspaper Annual and Directory*, Feb. 8, 1954; *Pettingill's Newspaper Directory and Advertisers' Hand-Book for 1878* (New York, 1878), p. 171.

52 *Evening Post*, Dec. 5, 1878; personal letter from Daniel J. W. McAuliffe, Oct. 9, 1950, Nov. 10, 1953. McAuliffe, a former managing editor of the St. Louis *Republic*, was closely acquainted with the history of St. Louis journalism. William A. Kelsoe, "Missourians Abroad, No. 10: Florence D. White," *Missouri Historical Review*, XVI (Jan. 1922), 247-52.

cial attention will be paid to the local news of St. Louis." To carry out this purpose the new editor organized a young and capable staff of reporters who scoured the city for lively, readable items. The *Post* thus acquired a reputation as an alert sheet which published the latest local intelligence in an entertaining manner free from the inadequacies and biases of its afternoon competitor, the *Evening Dispatch*.[53]

Editorially, the *Post* adopted another tenet of McCullagh's journalism, declaring that it would be "wholly independent of parties and politicians," taking its stand, rather, upon issues.[54] These were the words of a new journalistic style known as independent journalism, whose votaries, unlike the "party organs" of the day, were unhampered by slavish devotion to partisanship. The *Post* was inclined to Republicanism, but its independence was evident in the November elections when it advised its readers to ignore party labels and vote for the fittest candidates for city offices.[55] Generally, the *Post* favored the reformist, or Silk Stocking, wing of the Republicans in St. Louis, which was hostile to "Grantism" in national politics and opposed to the local machine of Chauncey I. Filley. In state politics its attacks on the Bourbon Democrats gave it a reputation among Democratic organs as being a Radical sheet,[56] but the charge was undeserved, and in his good-tempered way Dillon told his critics that they would "find a purer article of Democracy in the POST than in any other paper."

> Our platform is simply that good old Democratic platform of "Free Trade, Hard Money and Home Rule". . . . By Free Trade we mean a revenue tariff as opposed to protection; by Hard Money we mean gold or its equivalent in value dollar for dollar, and by Home Rule we mean that the Federal Government shall not meddle in State functions, and that the city shall not undertake private business of any kind.[57]

In short, John Dillon could be classed as a Liberal Republican, although he had never been connected formally with that movement. He was a patrician reformer in old St. Louis, with a philosophy very similar to Joseph Pulitzer's more plebeian middle class views.[58]

Like the self-made Pulitzer, Dillon also disliked monopolistic corporations. When the St. Louis Gas-light Company sought to persuade the city fathers to restore an exclusive franchise for furnishing the city with illumination—cancelled because of high charges and

---

[53] *Evening Post*, Aug. 30, 1878; *Post-Dispatch*, Jan. 12, 1882.
[54] *Evening Post*, Aug. 5, 1878, Aug. 30, 1878.
[55] *Ibid.*, Oct. 18, 1878.
[56] *Ibid.*, Aug. 5, 1878, Aug. 9, 1878, Aug. 24, 1878.
[57] *Ibid.*, Dec. 9, 1878.
[58] *Ibid.*, Aug. 27, 1878, Sept. 14, 1878, Dec. 9, 1878. See also Goldman, *Rendezvous*, ch. 2, for a discussion of patrician reformism in the 1870s.

1. John A. Dillon, co-founder of the *Post-Dispatch*. (Photograph from Dillon's granddaughter, Miss Gertrude McDonald)

2. Edward Butler, political boss of St. Louis and the object of *Post-Dispatch* editorials and campaigns. (From James Cox, *Old and New St. Louis*, published 1894)

3. Florence D. White, reporter on Pulitzer's original staff. (From the *Post-Dispatch* files)

4. William C. Steigers, first advertising agent of the *Post-Dispatch*. (From the *Post-Dispatch* files)

5. John J. Jennings, star reporter of the first *Post-Dispatch* staff. (From *The Journalist*, October 11, 1884)

6. Henry W. Moore, first city editor of the *Post-Dispatch*. (From *The Journalist*, December 13, 1884)

7. John A. Cockerill, first managing editor of *Post-Dispatch*. (From *American Journalist*, 1883)

8. Mrs. Hannah D. Pittman, early *Post-Dispatch* society editor. (From Mrs. C. P. Johnson, *Notable Women of St. Louis*, published 1914)

poor service—most papers, including the *Globe-Democrat* and the *Republican*, made no objection, but the *Evening Post* was opposed; it warned the municipal assembly that "the city has had dealings with the gas company before, . . . and the gas company has invariably come out ahead and the citizens have come out behind." [59] Although he came from a class which profited from monopolistic privileges, something in Dillon's makeup, perhaps an innate fair-mindedness bred from quiet reflection or a patrician's temperamental dislike of the business world, led him to oppose the wealthy and powerful who enjoyed special privileges at the expense of the community. [60]

In the late summer of 1878 the *Evening Post* advanced an important step journalistically. Hitherto, it had been distinguished chiefly for a lively presentation of local news and an independent if somewhat passive editorial policy. On August 31, taking a leaf from the *Globe-Democrat*, the *Post* launched into a campaign exposing the gambling underworld which flourished "so bold and defiant of public opinion" in St. Louis. [61] Albert B. Cunningham, the *Post's* bibulous but able managing editor, detailed the members of his staff to grill officials and gamblers in an effort to find out why the dens were permitted to operate so openly. [62] This was the start of a vigorous three-month campaign in which the news columns were coordinated with the editorial page to arouse public opinion. The *Post's* campaign was what journalists called a crusade, a technique becoming popular among progressive papers, in which the news columns were used to systematically expose public abuses and achieve reform. [63]

Throughout this crusade Dillon showed unwonted aggressiveness, and his new-style journalism began to attract attention. Indeed, judged by an increased volume of advertising which crammed the *Post's* columns in the fall, the financial worries attendant upon launching a new paper appeared to be diminishing. On December 5 Dillon overcame his habitual pessimism in business matters to announce that the *Evening Post* intended to purchase its own press, enabling it to publish independently of the *Globe-Democrat*. [64]

---

[59] *Evening Post,* Nov. 28, 1878. For the early history of the city's dispute with the St. Louis Gas-light Company, see Soraghan, "History of St. Louis," pp. 38-40, 52-53.

[60] *Evening Post,* Oct. 14, 1878, Nov. 28, 1878.

[61] *Ibid.,* Aug, 31, 1878.

[62] Personal letter from D. J. W. McAuliffe, Oct. 23, 1950.

[63] Frank Luther Mott, *American Journalism: A History, 1690-1960,* 3rd ed. (New York, 1962), p. 573, defines "crusade." Major articles in the *Post's* crusade were in the following issues: Sept. 4, 1878, Sept. 8, 1878, Sept. 13, 1878, Sept. 14, 1878, Sept. 16, 1878, Sept. 19, 1878, Nov. 18, 1878, Nov. 21, 1878.

[64] *Evening Post,* Dec. 5, 1878; *The Journalist,* New York, Sept. 25, 1886; Moberly (Mo.) *Headlight,* as quoted in *Post and Dispatch,* Dec. 31, 1878. The *Headlight* noted that in its last days "the business of the *Post* had increased to a wonderful degree."

But on December 9 Dillon's hard-won confidence was shaken by Joseph Pulitzer's purchase of the *Dispatch*. Together with the establishment of the *Evening Star,* this meant the *Post* now faced serious competition. Pulitzer's well-known resourcefulness aroused Dillon's anxieties, for he thought he knew what his new rival had in mind. Only four years before, in 1874, Pulitzer had suspended his political activities long enough to swoop into St. Louis, purchase the bankrupt *Staats-Zeitung,* a German-language journal whose only asset was the possession of a coveted Associated Press franchise, and sell it almost immediately to the *Morning Globe*. This was the final stroke the *Globe* needed to force the *Democrat* into a consolidation. On his part, Pulitzer had made a quick profit of $20,000. Dillon, who had been on the *Globe* at the time, now painfully recalled the event in a similar situation; Pulitzer might combine the *Dispatch* with the *Star,* which would probably mean the end of his own venture.[65]

In a nervous effort to fathom Pulitzer's intentions, Dillon sent a reporter to the *Dispatch* office the morning after the sale, but the new proprietor, except for admitting ownership, remarked that he had not yet decided what to do. Thereupon Dillon wasted no time in getting in touch with Pulitzer himself, and together the two men agreed to a combination of the *Post* and *Dispatch*.[66]

Had Pulitzer planned this deft maneuver all along to force Dillon into consolidating the relatively sound and respected *Evening Post* with the bankrupt and worthless *Dispatch?* The knowing *Globe-Democrat* thought so, for the day following the merger it commented that

> Mr. Pulitzer's designs were shrouded in the mystery in which he loves to envelop himself, but now that they have reached their fruition the public can not but admire his wisdom and caution which were absolutely necessary to their fulfillment.[67]

Aware that he had bought "a journalistic wreck" at the courthouse sale, a sheet which "in the eyes of the experts [was] beyond resuscitation," Pulitzer was determined to provide his new career with a sound footing. In later years he loved to recall how he had purchased a bankrupt newspaper for only $2,500 and made of it a brilliant success. The true story is not so dramatic, although it reflects credit upon Pulitzer's business acumen. He was well aware that, except for an

---

[65] Johns, *Pulitzer,* p. 33. However, D. M. Houser testified the *Democrat* paid $37,500 for the *Staats-Zeitung,* and of this he heard $10,000 to $15,000 "had gone into a middle man's pocket. . . ." *Post-Dispatch,* Jan. 8, 1891.

[66] *Globe-Democrat,* Dec. 13, 1878; *Evening Post,* Dec. 10, 1878.

[67] *Globe-Democrat,* Dec. 13, 1878. That others thought this was the case, too, is apparent from a cartoon published Dec. 15, 1878, in *Die Laterne,* a German-language humor magazine. *P-D Notebook,* St. Louis, Dec. 1953.

Associated Press franchise, his *Dispatch* was worthless, and it would take more than his own slender resources to revive it. He needed to combine the *Dispatch* with a solidly established paper if he was to make a go of the gamble. Having just been founded, the *Star* was unsatisfactory for this purpose, but the *Evening Post* filled every need.

Whatever the motives, the union was satisfactory to both men. For Dillon it meant relief from shouldering alone business burdens he found distasteful; as for Pulitzer, his plans for a career in journalism were now on firmer foundations.[68]

On the afternoon of December 11, Pulitzer moved the salvageable effects of the *Dispatch* to the little office of the *Post* at 321 Pine Street, where for the first time Dillon's staff got a glimpse of him. As one reporter remembered, "When a tall, distinguished looking young man showed up in the *Post* news room and looked appraisingly about, I knew without being told that it was Joseph Pulitzer. He was more than six feet tall . . . [and] wore rimless glasses, a soft hat and a blue chinchilla overcoat, obviously tailored in New York." [69]

The next afternoon, December 12, the first issue of the *Post and Dispatch* appeared. Because it had no press fit for use, the four-page journal was printed on the presses of the *Globe-Democrat,* and the first day's circulation was 4,020 copies.[70] The event turned out to be a significant one in the history of American journalism, but so far as St. Louisans hurrying home on that December afternoon were concerned, the *Post and Dispatch* must have seemed only another of the flickering sheets hawked on the streets year after year with their bright promises and sterling platforms. If there were any distinguishing features to this little paper, they lay in the fact that it was the heir of the refreshing and independent *Evening Post* and that it had a dynamic new publisher.

---

[68] It takes nothing from the genius of Pulitzer, a brilliant businessman who created a new era of journalism with the St. Louis *Post-Dispatch* and New York *World,* to suggest that his career might have been cut short by failure had he not engineered the consolidation. The point seems to be worth noting, since Pulitzer's standard biographers neglect the significance of the *Evening Post* in his amazing early success. (See Seitz, *Pulitzer;* Johns, *Pulitzer;* and James Barrett, *Pulitzer.*) Pulitzer substantially repeated the strategy by buying an already established newspaper when in 1883 he bought the New York *World.*

[69] Charles Edmundson, "Pulitzer's Prime Minister," *Page One,* St. Louis, 1948, p. 26.

[70] *Post-Dispatch,* Dec. 12, 1883; Joseph Pulitzer to Florence D. White, Oct. 17, 1903, Pulitzer Papers (CU). The new paper inherited about 3,100 copies from the *Evening Post* and the remainder from the *Dispatch.*

Although nowhere have I found a direct statement that the *Post and Dispatch* used the presses of the *Globe-Democrat,* there is little doubt that such was the case. The admittedly dim recollections of the last surviving member of the original staff of the *Post and Dispatch,* Florence D. White, confirm my opinion. Personal letter from D. J. W. McAuliffe, Nov. 10, 1953.

CHAPTER II

Change and Conflict*

In 1878 St. Louis was the metropolis of the Upper Mississippi Valley, an unkempt city of 350,000 inhabitants which sprawled nineteen miles along the river front. In the past dozen years it had recovered remarkably from the disruptions of the Civil War and was now a teeming industrial and commercial center. In its swift expansion St. Louis resembled the region it served, the Trans-Mississippi West and Southwest. Yet, although much of its population and booming economic life were new, it was a city of old and sophisticated traditions stemming from a French colonial past and intimate associations both with the antebellum South and the Rhenish provinces of Germany. These gave St. Louis a cultured and conservative flavor not found in other Midwestern communities. In the words of Theodore Dreiser, who came to St. Louis a few years later, "Contrasted to Chicago, it was not a metropolis at all. While rich and successful it was a creature of another mood. . . . I learned in time to like it very much, but for the things that set it apart from other cities, not for the things by which it sought to rival them." [1]

Physically, St. Louis had changed much from the pre-war community whose lifeblood was the river. The riverfront itself had altered. There were only "half a dozen sound-asleep steamboats where I used to see a solid mile of wide-awake ones," Mark Twain complained in the

---

* The first pages of this chapter are an adaptation of my article, "St Louis in the Early 'Eighties," published in the *Bulletin of the Missouri Historical Society,* XIX (July 1963), 328-39. Adapted by permission.

[1] Theodore Dreiser, *A Book About Myself,* p. 88. A recent commentator makes a similar observation: "St. Louis is a city set apart in the Midwest; in the region yet not entirely a part of it. . . ." Graham Hutton, *Midwest at Noon* (Chicago, 1946), p. 155. The most satisfactory account of the rise and progress of St. Louis to 1882 is Scharf, *History of St. Louis.* See also, Soraghan, "History of St. Louis," for an account of the city's growth following the Civil War. James Cox, *Old and New St. Louis* (St. Louis, 1894), covers uncritically and in less detail the city until 1893. Useful material may also be found in Walter B. Stevens, *St. Louis: The Fourth City,* 3 vols. (St. Louis, 1909). Both Cox and Stevens were briefly reporters on the *Post-Dispatch* in the 1880s. A good, if somewhat episodic sketch of more recent history is to be found in Carlos Hurd, "St. Louis: Boundary Bound," *Our Fair City* (New York, 1947), Robert S. Allen (ed.), pp. 235-55. Hurd was a *Post-Dispatch* reporter for many years. See also, Orrick Johns, *The Time of Our Lives: The Story of My Father and Myself* (New York, 1937). The author's father was a longtime editor of the editorial page of the *Post-Dispatch.* A recent commentary on St. Louis by a *Post-Dispatch* editor is Ernest Kirschten, *Catfish and Crystal* (New York, 1960).

eighties.[2] In their place the St. Louis Bridge, spanning the river in three great arches, dominated the waterfront. It was indicative of the new railroad age which was dooming the picturesque stern-wheelers by altering the flow of commerce from a north-south to an east-west direction. From the bridge an incoming stranger noted that "the city itself is barely visible," because the skyline was overcast with a heavy pall of smoke streaming from tall factory chimneys and hundreds of unseen residences. Only "a dome or two, the outlines of a shot tower or an elevator, looms out vaguely [from the haze]. These Western cities exhale a tainted breath, stifle themselves in the fumes of their own prosperity," exclaimed the traveler.[3]

The railroads that eclipsed the importance of the river caused the city to move away from the bank. Instead of a ribbon-like settlement pressing close by the levee, St. Louis had begun to spread westward towards the rolling countryside beyond the terraces paralleling the Mississippi. The business district now encompassed Fourth and Fifth streets, and "that portion of Third street to the levee, and from the bridge to the foot of Chouteau avenue, is half deserted. The tall business houses on the levee have become rookeries, cheap boarding houses and groggeries." By 1879 the situation was such that "those who have possession of Third, and even Fourth feel a little nervous over the general tendency to move westward."[4] Once the heart of the town, the harbor district now had a tumbledown, slovenly appearance, "rotten with bagnios and filled with a dangerous and criminal population."[5] In some places the district east of Fourth was picturesque; it was here, south of Olive, that the ancient enclave of "Frenchtown" still could be made out. It was "a labyrinth of blind alleys and courts," of dilapidated houses, some pitched at crazy angles, where now dwelt the very poor. The "old" French cathedral—it was only forty-four years old in 1878—with its classic columns, stood out boldly to remind St. Louisans of the city's proud Gallic origins. For the rest, the original business district was one of narrow streets along which small shops, warehouses, and slum quarters were jostled together.[6]

2 Samuel Clemens (Mark Twain), *Life on the Mississippi*, Harper and Brothers edition (New York, 1917), p. 193.

3 W. H. Bishop, "St. Louis," *Harper's New Monthly Magazine*, LXVIII (Mar. 1884), 497-98. The heavy smoke pall blackened every building in the city. Mark Twain remarked that "in St. Louis, as in London and Pittsburgh, you can't persuade a new thing to look new; the coal-smoke turns it into an antiquity the moment you take your hand off it." Clemens, *op.cit.*, p. 191.

4 *Post-Dispatch*, June 19, 1879, Dec. 22, 1880.

5 *Ibid.*, Jan. 6, 1880, Aug. 5, 1880.

6 *Post and Dispatch*, March 4, 1879; *Post-Dispatch*, June 19, 1879, April 12, 1880, May 11, 1880; C. M. Woodward, "The City of St. Louis," *New England Magazine: An Illustrated Monthly*, V (New Series) (Jan. 1892), 602-604.

The central business area was now Fourth and Fifth streets. Fourth had "an elegant retail trade, and [was] the promenade of shoppers with full purses," while Fifth, soon to become St. Louis's Broadway, was lined with shops of all descriptions.[7] Also on Fourth was the Merchants' Exchange, its interior large enough to house a national political convention in 1876. It was the city's grain trading mart and the scene of many civic and social gatherings. Here, too, occupying a full block was the ponderously domed courthouse where the *Evening Dispatch* had been put up for sale.[8]

Beyond Fifth to Twelfth, where a country market attracted "grangers," was a solidly built-up district filled with businesses and industries, boardinghouses and drab residences. These streets were unprepossessing except for a few official buildings, including the high-towered Four Courts, an imposing but unfinished post office, and the city hall. The Four Courts, the most interesting of the three, served as a combined jail, police headquarters, and palace of justice. This district, too, was honeycombed with neighborhoods of vice and poverty; as were many river towns, St. Louis was overrun with red-light districts, gambling dens, and slum areas. "Wild Cat Chute," a narrow alley hidden in the block west of Seventh, and "Clabber Alley," filled with a "frightful stench," were the most notorious neighborhoods, boasting "more crime and misery than all the rest of the town can show."[9] For the most part, however, St. Louis presented the appearance of a prosperous city with its myriad business establishments, small, medium, and large, struggling to grow in a friendly but competitive economy. Pulitzer's and Dillon's new paper was typical of hundreds of small concerns seeking a foothold.

Beyond Twelfth Street St. Louis had grown considerably by 1878. Between Seventeenth and Jefferson Avenue was a thickly settled working class district known as "Kerry Patch," cradled in a wide trough between the north-south ridges marking the western section. Kerry Patch was so called because most of its residents had come from County Kerry, Ireland. Its Irishmen entered enthusiastically into local politics, manned the city's police and fire departments and produced more than a handful of newspaper reporters. The Irish in the Patch and elsewhere constituted the second largest ethnic element in the population, outnumbered only by the Germans.[10]

---

[7] Bishop, "St. Louis," p. 499; *Post-Dispatch*, April 7, 1879.

[8] M. M. Yeakle, Sr., *The City of St. Louis of To-Day: Its Progress and Prospects* (St. Louis, 1889), p. 78; Woodward, "City of St. Louis," pp. 602-603.

[9] *Post-Dispatch*, May 26, 1879.

[10] Interview with D. J. W. McAuliffe, Jan. 17, 1951; *Post-Dispatch*, April 19, 1880, Oct. 18, 1882, Nov. 15, 1882; *Reedy's Mirror*, Sept. 30, 1897; Harold Zink, *City Bosses in the United States: A Study of Twenty Municipal Bosses* (Durham, N.C.,

West of Jefferson Avenue middle class families escaping from the smoke and noise of the central portion of the city built modest, comfortable brick or frame dwellings by the hundreds in the seventies and eighties.[11] Beyond Grand Avenue to remote Forest Park the population thinned out, and the scene became largely bucolic with wide spaces interposed between scattered real estate developments growing in size and number with each passing year.[12]

The city's aristocratic class, noticeable for its exclusiveness, clung to palatial residences downtown in oases of wealth like Lucas Place and Lafayette Park. Lucas Place, only three blocks long, was protected from encroachment by Missouri Park at Thirteenth Street. Here lived such old families as the Lucases, Lacklands, Turners, Morrisons, and Maffitts. Their mansions lined either side of the quiet, tree-shaded avenue in Victorian stateliness while at either end fashionable churches guarded the morals of the well-dressed faithful. Unfortunately, it was accurately predicted of the Place that "the city is fast growing towards it, and inside of twenty years it will be abandoned to keepers of first-class hash houses." [13] Already the elite had begun a western hegira which continued into the next century. Vandeventer Place, just west of Grand Avenue, was a "semi-private, oblong park" protected from the workaday world by ornate iron gates. It was to be a model for later, ultra-exclusive "places" still further out near Forest Park. A caste-like atmosphere was thus visibly imparted to the western section of St. Louis.[14]

In the less desirable districts of North and South St. Louis were the "Germans," who constituted the largest homogeneous element in the community. The census of 1880 listed 55,000 residents born in Germany but it was estimated that the German element actually totaled 150,000, or more than a third of the entire population. Partly because they enjoyed their own company and partly because the "old" families would not admit them to the upper echelons of society, there grew up in South St. Louis, particularly, a separate German community led by

1930), p. 5; Soraghan, "History of St. Louis," p. 2; Bishop, "St Louis," 509-510. See comments on Kerry Patch and related topics in Max Putzel, *The Man in the Mirror*, esp. pp. 11-14.

[11] *Post and Dispatch,* Dec. 13, 1878; *Post-Dispatch,* Aug. 20, 1879; Florence D. White to Joseph Pulitzer, July 23, 1900, Pulitzer Papers (CU).

[12] *Post-Dispatch,* Sept. 19, 1879; Charles Dudley Warner, "Studies of the Great West, VIII—St. Louis and Kansas City," *Harper's New Monthly Magazine,* LXXVII, (Oct. 1888), 749.

[13] *Post-Dispatch,* Oct. 16, 1880; St. Louis *Spectator,* April 19, 1890; Warner, "Studies of Great West," p. 749.

[14] Bishop, "St. Louis," p. 510; Warner, *loc. cit.; Spectator,* April 19, 1890, June 4, 1892.

rich beer barons and idealistic intellectuals.[15] But despite this mild ostracism the Germans made a powerful impress upon the life of the city. An industrious people, they added to the wealth of the community through their many economic enterprises. They also imparted a convivial old-world atmosphere to the city by such open-air beer gardens as Schnaider's, summer entertainment spots like Uhrig's Cave with their light opera, and numerous sidewalk cafes on the continental model where good conversation was mixed with good beer. The German love of music was everywhere evident in the brass bands and liederkranz societies; and German intellectualism—the St. Louis Movement, for example, devoted to the philosophic speculations of Hegel—became a characteristic of the city.[16]

Surrounded by an abundance of raw materials within easy reach and with access to rapidly growing markets, St. Louis by 1878 was a far cry from the relatively simple port of antebellum days; it was now a many-sided center of the industrial age.[17] Despite Mark Twain's lament, the river still played a considerable role, particularly when James B. Eads, fresh from his triumph as a bridge builder, in 1877 completed a jetty system at the mouth of the Mississippi permitting ocean-going vessels to ascend the river to New Orleans. This produced a renaissance in the shipment of grain from St. Louis—increasingly utilizing unromantic but efficient barges instead of steamboats—and once again the Merchants' Exchange hummed with proud activity.[18] Indeed, the commission business lay at the very center of the city's wealth, and great personal fortunes were amassed "on 'Change." "The prosperity of Missouri, as well as most of the States of the Mississippi Valley, depends mainly upon the . . . prices of corn, wheat, rye, oats and barley," said Pulitzer's new paper. As for St. Louis: "The grain trade is the largest and most sensitive industry of the city." [19]

Important as it was, however, the grain business—and its adjunct, flour-milling—was now rivaled by other forms of economic activity. Taking advantage of the rich beds of coal in nearby Illinois and the

---

[15] Florence D. White to Joseph Pulitzer, July 23, 1900, Pulitzer Collection (CU); Hamilton Basso, "St. Louis," *Holiday Magazine,* VIII (Oct. 1950), 44-48; *Spectator,* June 28, 1884, March 14, 1891.

[16] *Post-Dispatch,* May 1, 1880; Basso, "St. Louis," pp. 46-49, 72; "The Summer Beer Gardens of St. Louis," *Bulletin of the Missouri Historical Society,* IX (July 1953), 391-95; Snider, *St. Louis Movement; Spectator,* July 24, 1886, Aug. 27, 1887.

[17] Wyatt Winton Belcher, *The Economic Rivalry Between Chicago and St. Louis, 1850-1880* (New York, 1947). This book is an excellent study of St. Louis's economic development in the third quarter of the nineteenth century.

[18] St. Louis *Evening Dispatch,* Dec. 24, 1877; Scharf, *History of St. Louis,* II, 1,123-38; Soraghan, "History of St. Louis," pp. 110-15; Florence Dorsey, *Road to the Sea,* pp. 201-17, gives a vivid account of Eads' work constructing the jetties.

[19] *Post-Dispatch,* March 24, 1879.

deposits of ore in the Iron Mountain and Pilot Knob districts south-west of the city, heavy industry had taken root. At Carondelet, a suburb on the southern edge of St. Louis, after four or five years of depression, the night skies were again aglow from steel works producing goods for western railway construction, and scattered throughout the city were stove, farm implement, and pipe manufacturing establishments.[20] From the pine forests of Wisconsin massive rafts of logs drifted down the Mississippi to provide material for the furniture and woodenware industries which were busily supplying products for the rapidly filling West and Southwest.[21] Contrariwise, the West and Southwest in the seventies made St. Louis a mecca for long cattle trains bringing in livestock for meatpacking and to provide hides for a booming leather goods industry.[22] For St. Louisans themselves, enterprising Germans were using Missouri's barley crop to build a large brewing industry. By 1881, 658 glasses of beer were produced for each man, woman, and child in the city, and enough were consumed in the 2,000 saloons, sidewalk cafes, and open-air gardens to give one the impression that St. Louis was a pleasure-loving community.[23]

Under the impact of this booming economy, St. Louis had become the fifth largest city in the country, leaping from a population of 160,000 in 1860 to twice that two decades later.[24] Inspired by such statistics, local boosters hailed their community as "the great city of futurity; the final Great City of the world"; even the intellectuals of the St. Louis Movement were caught by the spirit of the time, equating the historical philosophy of Hegel with a seemingly inevitable process assuring "the future supremacy of St. Louis."[25] The city acquired the sobriquet of "the Future Great" which Chicago newspapers loved to use in derision.[26]

For, despite the glowing statistics, St. Louis could not shake a reputation for being "slow-going and over-cautious," and "a sleepy old place."[27] True, it had grown greatly, but Chicago, the chief

---

[20] Shortly after 1880, Bessemer furnaces were installed in Carondelet mills. *Post-Dispatch*, Aug. 7, 1879, April 3, 1880, March 9, 1882; Scharf, *History of St. Louis*, II, 1,258-75; Bishop, "St. Louis," p. 514.

[21] Scharf, *op. cit.*, II, 1,322-28; *Post-Dispatch*, Aug. 27, 1879, May 31, 1880.

[22] *Spectator*, Aug. 29, 1891; *The Hornet*, Feb. 11, 1882; *Post-Dispatch*, Dec. 31, 1881.

[23] *Post-Dispatch*, Aug. 12, 1879; Scharf, *History of St. Louis*, II, 1,226, 1,330-33; Troy (N.Y.) *Times*, as quoted in *Post-Dispatch*, Feb. 26, 1881.

[24] Williams and Shoemaker, *Missouri*, II, 372.

[25] L. U. Reavis, *St. Louis: The Future Great City* (St. Louis, 1881). The quotation is taken from "A Word to the Reader."

[26] Snider, *St. Louis Movement*, pp. 70-137.

[27] Omaha *Bee*, as quoted in *Post-Dispatch*, March 25, 1879; *The Journalist*, Dec. 13, 1884; *Union Printer*, Dec. 30, 1893.

rival, had piled up even more impressive figures of population and commercial growth.[28] Basically, although wealthy and successful, St. Louis had depended too long on the rivers, those "natural avenues of commerce," while Chicago, less favored by nature, had surmounted its difficulties by constructing railroads in every direction in the decade before the Civil War.[29] After the war, it is true, St. Louis sought to catch up by constructing a western railway network of its own and, in 1874, by completing the St. Louis Bridge over the Mississippi to the east. But Chicago's lines, with their head start, continued to divert an ever-growing volume of traffic from the trans-Mississippi region, adding to that already captured in Illinois and Indiana, and its connections with the East were far superior to its rival's.

The problem was that, despite obvious and important exceptions, the general conservatism of St. Louis capitalists had permitted Chicago to forge ahead. Years of prosperity without undue risk when river traffic was supreme had bred a feeling of complacency in the community. Moreover, much of the economic development of St. Louis was in the hands of a small and unprogressive group of industrial, commercial, and financial leaders who controlled the banks, some of the larger businesses and much of the city's real estate. "This close connection between the bankers and other business men made it very difficult for new businesses to obtain sufficient capital to start operations, especially when they offered competition to the older firms." [30] In short, St. Louis was partially controlled by a conservative and monopolistic oligarchy.[31]

The jealousy of these men about local enterprise was sanctioned by the city's aristocratic atmosphere, mainly derived from the antebellum South. With a leadership whose ancestry was in large part Virginian and Kentuckian, St. Louis's upper circles were steeped in a caste-like tradition contrasting sharply with the egalitarianism of most of the frontier-descended Middle West. It was an attitude that placed weight upon status and social position and tended to give to men of birth, breeding, and wealth the privileges of a ruling class. In St. Louis this tradition buttressed the small, if fluid, oligarchy in its pretensions of exclusiveness and made them look upon the community as rightfully theirs to manage—and exploit—without

---

[28] Belcher, *Economic Rivalry*. The entire book is concerned with this theme.
[29] *Ibid.*, p. 75.
[30] *Ibid.*, p. 117.
[31] Claude H. Wetmore and Lincoln Steffens, "Tweed Days in St. Louis," *McClure's Magazine*, XIX (Oct. 1902), 577; William Cowper Brann, "Behind the Scenes in St. Louis," *The Complete Works of Brann the Iconoclast* (New York, 1898), X, 205-206; Orrick Johns, *Time of Our Lives*, pp. 66-67.

interference either from outsiders or the lower orders, whether small businessmen or the laboring classes. Though it should not be exaggerated, this aristocratic tradition aided its beneficiaries in controlling the city's economic, political, and social life without effective challenge for many years.[32]

The oligarchy had been formed in the era of untrammeled individualism shortly before and immediately following the war, when young men of talent and determination—sometimes aided by inherited wealth as in the case of Pierre Chouteau, but as frequently endowed only with wit and ambition as with Erastus Wells—took advantage of opportunities afforded by a rapidly expanding community to establish street railway lines, transfer companies, gaslight corporations, and other public services. Within a few years Chouteau, Wells, Julius Walsh, John Scullin, John Lackland, and others carved out de facto monopolies and legal franchises for themselves.[33] And since this was not a period when self-made men were inclined to feel a sense of public responsibility, their services were marked by high charges, callousness towards public needs, and resistance to competition or change. They had contributed a great deal to the growth of St. Louis, but by 1878 their monopolies were hampering continued growth, and objections were beginning to be voiced by such newspapers as the *Evening Post,* a spokesman, in effect, for smaller and competitive businesses who resented discriminations imposed by the monopolies.

The moneyed classes had entrenched themselves in other ways. With the help of the economy-minded Grangers they had framed a state constitution in 1875 which placed such sharp restrictions on the taxing powers of municipalities that local authorities could not undertake important civic improvements or keep those already in existence in decent repair. The city government of St. Louis could assess additional taxes only when two-thirds of the propertied citizens approved—a nearly impossible requirement. As a result, as late as 1889 there was only one thoroughfare improved its entire length to Forest Park and no sewer beyond Vandeventer Avenue, just west of Grand. In North and South St. Louis conditions were worse. "That Caron-

---

[32] Brann, "Behind the Scenes," X, 205-206. Basso, "St. Louis," pp. 42-44, 76, gives present impressions. William Marion Reedy, *The Makers of St. Louis* (St. Louis, 1906), contains sketches of many leading figures in St. Louis after 1880. Scharf, *History of St. Louis,* contains sketches for a somewhat earlier period. Interview with Frances Cabanne Saportas, March 10, 1951.

[33] For sketch of Charles P. Chouteau, see Scharf, *History of St. Louis,* I, 184; for Walsh, *ibid.,* II, 1,208-1,209; for Lackland, *ibid.,* II, 1,401-1402; for Wells, *ibid.,* I, 628-29. See also, Irving Dilliard, "Erastus Wells," *Dictionary of American Biography,* XIX, 638-39; and Dilliard, "John Scullin," *ibid.* (1935), XVI, 527.

delet and the whole southern part of the city has been shamefully neglected, is too well known to need comment. . . . South of Laclede avenue the tender care which has made the central part of the city so desirable [by 1896] has never been felt." In most of this district "the streets [are] badly paved, the sidewalks and gutters out of repair, and the alleys abominable." [34]

To protect their privileges the magnates were also firmly in control of local government. Either by electing men of their own class— "the best citizens"—to public office, or by combining with political machines manned by "ward bummers" and their "bosses," they protected their financial interests and franchises from popular attack. The alliance of "the Push" and "the Silks," as they were sometimes called, usually worked smoothly; but at regular intervals, when a long lease of office by the former produced a saturnalia of corruption, the "best citizens" would lead a campaign of reform, oust "the Push" and take direct control. But whatever the precise arrangement, the vital interests of the oligarchy were rarely disturbed. Normally it used the Democratic Party, dominant in Missouri though not always in St. Louis, to maintain its hold, but both parties were made up of combinations of "silks" and "ward bummers"; it appeared to matter little which one scored at the polls—the oligarchs were almost never on the losing side.[35]

Rumblings of dissatisfaction, however, were beginning to be heard. The growing body of ordinary businessmen in the city were becoming restless under the yoke of monopolism, and by 1878 middle class newspapers, breaking away from outworn practices of political journalism, were voicing demands for reform.

Greater St. Louis spilled across the Mississippi River into Illinois. Early in the nineteenth century a quiet village named Illinois Town had sprung up at the ferry landing opposite St. Louis. In the late 1850's the location became important when railroads from the East began to reach the Mississippi. They constructed their great switching yards on "Bloody Island," a bit of land between Cahokia Creek and the river adjacent to Illinois Town, rechristened East St. Louis. Bloody Island had been famous in the lore of early St. Louis as the scene of several famous duels. Attracting after the Civil War

---

[34] St. Louis *Life*, July 25, 1896; *Spectator*, July 16, 1892; *Reedy's Mirror*, Aug. 29, 1901; Williams and Shoemaker, *Missouri*, II, 279-99, gives an account of the framing of the constitution of 1875.

[35] *Spectator*, Sept. 3, 1892; Soraghan, "History of St. Louis," pp. 50-51; Wetmore and Steffens, "Tweed Days," p. 577; Orrick Johns, *Time of Our Lives*, pp. 137-39; Joseph J. McAuliffe, "From Blacksmith to Boss," *Leslie's Monthly Magazine*, LVIII (Oct. 1904), 636. McAuliffe was a political reporter for the *Post-Dispatch*. Later he became city editor and then managing editor of the rival *Globe-Democrat*.

brawny, hard-drinking, and turbulent railroad laborers, the Island became the site of almost daily altercations, riots, and strikes far bloodier than the duels which had given it its name. In time it lost its identity as the railroads covered the streams and sloughs separating it from the mainland, and the brawling island folk were merged with the older settlement. Numbering about 20,000, the community became notorious as a dingy, tough, scandalously corrupt place to which the epithet "Hoodlumville" was often applied.[36]

By 1874 nine roads terminated in East St. Louis, all of them equipped with warehouse facilities to transfer goods for shipment by ferry across the river. Consequently, when the new bridge was opened the same year the roads were reluctant to abandon these facilities; instead, they continued to unload in the East St. Louis yards, where the merchandise was picked up by a transfer company and taken over the bridge by wagon to St. Louis. This inconvenient arrangement, carried on at least partially out of consideration for the monopolistic interests of St. Louis which controlled the bridge, ferry, and transfer companies, made the bridge almost as much a monument to the backwardness of St. Louis as it was a symbol of progress.[37]

Stretching away from St. Louis in three directions—north, south, and west—lay the largely rural state of Missouri, not far removed from the raw frontier. In the dozen years since the Civil War farmers from neighboring states had flooded into the prairie-like corn belt of the northern tier of counties and the rolling country of Central and Western Missouri. The uninhabited territory, embracing all but the river valleys prior to 1860, had now receded into the southwest and some districts of the Ozarks.[38] Despite the disappearance of the frontier, however, "the country around St. Louis . . . is but in its infancy—sparsely settled and comparatively poor. There is no great city in America that has a tributary region capable of so much development." [39] There were only two other urban centers in the entire state—Kansas City, across the state, and St. Joseph, another cowtown on the Missouri River. For the rest, there were a number of stagnant river towns and a handful of new places strung out along the railroads. With railroad construction, however, and rural hardships, a drift towards urbanization had begun.[40]

[36] Agnes Wallace, "The Wiggins Ferry Monopoly," *Missouri Historical Review*, XLII (Oct. 1947), 1-9; *Spectator*, Dec. 19, 1885, May 8, 1886, April 2, 1887, June 28, 1890; St. Louis *Life*, June 4, 1896; *Post-Dispatch*, March 23, 1881, Dec. 6, 1881.

[37] Woodward, *History of St. Louis Bridge*, p. 595; Wallace, *op.cit.*, pp. 12-17.

[38] Williams and Shoemaker, *Missouri*, II, 339-521; Walter Williams, *The State of Missouri: An Autobiography* (Columbia, Mo., 1904), pp. 63-64.

[39] *Post-Dispatch*, Oct. 10, 1879.

[40] *Ibid.*, Feb. 20, 1880; Williams and Shoemaker, *op.cit.*, II, 393-94; *Spectator*,

Further testifying to the immaturity of the state in 1878, parts of Western Missouri still burned with the fierce hates of the border warfare of the fifties and sixties. Lawlessness, which had made Missouri a synonym for backwardness, still lingered in the country of the James Boys.[41]

Agriculture was the chief economic activity of Missouri. Corn, wheat, oats, and barley were the leading products, with livestock becoming increasingly important. But agriculture was undergoing a revolutionary change. Subsistence farming had largely disappeared; a capitalistic economy based upon a cash market was now the rule. The growth of railroads, bringing markets within a reasonable distance of the farm, the introduction of farm machinery which made large crops feasible, and the whetted desires of the farmer for an increased income all accounted for the change.[42] The new economy, however, did not bring contentment and prosperity. Instead, in the seventies rural Missouri became a region of unrest. Cash markets, railroads, and farm machinery only seemed to sink the farmer deep into debt, the helpless victim of spiraling costs and monopolistic charges. Prices had fallen primarily because of over-production, but the Missouri farmer was reluctant to admit that glutted markets in St. Louis and Chicago had contributed to his troubles. Instead, he blamed powerful corporations and high taxes.[43]

The fruit of frustration was revolt. Imitating farmers elsewhere in the Midwest, Missourians joined the Granger movement, which at its height in 1875, had 150,000 members in the state. They forced the adoption of a new constitution that, in addition to imposing restrictions on the taxing powers of state and local governments, gave to the legislature authority to regulate railroads. Together with the creation of a Board of Equalization, designed to secure an equitable assessment of corporation properties for taxation, these reforms satisfied the aims of the Missouri Grange. Its mission seemingly accomplished, it faded into obscurity.[44]

Unfortunately, however, rural prosperity did not return. The Granger reforms had not struck at such causes of depression as overexpansion and over-production, and the reforms themselves were

Aug. 30, 1890; Homer Clevenger, "Agrarian Politics in Missouri, 1880-1896," unpub. diss. (University of Missouri, 1940), pp. 29-34. This study is indispensable for an understanding of the postwar history of Missouri.

[41] Homer Croy, *Jesse James Was My Neighbor* (New York, 1949), pp. 36-37. Croy began his career as a writer on the *Post-Dispatch*.

[42] Clevenger, "Agrarian Politics," pp. 33-38.

[43] *Ibid.*, pp. 41-52.

[44] Williams and Shoemaker, II, 262, 279-99; Homer Clevenger, "The Farmers' Alliance in Missouri," *Missouri Historical Review*, XLV (Oct. 1944), 26; *Reedy's Mirror*, Dec. 13, 1900.

largely unenforced. The Democratic Party, which ruled Missouri after 1872, was controlled by the Bourbon oligarchy of St. Louis and elsewhere, and it prevented the passage of effective railway regulation or a fairer policy of tax assessment.[45] The failure of the Granger reforms, therefore, resulted in the rise of the Greenback Party in the late seventies. The agrarians now turned to the device of inflation as a means of relieving agricultural distress. The Greenback movement in Missouri—the strongest in the nation—made significant inroads into the hegemony of the Democratic Party in the state in 1878, capturing a seat in Congress and twenty-six in the legislature. A brief return of prosperity beginning in 1878, however, doomed the movement to a hopeless faction.[46]

But hard times were to descend again and again upon the embattled Missouri farmer, and agrarian unrest was to continue, producing not only third parties, but recurring efforts to capture control of the Democracy (as the Democratic Party was often called then). In fact, the Granger and Greenback movements signaled the beginning of a gradual change in Missouri politics. The emotions stirred by civil war and reconstruction for a long time prevented determination of elections on economic issues. The draconian reconstruction policy of the Radicals from 1865 to 1870 had driven thousands of ex-Confederates in outstate areas into the ranks of the Democrats, where they formed a die-hard "yellow dog majority" which Bourbon oligarchs used to dominate the state.[47] But almost as soon as it was formed the "yellow dog" majority began to be worn away by the winds of agrarian revolt. As depression followed depression in the seventies, eighties, and nineties more and more rural Confederates broke away from their stereotyped loyalties to join a succession of third parties, or more important, to form an unstable agitating element in the Democratic Party. Thus, the discontent of the seventies portended a turbulent future for Missouri politics.[48]

In the 1870s the same conflict between change and tradition was

---

[45] Clevenger, "Agrarian Politics," pp. 1-6, 26-27, 142.

[46] J. A. Leach, "Public Opinion and the Inflation Movement in Missouri, 1875-1879," *Missouri Historical Review*, XXIV (July 1930), 571-73; Williams and Shoemaker, II, 300-18. See also, Irwin Unger, *The Greenback Era: A Social and Political History of American Finance, 1865-1879* (Princeton, 1964), esp. ch. 6, for a general discussion of the Greenback movement.

[47] C. H. McClure, "A Century of Missouri Politics," *Missouri Historical Review*, XV (Jan. 1921), 324-30; Robert M. Crisler, "Missouri's 'Little Dixie'," *Missouri Historical Review*, XLII (Jan. 1948). 130-39; *Spectator*, Dec. 8, 1888; St. Louis *Life*, June 2, 1894; Clevenger, "Agrarian Politics," pp. 86-109. The term "Little Dixie" was coined in the seventies.

[48] Clevenger, "Agrarian Politics." This study is devoted to a development of this theme. See also McClure, XV, 324-36.

developing in the daily journalism of St. Louis. A new style, born in the East and filtering into the Middle West after the Civil War, had begun to stir the newspapers of the city. The old-style newspapers were "party organs," dedicated to partisanship and interested only in political news—which they normally colored outrageously. Their editors either were politicians themselves or were beholden to politicians. Judged by their small circulation, they had little popular appeal.[49]

Such a journal was the *Missouri Republican*. Until the midseventies it was the leading newspaper of St. Louis, if not of Missouri. It was the powerful organ of the Democratic Party in the state, and its publishers, George and John Knapp, spoke with authority in party councils.[50] More specifically, their paper was the spokesman of the conservative oligarchy of St. Louis, which so largely controlled the Democratic Party after the Civil War. The *Republican's* daily circulation, about 15,000, was small by modern standards, but it was read by St. Louis's "best citizens," and its weekly and semi-weekly editions had a far-flung readership in rural Missouri.[51] For decades the *Republican* had been "foremost in point of influence, circulation, [advertising] patronage and income" among St. Louis papers.[52]

In its time it had been a progressive journal. It was the first newspaper established west of the Mississippi, having been founded in 1808 when St. Louis was a fur-trading village. Its original name was the *Missouri Gazette,* but in 1822 it was rechristened the *Republican* to accord with the Jeffersonian sympathies of its publisher.[53] Before the Civil War, a period in which St. Louis proliferated with short-lived sheets, only the *Republican* grew and prospered.[54]

In the dozen years after 1865 the *Republican* reached the height

---

[49] The best study of the history of journalism in the United States is Frank Luther Mott, *American Journalism: A History, 1690-1960*. See esp., chs. 6-25.

[50] George Knapp was the paper's principal publisher for many years. See Walter Williams, "George Knapp," *Dictionary of American Biography*, X, 448-49. William Vincent Byars to James Byars, July 26, 1885, William Vincent Byars Papers. Scharf, *History of St. Louis*, I, 902-20, has a very full account of the *Republican* to 1881. As late as 1903, Champ Clark, seeking political preferment, wrote: "It is believed here that the *Republic* can nominate me, if it goes at it for blood." Champ Clark to Charles W. Knapp, Jan. 19, 1903, Miscellaneous Papers, Missouri Historical Society, St. Louis.

[51] Personal letter from R. Bruce Jones, Feb. 8, 1954.

[52] *Post-Dispatch*, Mar. 27, 1882.

[53] The name St. Louis *Republic* was adopted in 1888.

[54] Scharf, *History of St. Louis*, I, 902-20; Dorothy Grace Brown, "Early St. Louis Newspapers, 1808-1850," unpub. M. A. diss. (Washington University, 1931), pp. 1-33. See also, William Vincent Byars, "A Century of Journalism in Missouri," *Missouri Historical Review*, XV (Oct. 1920), 53-73; Williams and Shoemaker, II, 565.

of its influence. As the chief organ of the Democratic Party in 1870 it helped to overthrow the Radicals in Missouri, whose vindictive policies had proscribed the ex-Confederates and reduced the Democrats to a helpless minority. Its editor, William Hyde, persuaded his fellow Union Democrats—who were still eligible to vote—to combine with the Liberal Republicans in their campagin to put an end to reconstruction by electing B. Gratz Brown governor. Two years later, the rejuvenated Democrats, infused with thousands of reenfranchised, ex-Confederate votes, recovered control of Missouri and the *Republican* became the most powerful newspaper in the state.[55]

But its very success held within it the seeds of decline. After 1873 political journalism began to be challenged in St. Louis by the new style coming from the East, and the fact that the *Republican* was a party organ began to count against it. Editor Hyde spent too much time managing elections and too little seeking out news; as a result his paper was "not as aggressive as it should have been." Indeed, more and more after 1875 the *Republican* came to be looked upon as "somewhat 'sleepy' compared with its more enterprising rivals." [56] Moreover, its tendency to distort political reports in the interests of party gradually produced mistrust; the public came to believe the *Republican's* "news and views were colored to carry out the ends of its owners." [57]

Worse still, the solicitude displayed by the *Republican* for the interests of the St. Louis oligarchy gave it a reputation as "the organ of wealth and money." [58] Oligarchical influence on the paper's policies was glaringly revealed when in the late seventies the *Republican's* owners were forced to admit they had accepted $5,000 worth of securities for "publishing statistical information and local notices favorable to the construction of the St. Louis bridge. . . ." [59] Critics also maintained that the paper's successful efforts to control the municipal government, when it managed the election of Mayor Henry Overstolz in 1877, were in reality a policy of protecting and promoting the economic privileges of the city's monopolists. After 1878 slowly developing resentment of the *Republican's* political dictation and

55 Thomas S. Barclay, *The Liberal Republican Movement in Missouri*, pp. 195-96; Peterson, *Freedom and Franchise*, ch. 13.
56 Albert J. Stofer to William Vincent Byars, Dec. 7, 1919, William Vincent Byars Papers.
57 *Reedy's Mirror*, Feb. 25, 1897.
58 *Post-Dispatch*, Nov. 12, 1881.
59 *Ibid.*, Jan. 9, 1881.

the powerful coterie behind it started the venerable journal on a downward path which led to its disappearance in 1919.[60]

A new day in St. Louis journalism began to dawn in 1872 with the establishment of the *Morning Globe*. Launched as another political sheet by William McKee and Daniel Houser, who were bent upon destroying the *Morning Democrat* and recovering control of the dispensing of Republican patronage in Missouri, the *Globe* became the unwitting vehicle of change when Joseph B. McCullagh of the Chicago *Republican* and once of the Cincinnati *Enquirer* was hired as its editor.[61] McCullagh was short, ponderous, authoritarian, and one of the most inventive newspaper men of his time. He had been a war correspondent with General Grant, and afterwards, as a Washington reporter for the Cincinnati *Commercial*, was one of the originators of the interview story, a favorite device of the new journalism to impart a sense of immediacy to news articles.[62] As a writer "he saw the coloring of the events he covered, and he transferred that coloring to what he wrote. He was said to be sensational, but if he was, it was a sensationalism that was popular." [63]

In brief, McCullagh was attune to the new style of daily pub-

---

[60] *Journalist*, Nov. 14, 1885; *Reedy's Mirror*, Feb. 25, 1897; Walter B. Stevens, "The Tragedy of the St. Louis Republic," *Missouri Historical Review*, XXII (Jan. 1928), 139-49; interview with D.J.W. McAuliffe, Jan. 17, 1951. As reporter, city editor, and managing editor of the *Republic*, McAuliffe was able to recite chapter and verse the influence of the city's oligarchy on the paper. See also, Orrick Johns, *op.cit.*, pp. 67-68.

[61] The *Democrat* had been founded in 1852 by McKee as a Free Soil Democratic paper. In the late 1850s it migrated into the new Republican Party. (Scharf, I, 924-27. See also, Jim A. Hart, "The Missouri *Democrat*, 1852-1860," *Missouri Historical Review*, LV (Jan. 1961), 127-41.) McKee in the seventies was involved in the scandalous Whiskey Ring and was convicted, though pardoned, for his role in it. Gen. John McDonald, *Secrets of the Whiskey Ring, and Eighteen Months in the Penitentiary* (St. Louis, 1880), 39-40, 294-95. See also, Barclay, *Liberal Republican Movement*, pp. 245-46.

[62] Harry Wilson, "McCullagh of the Globe-Democrat," *Page One* (St. Louis, 1948), pp. 9, 24; Mott, p. 386; Bernard A. Weisberger, *Reporters for the Union* (Boston, 1953), pp. 118-19. See also, Walter Williams, "Joseph McCullagh," *Dictionary of American Biography*, XII, 5.

[63] Z. L. White, "Western Journalism," *Harper's New Monthly Magazine*, LXXVII (Oct. 1888), 695; M. Koenigsberg, *King News* (Philadelphia, 1941), pp. 171, 179-80. A leading newspaperman, Koenigsberg comments that "no journalist of McCullagh's time exceeded his contributions to the development and elevation of newspaper standards." See also, Dreiser, pp. 89-90; Wilson, pp. 9, 24; *Reedy's Mirror*, Aug. 15, 1894, Dec. 17, 1896; St. Louis *Life*, Sept. 13, 1890, May 6, 1893; *Spectator*, April 30, 1892. For an extended look at McCullagh by an associate, see Walter B. Stevens, "Joseph B. McCullagh," *Missouri Historical Review*, XXV (Oct. 1930), 3-9; (Jan. 1931), 245-53; (April 1931), 425-31; (July 1931), 576-84; XXVI (Oct. 1931), 40-53; (Jan. 1932), 153-62; (April 1932), 256-66; (July 1932), 375-86; XXVII (Oct. 1932), 50-62; (Jan. 1933), 151-56; (April 1933), 257-61; (July 1933), 337-43; XXVIII (Oct. 1933), 38-42; (Jan. 1934), 125-29; (April 1934), 206-10.

lication. It was a style which emphasized the paper as a vehicle of news rather than opinion, especially entertaining items found on the police blotter, in the courts, in society, and on the streets. Such news was scorned as "sensational" by the respectable, but it attracted a reading public hitherto neglected, the great mass of shopkeepers, clerks, and workers of the rising urban communities. An appetite for serious news also was growing, whetted especially by the cataclysmic event of war, and the new journals catered to this appetite by utilizing the telegraph and the war correspondent to provide the reader with the latest and fullest information. Thus newspapers, first in New York and more slowly elsewhere, began to reshape themselves from political organs into genuine newspapers.[64]

Another characteristic of the new style was a spirit of independence. As their revenues from circulation and, latterly, advertising increased, the new journals began to emancipate themselves from politicians. Printer-editors, once obligated to politicians for their livelihood, evolved into independent publishers. They exercised their freedom by taking positions of their own on questions of the day, more and more independent now of parties. This development was greatly stimulated in 1872 when President Grant sought reelection. Many a Republican journal meditated bolting the party's traces. Whitelaw Reid, Horace Greeley's successor as master of the New York *Tribune,* voiced the growing spirit when he exclaimed, "Independent journalism! that is the watchword of the future. . . ."[65]

McCullagh immediately set about making a live-wire journal of the *Globe.* "There was a snap in its editorial comments that St. Louis had not been accustomed to; there was an air of sensationalism about its news department that was new in the field" and which attracted attention; when, in 1874, the paper secured the much-needed Associated Press franchise from Joseph Pulitzer, the *Globe* quickly forced the rival *Democrat* into a union. Thus, in 1875, the St. Louis *Globe-Democrat* was born.[66]

In two or three years the consolidated journal surpassed the old-line *Republican* in public favor, and by 1879 even its rivals conceded that it was one of the "two most prominent papers in the West."[67] For the next score of years, until its creator leaped to

---

[64] Mott, chs. 13-24.

[65] *Ibid.,* p. 412.

[66] White, "Western Journalism," p. 695; Scharf, I, 927; Seitz, p. 76. For a history of the *Globe-Democrat,* see Jim Allee Hart, *A History of the St. Louis Globe-Democrat* (Columbia, Mo., 1961).

[67] *Post-Dispatch,* March 29, 1879. The *Post-Dispatch* named the Cincinnati *Enquirer* as the other paper.

his death from a St. Louis hotel window, the *Globe-Democrat* was the city's leading newspaper.[68]

McCullagh made his paper a purveyor of news without equal in the West. Saying "the truth—no matter which side it may help or hurt—is what we want for the news columns," the *Globe-Democrat* published the facts as it saw them. Accuracy was the editor's most stringent demand. Next, he sought to give his readers complete coverage of the happenings of the day. A large and competent local staff scoured the city for news, and the *Globe-Democrat's* annual telegraph tolls were larger than those of almost any journal west of New York.[69] Editor McCullagh was imaginative; among the new wrinkles he developed were elaborations of the interview technique. From the start the *Globe-Democrat* assigned a regular hotel reporter to converse with interesting visitors, and in 1877 "Little Mack"— as Eugene Field affectionately called him—advanced a step further when he invented the "mass interview." Often he hired a veritable army of reporters, armed it with a "catechism" and sent it onto the floors of conventions, legislatures, and even the Congress to interview members.[70]

Not merely different techniques, but new sources of news were discovered by the *Globe-Democrat*. Among these were religion and railroads. Without displaying sectarian preferences the paper devoted many columns of space to churches and reveled in publishing argumentative pieces by readers of different faiths. So proud was McCullagh of this feature that the *Globe-Democrat* referred to itself as "the Great Religious Daily." As for railroad news, the *Globe-Democrat* assigned a special reporter to produce a daily column on the subject. This was an adaptation of river news, long a staple item in St. Louis newspapers.[71]

Editorially, although the *Globe-Democrat* was staunchly Republican, it was far from a thick-and-thin party organ. Its pungent, often witty editorials constantly attacked Chauncey I. Filley, the party's boss in Missouri. The paper observed one day that "if hell were dosed with tartar emitic, the last dregs of its last vomit would be a few men of his kind." [72] Its social and economic opinions were conserva-

[68] *Spectator*, March 19, 1881; *Reedy's Mirror*, Dec. 17, 1896; St. Louis *Criterion*, Jan. 9, 1897.

[69] Walter B. Stevens, "The New Journalism in Missouri," *Missouri Historical Review*, XVII (April 1923), 323; Wilson, p. 9; Koenigsberg, p. 180; *Post-Dispatch*, March 12, 1880, Oct. 27, 1881.

[70] Wilson, pp. 9, 24; Stevens, "New Journalism in Missouri," *Missouri Historical Review*, XVIII (July 1924), 558; XIX (April 1925), 429.

[71] Stevens, "New Journalism in Missouri," *Missouri Historical Review*, XVIII (Oct. 1923), 60-61; XIX (July 1924), 559-60.

[72] Wilson, p. 9; *Hornet*, Feb. 25, 1882.

tive but ruggedly independent. Once, when a group of local business men planned to reward McCullagh with a $25,000 dwelling for his services in promoting the prosperity of St. Louis, the editor refused, growling that "some of them might come around afterwards and want to run the paper." [73]

Like most papers of the new journalism, the *Globe-Democrat* had a penchant for self-advertisement. In 1878, in an effort to smoke out the circulation of the close-mouthed *Republican,* Business Manager Daniel Houser published his paper's exact figures in a series of notarized statements and challenged his rival to do the same. Not caring to reveal its loss of first place, the *Republican* ignored the invitation. On another occasion the *Globe-Democrat* invited its readers to visit its offices to watch the papers roll from a new press. Such practices were rationalized as taking the public into partnership.[74]

Altogether, the audacious methods of the *Globe-Democrat* made it the fastest growing and wealthiest newspaper in St. Louis in the late seventies. In 1878 it reached the unheard of circulation of 24,000 for the daily, and its weekly was challenging the *Republican's* in the country. At the same time, the long-held domination of advertising by "Old 1808" was broken, and the *Globe-Democrat* earned for its stockholders a net profit of $120,000 on a $500,000 investment.[75]

The *Republican* could only wring its hands at the new journalistic style, "Audax! Audax! Toujours audax!" But a keen observer of "Little Mack's" originality, Joseph Pulitzer, took careful note of all that he did.

Together, the *Globe-Democrat* and the *Republican,* representing the old and the new, dominated St. Louis newspaperdom. It was no mere coincidence that they were morning publications, for the era of evening journalism had not yet arrived in the Midwest. In the period of political journalism, when news was secondary to opinion, papers reaching the reader at the breakfast table always had greater prestige than their afternoon competitors. But by 1865, when the public's desire for news began to outweigh every other demand, it was natural that the very latest intelligence should be preferred. This meant, since most of the affairs of the world occur during the hours of daylight, that alert afternoon dailies held an advantage over their long-established rivals.[76]

---

[73] Wilson, p. 24; Dreiser, p. 111.

[74] Stevens, "New Journalism in Missouri," *Missouri Historical Review,* XVII (April 1923), 323-24.

[75] *Ibid.; Journalist,* Dec. 13, 1884, Nov. 7, 1885. Personal letter from R. Bruce Jones, Feb. 8, 1954; *Spectator,* March 19, 1881; *Post-Dispatch,* Dec. 23, 1879.

[76] Mott, pp. 446-49, discusses the rise of evening journalism generally.

The growth of large cities also acted as a tonic to evening journalism. The head of a family found he had less and less time in increasingly distant residential neighborhoods to glance through the morning paper before catching a street car for his place of business downtown, and if he took the journal with him to read on the car his wife was deprived of the opportunity of perusing the advertisements in preparation for a shopping tour later in the day. If either waited until the leisurely after-supper hours to look over the paper, the contents had become stale. It was preferable to take an afternoon paper for reading at night when news and ads were fresh. Improved gas lighting in the home was also a factor in these recastings of habit. Aware of the rising circulation of evening journals after the Civil War, advertisers for the first time began to patronize them. Thus, evening journalism began to become profitable as well as popular.[77]

As with other innovations in newspaper publication, afternoon journalism developed first in the larger cities of the Atlantic seaboard and gradually spread westward.[78] In St. Louis, as we have seen, a member of Joseph B. McCullagh's *Globe-Democrat*, John A. Dillon, began to apply the precepts of the new journalism to the afternoon field early in 1878. McCullagh happily hailed the *Evening Post*, telling his readers that "the *Globe-Democrat* now sends forth another graduate to establish a first-class daily evening paper, such as St. Louis has long needed." [79] Dillon founded the *Post* "on the assumption that the field was vacant and the theory that if we made a newspaper worth supporting it would be supported." [80] Hitherto, it had been the belief that "an evening newspaper could not be made profitable in St. Louis," a conviction which was entirely justified on the basis of the history of the St. Louis *Evening Dispatch*, between 1862 and 1878 the city's principal afternoon organ.[81]

During most of its life the *Dispatch* was "a small blanket sheet with scarcely any enterprise, but [sic] little circulation and less advertising. The circulation rarely ever exceeded 5,000 copies daily, and there was a most decided strain to make it reach these figures. The real circulation was confined to the central part of the city and street sales. The subscribers on the outskirts of the city could

[77] *Post-Dispatch*, Jan. 16, 1880; Mott, p. 447. Interview with A. G. Lincoln, Dec. 15, 1949. Lincoln was circulation manager of the *Post-Dispatch* for forty years, beginning in 1895.

[78] Mott, pp. 446-49.

[79] Stevens, "New Journalism in Missouri," *Missouri Historical Review*, XIX (Jan. 1925), 331.

[80] *Evening Post*, Oct. 25, 1878.

[81] *Post-Dispatch*, Jan. 12, 1882.

easily be counted." [82] Unprogressive news policies and vindictively partisan editorials were responsible for this poor showing. Since its founding in 1862 the *Dispatch* had been a political journal, changing its allegiance as it was bought and sold by various politicians.[83]

The paper had been established as the *Union* by a group of loyal citizens in the dark days of the Civil War when the *Democrat* temporarily deserted Abraham Lincoln to support the radical policies of General John C. Fremont in Missouri. The *Union* strongly endorsed the views of General Francis P. Blair, one of its founders, who vigorously supported Lincoln's moderation in the slavery question.[84] By 1864, however, the *Democrat* was back in the fold as the administration's spokesman in Missouri, and the *Union* was shouldered out. Deserted soon after by its original owners, it was sold in 1864 to a group of Union Democrats led by Charles P. Johnson. Johnson was placed in charge of the sheet and renamed it the *Evening Dispatch*. The paper adopted the Democratic views of the new ownership.[85]

For most of the next fourteen years the *Dispatch* was the only afternoon paper in St. Louis, but lack of competition did not overcome the drawbacks of political journalism, and the paper's penchant for losing money, characteristic from the start, was constant. The *Dispatch's* history was filled with makeshift arrangements, changing owners, and mounting debts. Typical of its unending struggle with adversity was the experience of William McHenry and Peter Foy, who bought the paper in 1868 with high hopes, only to give it up five years later badly in debt. In a fit of exasperation and despair, McHenry wrote to his partner that the *Dispatch's* type was worn out, its office equipment in need of replacement, and the building in which it was published "in danger of falling down. . . . In short, it will take more than $20,000 to put the *Dispatch* entirely out of debt . . . we were dismally cheated and deceived in buying the concern. . . . According to my reckoning we would have been about $30,000 better off had we let the *Dispatch* go to the devil . . . and started an entirely new concern." [86]

In the mid-seventies another expedient was tried when Stilson

---

[82] *Journalist*, Sept. 25, 1886.

[83] These observations are made from a study of the files of the *Dispatch*, the originals of which are in the possession of the St. Louis *Post-Dispatch*. *Evening Post*, Oct. 7, 1878.

[84] Allan Nevins, *The War for the Union*, 2 vols. (I, *The Improvised War, 1861-1862*) (New York, 1959), pp. 331-41.

[85] *Post-Dispatch*, Jan. 12, 1882; Scharf, I, 926; James G. Randall, *The Civil War and Reconstruction* (Boston, 1937), p. 478.

[86] *Post-Dispatch*, April 21, 1881.

Hutchins, a skilled journalist who founded the Washington *Post* soon after, sought to lift the *Dispatch* from its "Slough of Despond" by publishing it in tandem with the *Morning Times*. Hutchins thought an around-the-clock arrangement might provide the magic touch, but he announced that "the *Times* and *Dispatch* are totally distinct from each other, though both run under the same management." His Jefferson City correspondent took advantage of this explanation to excuse himself for not covering a story. Hutchins had fired him for intoxication, and when the reporter pleaded illness, the publisher only remarked that this was the aftereffect of the bottle. "You go back and tell 'Hutch,'" the reporter told a friend, "that that drunk and this sickness are like the *Times* and *Dispatch*, totally distinct although both run under the same management." [87]

The public, however, continued to shun the paper, and at length Hutchins wearied of trying to make a success of it and sold it in 1875 to a successful Ohio newspaperman, W. L. Allison, who lost $25,000 in three years on this venture. Late in 1877 he unloaded an almost worthless sheet on the firm of Hume & Wolcott. Desperately the new owners cut costs, reducing the staff to a reporter or two and hiring low-wage female compositers; their paper took to stealing news from competitors and loaning its editorial columns to the ambitions of local Greenbackers. But it was all in vain. The paper's patronage dwindled towards the vanishing point. [88]

The appearance of the vigorous *Evening Post* early in 1878 was in the nature of a coup de grace which brought the *Evening Dispatch* to the auction block in December. The *Post* crowed that this was what happened to newspapers that published "on the cheap and nasty plan. . . . The History of journalism in this country shows that while a cheap newspaper always loses money, a newspaper which spends money for news succeeds. . . ." [89] It was this philosophy—emphasis upon news, integrity, and editorial independence—expressed by the first afternoon paper in St. Louis to practice it, which brought the final demise of the city's last important evening paper published on the old plan.

---

[87] *American Journalist*, July 1884.
[88] Scharf, I, 936; *Evening Post*, Dec. 10, 1878; *Post-Dispatch*, Jan. 12, 1882.
[89] *Evening Post*, Dec. 10, 1878.

CHAPTER III

The First Three Months

The new *Post and Dispatch* appeared on a Thursday afternoon. The mail and home edition, printed at three o'clock, attracted little notice, but the street edition at five o'clock, distributed to a knot of newsboys at the paper's "dingy old rooms . . . on Pine Street," caught the attention of several hundred persons who bought copies as they boarded horse-drawn cars for the slow, jerky ride home.[1] In the gathering darkness of early winter there was only time to glance at what seemed to be a reproduction of the *Evening Post*. The clean, well-printed front page was neatly divided between advertisements and the news. Even the numbering was a continuation of the *Post's;* this was the 286th issue of volume one.

In their gas-lighted homes St. Louisans gave their copies closer inspection. It was true: under VAGARIES OF VICE were the same short, bright squibs about the petty criminal cases disposed of that morning at the Four Courts, and, like the *Post,* the new paper did not neglect serious readers; under FOREIGN NEWS stories ingeniously datelined "Special by Cable to the Post and Dispatch" told of the occupation of parts of the Balkans by Russian troops, and a typically alliterative head, TRAIL OF THE TIDE, captioned a flood story from the East.

It was the editorials on page two of the four-page sheet which revealed that here was a new publication. In a column of rapid-fire paragraphs contrasting sharply with Dillon's deliberate and polished prose of the day before, Joseph Pulitzer proclaimed the policies and promises of the new paper. Declaring that "the union of the POST with the DISPATCH . . . takes place to-day under circumstances which render the paper one of the best established among the newspapers of the country," Pulitzer exhibited his characteristic style:

> The POST and DISPATCH will serve no party but the people; will be no organ of "Republicanism," but the organ of truth; will follow no caucases [sic] but its own convictions; will not support the "Administration," but criticise it; will oppose all frauds and shams wherever and whatever they are; will advocate principles and ideas rather than prejudices and partisanship. These ideas and principles are precisely the same as those upon which our Government was originally founded, and to which we

---

[1] St. Louis *Spectator,* Feb. 5, 1881.

owe our country's marvelous growth and development. They are the same that made a Republic possible and without which a real Republic is impossible. They are the ideas of a true, genuine, real Democracy. They are the principles of hard money, home rule, and revenue reform.

Pulitzer's ambitious personality was evident in other ways. A brief but significant paragraph indicated that he, not Dillon, would have the final word in editorial policy. A local official, John G. Priest, whom the *Post* had attacked for weeks, now found that he was "the only politician who will gain by the union of the POST and DISPATCH. . . . We will support him for any office in the United States."

Also present was an impatient note:

> For the present the paper will be issued from the office of the POST, but only for the present. We shall immediately enlarge the size of the paper, and make use of our own presses, having no relations or connections with any other establishment.

Despite slender means, Pulitzer intended to shed as soon as possible the compromising arrangement whereby the *Post and Dispatch* used the *Globe-Democrat's* press and office space. As if to show that his promises of an improved paper were not mere vaporings, he announced that the very next Saturday the *Post and Dispatch* would contain ten pages, making it "the largest evening paper ever published in St. Louis." Unlike the large morning journals the little *Post and Dispatch* would have no Sunday issue, but this one "will be a Sunday paper published Saturday afternoon."

In short, although in appearance the *Post and Dispatch* was a continuation of the *Evening Post*, its tone was entirely different. Audacity replaced caution, and a headlong plunge into politics replaced the *Post's* Olympian detachment. Two vestiges of the old *Evening Dispatch* remained: a few columns of legal notices on page four denoted the advertising contract with the city, and an announcement that its telegraph news had come over the wires of the Western Associated Press showed that the *Post and Dispatch* possessed this "indispensable . . . basis of evening journalism in St. Louis."

The first issues sketched the main outlines of the paper's editorial policies. Exhibiting the interests of its dynamic new proprietor, the *Post and Dispatch* turned to politics. It intended to be vigorously Democratic, as it made clear on the second day of publication:

> All local or temporary issues are finally settled by their relation to the control of Federal power, and we consider the continuance in power of Republicanism is dangerous to the country. Its only

title to the power it holds is a glaring fraud, and that closes all argument and sets the seal of condemnation on the party.[2]

In the days that followed the paper went into further detail, revealing the old Liberal Republican dislike of the Radicals whom the paper believed controlled the policies of the Hayes administration. The *Post and Dispatch* would be A DEMOCRATIC PAPER because

a change in our National Government is imperatively needed. Real prosperity will never come until the people have restored real, popular self-government. . . . Grantism completely rules the Republican party. Grantism means an end to the Republic. Grantism, therefore, must . . . be . . . rooted out. The Government must once more belong to the people, and not the people to the Government. The President of the Republic must again be elected by the people and not by the four convicted jail-birds called a Returning Board. Political frauds must be punished, not honored, as at present. . . . The large majority must rule, and not the small minority of the nation. The Constitution must be observed, not violated. . . . The return to these principles of true Democracy upon which our country, our government, our liberties and our prosperity were founded, can alone give us what we need—regeneration and reform, peace, prosperity and patriotism.[3]

Aside from "extravagance, profligacy, wastefulness, corruption, peculations, defalcations and dishonor of every description," the principal sin "for which Grantism will ever be known," the *Post and Dispatch* declared, was its determination to centralize all political power in the national capital and thereby reduce state and local governments to nonentities.[4] This was the real significance of the party's policies towards the South. While the worst excesses of Reconstruction had been abandoned, the recent demand by James G. Blaine that intimidation of Negro voters in the South should be investigated showed that the policies of the Republican Party had not changed:

The real question at issue behind the Blaine debate is not whether the elections in the South were conducted fairly and peaceably, but whether each State, South and North, shall be allowed to decide whether its elections . . . are valid. On this question there cannot be two opinions. Grant the worst that is charged by Blaine, concede that in more than one Southern State elections are habitually decided by intimidation—is it not a

2 St. Louis *Post and Dispatch*, Dec. 13, 1878.
3 *Ibid.*, Dec. 23, 1878.
4 *Ibid.*, Dec. 18, 1878.

lesser evil to endure local terrorism than to invite centralized terrorism? Localizing the evil restricts it, begins to cure it, sets it forth for reprobation at the great bar of public opinion, brings it under the ban of that sense of justice which must conquer in the end. On the other hand, to apply the only remedy in reach under the Blaine plan, to allow the Federal Government at Washington to decide what are and what are not legal elections, is a total subversion of our Government, a destruction of its form, an abandonment of its fundamental principle, the principle of liberty.[5]

However, although the *Post and Dispatch* would be Democratic, it did not intend to be an old-style party organ. Announcing in its initial platform that it would "follow no caucases but its own convictions," from the start the paper expressed a spirit of independence, especially in state and local matters. On the second day of publication it announced:

The POST and DISPATCH is perfectly independent in politics. If Democracy means assent to the corrupt management of the State treasury, we are not Democratic; if it means greenbackism in national finance or repudiation of local debt, we are not Democratic.[6]

In the elections of the preceding November, the Greenback Party had made serious inroads into the Democratic domination of rural Missouri, and in order to stave off still greater defections, the Democrats, too, had moved in the direction of soft money. They demanded that Congress repeal the Resumption Act of 1875 and that greenbacks should be issued "sufficient to supply the wholesome and necessary business demands of the whole country." At the same time, the first suggestions that silver might better be used as an instrument of inflation began to be heard. Richard P. Bland, a Democratic congressman from Missouri, was pressing for a silver purchase act in Washington.[7] Notwithstanding, the *Post and Dispatch* declared,

The friends of honest money may rejoice in the assurance that the greenback heresy and the silver craze will receive no encouragement from the POST and DISPATCH. . . . In the cause of honesty our fingers will be ready to touch the tuneful pipe of hard money.[8]

[5] *Ibid.*, Dec. 13, 1878.

[6] *Ibid.*

[7] Leach, "Public Opinion and the Inflation Movement," *Missouri Historical Review*, XXIV (July 1930), 577-81; XXV (Oct. 1930), 116-35. Homer Clevenger, "Agrarian Politics," 16-18. *Post-Dispatch*, Nov. 5, 1879.

[8] *Post and Dispatch*, Dec. 13, 1878.

Accompanying the paragraph was a three-column feature article expressing enthusiastic approval of the Resumption Act on the part of local businessmen. The *Post and Dispatch* also defended the gold standard in a vehement column-length editorial. It asserted roundly that even a fifty percent advance in the price of gold

> and its exclusive use as the standard of value would not do the country half the damage that the promoters of the silver fraud have already inflicted upon us by their desperate and unscrupulous assaults upon credit, contracts and the right of property. . . . [The silver agitation] paralyzes business and cripples enterprise by destroying confidence and keeping the rate of interest higher (through the constant menace to lenders) than any man can afford to pay for the use of capital in productive industry, thus keeping in idleness . . . thousands of laborers that would, under the *regime* of an honest and stable standard of value, be engaged in the production of wealth.[9]

The radicals of rural Missouri were not the only adversaries the *Post and Dispatch* attacked in the ranks of the Democracy. Very early it expressed a distaste for the oligarchs who dominated the party locally. "The trouble in St. Louis," it declared, "is not with either our masses or merchants or middle classes, but those whose wealth would seem to make it their own interest to lead in every measure of enterprise, but who do not lead, nor even sometimes follow." [10]

In the last hours of 1878 the little *Post and Dispatch* showed the first flash of aggressiveness that distinguished its new owner. Early in January the legislature of Missouri was to elect a United States senator, and the various elements composing the state's Democratic Party girded for a fight. The rural ex-Confederates were lined up solidly for George G. Vest, a lawyer who had served in the Confederate Congress. The commercial and moneyed interests—the Bourbons—of St. Louis, led by the *Republican*, favored Samuel Glover, a prominent local attorney. Another Bourbon candidate was Thomas Allen, president of the Iron Mountain Railroad. In the struggle that rapidly developed the *Post* and *Dispatch* for the first time challenged the conservative clique that controlled the state Democratic Party. It is true that Pulitzer had little sympathy for the agrarians, but he had even less for the social and financial oligarchy of St. Louis, against whose domination small business was beginning to grow resentful.

---

[9] *Ibid.*
[10] *Ibid.*, Dec. 19, 1878.

On December 30 the paper announced its choice. "If it is a crime to sympathize with the struggle of a poor but pure and brilliant man like Vest against the combined power of money, offices, patronage, newspaper influence and slander, we plead guilty." With that, the *Post and Dispatch* plunged into the fray with a lack of restraint and a persistency which were to be two of its most striking characteristics. In the heat of the battle it forgot a pledge it had made at the outset: "We prefer to publish a real newspaper to the mere blind puffery of candidates. We prefer telling the truth to bolstering up anybody's chances by falsehood." [11] The precepts of the new journalism which Pulitzer and Dillon much admired were soon lost in a resurgence of old-fashioned personal journalism so typical of party newspapers. Headlines became slanted, news stories biased, and editorials made Vest progressively purer while the characters of Glover and Allen were painted in ever blacker hues. The tone of the editorials became biting, personal, exaggerated, and always couched in Pulitzer's excited prose. Nevertheless, although the style was antiquated, the philosophy of reform was not. Vest was not the ideal candidate for a city journal, but at least his victory would administer a rebuke to the local aristocrats who assumed the right to run St. Louis to suit themselves.

The *Post and Dispatch* vigorously defended Vest against attacks by the *Republican,* organ of the powerful group promoting Glover. The *Republican's* accusation that Vest was corrupt was labeled "an unmitigated lie" and hints that he had a liking for alcohol were scorned as "a gross slander" which had been used to defame "nearly every prominent man in the history of this state . . . ." [12] The *Post and Dispatch* ridiculed Editor Hyde's frantic lobbying for Glover at the capital and charged that the entire resources of the state administration were being used against the man who was supported by "the masses of the people." [13]

The candidacy of Thomas Allen, the railroad magnate, was opposed with equal vigor and for even more explicit reasons: "With Tom Allen as Senator the railroads would rule this State very satisfactorily—to themselves." Allen's entire career was "involved in corporations, whose influence upon the government is daily growing to be more demoralizing and dangerous." [14] In a blunt editorial labeled THE GREAT ISSUE, the paper developed this theme in detail:

What is the great demoralizer of our public life? Of course, corruption. And what causes corruption? Of course, the greed

---

11 *Ibid.,* Dec. 27, 1878.
12 *Ibid.,* Jan. 2, 1879, Jan. 8, 1879.
13 *Ibid.,* Jan. 2, 1879.
14 *Ibid.,* Jan. 4, 1879, Jan. 7, 1879.

for money. And who offer the greatest temptation to that greed? Corporations. And what are corporations? All monopolies, all special privileges, all classes favored by law.

Democracy means opposition to all special privileges. Republicanism means favoritism to corporations. The tremendous power and influence of nearly all corporations and favored classes, whether railroads or banks or protected interests, are notoriously on the Republican side. Without their united great aid that party would not be in power today. . . .

Money is the great power of to-day. Men sell their souls for it. Women sell their bodies for it. . . . Others worship it. . . . It is the growing dark cloud to our free institutions. It is the natural great enemy of Democracy. It is the irresistible great conflict of the future.

The money power has grown so great that the issue of all issues . . . is whether the corporations shall rule this country or the country shall again rule the corporations. . . . [Corporate influence] reaches into almost every County Court and City Council, extends to every State Legislature, every Congress, every Senate, nay reaches the Supreme Court, and the White House itself! . . .

Yet it is seriously proposed by purchased papers and political prostitutes to send . . . the most conspicuous creature of "capital and privilege" in this State to the Senate of the United States . . . . as the representative of the Missouri Democracy! What would be said of the Republicans if they elected Tom Scott Senator from Pennsylvania. . . . And is there, relatively speaking, any difference between Tom Scott and Tom Allen? [15]

All the efforts of the Glover and Allen forces failed to avert defeat. On January 16 the *Post and Dispatch* joyfully carried the news, VEST VICTORIOUS, under six decks of subheads, and the next day the paper preened itself on its first major triumph, although its small circulation scarcely justified its claim of influence. Shrilly it declared that

our readers alone were not surprised by the result, as the POST AND DISPATCH was the only journal that daily predicted [the outcome] against the loud and lying contradictions of all the other papers. We mention this in no spirit of vanity, but because our reference and prediction about the past and present may entitle our predictions about the future to more absolute confidence.[16]

[15] *Ibid.*, Jan. 10, 1879.
[16] *Ibid.*, Jan. 17, 1879.

The contest left a legacy of bitterness in the relations between the brash new sheet and the venerable *Republican*. The *Post and Dispatch* had scored attempts by the *Republican's* owners and editor to manage the election by manipulation of the party caucus, and it declared that its opponent

> believes that the politics of a State shall be controlled by a newspaper; that whoever has control of such newspaper shall have the power to say who shall and who shall not be Governor or Senator; that a political party, or convention, or caucus, is simply to obey the dictum of such paper or person; that whoever dares to oppose this policy is foolish.[17]

The bruised feelings of the *Republican* after the humiliating defeat of its candidate were not improved by such *Post and Dispatch* jibes as: "They live high around at the *Republican* office now: mostly crow." [18] This was the opening round in a long, eye-gouging brawl between the two papers, one representing the old and the other the new in American journalism.

To keep its name before the public, the little *Post and Dispatch* next turned to the local scene for an issue. It found just what it wanted in the maneuverings of the venerable St. Louis Gas-light Company to recover an old monopoly of illumination. The company had been chartered in 1837, and for years afterwards had exploited the exclusive privilege granted to it by forcing up rates until St. Louisans paid the highest rates in the nation for heat and light. It was estimated that in 1870 the company's profits amounted to seventy-three percent of the stockholders' $600,000 investment. For this lucrative monopoly it paid the city annually only $16,000.[19] The situation became so intolerable that in 1870 legal proceedings were begun to deprive the company of its franchise. The company was saved temporarily when the Democrats, dominated by the local oligarchy, recovered control of the city in 1872, electing Joseph Brown, president of the Atlantic and Pacific, and Missouri Pacific Railroads, mayor of St. Louis. The proceedings against the company were dropped, and in 1873 Brown and a small coterie of pro-monopoly lawyers and politicians negotiated what was called the Tripartite Agreement between the city, the St. Louis Gas-light Company, and the Laclede Corporation which was organized in 1871 and had briefly threatened to compete with the older company. With the approval of the city the

---

17 *Ibid.*, Jan. 6, 1879.
18 *Ibid.*, Jan. 18, 1879.
19 *Ibid.*, Jan. 17, 1879, Jan. 24, 1879; *Post-Dispatch*, March 12, 1881. Scharf, *History of St. Louis*, II, 1,438-39; Soraghan, "History of St. Louis," p. 38-40, 52-53.

9. Alfred H. Spink, first sports writer of the *Post-Dispatch*. (Courtesy C. C. Johnson Spink)

10. Alonzo W. Slayback, shot to death in *Post-Dispatch* offices by John Cockerill. (From A. W. Slayback, *A Memorial Volume*, published 1883)

11. John McGuffin, first *Post-Dispatch* business manager, who, along with Pulitzer, Moore, and Cockerill, put together the *Post-Dispatch*. (From the *Post-Dispatch* files)

12. Cartoon published in *Die Laterne*, a St. Louis publication, at the time Pulitzer bought the *Dispatch* at a courthouse auction. The cartoon speculates that Pulitzer plans to combine the *Dispatch* with the *Post*. (From the *Post-Dispatch* files)

13. Drawing of Missouri Governor Thomas T. Crittenden published in the *Post-Dispatch* on August 4, 1882, during the paper's attacks on him in its anti-gambling crusade. (From the *Post-Dispatch* files)

two companies divided the community into two districts—the boundary being set at Washington Avenue—and reestablished the monopoly as of old. In accordance with the division, the old Gas-light Company renewed its grasp upon the downtown business district where its rates remained outrageously high. At the same time, the Tripartite Agreement permitted both companies to boost their charges to the city for municipal lighting to higher levels than ever before—a fact which taxpayers soon discovered.[20]

The Tripartite Agreement produced such an outcry that in 1876, when Mayor Brown retired, the city revived its suit to cancel the franchise and took over the gas works as a public utility. The company took the case to the courts on the plea that the agreement, which had extended the franchise for twenty years, had been violated. After two adverse decisions in the lower courts, late in 1878 the stockholders of the defunct company without much hope appealed to the Missouri Supreme Court.[21]

In desperation they also turned to the Municipal Assembly where they presented what they described as a "compromise," a proposal to shoulder all the legal expenses and court costs incurred by the municipality since 1876 if the city would return the charter to the company. The monopolists planned to slip their "compromise" through the assembly with little or no debate, a strategy which was proceeding satisfactorily when late in January the little *Post and Dispatch* suddenly turned its attention to the matter.

On January 30 it published a blunt statement entitled NO COMPROMISE:

> The more the proposition of the Gas Company is looked into the more it looks like the division of that ancient turkey and buzzard between the white man and the Indian. Whichever way the proposition is turned, it is the same—the city gets the buzzard, the Gas Company all the turkey.

The editorial declared "we might support some fair and just compromise. But the present proposition is no compromise at all. It is . . . almost an unconditional surrender of the city to the gas company." And it concluded:

> The argument that the city should not run the Gas-works is no argument at all. We do not wish the city to run the Gas-works. No sensible man does. But that is no reason why the city, if the suit [in the Supreme Court] is decided in her favor as it has already been by two tribunals, should not sell the Gas-

---

[20] Soraghan, pp. 50-53.
[21] *Post and Dispatch,* Jan. 17, 1879, Jan. 24, 1879.

works for several millions of dollars in cash and under conditions securing cheaper gas in the future. . . .

We say to the Gas Committee [of the assembly]: This is no compromise. Hands off! No surrender to the monopoly.

The next afternoon, once more under the heading NO COMPRO-MISE, the *Post and Dispatch* attacked the heart of the proposal:

The most objectionable feature of this business is that its only possibility of success depends upon bribery. Yes, we write it deliberately, bribery. . . . We do not mean any of the numerous and dark practices that are undoubtedly resorted to by the high-toned money bags who represent the gas monopoly. We mean what the monopolists have already announced as an inducement for the city to make the compromise—that the gas monopolists will pay all the expenses of the suit and all the fees of the lawyers of the city, amounting to one hundred thousand dollars.

This is an open and unblushing bid to bribe the lawyers of the city by the payment of large fees. . . . Let them [the city's attorneys] be paid by the city and not be bribed by the gas monopolists. Let them remember how the city was sold once before in the tripartite agreement by her own lawyers.[22]

In this campaign the *Post and Dispatch* continued to display the aggressiveness it had first shown in the senatorial election. Its policy was always to attack, never to be pushed on the defensive. The company's proposition, it said, should never be considered other than "an impertinent, insolent request for a surrender on the part of the city. . . ."[23] And to the question, "What are your reasons for opposing the gas compromise?" the paper replied:

But this is bad logic from the start. The question is not, what reasons are there for opposing the so-called compromise? but it is the reverse—what reasons are there in favor of it?[24]

NO COMPROMISE! NO COMPROMISE! NO COMPROMISE! appeared day after day for more than two weeks at the head of hard-swinging editorials, feature articles which exposed the company's long record of inefficiencies, greed, and arrogance, and interview stories which publicized the hostility of consumers—especially downtown businessmen—to a renewal of the franchise. Pulitzer was certainly no advocate of public ownership. But his dislike of privilege in this case outweighed his fear of government. The *Post and Dispatch* did not contemplate permanent municipal operation of the gas works, but, for

---

22 *Ibid.*, Jan. 31, 1879.
23 *Ibid.*, Feb. 4, 1879.
24 *Ibid.*, Feb. 1, 1879.

the sake of businessmen-consumers like himself, he vigorously defended the city's cancellation of the franchise. Franchises did not come under the heading of private property.

In contrast to the senatorial campaign, the *Post and Dispatch* could truthfully claim to be "solitary and alone" in the fight against the gas monopoly. As the organ of the entrenched interests, the *Republican* thought the compromise was eminently fair, while the *Globe-Democrat* failed to break an embarrassed silence until the eve of the vote in the assembly when it made a mild request for further study. Only the *Westliche Post*—Pulitzer's old paper—wholeheartedly sided with the *Post and Dispatch,* condemning the compromise with righteous wrath.[25]

It was with justifiable pride, therefore, that on February 20 the *Post and Dispatch* recorded the news under NO COMPROMISE that the assembly had rejected the St. Louis Gas-light Company's proposal. There was no doubt that this victory belonged to this aggressive new sheet, or that it was important. The paper had administered an unaccustomed check to the powerful interests of St. Louis.[26]

The crusade against the gas "compromise" had not reached its climax when the *Post and Dispatch* suddenly launched another campaign. It was doubtless the result of an inspiration from City Editor Moore or News Editor Jennings, one of whom remembered that the tax returns for 1878 were on file in the assessor's office. One Saturday afternoon in mid-February readers were startled to find on the front page a two-column story under heavy Gothic lettering, TAX-DODGER, which revealed—as subheads proclaimed—"Wholesale Perjury as a Fine Art," "An Alarming Scarcity of Personal Property," "Wealthy Paupers—not a Cent in Pocket nor a Dollar in Bank," "Specimen Samples of the Returns of Some of our Richest Citizens." [27]

"As a sample of how the returns are filled out by tax-payers," the *Post and Dispatch* said, "we give the following copies of the returns for this year of some well-known citizens."

The tax return of J.B.C. Lucas, the wealthiest man in the city, read:

Two horses, mares and geldings	$100.00
One cow	25.00
Two clocks	20.00
Two watches, chains and appendages	50.00
One sewing machine	15.00
Gold and silver plate	500.00

[25] *Ibid.,* Feb. 15, 1879.
[26] *Ibid.,* Feb. 20, 1879, Feb. 22, 1879.
[27] *Ibid.,* Feb. 15, 1879.

Jewelry, all kinds	250.00
Household, kitchen furniture	1500.00
One library	75.00
Two carriages	200.00
	$2735.00

Commented the *Post and Dispatch*:

Money on hand—NOT A CENT.

Money deposited in bank or other safe place—NOT A DOLLAR.

Aggregate statement of solvent notes unsecured by mortgage or deed of trust—nothing.

Aggregate statement of all solvent notes secured by mortgage or deed of trust—nothing.

Aggregate statement of all solvent bonds, whether State, County, town, city, township, incorporated or unincorporated companies—nothing.

He also possesses no pianos or musical instruments, no asses or jennets, mules, sheep, hogs, and other livestock, and has no stock in steamboats or other vessels.

Moralizing comment was left for the editorial page:

Millions and millions of property in this city escape all taxation. When persons like Charles P. Chouteau, the Lucases, or Gerard B. Allen, swear that they do not have one cent in cash, or in bank, don't own one cent's worth of bonds or stocks or notes or other securities, they commit . . . a falsehood, both ridiculous and monstrous. And a much stronger term could be used without danger of libel suits. Tax-dodging has become so . . . universal, thanks to the indifference of the press and the officials, that change is imperatively demanded. The grand jury could do no better service than to investigate the matter.

Here was a new development in *Post and Dispatch* journalism. The previous campaigns had been chiefly editorial. In this one, for the first time Joseph Pulitzer discovered "the means of fighting popular causes in the news columns." [28] The *Post and Dispatch* editors and reporters had dug beneath the surface of events to ferret out abuses hidden from public view. Crusading by news exposure was not new. The New York *Times* had resorted to this technique several years before in

---

[28] Will Irwin, "The American Newspaper, Part III," *Collier's Magazine*, XLVI (Feb. 18, 1911), 14. Both the St. Louis *Democrat* and Emory Foster's ephemeral *Morning Journal* exposed the notorious Whiskey Ring in 1875. Mott, *American Journalism*, p. 415; McDonald, *Secrets of the Great Whiskey Ring*, pp. 126-218, 294-95; Augustus Thomas, *The Print of My Remembrance* (New York, 1922), p. 127; Hart, *History of the Globe-Democrat*, ch. 10.

smashing the Tweed Ring, and in St. Louis the *Globe-Democrat* and even Dillon's *Evening Post* used it to attack gambling. Now the *Post and Dispatch* incorporated the device into its own developing style of crusading to expose wrong-doing by the city's "best citizens." It produced a sensation—a result devoutly hoped for by the paper's directors.[29]

The "best citizens," whose questionable behavior was bared to the public, were not accustomed to disrespectful treatment. There was bitter resentment even among thoughtful elements in the community. Powerful interests resolved to destroy the insolent *Post and Dispatch*. Valuable advertising was withdrawn with every expectation that the paper would soon wither and die.[30] But the paper persisted, published day after day additional tax returns, and whenever a faulty declaration invited it, the *Post and Dispatch* would say:

Money on hand. . . . . NOT A CENT.
Money deposited in bank or other safe place. . . . . NOT A DOLLAR.

On the editorial page each day appeared the taxpayer's oath together with dozens of short paragraphs expressing scorn at the dishonesty of the rich. The cry of outraged citizens only made the paper more determined:

It is said that we go too far in our exposure of taxdodging and our criticism of the most "prominent and powerful" citizens of St. Louis.
We say that we have not gone far enough. . . .
When men like Chas. P. Chouteau make a sworn return that they do not own a bond, a mortgage or a note of any kind, or have not a penny in hand, in bank or anywhere else in the world, the public interest demands exposure and correction.
We are not after the men who have furniture or pictures. But we are after the men who in the aggregate have millions and millions of bonds, notes, mortgages and money without paying one penny upon them, in violation of honor and truth, law and oaths.[31]

To complaints that it was invading the privacy of individuals, the *Post and Dispatch* pointed out that

the tax returns are not private secrets; they are public documents; and if the publication of them hurts any one it is not our fault.

---

[29] Irwin, *loc. cit.*
[30] Creelman, "Joseph Pulitzer," p. 239. George S. Johns, *Joseph Pulitzer*, pp. 70-71.
[31] *Post and Dispatch*, Feb. 21, 1879.

We would not willingly injure an honest man, but we do not care how many dishonest men are injured by the publication of their own sworn statements. . . . The matter is one in which our own journalistic enterprise keeps step with public duty, and we shall not consider our enterprise exhausted, or our duty discharged, until we have put an end, as far as possible, to tax-dodging.[32]

The *Post and Dispatch* spoke for the ordinary citizen: "If the rich would pay their taxes as the poor or middle classes do, St. Louis would be rich indeed." [33] But because wealthy individuals refused to declare $70,000,000 in personal wealth, the burden of public expenditures fell upon honest citizens less able to pay.[34] To prove its point the paper published long lists of returns made out by men in humbler pursuits, such as lawyers, ministers, teachers, and small businessmen who were found to have made honest declarations. Said the *Post and Dispatch*:

> Prejudices against the rich are as unworthy as prejudices against the poor. Both should be treated alike. Both are alike before the law. It is not catering to the prejudice of the many against the few, the rich as against the poor, when we state the obvious truth that the latter are infinitely more conscientious, truthful and honorable in their returns. . . .[35]

For more than three weeks the paper carried on its campaign of exposure, at the end of which it insisted upon an investigation.

> We have published the returns of poor men, of mechanics, printers, plasterers, widows and others, showing that the scanty and hard-earned savings of the poor are made to contribute their full share of taxation. In the face of such a fact it is a shame that property of notoriously great value . . . should escape taxation because its owners have elastic consciences and because the assessor cringes pliantly before the pressure of wealth. . . . It is time for the grand jury to step in and find the reason and the remedy. . . .[36]

When the grand jury was convened next day, Judge Laughlin delivered a thoughtful charge to the jury, whose foreman was the redoubtable Joseph B. McCullagh. The judge declared he had looked carefully into the tax-dodging matter but had concluded that the statute itself was full of "flagrant defects" making enforcement impossible. Therefore, he felt a probe by the grand jury would accomplish

---

[32] *Ibid.*, Feb. 22, 1879.
[33] *Ibid.*, Feb. 19, 1879.
[34] *Ibid.*, Feb. 21, 1879.
[35] *Ibid.*, Feb. 17, 1879.
[36] *Post-Dispatch*, March 10, 1879.

little. The *Post and Dispatch* protested, declaring that the law was written with "complete clearness" and that the jury had "ample power to indict for perjury" the worst offenders.[37]

But Laughlin's opinion was the turning point in the paper's sensational campaign; in grudging acquiescence to the judge's objections the *Post and Dispatch* soon lost interest in its crusade. It carried on for two or three weeks more and finally dropped it. In later years Pulitzer liked to remember the crusade as a success, but no reform resulted from it and assessments continued to decline.[38]

Journalistically, however, the tax-dodger crusade was a master stroke. The *Post and Dispatch* was the most talked about sheet in the city. Moreover, it was responsible for bringing to the paper what Pulitzer was trying hardest to obtain—an increase in circulation. Early in the campaign the paper announced that it had suffered a loss of two subscribers on Lucas Place but had gained 568 elsewhere, and a few days later it observed defiantly:

> The increased demand for the POST AND DISPATCH is the best evidence of the interest our citizens take in the great question of tax dodging. We propose to continue the work, in spite of the indignation of some of our "best"—because richest—fellow citizens of eminent respectability, who think they know as much about running a first-class newspaper as they do about swearing to false returns.[39]

To attract a larger readership Pulitzer turned more and more to sensational exposures. One was a story headed THE SOCIAL EVIL, culled from a year-old jury report on the spread of prostitution in St. Louis. It concerned property owners, some of them unsuspecting, "who rent and lease homes to the frail sisterhood for immoral purposes."[40] But the most spectacular sensation was a story gained by careful planning and sheer audacity on the part of the news staff. The governor of Missouri had appointed to the local police board two men suspected of having connections with the local gambling fraternity. Consequently, the state senate sent an investigating committee to St. Louis to conduct secret hearings on their fitness. The hearings were to be held in the Lindell Hotel.

The editors of the *Post and Dispatch* were determined somehow to

---

[37] *Ibid.*, March 11, 1879, March 12, 1879.

[38] In 1877 the total assessment on personal property in St. Louis was $33,338,000; in 1879, following the crusade, it fell to $27,742,000; and a year later it slipped still further to $24,668,000. The paper was to return to the matter again. *Ibid.*, Jan. 12, 1882, Feb. 18, 1882.

[39] *Post and Dispatch*, Feb. 20, 1879, Feb. 24, 1879.

[40] *Ibid.*, Feb. 11, 1879.

defeat the ban on publicity. Their paper "was just taking a start to grow, and proprietors as well as subordinates were straining every nerve to make it interesting to the public." [41] The day before the hearings Dillon and Pulitzer met with their city editor, Henry Moore, in the small *Post and Dispatch* office. Moore suggested that a reporter could be hidden in a physician's waiting room where an old sealed up door permitted sounds to be heard from the other side of the wall. The doctor in question agreed so long as his parlor was not locked, "as patients were constantly calling to see him."

Next morning "Jenkins," as the reporter was referred to, took up his station.[42] Although the hallway outside swarmed with reporters, policemen, and curious onlookers, for a day and a half he crouched in a cramped position listening to unvarnished testimony. "At a certain point about five feet from the floor, he could catch all of what was said . . . by drawing his ear up very close and holding it in a sort of funnel shape." He could not take notes, but "kept what he had heard . . . running through his mind, something after the style of a school-boy learning a Greek conjugation." At dawn the next morning he met the city editor who transcribed all that was heard and hurried to the office. The feature of the reporter's work was that he was so well acquainted with the interrogating senators and witnesses that he ascribed to the proper persons all questions and replies.[43]

Moore wrote an exciting account which ran to eight full columns. Fourteen decks of headlines were set over the story—the equivalent of a modern eight-column streamer—and atop the entire piece was the heading, THE VEIL IS RENT.[44]

At three o'clock the edition was rushed onto the street where newsboys shouted, "secret proceedings of the committee!" and "exposure of the gambling ring!" One boy hurried to the hotel and ran unstairs to the hallway outside the committee room where the hearing was still in progress. "Somebody read the first line of [Bob] Pate's testimony, . . . and then gave the alarm." The chairman of the committee came out, bought a paper, and his jaw sagged in astonishment. There, staring at him was the entire story, "more complete than . . . [his] own secretary had recorded it." Crowed the *Post and Dispatch,* "the cat was really out of the bag, the dog was really dead. . . ." [45]

On all sides this was accounted the most sensational journalistic feat in many a year. Morrison Munford, a leading Kansas City editor,

---

41 *Spectator,* Feb. 5, 1881.

42 "Jenkins" was a nickname often given to reporters who invaded the privacy of others for sensational news. Mott, p. 386.

43 *Spectator,* Feb. 5, 1881.

44 *Post and Dispatch,* Feb. 18, 1879.

45 *Ibid.,* Feb. 19, 1879.

exclaimed that it was "the finest piece of work I have seen in a long time; it stamps the POST AND DISPATCH as one of the most enterprising papers in the country," and the editors of the other St. Louis papers lamely reprinted the story, wryly giving credit to their lively competitor.[46] For days afterwards, under THE GREAT SCOOP, the *Post and Dispatch* modestly printed columns of tributes from journals across the land. It told its readers that the story proved that it "does not stop at bolts and bars, stone walls or wooden bulwarks when there is news to be obtained." [47]

The editorial page, too, in February took on a spectacular tinge when it launched into a campaign to shock St. Louisans into a realization that the city was dropping behind Chicago in the race for supremacy of the Middle West. Misleading statistics and confident predictions of future greatness had made the local citizenry complacent, satisfied with the unprogressiveness of their business habits and civic slothfulness. This was the period of the "Great Illusion," a false optimism which Pulitzer himself shared to some degree. Nevertheless, he hoped to awaken the city by an editorial barrage which, by its sensational tone, would also bring the *Post and Dispatch* new readers.

The campaign began with a long piece entitled ST. LOUIS AS IT IS, and its exaggerated, free-swinging style must have caused the sensation Pulitzer hoped for.

> St. Louis is in point of population the third city in the Union, and claims to be second to none in cultivation, intelligence, sagacity, enterprise, or anything that might stamp it at once cosmopolitan and metropolitan, [the paper began]. We have never thought it worth while to take an inventory of the assets which make up our collected wealth.[48]

The *Post and Dispatch* proposed to do so now, pointing out that culturally the city lagged far behind Chicago, boasting only two small bookstores, two small libraries, and two theaters where empty seats were more noticeable than good performances. The paper concluded that these remarks were only the beginning, but

> enough has been said to furnish food for thought, and if the food is bitter, the thought may be wholesome. The great point is not whether this is pleasant, but whether it is true. If we are mistaken, have exaggerated or erred we invite correction. . . . . But the contrast between the braggart pretense and the beggarly performance grows less endurable when one thinks that

---

46 *Ibid.*
47 *Ibid.*, Feb. 18, 1879, March 1, 1879.
48 *Ibid.*, Feb. 12, 1879.

the puffery of the press may have helped to swell a conceit as ridiculous as it is empty. Perhaps the truth would be more pleasant if we indulged in it more freely and frequently.

Two days later the paper blasted as "untenable" St. Louis's claim to commercial supremacy.

The plain fact is that we not only do not compete with Chicago in her specialties, but we are left behind in . . . our own specialties. The disproportion in the comparative receipts of grain, live stock and lumber might be endured if we could only handle as much in boots and shoes, dry goods or other great staples. With ordinary energy and ordinary management St. Louis would have been the center of a system of railway transportation that would defy competition, but thanks to our jealousy of each other, our opposition to foreign capital and our long series of mistakes in over-rashness and over-timidity, our cheapest way to the Pacific is via Chicago, while Chicago outbids us alike for the trade of Texas, of Kansas and of California. With the exception of our milling business and our cotton trade we have been left behind in every struggle for commercial supremacy. . . .

With facts such as these . . . it is "playing baby" to console ourselves with dreams of future greatness and assumptions of natural advantage. . . . No natural advantage can atone for the natural disadvantage of not having any sense. In the fierce struggle for supremacy, in the fierce competition for business, not to advance is to recede.[49]

Unprogressive businessmen were not the only reasons for backwardness. Worse still was corruption in municipal government.

The curse is that we are ruled by the alliance of whisky and gambling; and the corruption bred by these noxious influences permeates our whole local government and our local politics. For the rank and file of the voters two thousand dramshops open their seductive portals; for the leaders of the gamblers' ring offer at once the means of achieving success and . . . substantial rewards. . . . The pollution of its bribery has silenced a servile press, has corrupted an obsequious police, has defiled the very judgment seat of justice itself. The congenial alliance between the gambling hell and the brothel, the convenient service of the pander and the capper, the coercion of the spy and the blackmailer—these have been the influences which have ruled St. Louis,

---

[49] *Ibid.,* Feb. 14, 1879.

mocking at honesty, insulting purity, defying decency—our burden, our shame, and our ruin.

These conditions were borne by "tens of thousands of pure and peaceful" citizens who "have no feeling but loathing and horror and hatred for the corrupt and malignant influences that sway our Government and our local politics. Their deepest wish is to throw off the disgrace which oppresses them." Indeed, asserted the paper, "all they need is an organ, a voice to speak what their heads think, what their hearts feel" to unite and lead them. "Well!" the *Post and Dispatch* exclaimed:

> Six days in the week at least the truth will be spoken for them without fear or favor; the work of purgation is begun as soon as the secret evil is dragged into the light of day. The unpleasant truth has long wanted the ripe occasion to make its publication felt with telling effect. We have commenced to publish the true story. The friends of decency may rest assured that we will not close our record until the end of the last chapter.[50]

As has been seen, this sort of frantic—sometimes exaggerated— journalism by the end of February, two and a half months after the paper started publication, at last began to produce results; there was an upturn in circulation. This was a necessity if the paper hoped to survive, for as an adherent of the new journalism it had no support from parties or politicians. Moreover, its unrestrained attacks upon the "best citizens" already had begun to earn for it the enmity of those who, in considerable degree, controlled the politics and wealth of the city. Only with a broad popular base—in the form of a large circulation—could the *Post and Dispatch* prosper as an independent business. Pulitzer hoped he had found the formula for success in spectacular journalism.

Other handicaps in addition to a small readership faced the proprietors. There were fewer than twenty carriers to distribute the home edition of the paper; subscribers were poorly served by long, winding routes through the residential districts. Street sales downtown were similarly handicapped by a shortage of newsboys; only about fifty hawked afternoon papers, although to some extent they made up for thin ranks in noise and activity.[51]

Moreover, the new *Post and Dispatch* faced a fight for survival in

---

[50] *Ibid.*, Feb. 18, 1879.

[51] Frank R. O'Neil to Joseph Pulitzer, 1903, Pulitzer Papers (CU); *Post-Dispatch*, Dec. 24, 1879, Aug. 18, 1881. Newsboys bought their copies from the *Post and Dispatch* for two and a half cents per copy and pocketed whatever they made from hawking them at five cents. *Ibid.*, April 21, 1881.

a struggle with the *Evening Star,* a paper of strong financial resources provided by Thomas Allen, the railroad owner, and a coterie of politicians about him. The *Star* and the *Post and Dispatch* staged a brief but sharp encounter worthy of far larger newspapers. An acute crisis occurred almost immediately when, because of confusion caused by the consolidation of the *Dispatch* and *Post,* several hundred sub-scribers, waiting in vain for the new paper, shifted to the *Star.* It was a loss the *Post and Dispatch* could ill afford, which threatened its existence at the very start. The paper pleaded for patience: "In readjusting the carriers' routes . . . a great many carriers find themselves on unfamiliar ground. Any of the subscribers to the POST AND DISPATCH who fail to receive the paper or who receive it irregularly will confer a favor by informing us of it." [52]

Fortunately, the *Star* was even more vulnerable, for it lacked an Associated Press franchise, and when it took to pirating cable news from the *Post and Dispatch* the latter used an old trick to expose it. A fictitious cable was concocted by the telegraph editor about a revolt against British forces in Afghanistan, and when the *Star* published the report as its own, its rival icily remarked:

We do not propose to moralize on the sinfulness of stealing . . . but we must firmly insist that the way of the transgressor is hard, and though there is no law to punish the larceny of news once published, there is a sterner justice lying in wait for newspapers which are exposed in the publication of bogus news and in the attempt to gain readers under false pretenses.[53]

After this the *Star's* threat withered, and the *Post and Dispatch* entered the new year with a circulation of 3,160 copies.[54]

Another problem was to persuade local businessmen of the ad-vantages of advertising in the afternoon *Post and Dispatch.* Making a virtue of the fact that its circulation, however small, at least con-sisted of city readers, Pulitzer argued that "quality [is] more im-portant that quantity . . . especially so with regard to the quality of newspaper circulation." He pointed out that "a merchant wants to sell" his goods. Therefore, what benefit does a merchant receive "if his advertisement goes to people in Illinois, Iowa or Kansas, who can not come here to buy their Christmas presents? The

---

[52] *Post and Dispatch,* Dec. 13, 1878, Dec. 20, 1878.

[53] *Ibid.,* Jan. 2, 1879. The Chicago *Daily News* disposed of a competitor with a similar trick two or three years earlier. Melville E. Stone, *Fifty Years a Journal-ist* (New York, 1923), pp. 63-64.

[54] *Post-Dispatch,* Jan. 12, 1882.

readers of the POST AND DISPATCH, however, are . . . right here in this city. . . ." [55]

Turning to the readers of the morning papers, Pulitzer also sought to persuade them to switch to his journal.

One of the unsettled questions of journalism is the relative importance of the morning and evening paper. It has commonly been supposed that as a medium for diffusing the news of the day, the advantage was wholly on the side of the morning paper. But . . . in the matter of cable news the evening papers always have the start. Whether it be a collision in the Sea of Marmora, a battle in the Pelwar Pass, a revolution in the Sultan's palace, or a row in the British cabinet, the evening paper is invariably the first to give the news. In the financial and commercial reports it has the whole field to itself . . . at least fifteen hours before the morning papers have them. The court proceedings and criminal items are matters of great local importance, and nearly all the important decisions, verdicts and trials are in time for the evening paper. In a word, the evening paper chronicles everything that happens between 4 a.m. and 4 p.m., leaving to the morning papers such events as happen between 4 p.m. and 4 a.m.[56]

The new paper concluded this plea with a characteristic statement:

In a city, at least, there are about three times as many people who have leisure for an evening paper as there are for a morning paper. It is merely a question whether the evening paper can occupy the field, and we propose to occupy it.

It was also characteristic of Joseph Pulitzer that immediately upon launching the *Post and Dispatch* he persuaded his cautious partner to gamble their meager resources upon the future, the acquisition of a building and equipment at the first possible moment. The paper must be totally independent of any compromising arrangements with the *Globe-Democrat*. Although the Dispatch Publishing Company was capitalized at $250,000, it represented hopes, not actualities.[57] Between them, Pulitzer and Dillon actually possessed

---

[55] *Post and Dispatch*, Dec. 16, 1878.

[56] *Ibid.*, Dec. 21, 1878.

[57] The corporation which had published the old *Evening Dispatch* was the St. Louis Dispatch Company, which went bankrupt. The new organization, the Dispatch Publishing Company, was not a continuation of it. *Post-Dispatch*, Dec. 15, 1879, Jan. 12, 1882. Dillon and Pulitzer owned all but a few shares of the stock in the new company and constituted half the board of directors. The other two members were William Patrick and Blanche Valle Dillon. Early in 1879 Charles Parsons, president of the local bank where the funds of the new paper

only a few thousand dollars of ready capital; the former's amounted to $2,700 in cash and Dillon's, less easily available, was perhaps a bit more.[58] Despite this, at the very time when the paper was struggling for survival against the tiny *Evening Star*, it boldly announced it had ordered for immediate delivery a Bullock press from Philadelphia.[59] This must have fallen through, but in January, when it still had not caught public favor, the *Post and Dispatch* arranged to rent and renovate an old three-story residence at 111 North Fifth Street as a place of publication.[60] At the same time a press was again ordered, this one from the famous manufacturer, Richard M. Hoe and Company of New York. It was a small, four-cylinder affair capable of printing 20,000 folio sheets per hour. New cases of type were also ordered, and on January 25 the paper announced it would move into its new quarters in February.[61]

The purchase of equipment, payments on the lease, and repairs to the new property entailed a drain on the paper's modest resources, and the proprietors had to dig deep into their private accounts to meet operating expenses. There were moments when it seemed as if their funds might be exhausted. Each morning during this touch-and-go period, as he hurried into the office Pulitzer held a whispered conference with Thomas D. Harris, the cashier, over the precarious situation. Reminded of it years later Pulitzer exclaimed dramatically, "Yes, and let me tell you, Harris so nearly exhausted . . . [my] personal account that I drew out of it $300 and put it in a trunk at home, against the coming expenses of the birth of my first child." At the end of February, however, the tide began to turn.[62]

Completion of alterations in the new building was delayed until the first week of March. On the first floor of the narrow structure was the counting room, and on the second, reached by an open stairway, was the newsroom with a curtained alcove for the editor's office. At the rear was a two-story ell, on the ground floor of which

---

were deposited, was added to the board as vice-president. *Post and Dispatch*, Dec. 26, 1878; Florence D. White to Joseph Pulitzer, March 21, 1905, Pulitzer Papers (CU); Scharf, II, 1,397-98.

[58] George Johns, *Joseph Pulitzer*, p. 49. Personal letter from D.J.W. McAuliffe, April 9, 1951. Barrett's belief that "Dillon was to share in the profits, but the running expenses were up to Pulitzer," is incorrect. James Barrett, *Joseph Pulitzer*, p. 50. Relying on the recollections of Florence D. White, McAuliffe wrote, "J. P. had access to a little ready money, and Dillon's was not so easily available, but Dillon always paid his share."

[59] *Post and Dispatch*, Dec. 23, 1878.

[60] *Ibid.*, Jan. 25, 1879; *Post-Dispatch*, Jan. 23, 1880. This location had been the home of the *Evening Dispatch*. A Mrs. E. A. Clark of New York owned the property.

[61] *Post and Dispatch*, Jan. 25, 1879, March 1, 1879; *Post-Dispatch*, Jan. 12, 1882.

[62] George Johns, *Joseph Pulitzer*, pp. 68-69.

were installed the press and a boiler, while the heavy type cases were on the second floor in a crowded and ill-suited composing room. Altogether, the building was makeshift, but to the impatient Pulitzer it represented independence.[63]

Monday, March 10 was set for the grand opening. A special eight-page edition of 20,000 copies was planned and, more important, a change was to be made in the paper's name; after March 10 it was to be the *Post-Dispatch,* "the largest evening paper ever published in St. Louis." [64]

On the eve of its first milestone, the *Post and Dispatch* glanced with satisfaction over its brief past, remarking: "We have steadily published more news, telegraphic, commercial, local and miscellaneous, than any other evening paper in the country, and in spite of the expense we find it pays." [65]

At 2:30 Monday afternoon, as scores of well-wishers crowded into the refurbished rooms at 111 North Fifth Street to congratulate Dillon and Pulitzer "and to wish the enterprise a continuation of the brilliant success which has attended it from the start," the page forms were affixed to the cylinders of the new press, a ticklish task.[66] Steam was applied, and the press started to roll, slowly as the pressmen examined the first copies, and then faster and faster. Copublishers Dillon and Pulitzer looked on with obvious pride. The press roared steadily for several minutes when suddenly the racing sheet of white paper tore, and before the machinery could be stopped its rollers were a tangled mass of ink-splotched, ruined newsprint. The pressmen sprang to the task of cleaning the mess, but it was dark before the newspaper's subscribers received their first copies of the St. Louis *Post-Dispatch.*[67]

The mishap, however, scarcely dampened the enthusiasm or importance of the occasion. As exchange copies filtered into the office from journals outside the city, Pulitzer and Dillon were gratified by editorial comments on the special edition. The Farmington *Times* observed:

> The POST-DISPATCH has achieved a success that probably never has been equaled by any evening paper in that city. Its vigorous editorials, superior reports of local happenings and its

---

[63] *Post-Dispatch,* Jan. 23, 1880; George Johns, *Joseph Pulitzer,* p. 68.

[64] *Post and Dispatch,* March 1, 1879, March 5, 1879, March 7, 1879. Pulitzer had one superstition—that the number ten was lucky. This may explain why he chose March 10 for the grand opening of his new establishment.

[65] *Ibid.,* March 6, 1879.

[66] *Globe-Democrat,* as quoted in *Post-Dispatch,* March 11, 1879.

[67] *Post-Dispatch,* March 11, 1879.

latest telegraphic intelligence commend it to the people. Added to all this, it is an aggressive Western Democratic journal.[68]

Others noted that the *Post-Dispatch* "is gaining in popularity . . . and must and will have an immense circulation," and its "advertising patronage is such that it can not fail to prosper." [69]

The first and most critical period of any journal's history had been negotiated. In three months the audacious Joseph Pulitzer had made the *Post and Dispatch* an independent enterprise, no longer under the shadow of the *Globe-Democrat.* Although tiny and struggling and still precarious, it had already made good use of some of the new methods of successful journalism.

---

[68] As reprinted in *ibid.*, March 15, 1879.

[69] Moberly (Missouri) *Monitor* and Warrensburg (Missouri) *Journal,* as quoted in *ibid.,* March 15, 1879.

CHAPTER IV

A Style Develops

In new quarters on one of the city's main streets, Pulitzer and Dillon strained every nerve to keep the *Post-Dispatch* moving ahead, and during the remainder of 1879 the paper developed an individual style. Pulitzer's own daring and drive were chiefly responsible for the paper's success thus far. As he later remarked, "I worked on that carcass like a slave."[1] The conscientious Dillon, who was less aggressive than his partner, largely confined himself to the editorial page. In one respect, however, his contribution was notable. As editor of the *Evening Post,* he had gathered a young and resourceful staff who now served the new paper admirably.[2]

Since the *Post-Dispatch* was small, there was no formal managing editor. John J. Jennings, the news editor, came closest to filling the role, although his convivial and casual ways made him a poor choice for an editorial position.[3] Like many St. Louis reporters Johnny Jennings was born in humble Kerry Patch and educated in the classics at Christian Brothers College, a Catholic preparatory school. Before joining Dillon's *Post* in 1878 he had learned the newspaper trade under McCullagh on the *Globe-Democrat.* He was accounted on all sides the cleverest newspaperman in St. Louis, an entertaining, versatile writer and a quick-witted reporter. Jennings could uncover a sensational piece of news, produce an imaginative feature, or write a serious drama review with equal facility.[4] He was also a versifier, which made him much sought after by traveling theatrical troupes. At twenty-five, he was the star reporter of the *Post-Dispatch.*[5]

---

[1] *Post-Dispatch,* May 11, 1883.

[2] Pulitzer dismissed all but one of the staff of the old *Evening Dispatch* at the time of the consolidation. The one man he offered to retain refused to accept. *Post and Dispatch,* Dec. 13, 1878.

[3] *Gould's St. Louis Directory* (St. Louis, 1879), p. 510. As news editor Jennings assisted in supervising the flow of news but he had no voice in determining policy.

[4] Pulitzer had an exceedingly high regard for Jennings. He wrote to Don Seitz years later that he considered Jennings "exceptionally fertile [and] suggestive" and capable of "original work." By then, Jennings was a feature writer on the New York *World.* Joseph Pulitzer to Don Seitz, Feb. 4, 1905, Pulitzer Papers (LC).

[5] Joseph Pulitzer to Don Seitz, Feb. 4, 1905, Pulitzer Papers (LC). Personal letter from D.J.W. McAuliffe, Oct. 23, 1950; George S. Johns, *Joseph Pulitzer,* p. 72; *Reedy's Mirror,* June 28, 1900; *The Hornet,* Jan. 15, 1881; *Spectator,* Nov. 12, 1885, July 3, 1886, Oct. 2, 1886; *Journalist,* Oct. 11, 1884; *Who Was Who in America, 1897-1942* (Chicago, 1942), p. 633.

The real director of the news staff was Henry W. Moore, the city editor, a pale, nervous man of slight build and sensitive features. At twenty-nine Moore was a daring journalist and a competent executive. He was born in Devonshire, and had traveled widely before arriving in St. Louis in 1878, where he joined the *Evening Post* as a drama critic, a coveted position at that time. Moore's urbane manners gained him an entrée into society, but they were mostly evident outside the newspaper office. At work he was cold and calculating, cynically exploiting his acquaintances to ferret out sensational news. It was he who planned the paper's most electrifying scoops. With a caustic tongue he exacted strenuous efforts and deep respect from his newsroom subordinates. Altogether, Henry Moore was the sort of ruthless city editor demanded by the new journalism.[6]

Moore directed a handful of hustling reporters. Alfred H. Spink was the versatile police and sporting writer.[7] He was somewhat erratic, but was a genius in his way, and in the modern sports world there is more than one monument to his originality and promotional talents. When he came to St. Louis in 1878 he already had won prominence and a $5,000 check from James Gordon Bennett for reporting a yellow fever epidemic in New Orleans. His experience on Bennett's *Herald* and Dana's *Sun* made him a valuable man for the *Post-Dispatch*.[8] The prankster of the staff was John Tracy McEnnis, the son of a well-known local merchant. Blessed with a rollicking, sentimental Irish wit, in Theodore Dreiser's phrase, McEnnis was "a truly brilliant writer," a reporter with a gifted and fanciful pen and good-humored enterprise.[9] He, too, was a product of Christian Brothers College.[10] The cub of the staff was Florence

---

6 *Gould's St. Louis Directory*, 1879, p. 696; *Journalist*, July 19, 1884; *Spectator*, Jan. 15, 1881, Nov. 3, 1883, Dec. 8, 1883, Nov. 7, 1885, Feb. 13, 1886, April 2, 1892; *American Journalist*, Oct. 1883; *Post-Dispatch*, Sept. 6, 1879, Jan. 29, 1883; interviews with Harry Duhring, Nov. 1, 1950, and Richard J. Collins, March 20, 1951. Collins and Duhring were on the *Post-Dispatch* when Moore was managing editor.

7 Florence D. White to Joseph Pulitzer, Aug. 31, 1900, Pulitzer Papers (CU).

8 In 1886 Spink established the *Sporting News*, modern "bible of baseball," and in 1900 helped to found the American League. Personal letter from Alfred H. Spink, Jr., May 11, 1951, July 15, 1951; Florence D. White to Joseph Pulitzer, Aug. 31, 1900, Pulitzer Papers (CU); *Journalist*, July 31, 1897, Aug. 7, 1897; *The Billiard Reporter*, June 1928, p. 2; Frederick G. Lieb, *The St. Louis Cardinals: The Story of a Great Baseball Club* (New York, 1944), pp. 5-6; interviews with Richard J. Collins, March 20, 1951, and John E. Wray, Jan. 17, 1951. Both were sports reporters under Spink. See also, *Post-Dispatch*, May 8, 1966, and *The Sporting News* (St. Louis), March 19, 1966.

9 As managing editor of the Chicago *Globe* in the 1880s, McEnnis did much to encourage Dreiser. Dreiser, pp. 73-83.

10 William A. Kelsoe, *St. Louis Reference Record* (St. Louis, [1927]), p. 44; George

Dennis White who at sixteen had just come from Christian Brothers. Flory did odd jobs picking up routine news and running errands, but Pulitzer saw ability in his quiet industry and was soon giving him weightier assignments at the Four Courts and City Hall.[11]

Completing the news department were John R. Reavis, "an energetic hustler" of an intellectual type, the political reporter;[12] Alston L. Ryland, a veteran journalist, the river reporter and oldest man on the staff;[13] Mrs. Helen Starrett, the society editor, a vigorous suffragette whose stock address, "What shall we do with our daughters?" brought her fame among local feminists;[14] William F. Coulter, the experienced commercial editor;[15] and Gay Waters, a young minister, the *Post-Dispatch* correspondent in Jefferson City.[16]

The counting room force was even smaller and less formal. Although in later years he feigned ignorance of such matters, Pulitzer was his own business manager. After the paper was out each day he went to the counting room on the first floor where he consulted with the cashier on revenues and expenses.[17] His chief assistant on the business side was William C. Steigers, the advertising agent, who

---

Johns, *Joseph Pulitzer,* pp. 169-70; Frank R. O'Neil to William v. Byars, Jan. 2, 1895, William Vincent Byars Papers; John A. Dillon to Joseph Pulitzer, June 11, 1885, Pulitzer Papers (CU); *The Life,* May 13, 1893; *Spectator,* Sept. 1, 1883, June 27, 1885, Dec. 18, 1886; *Hornet,* Jan. 15, 1881, Feb. 26, 1881, March 5, 1881; *Journalist,* Oct. 30, 1886; *Reedy's Mirror,* Nov. 18, 1894.

[11] In time, White became Pulitzer's "prime minister," the supervisor of both the New York *World* and the *Post-Dispatch.* Personal letter from D.J.W. McAuliffe, Oct. 23, 1950; Kelsoe, "Missourians Abroad, No. 10: Florence D. White"; Edmundson, "Pulitzer's Prime Minister," pp. 25-26.

[12] Personal letter from D.J.W. McAuliffe, Oct. 23, 1950; *Post-Dispatch,* Sept. 4, 1879. Reavis was a founder and first editor of the St. Louis *Spectator* after he left the *Post-Dispatch. Hornet,* Dec. 11, 1880; Mrs. Charles P. Johnson, *Notable Women of St. Louis: 1914* (St. Louis, 1914), p. 185.

[13] St. Louis *Evening Post,* Nov. 8, 1878; *Post-Dispatch,* Feb. 20, 1883, Aug. 17, 1883.

[14] Mrs. Starrett left St. Louis in the summer of 1879 to join a Chicago newspaper. *American Journalist: A Magazine for Professional Writers,* April 1884; *Post and Dispatch,* Jan. 25, 1879; anon., "History of Woman Suffrage in Missouri," *Missouri Historical Review,* XIV (Jan. 1920), 294-95.

[15] *Gould's St. Louis Directory,* 1871, p. 177; 1873, p. 197; 1877, p. 228; 1879, p. 251; *Journalist,* May 17, 1884; *Spectator,* Jan. 22, 1881, *Hornet,* Feb. 12, 1881.

[16] *Post and Dispatch,* Feb. 28, 1879. R. B. Hayes probably was the first telegraph editor. *Evening Post,* Dec. 2, 1878. S. C. Sackett and William A. Brickenor, both on the original staff, remained but a few months. *Gould's St. Louis Directory,* 1879, pp. 177, 842.

[17] Reynolds, "Joseph Pulitzer," p. 66. Pulitzer's pose in later life that he had no interest in and always was ignorant of the business side of his papers has become part of the Pulitzer legend. (See George Johns, *Joseph Pulitzer,* p. 71.) That such was far from the case is readily apparent from the voluminous reports, letters, and memoranda which constitute the Pulitzer Papers. See also the tribute to Pulitzer's business genius by a St. Louis rival, Charles W. Knapp, publisher of the *Republic. Birthday Anniversary Dinner, Given by Joseph Pulitzer, April 10, 1907* (St. Louis, 1907), 38-39.

at thirty-three was a veteran of St. Louis counting rooms. Steigers already had shown his worth by securing a notable increase in advertising for the *Evening Post* the previous autumn. Billy was an energetic "go-getter" whose domineering ways made him difficult to work with but whose driving qualities assured for him a long, if stormy, career on the *Post-Dispatch*. Steigers was "ready to prey on anybody," an associate remarked. "If a man has a dollar, Steigers honestly feels robbed unless that man's dollar comes to him for advertising. . . . His most valuable assets are his power of earnest and picturesque speech, [and] a mind with but one side to it. . . . He believes thoroughly and heartily in the Post-Dispatch as the greatest advertising medium in the world. . . ." [18]

One of Pulitzer's first acts on Fifth Street was to alter the format. The paper was enlarged from seven to eight columns, and the sheets on which it was printed were three inches longer. In mid-May, the typeface of the headlines became lighter and somewhat smaller, and the practice of setting a dozen or more decks over important stories was modified; five or six became normal. This subdued the billboard effect of the front page—a common style of the day— and increased advertising and news capacity. Slightly larger body type for editorials and telegraph news made the paper a bit more readable, but small print, tightly jammed together long remained a bane to subscribers. [19]

With the increase in space Pulitzer sought to break into the "want advertising" business hitherto monopolized by the morning papers. The purpose was only incidentally to gain revenue, however. To Pulitzer the four- and five-line ads were more valuable for stimulating circulation; he wanted to encourage all kinds of people to advertise for "situations" in the *Post-Dispatch* and for businessmen and housewives to become accustomed to using his paper to find employees

[18] Report to Joseph Pulitzer, 1905, Pulitzer Papers (CU); *Gould's St. Louis Directory*, 1869, p. 739; 1874, p. 849; 1876, p. 842; 1879, p. 927; *Post-Dispatch*, May 25, 1923; interviews with Byron J. Dietrich, Dec. 15, 1950, Harry Duhring, Nov. 1, 1950, and F. A. Behymer, Nov. 14, 1949.

Others in the countingroom were the cashier, Thomas D. Harris, a competent keeper of accounts; William E. Williams, who assisted Steigers; a circulation agent; and "Reddy" Galvin, the freckle-faced, over-bold office boy. Completing the list of employees was the small mechanical force among whom were a number of female compositors under the direction of Charley Harris, foreman of the composing room. (*Post-Dispatch*, Jan. 8, 1880; *Gould's St. Louis Directory*, 1879, pp. 370, 433, 1,036; Dreiser, pp. 280-81; Reynolds, p. 77.) Two or three female compositors—vestiges of the original force—were still on the job in the nineties. Interview with Mary E. Peers, Dec. 8, 1950.

[19] *Post and Dispatch*, March 5, 1879; *Post-Dispatch*, March 10, 1879, May 15, 1879. The American Social Science Association in 1880 bitterly complained of the small type used by American newspapers. *Post-Dispatch*, Sept. 9, 1880.

and servants. His campaign, billed as a "new departure," commenced with the following announcement:

> We offer the use of our columns gratis to the thousands in St. Louis whose "Wants" of all kinds are checked in their expression by the high rates charged by the morning papers. Any advertisement of that description, and of an unobjectionable nature, not exceeding five lines in length, will be inserted in the first number of the POST-DISPATCH without pay and continued until its object has been obtained. It is our object to make the advertising colunms of the POST-DISPATCH not less varied and interesting than the news columns, and we have never failed in a single object yet.[20]

The offer of free insertions was continued throughout the summer and fall of 1879, and although the number printed did not exceed two or three columns daily—compared with nine to twelve in the *Globe-Democrat*—the *Post-Dispatch* had begun a long campaign to overcome the ancient prejudice against advertising in afternoon papers. Pulitzer lavished much attention on the want ads.[21]

Pulitzer was well aware, however, that in final analysis the popularity of his paper depended upon its main function. Announcing that "first and above all" the *Post-Dispatch* would be a *"news* paper," he sought to capitalize on the lessons he had learned in February. The paper must be talked about, and the way to achieve this was to continue unearthing sensations. He and Moore set the little staff to work, and before long the *Globe-Democrat* was severely condemning the *Post-Dispatch* for "mendacious fabrications of unscrupulous sensationalism."[22]

Typical of the paper's style was a half-column item headed DEATH'S DELILAH, which was subheaded: "The Startling Position a Frail Woman Awoke in This Morning," "A Well Known Citizen Stricken Down in the Arms of His Mistress," "The Death of Charles E. Spooner in an Apoplectic Fit—The Coroner's Inquest—Details of the Sad

---

[20] *Post and Dispatch*, March 5, 1879.

[21] Pulitzer's concern about want advertising was manifest throughout his career. Once, in reporting detailed figures of advertising in the *Post-Dispatch*, Steigers commented that he was aware of Pulitzer's "very deep, personal interest in the wants." (William C. Steigers to Joseph Pulitzer, Oct. 25, 1904, Pulitzer Papers (CU).) Pulitzer's interest in wants has been interpreted as sympathy for the lower classes. It may have been partly this, but it is more in keeping with his keen business sense to suggest that the stimulation of circulation was uppermost is his mind. Voluminous memoranda in the Pulitzer Papers strongly indicate this.

[22] St. Louis *Globe-Democrat*, June 6, 1879.

Story."[23] The "well known citizen" was actually an obscure sales-man who died the previous night in the arms of his mistress in a shabby downtown hotel. The episode was scarcely more than routine, but the paper sent a reporter to interview the distraught woman, and her pathetic tale was run on the first page. Philosophizing, the reporter said that at the end of the interview he "gathered up his notes, shut the door behind him and left the scene a wiser and perhaps a better man. Another lesson had been learned of the waywardness of humanity and the uncertain tenure of a man's life."

Another time Pulitzer heard a rumor that Miss Dolly Liggett, daughter of a wealthy tobacco merchant, had defied her parents by marrying the bookkeeper of a livery stable. Immediately, Pulitzer set two reporters on the story, but the angry Liggett family would see no one. In despair, as the paper's afternoon deadline neared Pulitzer turned to Flory White and asked him if he could get the news. "If I don't, I won't be back," was the cub's reply as he dashed out the door. Within two hours he returned with a "scoop," having been admitted by a maid to the palatial Liggett residence where he interviewed the tearful mother. The headline for that afternoon read: "A St. Louis Heiress Chooses a Husband Against Her Father's Will—And the Wrathful Parent Disinherits His Spirited Daughter."[24]

A final story of this kind, LOST THROUGH LOVE, brought strong criticism from competitors.[25] Prominently displayed on the first page, the tale concerned the suicide of an army officer in the Planter's Hotel. A letter found on the body indicating that the young man destroyed himself "in the agony of unfortunate love" was printed in full. In an editorial paragraph the *Post-Dispatch* clucked piously over its own prying journalism, but laid the blame elsewhere:

> There seems to be some room for improvement in the law regulating and defining the power of a coroner over the private papers and effects of suicides. Nothing but absolute necessity could justify even the coroner in reading private correspondence. . . . But even if a coroner should . . . become acquainted with secrets of a private and family nature, it is no part of his official duty to wound the feelings of the living and perhaps needlessly injure the reputation of the dead by making these secrets public property. The ends of justice are all fulfilled when the fact is established that the cause of death was a pistol shot. The attempt to pry

---

[23] *Post and Dispatch*, March, 1, 1879.
[24] George Johns, *Joseph Pulitzer*, pp. 69-70. Personal letter from D.J.W. Mc-Auliffe, Oct. 23, 1950; *Post-Dispatch*, June 21, 1879.
[25] *Post-Dispatch*, May 20, 1879.

further . . . is mere prurient curiosity with which a public official has nothing whatever to do.[26]

This effort to slough off responsibility was criticized as hypocritical by a rival journal. The *Post-Dispatch's* defense was revealing:

> The *Anzeiger des Westens* takes us to task for our censures of the Coroner. . . . But . . . there is a very wide difference between the responsibility of a public officer for his official duty and the responsibility of a newspaper for its publication. If the *Anzeiger* does not understand this it is not a newspaper.[27]

In a word, it was up to the public to maintain proper standards of conduct; the function of a live-wire newspaper was to take full advantage of the lapses.

The same sort of enterprise was resorted to in gathering crime news. In June a police officer was murdered by a young hoodlum who eluded the city's inept detectives. The *Post-Dispatch* set one of its own reporters on the trail, and in a series of page one stories it kept its readers apprised of his exciting adventures in search of the criminal.[28] The first installment was headlined A FRESH TRAIL, "Sanders, the Murderer, Probably Tracked to his Hiding Place" by "A Post-Dispatch Reporter in the Role of a Detective." It added portentiously: "The POST-DISPATCH has come into possession of information which will probably clear up the mystery of the whereabouts of the notorious murderer Sanders and lead to his arrest." [29] But Sanders was not found although the paper claimed to sight him almost daily for a week.[30] This was scarcely helpful to the police, but it advertised the *Post-Dispatch* as a paper to read.

The *Post-Dispatch* basked in its enterprise. "It is astounding," it exclaimed,

> how much energy is displayed by the morning papers in republishing the news from the POST-DISPATCH. Yesterday we gave a full account of the Flaven fire, losses, insurance, incidents and accidents, and a comparison of the morning papers shows that they have displayed a great accuracy in copying. And after we had found out in six hours the true inwardness of the Broadway Savings Bank [failure] from the cashier, together with the history

---

[26] *Ibid.*

[27] *Ibid.*, May 21, 1879.

[28] Dreiser, pp. 147-49, comments on the role of St. Louis reporters as amateur detectives in the nineties. See also, *Spectator*, July 6, 1889.

[29] *Post-Dispatch*, June 18, 1879.

[30] Actually, all the leads offered by the *Post-Dispatch* were false. Sanders fled from St. Louis to Canada immediately after the crime. He was caught four years later in Chicago. *Ibid.*, April 6, 1883, April 10, 1883.

of the bank, the list of its depositors, etc., nearly every morning paper was enabled to publish the same news some twelve hours later. If there was any copyright on afternoon papers the morning papers could not live.[31]

Occasionally, as it was bound to do, this high-pressure journalism went too far. Once, under A GRAVE CHARGE, the paper printed an account of what it presented as an abortion case, saying flatly that the evidence "proved conclusively" that a criminal operation had been performed. Twenty-four hours later it hastily retreated:

> The account about an alleged case of malpractice . . . which appeared in our local columns of yesterday, appeared without the knowledge of the editors of this journal, by an accidental escape of editorial supervision, which will not occur again.[32]

In December the *Post-Dispatch* was sued for libel by a singer named Mme. Carlotta Patti for publishing a report that she had been intoxicated during a performance in Leavenworth, Kansas. This time, feeling sure of the facts, the paper added spicy details to the original piece in a story headlined "FULL AS A TICK," while paying its respects to the attorney who had persuaded Patti to sue:

> Mr. Hermann is not so well provided with character himself that he can afford to be dancing in front of newspaper offices in war paint and feathers, and we may take a notion one of these days to set him up where the public can admire his beautiful moral proportions.[33]

Despite its sensationalism, in 1879 the *Post-Dispatch* won every case filed against it.

Pulitzer was aware, however, that to prosper the *Post-Dispatch* must be more than a mere purveyor of sensations. It must also provide substantial information, particularly to the commercial community. The paper promised to make itself

> indispensable to every merchant and business man who buys or sells, who is interested in the state of trade, in the latest financial and commercial quotations or the latest market reports, all of which we will present regularly, reliably, early and fully.[34]

Each day, therefore, it carried several columns of statistics of trade gathered from the Merchants' Exchange and the Third Street produce

---

31 *Ibid.*, May 23, 1879.

32 *Ibid.*, May 14 and 15, 1879.

33 *Ibid.*, Dec. 5, 1879, Dec. 15, 1879, Dec. 16, 1879, Dec. 24, 1879, Dec. 26, 1879. The *Post-Dispatch* won this case when the trial judge dismissed the complaint. *Ibid.*, April 6, 1880.

34 *Ibid.*, March 25, 1879.

markets, together with clearances of steamboats on the waterfront. Special reporters were assigned to each of these news sources. And in October it became the first journal in the city to publish quotations on stocks issued by local firms. Typically, it did not fail to bring this to the attention of its readers:

> All of the Sunday morning papers had detailed accounts of the sale of stocks on 'Change on Saturday. It is the first time they have ever noticed such an item, and the reason they were successful in getting it was that they only had to copy it out of the Saturday POST-DISPATCH.[35]

Oddly enough, for all its boldness in news, the feature columns remained dull carryovers from the genteel *Evening Post*. "Our Book Column" and "The Home," regular columns inherited from the *Post*, filled much precious space in the Saturday Supplement. "The Home" was devoted to decidedly unsensational domestic problems of comparatively affluent households; it had little popular appeal. Only the drama column exhibited the intimate, gossipy writing calculated to have wide reader interest, and in this the *Post-Dispatch* only imitated a common newspaper practice. The paper printed comments upon and interviews with matinee idols and beautiful actresses written by reporters who were acquainted with—as one headline phrased it— the SECRETS OF THE AMERICAN STAGE.[36] Characteristic was an interview with the reigning "queen of American society-drama," Fanny Davenport. Headed FAIR FANNY, it had the cozy intimacy of a modern screen article. Alone with the *Post-Dispatch* man in her Lindell Hotel suite

> Miss Davenport . . . seated herself . . . and drawing near the fire place, proceeded to warm a beautiful pair of little feet, which were encased in the neatest and most perfect fitting of slippers. She was attired in an elegant princess morning dress of black satin with a long flowing train, which allowed the greatest freedom of movement with a perfect-fitting garment. . . . As she reclined against the crimson plush, Miss Davenport made a picture in every sense artistic.[37]

Interspersed with offhand comments about her romantic experiences in faraway places, the interview consisted chiefly of advice from the sultry lady to young girls seeking careers on the stage.

---

[35] *Ibid.*, Oct. 20, 1879.
[36] *Ibid.*, Sept. 27, 1879.
[37] *Post and Dispatch*, Jan. 10, 1879. The interview likely was conducted by John Jennings, himself considered an authority on theater gossip. Not long after this, he wrote a gaudily illustrated book, *Theatrical and Circus Life; or, Secrets of the Stage, Green-Room and Sawdust Arena* (St. Louis, 1883).

For the rest, the paper's features consisted of a weekly sporting column, a church column, an entirely respectable listing of the doings of local society and dull syndicated "letters" from special correspondents in other cities, particularly New York and Washington. These were published under unoriginal "label heads" and must have had little appeal to St. Louisans.

Editorially, the *Post-Dispatch* began to build a definite policy and reputation as a crusading newspaper. In so doing it revealed itself as a middle class journal whose principal interests lay in protecting the community from organized vice on the one hand and the malpractices of the wealthy on the other. In particular, the paper continued to attack local monopolies injurious to trade and small business. The crusades were not many, since Pulitzer was becoming absorbed in the approaching political campaign, but they were indicative of the paper's emerging style.

The first crusade on Fifth Street was still rather crude. It was launched against lotteries which operated openly and semi-legally in the city. Stemming from raw frontier days, all forms of gambling flourished in St. Louis in the post-Civil War period; the old river port was one of the most wide open towns in the country. But what had been a picturesque by-product of river life was now becoming a serious menace to the good order of urban society. The city no longer could afford to be lax and tolerant. Joseph Pulitzer himself represented the changing attitude. Whereas in 1871, when he served briefly as a police commissioner, he had advocated leniency on the plea that gambling was a natural instinct, in 1879 he and his little newspaper joined the *Globe-Democrat's* campaign to break up the lottery racket.[38]

Lotteries had been a common and entirely respectable device for raising money in antebellum America, and like many states Missouri had tolerated and even authorized schemes of chance to raise funds for worthy public projects, and the charters of a few of them, now taken over by professional gamblers, were still in existence. The most important of these was the Missouri State Lottery, chartered in the forties to finance construction of a plank road from the village of Franklin to the Missouri River. Although the road had long since fallen into disuse, in 1879 the lottery, now operated by an ex-river gambler named William C. France, sold chances in cigar stores and saloons in every neighborhood of St. Louis, and its annual profit of $180,000 was a source of corruption. The *Globe-Democrat* and even the *Republican* had protested against the Lottery; interested citizens

---

[38] Walter B. Stevens, "New Journalism," XVIII (Jan. 1924), 200-201; *Evening Post*, Sept. 4, 1878, Sept. 7, 1878; Soraghan, "History of St. Louis," pp. 32-34; Darrell Garwood, *Crossroads of America: The Story of Kansas City* (New York, 1948), p. 128.

had brought suit attacking its legality; but it was upheld by the state supreme court.[39]

This was the situation early in 1878 when Alanson Bankson, alias Alanson Wakefield, formerly a "three-card monte man" on steamboats to New Orleans and presently the operator of a gambling room in a waterfront bawdy house, mysteriously gained control of the lottery and keno interests in the city. His next move was to use his money to influence local law enforcement by securing the appointment of a friendly police board. It was Wakefield's ambition to "run the town." [40]

Matters began to reach a crisis in February 1879, when Governor Phelps, prevailed upon by local politicians, named to the board Dr. James C. Nidelet and David Ladd, both suspected of connections with Wakefield. This prompted an investigation by the state senate, the result of which was the masterful "scoop" of the committee hearings by the *Post and Dispatch*. The paper revealed that through Nidelet Wakefield had received foreknowledge of police raids upon gambling joints and with this information had extorted from Bob Pate —a leading gambler—one-third of the profits from keno as payment for "protection." This was followed within a few days by another exposure—Wakefield's use of Nidelet to extort a one-third cut from the Missouri Lottery's take. The police commissioner threatened to prosecute France's ticket vendors unless he acceded to Wakefield's demands. France submitted, and legal proceedings were quietly suspended.[41]

These exposures resulted not only in the rejection of Nidelet and Ladd by the legislature but in a grand jury investigation of Wakefield's operations. The jury, whose foreman was Joseph B. McCullagh, indicted Wakefield for perjury when he denied his extortions, and he was tried and sentenced to a two-year prison term. The McCullagh jurors also probed into Nidelet's complicity, but although they censured him for unbecoming conduct, no evidence of criminality could be discovered.[42] The Missouri Lottery was destroyed as a legitimate concern and never recovered. Within a year its charter

---

[39] Stevens, "New Journalism," XVIII (Jan. 1924), 200-201; *Post and Dispatch,* March 6, 1879.

[40] *Post and Dispatch,* Jan. 31, 1879; *Post-Dispatch,* March 11, 1879, June 2, 1881.

[41] *Post and Dispatch,* Feb. 18, 1879, March 4, 1879.

[42] Stevens, *op. cit.,* p. 201; *Post-Dispatch,* May 1, 1879, Oct. 29, 1879, Oct. 30, 1879. The extent of Nidelet's complicity in Wakefield's schemes was never cleared up. Some staunchly defended him as an honest man victimized by newspaper and underworld smears. (See Scharf, *History of St. Louis,* II, 1,540-41.) The *Post-Dispatch* itself was uncertain, as shown by an editorial appearing May 3, 1879. However, Nidelet and one or two confederates disappeared from St. Louis immediately after the investigations and remained away for ten years. *Spectator,* March 9, 1889.

was repealed by the legislature. The newspaper crusade thus was responsible for outlawing lotteries in Missouri.[43]

However, although legalized lottery was destroyed, the potency of organized gambling was only momentarily checked. After a few months the lotteries and the keno dens, not only along the levee, but in the respectable neighborhood of Fourth Street, sprang up again. The *Post-Dispatch* charged that practically "licensed gambling" was going on, winked at by the police. To prove it the paper boldly published a list of the principal casinos in virtually unconcealed operations to which its reporters had had no difficulty in gaining admittance.[44]

Following the lottery crusade the *Post-Dispatch* launched a new campaign which made even more effective and systematic use of the technique of exposure. The somewhat superficial sensationalism of the lottery campaign was replaced by a deadly efficient publication of facts and figures exposing defalcations by local insurance companies, a practice that victimized thousands of small business concerns and modest-income families in the city. The campaign began when the *Post-Dispatch* reported that the receiver of a defunct company, Columbia Life Insurance, had filed suit in circuit court demanding that the directors of the Life Association of St. Louis return to Columbia $1,000,000 in assets which the receiver charged were fraudulently appropriated when the two companies were merged. This deal, said the *Post-Dispatch,* was the climax to "the blackest record that has yet blotted the pages of the history of St. Louis," the final installment to a tale of systematic thievery which had forced out of existence six insurance companies with assets totaling $10,000,000. The paper announced that it had "detailed" one of its best reporters to dig out the facts behind this dismal story.[45]

In October the promised exposure began. The first article, entitled INSURANCE INIQUITY, related how Columbia had been ruined by a raid on its assets, carried out by its own directors and those of the Life Association. The attorney who engineered the deal received a $275,000 "fee" from Columbia's assets and then, by legerdemain, 9,000 shares of Columbia's stocks were retired, the profits going to the directors. This left only $100,000 to cover payments to policy-holders. "It was in this final act that the policy-holders were robbed and the Columbia made fit for the receiver." [46]

---

[43] Stevens, *op.cit.*, p. 200. Curiously, the *Post-Dispatch* continued to carry lottery advertising until the eve of Wakefield's indictment, when it was quietly dropped. The *Republican*, on the other hand, ostentatiously announced it no longer accepted such advertisements.

[44] *Post-Dispatch*, May 9, 1879.

[45] *Ibid.,* June 24, 1879.

[46] *Ibid.,* Oct. 13, 1879, Oct. 14, 1879.

Then came an editorial blast against the "EMINENTLY RESPECTABLE" ROBBERS who perpetrated the deal:

The funds of a life insurance company constitute the most sacred of trusts, since the money is paid in for the benefit of widows and orphans, and the life insurance robber is the worst of all robbers. . . .

We see no means of entire protection against life insurance robbery. It will probably continue as long as men are dishonest; but if a few of the most distinguished of these conspirators—who are all among our "best" citizens—against women and children were put in the penitentiary, it would have a most salutary effect.[47]

Under A STARTLING RECORD the *Post-Dispatch* next published a carefully compiled table of statistics revealing precisely how, between 1869 and 1876, local policyholders who had paid in $23,000,000 in premiums to six defunct companies had received only $8,000,000 in benefits.[48] Inquired the article, "Now, where has the money gone?"

Over fifteen million dollars systematically raised only to be systematically stolen! . . . Considering everything, even the James boys seem perfect heroes compared with the pious frauds and hollow hypocrites who under the very cover of respectability could perpetuate such robbery.

"Respectability!" What mockery upon it, upon all society, all law and all justice, that not one of these infamous scoundrels was punished, that not one of them is in the Penitentiary!

Who can wonder at the growing discontent of the poor? Who can fail to see that Socialism, or Communism, is bred not below, but above, not in the atmosphere in which the bread is stolen, but in the atmosphere above, where these "respectable" wreckers of insurance companies, banks and watered railroads steal their millions, to move, not into prison, but into "best" society.[49]

The *Post-Dispatch* did not stop with generalities. It asked, WHO WERE THEY? and published a list of directors implicated. One of these was John G. Priest, a member of the Democratic National Committee from Missouri, whose political fortunes until now had been enthusiastically promoted by the *Post-Dispatch*. At first the paper accepted his protestations of innocence, but soon it discovered additional evidence of his culpability involving "a deliberate case of life insurance

[47] *Ibid.*, Oct. 15, 1879.
[48] *Ibid.*, Oct. 16, 1879.
[49] *Ibid.*

77

wrecking" in connection with still another company, the National.[50] After this, the *Post-Dispatch* ceased to support Priest.[51]

The results of this crusade were mixed. None of the insurance wreckers were punished, but in 1880, no doubt partly as a result of this exposure, the state legislature tightened the laws regulating insurance companies.[52]

The same technique of painstaking and systematic documentation was used to expose the questionable manipulations behind the failure of a number of banks in St. Louis in the depression-ridden seventies. Once more men of "eminent respectability" were held up to public scorn. These "robbers," the *Post-Dispatch* declared, "are of the worst, since they not only defraud vigorous men who are able to bear the loss, but women, children, ophans, the helpless." [53]

More fundamental than exposures of mere dishonesty among the rich and powerful, however, was the paper's antagonism to local monopoly, already exhibited in the gas company case. On Fifth Street this characteristic hardened into a dominant feature of *Post-Dispatch* journalism. In Pulitzer's view, entrenched privilege violated a basic principle of freedom—equal opportunity—and hampered the city's commercial development.

In the spring of 1879 the *Post-Dispatch* vigorously attacked the horse-car street railway monopoly's stranglehold on local transportation. A combine was created in 1860 when five local companies led by Erastus Wells, president of the Olive Street line, persuaded the legislature to pass an act denying to future promoters the right to lay tracks within three blocks of an existing line. Because of the narrow configuration of the city—nineteen miles long and four across at the widest point—and because the monopolists had taken care to preempt all approaches to the downtown district, this act effectively prevented any sort of competition. At the same time, the monopolists refused to extend their own facilities to serve the new neighborhoods springing up on the edge of the city, leaving thousands of St. Louisans without direct connections to the shopping centers.[54]

It was not surprising, therefore, that following a series of mass meetings a member of the legislature from Carondelet introduced a

---

[50] *Ibid.*, Nov. 19, 1879.

[51] The paper's final comment in this case was "some explanation by Mr. Priest is eminently necessary." *Ibid.*, Nov. 21, 1879. Priest was forced by court order to repay $7,500. *Ibid.*, Jan. 5, 1880.

[52] *Ibid.*, Dec. 2, 1880. This was by no means the last time the paper came back to the subject. Mismanagement of insurance companies continued to be a favorite target.

[53] *Ibid.*, June 24, 1879.

[54] *Post-Dispatch*, April 9, 1879, Dec. 3, 1880; see Soraghan, pp. 75-86, for the early history of street railways in St. Louis.

bill to repeal the hated monopoly act. And it was still less surprising that under PEOPLE IN THE SUBURBS the *Post-Dispatch* immediately got behind the measure.[55] Indignantly it described the hold of the combine upon the city:

All north and south lines are barred by the Fifth street line, which at certain points comes near enough to the levee to crowd an opposition line into the river, and which at other points wanders westward to Seventh street. This is the backbone of the monopoly system, and between the Pacific Railroad and Cass avenue competition is forbidden by the Market street, Olive street and Franklin avenue lines with their branches and extensions, while a line facetiously dubbed the "People's Line" . . . takes in the southwestern district. . . .

So ingeniously yet so completely has the field been covered that, no matter what the needs of any locality may be, no matter what may be the desire of the people for a railroad connection, no matter what may be the opportunities for investment by capital, *not another mile of street railroad can ever be built in St. Louis unless the law of 1860 is repealed.* Leave that law standing and St. Louis, already crippled and hampered and thwarted in many ways, has an iron band shrunk about her growth. . . . Either St. Louis must be left free to govern itself . . . and adapt itself to the needs of its development, or else we shall stand bound hand and foot, the slaves of monopoly. . . .[56]

The *Post-Dispatch* brushed aside as "purely imaginary" the monopolists' claim that the act of 1860 protected such streets as Pine and Lucas Place from the defilement of unsightly tracks. Also "too flimsy to be noticed" was the argument the repeal bill would "frighten capital away from St. Louis." In reality, asserted the *Post-Dispatch,* car line owners feared repeal would "cause capital to be invested in competition with them." The most "utterly absurd . . . pretense" of all was the claim that repeal would violate a "contract" the car lines claimed to have with the city. Franchises are not inviolable contracts, the *Post-Dispatch* declared, and to show the hollowness of this argument

it is only necessary to say that within a month the street car interest tried to have the city charter amended so as to exempt them [from having to repair the streets they used]. . . . In other words, when they see a chance of escaping from it, it is not a

[55] *Post-Dispatch,* March 29, 1879.
[56] *Ibid.,* April 9, 1879.

contract, but . . . when it may serve to prevent competition, it is a contract which the Legislature cannot annul. . . .[57]

Vehemently the *Post-Dispatch* contended *"there can be no such thing as an exclusive right to use the streets of a city for any purpose whatever.* A street . . . is a public thoroughfare, freely open to the use of all citizens . . . and no city government and no Legislature possesses authority to say that a track laid in a street . . . shall be the exclusive property of a private corporation."[58] It called upon the legislature to free St. Louis from the "horse-car corporations which own the three hundred miles of streets in St. Louis and . . . its half-million inhabitants as absolutely as they own their own mules."[59]

But the legislature moved slowly, pressured by a powerful lobby. In disgust the *Post-Dispatch* watched the debate in Jefferson City where

all the resources of corporate influence have been brought to bear; Congressmen and ex-Congressmen and bank presidents and ex-Governors and ex-Judges and practical politicians and amateur millionaires have swelled the ranks of the lobby. . . .[60] We commend the study of the opposition . . . to all students of our institutions, as a very good illustration of the causes which are sapping our public morality and destroying our private prosperity.[61]

After a long fight the measure passed, only to have the governor—controlled by the Bourbons—veto it.[62] In a fit of exasperation a *Post-Dispatch* editorial vowed to continue the struggle to DESTROY THE MONOPOLIES! [63]

In November another blow fell when, despite two adverse decisions in the lower courts, the state supreme court returned to the St. Louis Gas-light Company its monopoly of the city's illumination. Thunderstruck, the *Post-Dispatch* could only comment, "The gas company gains everything—the city nothing. Sufficient for the day is the evil thereof." [64] A reporter found the majority of the merchants, hotel managers, and other businessmen interviewed "felt very sore and vexed at the result. Their anticipation had been so hopeful and now they were so hopeless." [65]

---

[57] *Ibid.*, April 3, 1879.
[58] *Ibid.*
[59] *Ibid.*, April 12, 1879.
[60] *Ibid.*, April 9, 1879.
[61] *Ibid.*, April 8, 1879.
[62] *Ibid.*, April 24, 1879, Dec. 3, 1880.
[63] *Ibid.*, June 30, 1879.
[64] *Ibid.*, Nov. 17, 1879. The *Republican*, of course, jubilantly "gushed" its praises of the supreme court. *Ibid.*, Nov. 21, 1879.
[65] *Ibid.*, Nov. 17, 1879.

The *Post-Dispatch* was critical of the supreme court, conceding that although it "had a right" to its own conclusions, the appeals court which had been overruled was composed of able jurists, while "it is a tolerably well-known fact that our Supreme Tribunal is a corporation court." [66] The paper then paid its respects to James O. Broadhead, a distinguished corporation lawyer who had been unaccountably hired by the city in the early seventies to handle its case against the gas company. Broadhead's contribution at that time had been to persuade the city to accept the notorious Tripartite Agreement as a "compromise," although, in fact, it was a renewal of the monopoly. Then Broadhead had switched sides and in 1878 and 1879 represented the gas company before the courts. These questionable ethics were now raked over on the first page of the *Post-Dispatch* in a series of letters from city officials. Ostensibly neutral, the *Post-Dispatch* published Broadhead's denials, but its true intent became clear when it borrowed an editorial from the *Westliche Post* to attack Broadhead as a "sharphead [who] betrays and sells the city's interests to a gas monopoly. . . ." [67]

The "best families" on Lucas and Vandeventer Places by the end of 1879 were coming to dislike intensely the upstart sheet on Fifth Street, and their reasons were not confined to the assaults on their economic privileges. Reflecting Pulitzer's plebeian views, the *Post-Dispatch* never neglected a chance to heap scorn on the pretensions of the elite:

We do not believe in favoritism on account of family or birth. On the contrary, the man who raises himself to a respectable position from the gutter is entitled to more respect than the man who by the accident of birth alone receives fortune, education and family prestige.[68]

And in the summer of 1879, when the young men and women of the Southernish local gentry staged a medieval tournament complete with jousting knights and fair damsels in the amphitheater of the Fairgrounds, the *Post-Dispatch* laughed uproariously. Bedecked in the regalia of the British Indian cavalry, "the young knights sabred wooden heads right and left, and captured rings on their swords in quick succession as they rode furiously around the arena." [69] The climax came when a Queen of Love and Beauty was crowned by St. Louis's equivalent of Brian de Bois Guilbert.

---

[66] *Ibid.*, Nov. 18, 1879, Dec. 11, 1879.
[67] *Ibid.*, Nov. 21, 1879.
[68] *Ibid.*, Dec. 10, 1879.
[69] Woodward, "City of St. Louis," *New England Magazine*, V (Jan. 1892), 600-601.

At first glance it would seem as if the difficulties of reviving the glories of medieval chivalry in this prosaic end of the nineteenth century would be almost . . . insuperable. One would naturally think that full-grown men who wear pants and suspenders, and who show no lack of sense in the ordinary avocation of plodding trade, would object to making guys of themselves . . . and anyone would be justified in refusing to believe that the modest . . . young females of good society would object to competing for the chance of rivaling the pomp of the circus by being driven around in a four-horse chariot and being crowned. . . . Queen of Love and Beauty.[70]

The sting of ridicule was also noticeable in an article headed "SNOBS!" Written in sarcastic vein, it exposed the new popularity of heraldic devices among the city's blue bloods. St. Louis, in fact, "is becoming one of the centers for the diffusion of high lineage and great names." The piece continued,

In the olden countries the fountain of honor is the king, and arms are granted nowhere but from the throne. In democratic America, where the people have gone short on crowns and sovereigns, the aching void . . . is supplied by the engravers, and here in St. Louis honorable charges and armorial devices are granted by the firm of Scharr Brothers and Saxton and by F. Kershaw, with . . . ease and address.[71]

"Who are These Self-Constituted Aristocrats and Blue-Bloods?" the paper asked and sent a reporter around to Scharr's to find out. He discovered that Henry O'Fallon, member of a wealthy family, among others, had ordered a "complete coat of arms." The engraver told the *Post-Dispatch* that he was perfectly willing to supply with a coat of arms "every man, woman and child in America without regard to rank, color or previous condition of servitude."

It was natural that the city's "best families" should have disliked the *Post-Dispatch,* looking upon it as a dangerously radical sheet whose attacks on privilege constituted assaults on property. Nothing could have been further from the truth. For all his attacks upon monopoly and social pretension, Joseph Pulitzer was a middle class businessman, and his paper was as hostile to the labor movement as it was to the elite. This became abundantly clear in the spring and summer of 1879 when St. Louis was engulfed by a wave of strikes as the depression that had buffeted the nation for several years slowly lifted.

---

[70] *Post-Dispatch*, Sept. 19, 1879. Perhaps this was the origin of the "Queen of Love and Beauty" who annually presides over St. Louis's Veiled Prophet festivities.
[71] *Ibid.,* Dec. 12, 1879.

It was true, a spirit of liberal humanitarianism—and perhaps a desire to increase circulation among working class elements—at first inclined the *Post-Dispatch* to sympathize with the efforts of St. Louis workingmen to force a raise in what, after six years of depression, was barely a subsistence wage level. Impulsively, the *Post-Dispatch* came to the support of the coopers who struck against the millers. Under the headline, SENSIBLE STRIKE, a page one story informed the public that the coopers were striking for a justifiable raise from $6.25 to $8.50 per week. The paper said they were family men who "find it a hard struggle to support their wives and children upon the small wages which they earn." Mostly of German or Bohemian extraction, they were "an intelligent body" and the remarkable feature of their strike (an item on which the *Post-Dispatch* laid great stress) was its orderliness. They "discountenance all violence" and, although their meeting hall was over a saloon, "the reporter did not see a single striker patronize it." [72]

Amazed that a respectable journal could sympathize with a workmen's strike, "a gentleman of intelligence and character" wrote a letter of protest to the paper. Somewhat defensively, the *Post-Dispatch* asked, HOW MANY PERSONS CAN LIVE ON $5 A WEEK?

> We are as much opposed to unreasonable strikes as anybody can be. But there is no rule without exception and there is nothing unreasonable in the strike. . . . The wonder to us is how anybody can refuse sympathy to people who do ten hours' hard work every day for *less than one dollar* and with that have to support a family. Our reporters were especially instructed to ascertain this point accurately and exactly. . . .
>
> We hear mutterings of "market rates of labor," and the "laws of supply and demand," etc. But we hear nothing of humanity. . . . Behind all the laws of society is the great law of nature, of necessity, of humanity, of sympathy for mankind. We care not what people may think or say, or whether it is prudent or popular to say it—we do sympathize with the hard working men who get but one dollar a day with which to support a family.[73]

Despite this, however, Pulitzer was not happy supporting a strike. The truth was, collective action violated his individualistic temper. Consequently, as strikes multiplied and violence occurred here and there, the *Post-Dispatch* suddenly burst into an editorial expression of its true feelings:

---

[72] *Ibid.*, July 17, 1879.
[73] *Ibid.*, July 19, 1879.

... Of all ways of securing an improvement in his [the worker's] condition, a strike is about the worst. The coopers' strike secured an increase of wages, but secured it only for those coopers who would have had it without a strike, while it inflicted quite a serious loss on those coopers who, instead of securing an increase in wages, merely secured no wages at all. . . . The idea that the employers are the natural enemies of their workmen . . . is so absurd that any action based on it is doomed to failure, but it seems to be the basis of all the workingmen's movements recently, and indeed to constitute the stock in trade of many of the leaders.[74]

The paper went on:

If we were to listen only to the complaints of the labor agitators and professional disturbers in the country, we would think that we were in a condition of exceptional misery, and that misery was the result of class legislation and class tyranny. When we turn from sentiment to facts, we find out that there is no country under the sun so prosperous as ours, none in which labor is as well paid and as well secured in its payment.[75]

Now pursuing a policy congenial to his outlook, Pulitzer lectured local workers on the facts of economic life and bemoaned their actions in arresting the upward movement of prosperity by striking just when wages "were working their own cure."[76] Instead of following "the trifling agitator" whose advice would "destroy the industry on which workers . . . depend for a living," they should remember that "the only rate of wages which can be paid . . . is the rate which will enable the manufacturer to compete with similar industries." The *Post-Dispatch* added bitterly that "no community can flourish if its members are not endowed with common sense and it looks as if common sense were wanting in a community . . . in which workmen are willing on a moment's notice" to leave their jobs.[77] In short, the iron laws of "supply and demand" and the "market rates of labor" were valid after all, and even the great monopolies which the *Post-Dispatch* accused of destroying competition had no influence over wage levels.

Moreover, any suggestion that government on any level should have the slightest authority over the relationship between employer and employee was summarily rejected. The paper's comment upon a pro-

---

74 *Ibid.*, Aug. 15, 1879.
75 *Ibid.*
76 *Ibid.*, Aug. 23, 1879.
77 *Ibid.*

posal in the Illinois legislature to outlaw payment of employees in company scrip illustrates this:

> . . . We beg to call attention to a little measure now pending before the Springfield Solons which proposes to make it illegal to pay wages in anything but lawful money. The idea that employers and employes should have any freedom in making contracts or agreements seems to be too much for the Illinois legislator to accept, yet one which it is simple nonsense to reject.[78]

But if it was no admirer of unionism, the *Post-Dispatch* was a warm friend of the weak and the oppressed. The liberal humanitarianism that animated the early stand on the coopers' strike did not disappear. In many editorials the paper spoke out sharply for the rights of the ordinary man or sought for the poor acts of Christian charity. On two or three occasions in 1879 the police were censured for unnecessary brutality, once for wantonly shooting down a Negro on Pine Street for resisting arrest, although he "had not committed any offense at all," and another time, under POOR EDDIE NAHLICK, for such callous treatment of an eleven-year-old boy that he died in a Four Courts jail cell.[79] A strong editorial in 1880 castigated downtown department stores for perpetrating "the petty tyranny" of forcing female clerks to stand for hours while waiting upon customers. The paper called upon "the ladies of St. Louis" to insist that seats be provided for the clerks, and it pointed out that "if the ladies who are foremost in every other good work in this city will add to the roll of their charities the bettering of the shopgirls' condition, it will soon be done. . . ." [80] Still another editorial commented that "the poor people and the working classes of St. Louis are virtually deprived of frequent excursions on the Mississippi by the high tariff placed on steamboats by the owners. We ought to have half a dozen boats carrying children and their guardians up and down the river every evening," and it suggested that boat owners should loan their craft to charitable agencies "at reasonable rates" for this purpose.[81] The *Post-Dispatch* even defended the tramps swarming into the city's parks and public buildings from arbitrary treatment by municipal officials:

> The sudden vaccination of three hundred tramps at the order of an official who has no more authority to vaccinate tramps than he has to paint the Mayor's nose sky-blue . . . is [only] exceeded by some of the vagaries of the police in enforcing the ordinance against vagrants.[82]

[78] *Ibid.*, March 28, 1879.
[79] *Ibid.*, Aug. 6, 7, 11, 12, 1879.
[80] *Ibid.*, July 27, 1880.
[81] *Ibid.*, July 28, 1880.
[82] *Post and Dispatch,* Jan. 10, 1879.

Thus did the character of the *Post-Dispatch* take shape. Its resort to sensationalism and its pugnacious campaigns brought it gradually increasing popularity; by the end of 1879, although still small, it was firmly established, prosperous and growing. In May the paper's only opposition in the afternoon field, the *Evening Star,* ceased to exist. After its encounter with the *Post and Dispatch* in January the *Star* steadily declined and was finally abandoned by its politician-backers. Its failure was a cue for the *Post-Dispatch* to remark that failure was sure to be the fate of publishers "who think that influence can be purchased with money, or that support which can be bought at any price is worth any price at all." [83] The *Post-Dispatch* purchased the *Star* at auction for $790 and now had a monopoly of the afternoon field.[84]

The absorption of the *Star* was accompanied by a shuffling of the *Post-Dispatch* staff. Albert Cunningham, the *Star's* managing editor, replaced Henry Moore as city editor and John M. McGuffin, its business manager, became the cashier of the *Post-Dispatch* in place of Thomas Harris who withdrew because of poor health.[85] A broad-faced, extremely nervous man who sported a large black mustache and beetling brows, Cunningham was an experienced journalist, having learned—as so many did—his trade under McCullagh. He had been Dillon's city editor on the *Evening Post,* and no doubt it was Dillon who recommended him to Pulitzer.[86] McGuffin, plain and unpretentious, was a more important addition. He also was a veteran of St. Louis journalism, and his keen, original mind lent strength to the business end of the paper.[87]

In July the paper announced:

> Our increase in circulation during the past six months has been of such a character as to compel us to buy a new press, and within a month we expect to have a double four-cylinder press, double the size and capacity of our present one.[88]

The new $20,000 press could print 10,000 eight-page copies per hour. It also was equipped with stereotyping plates, a new device which

[83] *Post-Dispatch,* May 10, 1879.

[84] *Ibid.,* May 10, 12, 14, 1879. The *Post-Dispatch* claimed its circulation was increased by 2,000 with the acquisition of the *Star,* but this seems excessive. *Ibid.,* May 15, 1879.

[85] Moore remained with the paper as dramatic critic.

[86] Personal letter from D.J.W. McAuliffe, Oct. 23, 1950; *Spectator,* Feb. 5, 1881; *Journalist,* Sept. 25, 1886; *Post-Dispatch,* Sept. 11, 1880; *Gould's St. Louis Directory,* 1875, p. 232; 1877, p. 238; 1878, p. 232; 1879, p. 260.

[87] *American Journalist,* Aug. 1884, p. 346; *Spectator,* Feb. 5, 1881; *Gould's St. Louis Directory,* 1870, p. 578; 1873, p. 546; 1877, p. 610; 1879, p. 635; *Post-Dispatch,* Aug. 8, 1884.

[88] *Post-Dispatch,* July 10, 1879.

greatly increased its efficiency.[89] When it arrived in September, the mechanical force quickly dismantled the old one after the last edition on Saturday, and by working all day Sunday had the new one ready Monday afternoon. Then, taking a leaf from McCullagh, the publicity conscious Pulitzer cordially invited his readers to attend "a printing matinee" to see the latest mechanical marvel.[90]

Increased capacity permitted additional innovations. Features such as a weekly railroad column were added to the Saturday edition, now regularly enlarged to eight pages, and the paper could now publish "extras," the first one appearing at six o'clock on the afternoon of October 2 with the latest race results of the St. Louis Jockey Club.[91] Pulitzer even tried to challenge the established morning journals for rural readership. A *Weekly Post-Dispatch* made its appearance on September 10 at a subscription price of $1.25 a year. Appealing to Missouri's farmers, the *Post-Dispatch* declared "the Democrats of the West and South need a paper that they can trust; a paper that will serve Democracy from the standpoint of principle and conviction, that will not . . . sway and swerve like a weathercock" [92] Pulitzer hoped for a circulation of 20,000 for the weekly—about half that of the *Republican* or *Globe-Democrat*. It was "specially edited to give a complete history of the week brought down to 4 o'clock of the day of issue [Thursday]" for the isolated farm families who could not receive a daily.[93] However, although it was pushed hard and the paper claimed for it a growing popularity "from Iowa to Texas and from Indiana to Colorado," the weekly evidently did not prosper. In December its rate was reduced to one dollar. The paper's tendency to publish mostly news of local happenings had little appeal to the people of the Mississippi Valley and the Plains were readers continued to prefer the morning papers which placed more emphasis on rural events.[94]

In the city, however, the story was different, although here, too, it was not easy to break down long-established habits; conservative

[89] *Ibid.*, July 10, 1879, Aug. 18, 1879, Sept. 9, 1879. This was one of the earliest presses using stereotyping plates in St. Louis, perhaps the first. On the older press the type forms themselves were affixed to cylinders, a ticklish task. Floyd Calvin Shoemaker, *Missouri: Mother of the West* (Chicago, 1930), II, 571. See also, Mott, p. 401.

[90] *Post-Dispatch,* Sept. 9, 1879.

[91] The daily remained usually four pages.

[92] *Post-Dispatch,* Aug. 30, 1879.

[93] *Ibid.,* July 10, 1879, Jan. 2, 1880.

[94] *Ibid.,* Dec. 18, 1879, Jan. 2, 1880. The same reason was advanced for poor country circulation in 1900. A *Post-Dispatch* executive wrote Pulitzer, "I am convinced that a daily paper made to please St. Louis people will not please the country people. . . ." William E. Taylor to Joseph Pulitzer, Nov. 10, 1900, Pulitzer Papers (CU).

St. Louisans continued to prefer the morning journals. In a candid moment the *Post-Dispatch* ruefully admitted "there is nothing easier for a newspaper than to claim 'a large and constantly increasing circulation,' but nothing harder than to gain it." [95] Nevertheless, the paper's aggressive style gradually attracted new readers, and by December 31 its average daily circulation was 4,984 copies, an increase of nearly 2,000 during the year.[96]

But if growth in circulation sometimes seemed slow to the impatient Pulitzer, advertising volume was remarkable. Financially the paper's first year was an amazing success. As early as April the paper begged "the indulgence of our readers for the absence of a great many items of news." It exclaimed, "If we may judge the condition of business in St. Louis by our own advertising business it must be very lively. In spite of the . . . summer season the advertising of the POST-DISPATCH last week was greater in amount and more varied in its character than during any week of its existence." [97] Large display ads, some several columns wide, crowded news off the front page, especially as Christmas approached. By December the paper complained that even the enlarged Saturday edition was cramped for space.[98] Altogether, subtracting the operating expenses, which amounted to perhaps $100,000, in 1879 the *Post-Dispatch* achieved a profit of approximately $80,000.[99]

The partnership which achieved this success, however, was not altogether congenial. This became public on November 29 when the paper ran an ANNOUNCEMENT on the editorial page. It read in part:

> Our readers will hear—no doubt with regret—that Mr. John A. Dillon has withdrawn from the management of this journal, having disposed of his interest to Mr. Joseph Pulitzer, who is now sole proprietor.[100]

Other papers speculated about the reason for the parting, but probably the *Globe-Democrat* came closest to the truth when it

---

[95] *Post-Dispatch,* March 17, 1879.
[96] *Ibid.,* Jan. 12, 1882.
[97] *Ibid.,* April 12, 1879, June 16, 1879.
[98] *Ibid.,* Dec. 1, 1879, Dec. 17, 1879.
[99] Daniel W. Woods to Joseph Pulitzer, Feb. 25, 1903, Pulitzer Papers (CU). Woods told his chief that the figures for 1879 were not entirely clear because the books for that year had not been closed, but his best estimate was that the paper earned $87,178.82. However, the *Post-Dispatch,* Dec. 31, 1879, remarked that its profits by that time amounted only to $800 weekly. (But see Creelman, "Joseph Pulitzer," p. 239.) The estimate of $100,000 for operation costs is based on an observation in the *Post-Dispatch,* May 24, 1879.
[100] *Post-Dispatch,* Nov. 29, 1879.

commented that "incompatability of temper, superinduced, perhaps by an excess of talent" was the cause. Cautious and deliberate, Dillon had been swept along, unwillingly at times, by his energetic partner.[101] Also, after two years of business responsibilities for which he had little talent and no liking, Dillon was anxious to return to purely editorial and literary pursuits.[102] For Pulitzer, this was his experience as part-owner of the *Westliche Post* repeated, though with the opposite result. His urge to dominate whatever he undertook made it impossible for him to work for long in partnership with anyone, whether with Carl Schurz in 1873 or John Dillon in 1879.[103] Nevertheless, the two men remained on good terms, and the parting was arranged in a friendly spirit. Dillon sold his half interest to his dynamic associate for $40,000.[104] Joseph Pulitzer—a singular genius—was now the sole proprietor of the *Post-Dispatch*.

---

[101] On at least one occasion Pulitzer's penchant for sensations was a definite embarrassment to his partner. In the tax dodger crusade Dillon had to admit that his own sworn return was not entirely correct. The discrepancy was minor, but the incident no doubt was painful to the sensitive Dillon.

[102] Interview with Gertrude McDonald, Jan. 16, 1951.

[103] Creelman, p. 238; George Johns, *Joseph Pulitzer*, p. 59.

[104] Personal letter from D.J.W. McAuliffe, Oct. 23, 1950; interview with Gertrude McDonald, Jan. 16, 1951.

CHAPTER V

Single Ownership

Immediately upon Dillon's withdrawal Pulitzer reorganized the *Post-Dispatch*.[1] He selected John M. McGuffin as his business manager. In the six months since he had joined the force McGuffin's unostentatious industry had strongly impressed Pulitzer who especially liked his bold plans to increase circulation. A circulation agent, Sam Bothwell, was added to assist him.[2] The news and editorial departments also underwent considerable change. News Editor Jennings shuttled back temporarily to the *Globe-Democrat,* and City Editor Cunningham, whom Pulitzer found too easy-going, was dismissed.[3] Henry Moore was returned to the city desk where he built a reputation for himself as the most ruthlessly sensational editor in St. Louis.

Most important, John Albert Cockerill, editor of the Baltimore *Gazette,* was hired as the first formal managing editor of the *Post-Dispatch*. On his arrival in December 1879 he began an association with Joseph Pulitzer which was to last for fifteen years and become one of American journalism's legendary combinations. As "Joe

---

[1] The board of directors of the Dispatch Publishing Company was reconstituted, with Pulitzer as president, and his wife, Kate, vice-president. However, since he controlled all but a few shares of stock, Pulitzer practically ignored the board, calling the directors together only to rubberstamp decisions already made or transactions already completed. The other two members of the original board, William Patrick and Charles Parsons, remained, each with a single share of stock. Mrs. Pulitzer held only one share until 1881 when her holdings were increased to 200. She resigned from the board in 1883 but continued as a stockholder. *Post-Dispatch,* Dec. 16, 1879; Florence D. White to Joseph Pulitzer, March 21, 1905, and memorandum, 1906, Pulitzer Papers (CU).

[2] *American Journalist,* St. Louis, Aug., 1884; *Post-Dispatch,* Jan. 23, 1880, June 18, 1880; Sam C. Bothwell to Joseph Pulitzer, Aug. 26, 1886, Pulitzer Papers (CU). Ignatz Kappner, a courtly and elderly foreign-born bookkeeper, replaced McGuffin as cashier. *Gould's St. Louis Directory,* 1880, p. 554.

[3] Personal letter from D. J. W. McAuliffe, Oct. 23, 1950. Cunningham founded and briefly edited *The Hornet,* a weekly, after leaving the *Post-Dispatch*. About 1884 he moved to Washington, D.C., where he became a capital correspondent for a number of journals. Finally, he entered into a highly successful career as managing editor of, first, the Baltimore *Herald,* and later, the Baltimore *News. Gould's St. Louis Directory,* 1881, p. 284; 1882, p. 289; 1883, p. 277; *Editor & Publisher: A Journal for Newspaper Makers,* VI, Sept. 22, 1906; *The Journalist,* Dec. 15, 1888.

and John" they became inseparable in developing first the *Post-Dispatch* and later the New York *World*.[4]

John Cockerill, a big-framed and handsome man, had at thirty-four already achieved considerable success in the newspaper business. He was the son of an Ohio politician-soldier who had commanded a Union regiment during the Civil War—in which John himself had served as a drummer boy. Cockerill began his newspaper career as a printer's "devil" in his home town of West Union, Ohio. After the war he was editor of a small sheet in nearby Hamilton, the *True Telegram*. In 1869 he advanced to a city newspaper, the Cincinnati *Enquirer*, where he revealed his talents and rapidly rose to the managing editor's chair. According to Lafcadio Hearn, one of the *Enquirer's* reporters, Cockerill was "a hard master, a tremendous worker, and a born journalist." Hearn added that his editor was "not a literary man, nor a well-read man, nor a scholar—but he has immense common sense, and a large experience of life, besides being, in a Mark Twainish way, much of a humorist." [5] Cockerill's aggressive use of the methods of the new journalism made the *Enquirer* in a few years a leading paper in the Middle West before he was sent abroad to report the Russo-Turkish War in 1876 as one of America's first foreign correspondents. When he returned, he became a member of Stilson Hutchins' new journal, the Washington *Post*. From there he went to the Baltimore *Gazette* where a wire from Joseph Pulitzer found him.[6]

Cockerill's remarkably free and easy style, full of a spontaneous wit, immeasurably improved the *Post-Dispatch* editorial page, hitherto characterized by Pulitzer's screechy prose. At the same time, when the occasion demanded, Cockerill's editorials could be biting. He developed a reputation as the most effective paragraphist in St. Louis journalism.[7] Bold to the point of recklessness, Cockerill carried on the crusades of the *Post-Dispatch* with a gay disregard

[4] A good study of Cockerill is Homer W. King, *Pulitzer's Prize Editor: A Biography of John A. Cockerill, 1845-1896* (Durham, N.C., 1965). See also, John M· Lee, "John A. Cockerill," *Dictionary of American Biography*, IV, 256; Seitz, *Joseph Pulitzer*, pp. 104-106; George S. Johns, *Joseph Pulitzer*, pp. 65-66; Walt McDougall, *This is the Life!* (New York, 1926), pp. 101-102, 206-208.

[5] Elizabeth Bisland, *The Life and Letters of Lafcadio Hearn*, 2 vols. (New York, 1906), I, 53-54. See also, Elizabeth Stevenson, *Lafcadio Hearn* (New York, 1961), p. 43 *passim*.

[6] *Journalist*, Sept. 12, 1885, March 3, 1888; *Post-Dispatch*, Oct. 14, 1882; *Spectator*, May 26, 1883; Homer Gard to James Cox, April 14, 1922, Pulitzer Papers (LC); George Johns, pp. 65-66. Pulitzer had first met Cockerill in Cincinnati in 1872 and became well acquainted with his great abilities. King, pp. 77, 89-94.

[7] It was a general opinion, however, that McCullagh was St. Louis's best all-around editorial writer. *Reedy's Mirror*, April 16, 1896.

for consequences.[8] Within the newspaper's organization, his booming personality very soon made him indispensable; he became the idol of the staff, instilling it with an eager pride and spirit akin to Pulitzer's own inspirational qualities. For the publisher, too, Cockerill was the man for the occasion. Still very much a politician, Pulitzer intended to be away from the office for protracted intervals during the campaign of 1880, and his new editor was a man who would fearlessly maintain the paper's crusading policies and loyally devote his talents to promoting the *Post-Dispatch*. Cockerill was a career journalist with no other ambition than to serve his newspaper with all his energies.[9]

For the next three and a half years Cockerill, Moore, and Mc-Guffin, together with Pulitzer, constituted the directorate of the *Post-Dispatch,* making this upstart sheet the rival of the established morning dailies and perfecting the brand of newspaper publication which one day would revolutionize American journalism. The group was a prototype of all subsequent directorates of Pulitzer newspapers. It was resourceful, energetic, and intensely loyal to the *Post-Dispatch* and its proprietor. Pulitzer made use of it in the same way he utilized his later editors and managers. Not original himself, he surrounded himself with men who were, "picking their brains" and allowing them great freedom to develop their ideas.[10] Pulitzer en-

---

[8] Typical of Cockerill's offhand fearlessness was an incident that occurred on the New York *World* later. A pastor who objected to what he regarded as an irreligious cartoon was told: "My Dear Sir: Will you kindly go to hell?" McDougall, p. 138.

[9] There are many sketches of Cockerill in contemporary sources. The best are the following: St Louis *Spectator,* May 26, 1883; *Journalist,* Sept. 12, 1885, May 8, 1886, Oct. 1, 1887, Oct. 14, 1893, Oct. 1, 1897; *Reedy's Mirror,* April 16, 1896; *The Fourth Estate: A Newspaper for the Makers of Newspapers,* III, April 16, 1896.

[10] Pulitzer's personal lack of imagination and his habit of adopting the ideas of others is alluded to in Seitz, *Joseph Pulitzer,* p. 4, and more acidly in Mc-Dougall, *This is the Life!,* p. 166. See also, *Spectator,* Dec. 29, 1888. There is a difference of opinion on this point, however. W. A. Swanberg, who has examined the Pulitzer Papers, remarks that "it seems to me that JP's own letters reveal a mind simply teeming with ideas. Of course it's also true that he insisted that his men produce ideas, that he had no use for men without ideas, and that many of his crusades sprang from the brains of others. Yet (I speak really of his work on the *World*) he supplied a good share of them. . . ." (Personal letter, April 15, 1966.) My own view, derived from examining Pulitzer's correspondence with *Post-Dispatch* editors through the years until his death in 1911, is that he was not particularly productive of, or original in, ideas. He constantly admonished his editors to think of new approaches and he had much to say to them about their policies—lecturing, cautioning, exhorting them. I should add, however, that after 1883 Pulitzer lavished most of his energies on the *World,* although the observation sometimes made that he paid little attention to the *Post-Dispatch* is a gross error, as the volume of his correspondence with his St. Louis lieutenants vividly testifies.

couraged originality in every way possible, from violent give-and-take discussions to generous pay and bonuses. Cockerill, for example, was given a small stock interest, and Billy Steigers was granted generous commissions on advertising.[11]

It was one of Pulitzer's most striking characteristics, evident from the beginning, that he was capable of inspiring a fierce pride among his employees.[12] *Post-Dispatch* editors were noted for their esprit de corps and their eagerness to spend their energies in the service of the paper. Partly, this was traceable to the atmosphere of unconventionality, always stimulating to creative minds, but there were other factors. A feeling of comradeship pervaded the establishment, from the editors to the janitors. Pulitzer was one of the few editors of his time to appear in shirtsleeves and work among his employees as one of them.[13] In addition, as one observer noted later, Pulitzer always gave "loyalty for loyalty to his staff and friends who aided and supported him." [14] Once an editor showed the qualities Pulitzer desired—initiative, loyalty, industry—the publisher stood by him and overlooked both personal foibles and well-intentioned mistakes.[15]

Perhaps most important of all was the fact that Joseph Pulitzer actually sought to publish a newspaper in keeping with his grandiloquent pronouncements: a newspaper which refused to be the organ of special interests, classes, or political parties, a newspaper displaying a sleepless vigilance for the public good. To belong to the staff of such a sheet was as inspiriting—and as rare—an experience then as it is today; from the start it produced a sense of pride and purpose.

For all his dependence on resourceful assistants, however, Pulitzer observed no chain of command punctiliousness in his conduct of the *Post-Dispatch*. Instead, he was restlessly active in every part of the establishment. "He was everywhere in the office—appearing most unexpectedly and at odd times, now arguing with a reporter in the city room on some story—anon dashing into the composing room to give orders, dashing into the counting room. . . ." to confer with the business manager about circulation problems or consulting the advertising agent about want ads.[16] He seemingly never tired, appearing before anyone else early in the morning and "every night . . . working at his desk alone in the *Post-Dispatch* editorial

---

[11] Ignatz Kappner to Joseph Pulitzer, Nov. 29, 1886, Pulitzer Papers (CU).

[12] McDougall, pp. 163-64.

[13] Undated clipping, Pulitzer Papers (LC).

[14] Charles Parsons to Joseph Pulitzer, Oct. 26, 1903, Pulitzer Papers (CU).

[15] George Johns, p. 72.

[16] The quotation is from a member of the original staff of the New York *World* and is an observation of the way Pulitzer acted fresh from St. Louis. Obviously, he learned these habits while the active owner of the *Post-Dispatch*. New York *Times,* Nov. 5, 1911.

room . . . writing by the light of one gas jet." [17] An acute appraisal describes this volatile editor:

> From the very beginning Mr. Pulitzer seemed like some human dynamo, pouring energy and heat into all about him. His sanctum was a corner cut off by a dusty curtain from the room in which his city editor and reporters sat. And about every twenty minutes a long arm would sweep the curtain aside, the proprietor's head and long neck would be thrust out, and his shrill voice would shower suggestions mixed with violent condemnation or praise. . . . Nothing escaped his keen, gray-blue eyes. He wrote editorials, edited the news and contrived striking headlines. What he wrote himself he altered and polished and condensed, and sometimes the press had to wait while he worked on proofs with such eagerness to improve on himself that his corrections amounted practically to a rewriting of the article. No such worker had ever been seen in a St. Louis newspaper office before. [18]

Such an energetic employer was also not easy to work for. There were times when his subordinates became exasperated with the frenzied flow of orders and suggestions and the constant interference with office routine. John Cockerill growled once that "Mr. Pulitzer was the damndest best man in the world to have in a newspaper office for one hour in the morning. For the remainder of the day he was a damned nuisance." [19]

Moreover, despite his show of comradeship and appreciation of his subordinates, Pulitzer was always careful to reserve final authority for himself. No one exercised general control over the *Post-Dispatch* except himself. Even Cockerill admitted that he had "very little to do with the business department," and he might have added that he had comparatively little to do with Henry Moore's news force or that McGuffin had little authority over Steigers' activities in advertising. [20] To be sure, the proprietor was an extremely active newspaper man, but in addition, he was jealous of his authority and fearful of delegating too much of it. The newspaper was his, an extension of himself. Consequently, the positions of managing editor and business manager meant much less in terms of actual authority on Pulitzer's newspaper than they did on other journals. In short, although he sought men of bold and creative spirit to

---

[17] George Johns, pp. 67-68.

[18] Creelman, XXI, (March 1909), pp. 238-39.

[19] George Johns, p. 68.

[20] *Post-Dispatch*, Jan. 11, 1883. Personal letter from D. J. W. McAuliffe, Oct. 23, 1950.

run his newspapers, Pulitzer always had a lurking suspicion of their ambitions. As long as his health was good his fears were held in check, but when blindness and nervous illness overtook him in later years, the suspicious streak in his nature took strong hold. The results were an encouragement of tale-bearing, a demand for constant reports, unexpected visitations by personal secretaries, and an excessive division of authority in the management of the *Post-Dispatch* and the *World*, which often damaged the morale of the staffs of both newspapers.[21]

Always in a hurry, Pulitzer scarcely paused for breath when he assumed sole command of the *Post-Dispatch*. The very day he took over he announced that

> in a few days, or as soon as the necessary mechanical improvements are completed, the POST-DISPATCH will appear greatly enlarged and improved in every respect. It will be changed to the size of the New York *Herald* and Cincinnati *Gazette*, and appear as an *eight-page paper every day*. It will be full of special dispatches from all parts of the Union and the world. . . . It will continue to tell the truth about public affairs and about both parties, disregarding mere partisanship. . . . The sole ownership of this journal is regarded by its proprietor only as an additional incentive . . . to continue its improvement unceasingly, until it has become not alone the only and best evening paper—but the best of any kind St. Louis ever had.[22]

True to his word, Pulitzer enlarged the daily to eight pages and the Saturday to ten, and when "the spring business tide" rolled in in 1880 with its increased volume of advertising the size was boosted again, to ten and twelve pages respectively. This prompted the *Post-Dispatch* to burst out characteristically that its "growth and enlargement [is] without parallel in journalism." [23] At least it now bore a respectable resemblance to the morning journals.

Increased space permitted an improvement in coverage, particularly of local news. The *Post-Dispatch* acquired a reputation for publishing news ignored by its morning contemporaries. Labor news became regular fare in the *Post-Dispatch* which, in times of industrial strife, assigned regular "labor reporters" to cover strikes and union meetings at Vorwaerts Hall, and, whereas a parade of Negro militiamen through

---

21 See scattered but trenchant observations on this aspect of Pulitzer's character in McDougall, and briefer and kindlier comments in Seitz, ch. 1.

22 *Post-Dispatch*, Nov. 29, 1879.

23 *Ibid.*, Dec. 1, 1879, Dec. 4, 1879, Feb. 12, 1880, Feb. 28, 1880, April 10, 1880, April 17, 1880. The number of columns per page fluctuated between six and seven.

the downtown streets received ample mention in Pulitzer's news-paper, neither the *Globe-Democrat* nor the *Republican* considered it worthy of notice.[24] At the same time, it began to print personal items from each of the districts comprising Greater St. Louis. Every day dozens of ordinary citizens leading otherwise anonymous lives found themselves mentioned in sentence-length squibs in columns devoted to neighborhood events. And although on some days this gave the *Post-Dispatch* the aspect of a small-town weekly and much trouble and expense attended the collecting of news from country towns like Belleville and Collinsville, these inconveniences were overlooked by Pulitzer, whose aim was to build circulation.

The new interest in the ordinary citizen was accented in the changed character of the paper's "miscellany." Because of their limited appeal, the genteel features of the old *Evening Post* were dropped altogether or relegated to out-of-the-way corners, and new ones were added to appeal to unsophisticated tastes.

Typical of the change were items published for women readers. The staid "Home" column, which appealed chiefly to society ma-trons, gave way to articles like one headed CHEAP DRESSES written for "The Girl Who Puts a Small Sum to the Best Advantage." Said the *Post-Dispatch,* "a practical economist buys every dress with a view to its reappearance afterward in a new form, and it is unwise for any but a wealthy woman to purchase an expensive dress which can not be made over." [25] A dash of spice was evident in another article labeled THE FAIR SEX, which was "About Women of All Climes, Ages and Degrees—Good Women, Foolish Women and Frivolous Women—Grass Widows." [26]

In March a fiction column made its appearance in the large Satur-day edition. Later, when it proved popular, it ran in the daily. Occupying as much as two and a half columns, it consisted of sac-charine tales of romance and spine-tingling adventures. One piece, entitled A MYSTERIOUS TELEGRAM, was a pleasantly chilling yarn about a brave telegraph clerk who frustrated a gang of robbers in a lonely, rural railroad depot on a dark and stormy night; a second, THE CHILD WITNESS, was climaxed by the lisping testimony of a small boy which solved a double murder; and a third, TAKING BOARDERS, told how a pair of childhood sweethearts, now silvery with age, were reunited in a drab boardinghouse after a lifetime of loneliness.[27] This feature,

[24] *Ibid.,* Feb. 23, 1880, Aug. 30, 1880. See also, Louis Star, "The Press and Labor News," *The Press in the Contemporary Scene (The Annals of the American Academy of Political and Social Science,* CCXIX) (Philadelphia, Jan., 1942), 108.

[25] *Post-Dispatch,* July 3, 1880.

[26] *Ibid.,* July 8, 1880.

[27] *Ibid.,* May 8, 15, 29, 1880.

no doubt, greatly increased the popularity of the *Post-Dispatch* in many homes.

Still another new feature was the secret society column, of which the *Post-Dispatch* was inordinately proud. Written by a reporter reputed to have a wider acquaintance than any other newspaperman in the city, it detailed the myriad events of the fraternal orders that proliferated in St. Louis after the Civil War. Usually labeled THE MYSTIC ORDERS, it often filled an entire column in Saturday's paper. On one occasion the *Post-Dispatch* noted happily that this feature was so popular that it was "habitually copied, almost verbatim, by our enterprising English morning contemporaries. This shows rare discrimination." [28]

In a more serious vein the paper printed a weekly roundup of comment on economic conditions in the St. Louis area. Comments like the following reflected the lingering effects of depression:

> At the present time, although there appears to be plenty of work, outsiders are not advised to come here with the expectation of finding employment. [However] wages compare favorably with any of the large manufacturing centers of the Union. . . . The lowest wage reported as being paid is $1.15 per day, which is given to section hands on railroads, but for laboring work directly in the city the prices paid average from $1.25 to $1.75 per day. There is at present no prospect of a decline in any wages until winter sets in.[29]

Despite the paper's concentration on urban news, it also attempted an agricultral column which it pushed chiefly in the weekly edition. Variously captioned "Farm Management, The Farmer's Nook," or simply "The Farm," it consisted of "Suggestions Which Will Enrich the Wise Agriculturist."

Humor and sensation also were utilized to increase popularity. The dull "letters" from Eastern correspondents inherited from the *Post* were supplemented with syndicated commentary on the national scene by George Alfred Townsend who was best known to his readers countrywide as "Gath." [30] The drama review—standard fare in all American newspapers—became particularly distinguished in the *Post-*

---

[28] *Ibid.*, July 12, 1880. The reporter was Frank Bigney, who inaugurated this feature on the St. Louis *Times* a few months before Pulitzer hired him to obtain the column for the *Post-Dispatch*. Kelsoe, p. 296; *Journalist*, Nov. 13, 1886, July 2, 1887.

[29] *Post-Dispatch*, June 12, 1880.

[30] *Ibid.*, March 13, 1880. Townsend began his career in St. Louis in the 1870's. Pulitzer admired him greatly and later employed him on the New York *World*. Kelsoe, p. 39. Edith Merwin Bartow, *News and These United States* (New York, 1952), p. 203.

Dispatch for raciness. Characteristic was a minor triumph, THE AB-
BOTT KISS, scored by the ebullient John McEnnis, who was assigned
to pass an evening behind the stage viewing the performance of Romeo
and Juliet, "especially the osculatory manipulations" of Emma Abbott,
a popular actress.[31] The result was an article which began

> Kissing and being kissed are the accented words in the screed
> of human life. They are the oases in the desert, the coral islands
> in the waste of waters, strawberries and cream in December. . . .
> Just imagine a divine girl with real warm blood glowing in every
> vein of her body, and a flush of health on her beautiful, upturned
> face, her red lips protruding in the slightest possible pout, and
> her whole attitude meaning expectancy and waiting, and then
> fancy how that ripe, tender mouth would taste when you begin
> to feed on it, young man . . . . How would it strike you to play
> Romeo to Miss Abbott's Juliet? [32]

Following this torrid introduction were interviews with all the
principals, excluding, however, the actress's husband, although the
reporter admitted that "he probably knows as much about the kisses
as . . . the other gentlemen." The story reverberated in the exchange
columns of the nation's press.[33]

Gaily the *Post-Dispatch* pushed its new wares, particularly in the
Saturday supplement, which was crammed with lively "miscellany."
This popularization of news and features, making the paper for the
first time a source of entertainment as well as information, was an
important reason why in 1880 the *Post-Dispatch* enjoyed a remarkable rise in circulation.

There were other reasons as well. The *Post-Dispatch* experimented
with a number of ideas whose novelty attracted attention. One was
illustration. Woodcuts had appeared occasionally in daily newspapers for many years, but difficulty in producing them quickly and
attaching them to high-speed cylindrical presses limited their utility
for daily papers. Not until the zincograph was borrowed from Europe
in the seventies was it possible to incorporate illustration into daily
journalism, and even then before 1880 only one or two New York
papers attempted it.[34] It was cause for comment, therefore, on the

---

[31] *Spectator,* June 11, 1881.

[32] *Post-Dispatch,* Jan. 17, 1880.

[33] *Ibid. Spectator,* June 11, 1881.

[34] Mott, pp. 501-503. See also, Alfred McClung Lee, *The Daily Newspaper in America: The Evolution of a Social Instrument* (New York, 1937), pp. 129-31; and *Journalist,* Jan. 17, 1885. James Gordon Bennett, Sr., was the first to use illustration in a daily paper, in 1837. Horace Greeley first used a cartoon sketch, in 1840. *Ibid.,* Dec. 14, 1889.

afternoon of December 4, 1879, when the Post-Dispatch carried a humorous cartoon sketch of the *Globe-Democrat's* Joe McCullagh about to square off with an opponent in a libel case.[35]

Illustrations appeared only infrequently at first, but Pulitzer's experience with them convinced him of their value in attracting circulation. Generally, they were printed from cuts distributed by national agencies, as with the likenesses of the presidential and vice-presidential candidates.[36] But two or three times a local artist fashioned portraits illustrating local events: once when a pair of criminals was hanged in the Four Courts jailyard and again when Phelim Toole, a fireman celebrated for heroic exploits, was killed fighting a blaze.[37] Their publication produced bursts of circulation increase. In March, for example, when Charles Stewart Parnell visited St. Louis to plead the cause of Ireland, the *Post-Dispatch* for the first time cleared the front page of advertising and published a three-column portrait of the bearded patriot. These innovations "sold an extra edition of nearly three thousand papers for us." [38] Again, in August, when the paper carried sensational facsimiles of three letters purporting to implicate former President Grant in the Whiskey Ring scandals of a few years before, and in December when it carried a large engraving depicting the vast extent of Jay Gould's new St. Louis-based railroad empire, circulation boomed.[39] Thus, though

---

[35] This was not the paper's first illustration. Many woodcuts—some of them spectacular in size—had appeared in advertisements from the first. Nor was it, broadly speaking, even the first editorial drawing, for on two or three occasions in 1879 the *Post-Dispatch* published diagrams to illustrate important stories. In April the extent of "the greatest fire that has ever been known in St. Louis" was portrayed, though not very graphically, in a geometric figure, and when a skeleton was discovered in the charred ruins of the Southern Hotel a diagram was published in which "A" marked the spot of the gruesome find. *Post-Dispatch*, April 5, 1879, July 11, 1879. A third diagram was a prominent feature of a special edition published July 4, 1879. December's cut, however, was the first cartoon drawing.

[36] *Ibid.*, June 9, 1880, June 24, 1880, July 10, 1880.

[37] *Ibid.*, April 23, 1880, July 7, 1880.

[38] *Ibid.*, March 6, 1880. The cut appeared March 4. On the same day the *Globe-Democrat* also printed a picture of Parnell. Of this the *Post-Dispatch* remarked: "A more wretched job of picture-making was never seen. . . . An ordinary wood-chopper with a dull hatchet could come as near turning out a wood-cut as did the artists in this case. . . . We are glad that this botch appeared this morning, for it will assist the judicious public to an appreciation of the very able and artistic picture of the Great Agitator which we print to-day." The St. Louis *Times*, however, thought the cuts of both "esteemed contemporaries" looked as though they had been done "with a jack-knife on a pine-knot." *Ibid.*, March 5, 1880.

[39] *Ibid.*, Aug. 9, 1880, Dec. 25, 1880.

technical problems reduced the frequency of illustrations, their obvious popularity presaged increasing use of them in the future.[40]

The *Post-Dispatch* also experimented with another device—borrowed from James Gordon Bennett's New York *Herald*—and though the results were not entirely satisfactory, it, too, pointed the way to the future. In keeping with his policy of identifying the paper with the public interest, Pulitzer launched several fund-raising projects. The first occurred in Januray 1880, when Pulitzer associated his paper with the New York *Herald's* Famine Fund to help the destitute of Ireland.[41] Unfortunately, just as the *Post-Dispatch* drive got underway, the Merchants' Exchange staged a campaign of its own which quickly raised $5,000—enough to send a shipload of supplies to the Emerald Isle. The *Post-Dispatch* ruefully admitted that "not a nickel has been subscribed . . . to our Irish Relief Fund. We do not remember to have even seen a politician looking at the beautiful blank." [42]

The paper's second effort, although ultimately no more successful than the Relief Fund, was better planned and sustained. This one sought to mobilize the local citizenry behind a *Post-Dispatch* project to relieve the distressing condition of the city's streets. By 1880 the thoroughfares of St. Louis had degenerated into the worst of "any great city in the country." [43] Like many a metropolitan center following the Civil War, St. Louis encountered the problem of expanding municipal services to take care of a rapidly growing population, but it labored under the handicaps of a state constitution, buttressed by a city charter, which prevented it from raising the funds necessary even to maintain properly services already in existence.[44] This was particularly true of the streets. The coalition of economy-minded agrarians and moneyed interests in St. Louis who controlled the state's Democratic Party placed almost intolerable limits on the taxing and borrowing powers of municipalities, so that St. Louis had only about $60,000 annually to spend on street repair—a mere pittance.

---

[40] The first artist for the *Post-Dispatch* was a youth, Saunders Norvell, who became a prominent merchant and public figure in St. Louis. At sixteen he brought a drawing of a well-known local personality to Pulitzer. Looking up, the publisher said, "Young man that is very good. We'll put it in the *Post-Dispatch* and pay you $5 for it. See if you can do as well again." Several subsequent sketches were accepted before Norvell, anxious to receive payment for his work, demanded remuneration. Pulitzer wrote out an order for the cashier and as Norvell retreated towards the door he called out, "Young man, you've missed your vocation. You were born to be a collector." St. Louis *Times*, April 15, 1908. See also, Kelsoe, p. 276.
[41] *Post-Dispatch*, Feb. 9, 1880.
[42] *Ibid.*, Feb. 12, 1880.
[43] *Ibid.*, May 19, 1880.
[44] Barclay, *The Movement for Municipal Home Rule*, pp. 56-58.

Consequently, only a fraction of the city's three hundred miles of roadway were paved at all, and these were surfaced with cheap limestone macadam which rapidly disintegrated under the steady pounding of horses' hooves and grinding wheels. Thus, in wet weather "great pools of slime" several inches deep covered the main streets from curb to curb, and when the dry winds of summer blew in from the Plains the macadam was "converted to powder and blown over into Illinois." [45]

Although the *Post-Dispatch*, like everyone else in St. Louis, deplored this dismal situation, it looked askance at proposals to increase the city's taxing powers in order to resurface the streets.[46] The city charter, the paper declared,

> wisely limits the amount of special taxes to twenty-five per cent of the assessed value of property, yet to lay a granite pavement on any newly opened street would call for a special tax from the individual property owner to the full limit of the law, and for an equal amount to be taken from the general body of the tax-payers. Such an improvement on the face of it is not worth its cost. . . . If property-owners had any assurance that their investments in St. Louis real estate had any future worth thinking of, they might be willing to meet the outlay for granite. But . . . they are not to be blamed if they refuse to saddle themselves with so heavy an expense, and if they insist on deferring costly experiments in street paving, until they are in better condition.[47]

But the *Post-Dispatch* was willing to support a palliative which was introduced into the city assembly early in 1880, authorizing a private concern to charge property owners two cents per foot for sprinkling surfaces in front of their homes. This, the paper thought, would allow St. Louisans "to get along next summer without eating more than a half pound of pulverized limestone per day." [48] Unfortunately, it soon learned with disgust that the powerful real estate interests of the community opposed even this mild measure and prevented it from passing.[49]

In this dilemma the *Post-Dispatch* was suddenly struck with an idea which it communicated enthusiastically to the public in an editorial entitled A DOLLAR A MONTH.

---

[45] *Post-Dispatch*, Jan. 9, 1880, Feb. 6, 1880. See also, *ibid.*, Jan. 3, 1880, Jan. 9, 1880, April 29, 1880, Dec. 20, 1881; and Soraghan, pp. 66-71.

[46] *Post-Dispatch*, Aug. 1, 4, 1879.

[47] *Ibid.*, Aug. 4, 1879.

[48] *Ibid.*, Feb. 11, 1880, March 28, 1880.

[49] *Ibid.*, March 31, 1880.

There is nothing that St. Louis is so deficient in as attractive summer drives. Forest Park has a labyrinth of well-paved, compact roads, and once there the oppressed victim of summer heat . . . [may] enjoy the fresh air and the delicious exercise which comes of buggy and carriage riding. But the park is robbed of more than half its beauty by this villainous dust which lies between the city and the park gates. To have these stifling, suffocating clouds laid would be a blessing indeed. . . .

A number of gentlemen are interesting themselves in a sprinkling boom. They propose to secure for the citizens of St. Louis ten miles of delightful drive by private subscription. By sprinkling Page avenue, Union avenue and Lindell avenue a pleasant circuit can be secured from the sprinkled streets of the city to the cool roads of the park. . . . It is fair to assume that there are 6,000 people in the city who either own carriages or drive more or less during the summer months. The sprinkling . . . can be done for about $1,000 a month—or $6,000 for the season. A small monthly subscription from those who ride and drive would secure this great boon . . . .

Assuming that all the readers of the POST-DISPATCH are fond of riding to and from the park, we will manifest our appreciation of this worthy enterprise by making a monthly subscription of $10 to the cause of anti-dust. We would suggest that all persons who are willing to subscribe to the sprinkling fund send their names to this office. . . . Surely one thousand gentlemen can be found willing to contribute a dollar a month toward such a desirable end. . . . Send in your names, gentlemen! One dollar a month will do it.[50]

During the next few days the *Post-Dispatch* vigorously beat the drums for its proposal under such provocative headlines as DOWN WITH THE DUST and "Wanted: A Dollar a Month—Who is Stingy Enough to Refuse it?" while prominent feature articles and lengthy editorials exhorted St. Louisans to "sit down at once and drop a postal-card to the POST-DISPATCH simply saying: 'Put me down for a monthly subscription of $1 in aid of the Sprinkling Fund.' "[51] Its aim, the paper said, was "to make this a popular movement. Every home and carriage owner in the city is expected to be a dollar-a-month man in the Anti-Dust Association."[52]

At first contributions poured in. Within a week the *Post-Dispatch* announced, with some exaggeration, that half the needed amount was

[50] *Ibid.*, April 12, 1880.
[51] *Ibid.*, April 12, 13, 15, 1880.
[52] *Ibid.*, April 14, 1880.

pledged and "there should be no difficulty in securing the remainder." [53] A committee of "substantial business men" was appointed to administer the fund. But the paper's optimism was premature. Despite all its pleas and exhortations, by the end of April it was still far short of its goal and had to admit "the soft reverberations of the Anti-Dust Boom are growing faint upon the evening air." [54] In despair it asked:

> Can't something be done to make the anti-dust boom a success? . . . A committee should be organized to solicit additional subscriptions. We have done our part of the work and . . . it is not likely that we can raise much more. Where are the active gentlemen who are willing to take hold of our good beginning and carry it through to success? [55]

Apparently there were none, and although the plan was scaled down to more modest proportions, the *Post-Dispatch* finally had to confess defeat.[56]

This was the most ambitious of the paper's fund-raising campaigns, and its failure made the *Post-Dispatch* chary for a time about launching new ones, although it joined with other organizations once or twice in collecting funds for worthy causes.[57] Pulitzer did not abandon the idea, however, and it remained a part of his journalistic style.

Fund-raising to support worthy civic projects illustrated Pulitzer's attitude towards government at this stage. As far as possible, he thought, governmental activity should be kept at a minimum, particularly in matters of economic welfare, and a liberal journal should mobilize private efforts to solve problems of economic and social distress as much to prevent the expansion of government as to serve humanitarian causes. For to Pulitzer—still largely conditioned by Liberal Republicanism—it was axiomatic that to permit the expansion of government inevitably would mean the blighting of individual liberty. This viewpoint was expressed by the *Post-Dispatch* in the spring of 1880 when a tornado virtually destroyed the community of Marshfield. The mayor of the little town issued an agonized plea for assistance, and St. Louis, led by the Merchants'

---

[53] *Ibid.*, April 20, 1880.
[54] *Ibid.*, April 29, 1880.
[55] *Ibid.*, April 30, 1880.
[56] *Ibid.* The next year the *Spectator* was somewhat more successful in a similar campaign. *Spectator,* April 16, 1881, June 4, 1881.
[57] In one case the *Post-Dispatch* joined with the Merchants' Exchange in a highly successful drive to raise a fund for the bereaved family of the heroic Phelim Toole, whose funeral was a public event in St. Louis. *Post-Dispatch,* July 7, 1880, July 29, 1880.

Exchange, responded with a gift of $6,000. The *Post-Dispatch* supported the drive and was disappointed when the total raised was merely the Exchange gift; the distress of Marshfield was acute. But when a reader suggested that the state should appropriate funds to take care of the emergency, the *Post-Dispatch* indignantly replied that the demand was AN ABSURDITY:

> The idea . . . seems to be based on the paternal theory of government. The State of Missouri has nothing to do, as a State, with the visitation of God. In exchange for taxes received the State guarantees to protect its citizens in their lives and their rights in property as against the machinations of man. It has no more business to be paying for property destroyed by wind than it has to be paying for property destroyed by fire. If the plan . . . could be carried into execution it wouldn't be long before the State Treasury would be called upon to make good the shortage of crops. Droughts and grasshoppers are as much the agents of Providence as . . . cyclones. . . . A great many people have no idea of the province of governments based on the mutual plan, like ours. . . .[58]

The *Post-Dispatch* toyed with one more device for attracting readers, a resort to "stunt journalism." [59] In April a daring St. Louis aeronaut announced his intention of taking a cross-country jaunt in a balloon. Balloon ascensions were a stock attraction at county fairs after the Civil War, and because of their risky nature always drew publicity. Resolving to profit from the fanfare sure to accompany this one, the *Post-Dispatch* arranged for one of its reporters to accompany it, reporting his impressions by dropping dispatches from the balloon in flight. No doubt it was with a sigh of relief that the reporter told his readers an accident prevented the expedition from leaving the ground one Sunday afternoon in Lindell Park. His editors might not have been equally pleased, but at least the *Post-Dispatch* enjoyed a spate of publicity for the idea. Good-naturedly it chided the lordly *Globe-Democrat* for refusing to join in the praise, remarking that "it is impossible to print a live newspaper in this community without mentioning the POST-DISPATCH." [60]

These innovations and experiments brought the results Pulitzer coveted most, an acceleration in circulation. Readership almost doubled in 1880, jumping from a daily average of 4,984 on December

---

[58] *Ibid.,* April 27, 1880.

[59] "Stunt journalism" became one of the trademarks of Pulitzer's journalism on the New York *World*. It was climaxed by Nellie Bly's famous dash around the world in 1890. Mott, pp. 436-37.

[60] *Post-Dispatch,* April 19, 1880.

31, 1879, to 8,740 a year later.[61] On January 1, 1881, the paper announced in boldface type

The POST-DISPATCH has the largest BONA FIDE circulation ever attained by any afternoon paper in St. Louis; it has a larger circulation than any morning paper in St. Louis (except one); it sells ten times as many copies on the streets, by newsboys, than all other afternoon papers combined. . . .[62]

To some degree this startling growth was produced by the creation of a circulation system where virtually none had existed before.[63] This was largely the handiwork of John McGuffin, the new business manager. McGuffin established branch offices to stimulate sales in outlying neighborhoods, the first being located at Eleventh and Exchange streets in North St. Louis. The results were gratifying. "The week just closed has added another fine array to the subscription books of the POST-DISPATCH," the paper chortled in May. "Our circulation in North St. Louis and Carondelet has more than quadrupled in a fortnight." [64] McGuffin also expanded the carrier force until, within eighteen months, there were three times as many newsboys "delivering papers promptly in every district of the city" than in 1879 and more than two hundred "little street gamins" shouting "with peculiar abbreviation" the name of the *Post-Dispatch* downtown.[65] Tirelessly McGuffin sent agents "in every direction, east, west, north and south of the city," offering trial subscriptions and placing newspapers for sale in every depot and hotel and on every newsstand.[66] And whereas the morning papers passed on to their readers a boost in the price of newsprint, the *Post-Dispatch* absorbed the cost and maintained its subscription rate at twenty cents per week, making it "the cheapest daily paper in St. Louis. Don't forget it." [67]

In a further effort to increase its popularity, early in April the *Post-Dispatch* borrowed a practice from the *Globe-Democrat*, publishing a notarized statement containing sworn proofs of its rapid advance in circulation. "The interesting relations existing between

---

[61] *Ibid.*, Jan. 12, 1882.

[62] *Ibid.*, Jan. 1, 1881.

[63] Frank R. O'Neil to Joseph Pulitzer, [1903], Pulitzer Papers (CU). O'Neil remarked that when he helped to establish the rival *Evening Chronicle* in 1880, "I organized its carrier system—the first system of routing in evening journalism there [St. Louis]."

[64] *Post-Dispatch*, May 3, 1880, May 15, 1880.

[65] *Ibid.*, Dec. 24, 1879, Dec. 30, 1879, May 3, 1880, Aug. 18, 1881.

[66] *American Journalist*, Aug., 1884.

[67] *Post-Dispatch*, Jan. 13, 1880, Jan. 14, 1880. The morning papers raised their rates from twenty-five to thirty cents.

the publisher and his patrons," the paper explained, "make it exceedingly appropriate that we should make public the prosperity of a journal which to a certain degree is public property." [68] Other sworn statements followed from time to time, especially in the fall when, in a renewal of its smoldering quarrel with the *Missouri Republican,* the *Post-Dispatch* claimed that "we now print and circulate in St. Louis twenty-five per cent more copies than the *Republican."* Only the *Globe-Democrat* outsold the afternoon paper in St. Louis and "at the present rate of growth it will not be necessary to make this exception after the first of January." [69]

As circulation increased, so, too, did advertising and profits. In the prospectus for 1881 the *Post-Dispatch* declared that "its position is assured. Both its circulation and its revenue doubled during the last year." [70] Costs of running a journal "on the sensational, high pressure principle" rose also—by at least thirty percent—but when the cashier, Ignatz Kappner, closed the books at the end of the year the paper had made $112,932 or $25,000 more than the year before.[71] Largely, of course, financial prosperity simply bore out Pulitzer's dictum that "the life of the paper is in the news columns—advertising will come if you improve the paper." [72] But, as was his wont, the proprietor did not sit back and wait for advertisers to come to him. Rather, he worked hard to increase business. Never one to delegate responsibility, even in minor details, he worked closely with his aggressive advertising manager, Billy Steigers, as the following letter suggests:

> My dear Steigers: Glad you got Vogelers renewal. I want [higher] rates as much as you but insisting on rates must not be carried too far. We *must* get more of this Eastern business. There is a regular boom of medical ads of which we have very little. We must get at least those big advertisers to *commence* with us. . . . We must walk before we can run. You can always refuse to renew. One may stoop to start. . . . This is all said in the friendliest spirit I assure you—not that of carping criticism—and I hope you will not misunderstand it. . . .[73]

---

[68] *Ibid.,* April 10, 1880. Other notarized statements, more detailed, followed, but it was not until 1881 that the *Post-Dispatch* felt sufficiently confident of its advertisers to reveal fully its precise circulation, although "our books are always at the service of those who doubt . . . the growth of our circulation." *Ibid.,* Sept. 1, 1880.

[69] *Ibid.,* Sept. 1, 1880, Oct. 16, 1880.

[70] *Ibid.,* Nov. 5, 1880.

[71] *Ibid.,* Feb. 3, 1880; Daniel W. Woods to Joseph Pulitzer, Feb. 25, 1903, Pulitzer Papers (CU).

[72] Joseph Pulitzer to Florence D. White, Feb. 26, 1905, Pulitzer Papers (CU).

[73] Reynolds, "Joseph Pulitzer," p. 66.

The same determination was shown in the paper's attempts to break the grip of the morning dailies on want advertising. The bold policy of publishing "wants" free of charge the year before had achieved modest success, enough, apparently, to persuade Pulitzer to risk setting a rate of twenty-five cents for each insertion. But when, after a four months' trial, the number diminished, the *Post-Dispatch* announced again in heavy type that "all 'Wants' . . . will be inserted free of charge." [74] And to emphasize the importance of this kind of advertising, the *Post-Dispatch* gave it choice space, often printing columns of wants on the first or third pages. These efforts at last began to pay dividends, for by the end of the year the volume of classified matter increased by more than one-third.[75]

Many of the wants the paper carried would offend a modern publisher, especially in the "Personal" column. One insertion, for example, read

> A gentleman would like to make the acquaintance of a handsome widow or a pretty young lady.

Within a few days, the paper reported, replies "poured in . . . at a rate which would give one a very lively idea of the unsettled female population of this city," and it added:

> Just why they [the ladies] voluntarily put themselves in a position which they might have regretted keenly does not appear; for it is quite certain that the great majority of 'personal' writers are not gentlemen who are acting from a desire for information or from a wish for innocent acquaintanceships.[76]

In publishing such notices the *Post-Dispatch* exhibited standards no worse than most newspapers.[77] In many respects it was, indeed, a typical journal of the time. Like its contemporaries it used some advertisements which so closely resembled news stories that only careful reading revealed their true contents. AT IT AGAIN read the headline over one such ad in type used for genuine news items. "The Train Robbers Operating in Southwest Missouri," "Farmers and Miners on the Track of the Offenders." Not until the second paragraph did the reader find that he had been tricked into reading

[74] *Post-Dispatch*, Dec. 29, 1879, May 3, 1880.

[75] Memorandum [1905], Pulitzer Papers (CU). The number of wants, though still modest, increased from 16,630 in 1879 to 27,740 in 1880.

[76] *Post-Dispatch*, April 3, 1880. Now and then objections were raised against this sort of advertising, as when a St. Louis weekly complained that such notices in reality were for the purpose of arranging immoral assignations. *The Criterion*, Feb. 10, 1883.

[77] The *Globe-Democrat*, for example, was accused of printing questionable "personals," *Post-Dispatch*, Jan. 4, 1881. But both the New York *World* and the *Post-Dispatch* seemed especially culpable. *Journalist*, May 24, 1884, Aug. 9, 1884.

a testimonial for St. Jacob's Oil, a patent medicine.[78] Advertising copy in the *Post-Dispatch,* as in all papers of the time, was in a transitional stage. The "card" type of ad still was common with its small and tightly jammed print, but they were interspersed now with large half-page layouts using much white space and attractive and varied type.[79] And like all other papers, the appearance of the *Post-Dispatch* was largely determined by advertising. Normally the front page was divided between advertising in the left hand columns and news in the right. On such occasions as Fair Week and the Christmas season news was crowded off the page altogether. Only twice during 1880 was it cleared of advertising and devoted entirely to news.[80]

The growing prosperity of the *Post-Dispatch* in 1880 was not unattended by difficulties, two of which were serious. On a wintry night in January, just as the reorganized staff was taking hold, a fire came uncomfortably close to wiping out the enterprise. As it was, the rear of the building, which housed the press and the composing room, was gutted and equipment badly damaged, some of it beyond repair. Although he put up a brave front by publishing an issue the very next day, Pulitzer was momentarily dismayed. "The POST-DISPATCH is a thoroughly well-established institution," the paper said in an editorial labeled OUR BLACK FRIDAY,

> and is able to survive the ordinary vicissitudes of life. It is an embarrassment to have its strength and vigor shorn at a time when its growth is most marked, but all that energy and enterprise can do will be done to heal the wounds of this disaster and in a fortnight we will be ourselves again.[81]

At the invitation of Joe McCullagh, extended the very night of the fire, the *Post-Dispatch* renewed its use of the *Globe-Democrat's* presses and moved its composing room back to the office of the old *Evening Post,* and for the next two weeks it hobbled along with one four-page edition a day.[82] But, early in February the *Post-Dispatch* cheerfully

---

[78] *Post-Dispatch,* Sept. 24, 1881. This was a common device until the nineties. See complaints in *National Editorial Journalist,* V (March 1888), 17; and Mott, p. 506.

[79] See article in *Printer's Ink,* III (Dec. 17, 1890), 642, on St. Louis advertising practices.

[80] *Post-Dispatch,* March 4, 1880, Aug. 9, 1880. The *Post-Dispatch* remained orthodox, too, in never breaking column rules so that headlines, even if spectacular in phraseology, never were more than one column in width. Not until 1889 did the *Post-Dispatch* begin to break column rules and publish two-column headlines.

[81] *Ibid.,* Jan. 23, 1880.

[82] *Ibid.*

announced: "We are back again on our fire-tried press, though surrounded with hammering carpenters and annoyed by the dust and
confusion to rebuilding. . . . Our circulation has more than held
its own in the half-sheet period. . . ."[83]

Less immediate but in the long run a far more significant threat
materialized in July when, for the first time in over a year, the *Post-
Dispatch* encountered competition in the afternoon field. This was
no ordinary opposition. Edward W. Scripps, fresh from successes in
Detroit and Cleveland as spectacular as Pulitzer's, invaded St. Louis
with a new paper, the *Evening Chronicle*. He planned to repeat his
previous triumphs by selling the *Chronicle* for two cents and taking
up the cause of militant unionism, thereby building a mass circulation
among the city's working classes. Pulitzer had never contemplated
such a step. His *Post-Dispatch* sold for the usual five cents on the street
and, for all his dedication to the common man, he had little love for
labor militancy. A strong individualist, he disliked the concept of class
altogether, high or low. Consequently, although Pulitzer's aim was to
gain a large circulation for the *Post-Dispatch,* it never seemed to occur
to him that he should alter the street price of his paper any more than
his editorial policies to achieve it. In reality the "common man" Pulitzer sought to attract to his paper was the stable householder of whatever
class, hence the low price for weekly subscribers. In any case, the working class, as such, he thought of—until now at least—as "indifferent"
to newspapers.[84]

Scripps, too, sought mass circulation, but he concluded that the
way to achieve it was to frankly ally his newspapers with the working
class and in circulation, news, and editorial policies appeal to it as
a class, endorsing unionism and attacking employers of all types,
including small employers of Pulitzer's kind. His *Chronicle* became
an aggressive protagonist of the union movement in St. Louis and
its two-cent price was intended to reach this most humble segment of
urban society.[85]

Hoping for the same quick success he had enjoyed elsewhere, Scripps

---

[83] *Ibid.*, Feb. 5, 1880.

[84] Professor George Juergens of Amherst College, who has made a careful study
of Pulitzer's journalistic policies on the New York *World* in the 1880's comes to
rather different conclusions. See George Juergens, *Joseph Pulitzer and the New
York World* (Princeton, 1966).

[85] Milton A. McRae, *Forty Years in Newspaperdom* (New York, 1924), pp. 26-32.
See also, Mott, pp. 460-62, 551-54; Charles R. McCabe, ed., *Damned Old Crank*
(New York, 1951); and Nagley D. Cochran, *E. W. Scripps* (New York, 1933),
pp. 54-60.

hired an able staff, and on July 31 commenced publication.[86] At first the *Post-Dispatch* was inclined to be hospitable. A thoughtful editorial said:

> The experiment of cheap journalism is about to be attempted again in this city. The *Evening Chronicle* makes its appearance to-day. . . . The POST-DISPATCH has for nearly two years occupied exclusively and successfully the afternoon field. . . . Having established our paper firmly and made it a necessity to the business and reading public, we will regard honorable competition as something likely to prove beneficial. . . . The experiment of cheap journalism in St. Louis is one we shall watch with interest. There is a large population here which is indifferent to the daily press. This element may be induced to patronize a paper which commands itself through its cheapness. . . . If they can introduce their paper into non-reading circles and create an appetite for news the larger newspapers, such as the POST-DISPATCH, will be substantially benefited.[87]

The editorial added a practical note: the *Chronicle's* success "will depend on their [sic] ability to introduce and keep in circulation fractional currency in the shape of pennies." This, indeed, proved to be the new publication's Achilles' heel, for there was "a deep-seated prejudice against small coin west of the Appalachian range." Penny journalism, even in the most progressive Western cities, was just getting a start in 1880.[88] Consequently, the *Chronicle,* despite daring enterprise, was destined to experience years of hardship before it caught public favor in St. Louis.[89]

The cordiality of the *Post-Dispatch* began to cool almost immediately when the *Chronicle* proved to be hostile. In its effort to promote street sales the *Chronicle* inaugurated a policy of handing out copies free of charge to the newsboys, who pocketed as unencumbered profit the two-cent price to customers. This violated *Post-Dispatch* practice, common to all St. Louis journals, of wholesaling papers to vendors at two and one-half cents per copy. It was true, the newsboys profited two and one-half cents on each copy sold, but because of the fact that

---

[86] Florence D. White to Joseph Pulitzer, April 8, 1902, Pulitzer Papers (CU); *Journalist,* Sept. 25, 1886.

[87] *Post-Dispatch,* July 31, 1880.

[88] *Ibid.,* Aug. 14, 1880. Scripps himself had to solve this problem in Detroit and Cleveland, as did Stone in Chicago, before penny journalism succeeded in those cities. See Stone, *Fifty Years a Journalist,* for the experience of the Chicago *Daily News* in dealing with this problem.

[89] William V. Byars to James Byars, Sept. 5, 1882. William Vincent Byars Collection. The innate conservatism of St. Louis also no doubt militated against early success, as did the fact that a large percentage of the working class was German and preferred its own journals.

many copies often were not sold, the *Chronicle* plan seemed far preferable.[90]

At the instigation of the *Chronicle's* managers—or so the *Post-Dispatch* claimed—the "ragged, hungry and . . . energetic . . . gamins" suddenly demanded that three copies instead of two of Pulitzer's paper be wholesaled to them for five cents instead of two. When they were met with a blunt refusal a noisy strike ensued.[91] For two or three days the boys milled around the *Post-Dispatch* office, shoving and shouting and mobbing carriers who dared to deliver papers. But Pulitzer was adamant:

> There is no *raison d'etre* in the so-called newsboys' 'strike' against the POST-DISPATCH and the instigators of it must feel ashamed of their shabby showing. . . . The newsboys make as much on each copy . . . sold as we do, and we furnish the white paper, ink, presswork, type-setting and just enough brains to keep the thing going.[92]

Inexperience and lack of organization brought a quick collapse to the protest, but besides being publicly embarrassed at having to "argue with boys," the *Post-Dispatch* was angered by the *Chronicle's* demoralization of "this enterprising and useful body of young merchants." [93]

Relations between the two papers degenerated into a typical journalistic brawl when the *Chronicle,* determined to damage the reputation of its successful rival, accused Pulitzer of welshing on his debts. It asserted that the *Post-Dispatch,* far from enjoying prosperity, was laboring under heavy obligations. This brought a rejoinder of unusual venom; the *Post-Dispatch* called its tormentor a "journalistic hunchback" and charged it with pursuing "a persistent and offensive policy of personal abuse and defamation . . . against the editor of this paper."

The *Chronicle's* taunt stung Pulitzer in a sensitive spot; he was genuinely concerned over a mortgage of the old *Evening Dispatch* which he had refused to honor when he bought the paper. In 1877, when the *Dispatch* was staggering towards bankruptcy, its hard-pressed owners negotiated a loan of $15,000 from a lawyer-politician, Frank J. Bowman, which they secured with a note mortgaging all of the paper's possessions, including particularly its Western Associated Press franchise. The certificate conferring the franchise, in fact, was turned over

---

[90] The *Post-Dispatch* also encountered a newsboy strike in 1879 when it suddenly raised the wholesale price to three cents a copy. Although the strike was beaten, in the long run the newsboys won their point because the paper returned to the original price of two and one-half cents. *Post-Dispatch,* May 24, 1879.

[91] *Ibid.,* Aug. 3, 1880.

[92] *Ibid.,* Aug. 4, 1880.

[93] *Ibid.,* Aug. 3, 1880, Aug. 6, 1880.

to Bowman. Pulitzer insisted that the franchise was only a privilege of membership in a nonprofit organization, not negotiable property, and he pointed out that the Association's bylaws clearly stated that alienation of the certificate of membership was prohibited except to a purchaser of the newspaper.[94] The certificate Bowman held, therefore, was worth nothing. It seems likely that legal opinion agreed with Pulitzer because for a year nothing was heard of the matter. Then late in 1879 the note and the certificate fell into the hands of B. M. Chambers, publisher of the shaky *Morning Times* and a business promoter who had been attacked by the *Post-Dispatch* for questionable practices in connection with a recent bank failure. Needing money and determined to ruin his critic, Chambers insisted upon Pulitzer's liability and demanded immediate payment. The latter refused. Then Chambers announced in the *Times* that Pulitzer had forfeited ownership of the property, and he advertised that he intended to offer for sale at public auction

> the machinery, types, presses, cases, furniture, paper, forms and tools . . . of the St. Louis Dispatch, together with its interest in the Western Associated Press and all its other property, at the east front of the Court-house. . . .[95]

In outraged wrath the *Post-Dispatch* reported this news in an article with a large black headline, IS THIS MAN INSANE? At the same time Pulitzer filed suit in the circuit court of St. Louis to compel the Associated Press to issue to him a new certificate of membership in lieu of the one Chambers proposed to sell.[96]

When the time for the auction arrived, Chambers lost his nerve and failed to appear before the "small and cadaverous-looking crowd" which gathered to witness the proceedings, but Joseph Pulitzer took advantage of the occasion to mount the courthouse steps and announce in vigorous tones, "Well, let me make a statement. I declare here that the allegation made in the advertisement under which this sale is called is a falsehood. . . . It is stated . . . that the telegraphic franchise of the *Dispatch* will be sold to-day. Now look at this," he shouted, his voice rising to a note of triumph. "I want you all to look at this and see exactly the falsehood of the published statement." He brandished a new certificate of membership in the Western Associated Press, "beautifully embellished" with the signature of the president, Murat Halstead.[97]

---

[94] *American Journalist*, Sept., 1883; *Post-Dispatch*, Dec. 15, 1879, Dec. 16, 1879, Jan. 2, 1880.
[95] *Post-Dispatch*, Dec. 30, 1879.
[96] *Ibid.*, Dec. 17, 1879.
[97] *Ibid.*, Jan. 7, 1880.

For the moment Pulitzer had won. But the issue was not finally settled. The old certificate fell into the hands of other enemies created by *Post-Dispatch* crusades, and for several years it remained a source of embarrassment.[98] Such problems as these were but pinpricks, however, for a publisher who now had firmly established his small journal and, by experimenting with fresh ideas of news and entertainment, was bringing to it at last a growing readership among rank-and-file St. Louisans.

---

[98] John A. Dillon to Joseph Pulitzer, July 7, 1887, Aug. 5, 1887; B. D. Lee to Joseph Pulitzer, Sept. 20, 1887, J. F. Conroy to Joseph Pulitzer, Feb. 22, 1887, Pulitzer Papers (CU).

CHAPTER VI

National Politics

The *Post-Dispatch's* insistence time and again that it was independent of party caucuses was somewhat misleading. It was indeed free of party dictation, but the paper was intensely political, nonetheless; it even exhibited some of the characteristics of party journalism, a style it professed to disdain. The truth was that Joseph Pulitzer was still an ambitious politician when he bought the *Post-Dispatch* in 1878, and he intended to play a very active role for the Democrats in the coming national election. "I can never be president because I am a foreigner," he exclaimed to a friend, "but some day I am going to elect a president." [1]

As the election approached, the *Post-Dispatch* reflected its owner's growing preoccupation with politics. "We struggle conscientiously to provide a fine lot of miscellaneous reading matter for our non-partisan patrons," it said one day apologetically, "but the task is getting too much for us. Our exchanges team with politics." [2] And as the campaign got underway the *Post-Dispatch* joined the chorus of Democratic journals throughout the country in a supreme effort to break the Republican Party's twenty-year hegemony in Washington. For all of its lip service to objectivity, it never bothered to hide its sympathies, and such headlines as VICTORY; CHICAGO ALSO OURS; A DAY OF DISASTER; and ALL IS LOST appeared on the front page almost daily, while editorial attacks—particularly when the campaign moved into high gear— were notable for partisan venom. [3]

It was natural that Pulitzer, an ex-Liberal Republican, [4] should still consider "Grantism" as the great issue in national politics. "Grantism" was a one-word Liberal summation for the sins of the Radicals during Reconstruction, and although the simple old soldier

---

[1] Joseph Pulitzer, Jr. to Joseph Pulitzer, March 10, 1903, Pulitzer Papers (CU). According to Pulitzer's most exhaustive biographer, "In avowing a non-partisan independence Pulitzer varied a journalism then developing. . . . But Pulitzer was not non-partisan at heart; he was fiercely Democratic." Reynolds, "Joseph Pulitzer," p. 64.

[2] St. Louis *Post-Dispatch*, Sept. 17, 1880.

[3] *Ibid.*, April 2, 1879, Sept. 30, 1880, Nov. 3, 1880.

[4] Pulitzer proudly listed a number of blue ribbon figures who like himself had refused to follow Schurz from the Liberal Republican movement back into the Republican party in 1876, but who had gone into the Democratic Party. He named Governor Ewing of Ohio, George Julian of Indiana, and David Davis, Lyman Trumbull, and John M. Palmer, all of Illinois. *Ibid.*, July 31, 1879.

had retired, the *Post-Dispatch* insisted that "the Republican party is the same to-day as during Grant's reign." [5] To make the accusation stick, it blackened the administration of Rutherford B. Hayes, the colorless but well-meaning president who had done much to clean up the mess left by Grant. And it was altogether natural for the *Post-Dispatch* to dislike Hayes, for he was the symbol to Democrats everywhere of a stolen election; the paper sneered constantly at him as "the fraudulent President" who was "about as contemptible . . . as it is possible to be." [6]

But the paper went a great deal further. It charged that Hayes was the catspaw of the real masters of the party, the Conklings, Blaines, and Shermans, whom it identified with the Radicals, and declared that the administration was as guilty of wholesale corruption as Grant's ever was.[7] Even Carl Schurz, Hayes' Secretary of the Interior and Pulitzer's old friend, was not exempt from the paper's savage attacks. IS THIS REFORM? it exploded one day as it listed a series of scandals it claimed were besmirching the government.

> Is this reform? Is this the purification of the civil service promised by Mr. Hayes? If this is a clean administration, what is an unclean one. . . ? [8]

When Republican journals defended Hayes, pointing to his courageous removals in defiance of the spoilsmen, the *Post-Dispatch* was unimpressed. "For sublime impudence—impudence of really gorgeous magnificence," it fumed, "commend us to the Chicago *Tribune*." [9] Later on Pulitzer cooled considerably in his advocacy of a nonpartisan civil service, but in 1879 and 1880, in common with the Liberals of both parties, this was an important plank in the *Post-Dispatch's* reform platform. The paper justified AN AMERICAN REFORM BILL in Pulitzer's extravagant language on the ground that

> the present system constitutes the immense patronage of the President as a gigantic bait, and temptation, a most powerful lever and instrument of power and passion, a standing appeal to the lust for office-holding which a century of self-government has developed in the American people to a most extraordinary degree.[10]

---

[5] *Ibid.*, Aug. 10, 1880. The best treatment of the election of 1880 is Herbert J. Clancy, *The Presidential Election of 1880* (Jesuit Studies, IX, Loyola University) (Chicago, 1958).

[6] *Post and Dispatch*, Feb. 10, 1879, Feb. 12, 1879; *Post-Dispatch*, Feb. 12, 1880.

[7] For a balanced appraisal of Hayes' administration, see Harry Barnard, *Rutherford B. Hayes and His America* (Indianapolis, 1954), esp. chs. 61-72.

[8] *Post-Dispatch*, Jan. 31, 1880.

[9] *Ibid.*, July 15, 1879.

[10] *Ibid.*, Nov. 20, 1879; Reynolds, p. 85.

These accusations were paralleled by a similarly partisan denunciation of Hayes' policies towards the South. Scarcely noticing that he had put an end to Reconstruction by withdrawing the last of the Federal troops from Louisiana and South Carolina, the *Post-Dispatch* tried to link Hayes with a supposed Radical conspiracy to make use of the South in the elections of 1880 as it had in 1876. The occasion was a flare-up between the Chief Executive and the first Democratic Congress since the war. Under Southern leadership the Democratic majority sought to forestall any possibility of a revival of Federal intervention in the ex-Confederacy by attaching to appropriations measures riders denying the President authority to intervene in elections except at the request of the states. This maneuver failed, however, for although it would straiten the government financially, Hayes vetoed the bills.[11] To Hayes' admirers—and for once his party rallied to him—the vetoes were "pistol shots" protecting the integrity of the nation. To the *Post-Dispatch,* however, they were an abject surrender to the Grant "Hateites," the "bloody shirt" element of the Republican Party," and as a result,

> not since the close of the war have sectional passions, partisan hatred and prejudice and fanaticism of the North been so thoroughly aroused by false cries and infamous, systematic goading as just now. [Hayes' vetoes are a deliberate attempt to] draw the sectional lines, arouse the sectional passions . . . [and] thereby create the impression of a danger from the Democratic South, and thereby create a solid Republican North.[12]

When the Democratic majority, under the leadership of Ohio's Senator Allen G. Thurman, finally surrendered and passed the appropriations bills without the offensive riders the paper angrily dismissed Thurman as a Democratic presidential possibility. "Good bye, Mr. Thurman. You are off the Presidential track never to return again." [13]

The assault on Hayes was excessively partisan, but beneath it lay a genuine fear, justified by Republican policies since 1861. "Nothing is now so much to be dreaded as this manifest and avowed purpose towards centralization," the *Post-Dispatch* exclaimed. "It means a destruction of the Constitution." [14] The paper elaborated upon this theme in a number of editorials attacking the Stalwart scheme to

---

11 Barnard, pp. 481-85. See also, H. J. Eckenrode, *Rutherford B. Hayes, Statesman of Reunion (American Political Leaders)* (New York, 1930), pp. 260-62; and Matthew Josephson, *The Politicos, 1865-1896* (New York, 1938), pp. 271 *passim.*

12 Post-Dispatch, April 24, 1879, May 13, 1879, July 15, 1879.

13 *Ibid.,* June 6, 1879.

14 *Ibid.,* Aug. 10, 1880.

nominate Grant for a third term in 1880. "The danger to the Republic is not that if Grant is re-elected he will declare himself Emperor," it began,

There is no danger of this. The American style of murdering the Republic would be radically different—would adapt itself to our different situation and race.

The great danger is that the name and form of the Republic will be retained and used as the very weapons with which to destroy its real spirit, substance and character.

The danger is that under the very plea of preserving "law and order," freedom and local self-government will be sacrificed.

Already the traditions of Washington, Jefferson and Jackson are to be set aside under the supposed necessity for a strong, military government under Grant. Already the Presidency is occupied by a man who was never elected by the people. Already the Supreme Court is filled by violent partisans and notorious perjurors. Already a fraudulent Executive dares to resist . . . the will of the Congress and the plain spirit of the Constitution. Already centralization and imperialism are plainly visible behind Republicanism. Already the great majority of the people is treated with contempt by a desperate but able minority. . . . Already there is as much bitter feeling, fanaticism and sectional hatred as if the "South" and "the North" were two different countries inhabited by two different peoples. Already it is announced by the Vice-President of the United States that the South is in rebellion, that the Union is again in danger, that a stronger government is needed. . . .

And still this is supposed to be the same Republic, the same popular and local self-government we had twenty years ago.

Now suppose we were to advance twenty years more in the same direction. Suppose Grant should be elected to a third or fourth term, who is there, considering the growing corruption of the day, the power of corporations, the growing power of capital and its manifold ramifications, the growing power of Government itself, and the naturally growing audacity of the party in power—who is innocent enough to believe that the Republican leaders would peaceably surrender their power under any circumstances? [15]

Purged of exaggeration this was an expression of Liberalism which Pulitzer had inherited from Schurz and Preetorius in the early

---

[15] *Ibid.*, Sept. 17, 1879.

seventies.[16] The *Post-Dispatch* clung to traditional liberalism from the conviction that "a 'strong' government in peace always encroaches upon the liberties of the people. It is always in favor of the rich and against the poor. It is a 'strong' government that reigns at St. Petersburg, and that is driving the people of Russia to mad distraction." [17]

In the tradition of Jefferson and Jackson, the *Post-Dispatch* abhorred a "strong" central government as the principal threat to the American dream of equalitarian democracy. By means of tariffs, bounties and charters, it had fostered privileges for the few at the expense of the many—including particularly small businessmen like the publisher of the *Post-Dispatch*. The result, declared the paper, was that America was running the danger of creating a class-ridden society such as that from which Pulitzer had fled as a youth. The monopolists—industrialists, railroad kings, and bankers, mostly in New England—were becoming an elite, while the remainder of the American people were in danger of slipping back into a kind of second-class citizenship, the victims of "imperialism" in the case of the South and of "class legislation" in the case of the nonprivileged citizenry everywhere.

"Centralization is the . . . great danger of the day," the *Post-Dispatch* observed again and again.

> We see its tendency everywhere. Capital, corporations, protected interests, special privileges and classes favored by law all naturally form a corrupt alliance with the "powers that be," with the existing government and the ruling party. . . .
>
> The people are already ready for the logical result of centralization—an imperial sham republic.[18]

Obviously, the only escape from this dangerous tendency was a return to antebellum days when "local self-government" was supreme and the national authority sharply defined and limited.[19]

The most flagrant of the Radicals' policies that were sabotaging freedom, the *Post-Dispatch* believed, was their attitude towards the South. Published in a border state where the scars of war and reconstruction were deep and in a river community whose economic pros-

---

[16] See Sidney Fine, *Laissez Faire and the General-Welfare State: A Study of Conflict in American Thought, 1865-1901* (University of Michigan Publications: History and Political Science, XXII) (Ann Arbor, 1956), for an analysis of political and economic philosophies of the times; see remarks on p. 51 concerning liberalism.

[17] *Post-Dispatch*, Oct. 30, 1879.

[18] *Ibid.*, July 24, 1879.

[19] At times, the *Post-Dispatch* seemed to recognize the drift towards centralization as inevitable. "The tendency to centralization is not confined to politics," it said on one occasion. "It is probably the natural result of modern civilization and the development of the telegraph and steam power." *Post-Dispatch*, Nov. 24, 1879.

perity was still greatly dependent upon restoring the Mississippi Valley as a harmonious whole, the paper was particularly sensitive on this subject. Moreover, as an active politician, Pulitzer wanted a united Democratic Party. The *Post-Dispatch*, therefore, constantly urged the necessity of burying the past. It went so far as to deplore the observance of Memorial Day, and when an ex-Confederate conclave was held in St. Louis, it deprecated the playing of "Dixie" by the marching bands.[20] It deplored the revival of the Republican campaign device of the "bloody shirt," and when the local *Globe-Democrat* professed to hear "the old rebel yell" in the halls of the new Democratic Congress, the *Post-Dispatch* responded tartly:

> Does it, indeed? The old rebel yell is its sole political capital, . . . its stock in trade, furniture, fixtures, assets and good will. Without the rebel yell it could not keep the party together between elections, and if it did not set up the yell at least once a month the timid and honest souls of the party would be in danger of believing that the war was over and the country at peace.

Southern extremism met with no greater favor. When Senator Morgan of Alabama delivered a tirade accusing the North of having committed unprovoked aggression upon an innocent Confederacy in '61, the *Post-Dispatch* spluttered, "That Southern ass."

> [He has] made precisely the speech wanted by the Republican demagogues in the North and [is] sure to do more injury than forty speeches by Blaine and Chandler. . . . Common interest and common sense teach that national harmony, patriotism, love of country and fraternal relations are impossible until "bygones" are really "bygones," until the dead are really dead, until politics turn upon new issues, not the passions and hatreds of the late war. Whoever tears open these terrible but healing wounds is, in our opinion, unpatriotic and contemptible. We have said that dozens of times, when the Zach Chandlers and Blaines appealed for the war feeling of the North. We shall say so as promptly when an ass like Senator Morgan foolishly does the same in the South.

Nevertheless, the same editorial made plain the paper's belief that the Northern Radicals, not the ex-rebels, were chiefly responsible for the failure of the nation to heal the wounds of the war. Indeed,

---

[20] Another onlooker, the *Spectator*, thought the *Post-Dispatch* a bit ridiculous: "It is to be lamented that a good citizen is so sensitive. There is very little harm in 'Dixie' and the men who heard it on the battlefields twenty years ago are not now afraid of it." Besides, the *Spectator* reminded the *Post-Dispatch*, Lincoln himself "never tired of hearing it played, especially after he had 'captured it' . . . at the close of the war." St. Louis *Spectator*, Oct. 13, 1883.

we frankly confess that to us the course of the South, upon the whole, seems without parallel in history for the moderation, fortitude, good sense, patriotism and aptitude for local self-government displayed since the war. To-day we consider the South as the great conservative factor in our politics. We have been called extreme because we sincerely believe that, as a rule, the Confederates are now better union men than Republican stalwarts [are], and because the danger to the Union now comes from the North and the Republican rebels who howl for Grant, a third term and a military, strong, centralized imperial Republic.[21]

The Stalwart cry of the "bloody shirt" was undermining American liberty, the paper asserted, because it struck at liberty's taproots—local determinism and equal representation. When the rabidly Republican New York *Times* complained that nineteen ex-Confederates occupied seats in Congress, to four "who risked their lives for the old flag," the *Post-Dispatch* replied:

What was the purpose of suppressing the rebellion? Surely not to destroy but to preserve the Union and constitutional self-government. And would both not be practically as much destroyed as if the rebellion had succeeded, if the South had no representation in Congress, no equal place in the Union? And if the South is to be a part of this . . . common country, if the . . . Constitution is to be no farce, but to be enforced as to a common nationality and citizenship and real equality, who is to represent the South except its representative men? [22]

"The real issue," as the paper had declared in its first week of publication, "is not whether elections in the South are conducted fairly and peaceably, but whether each State, South and North, shall be allowed to decide whether its elections, carried on under its laws and controlled by its officials, are valid. . . . Grant . . . that in more than one Southern State elections are habitually decided by intimidation—is it not a lesser evil to endure local terrorism than to invite centralized despotism?" [23]

---

[21] *Post-Dispatch,* June 11, 1879.

[22] *Ibid.,* April 5, 1879.

[23] *Post and Dispatch,* Dec. 13, 1878. The *Post-Dispatch* was uncomfortably aware that the ending of Reconstruction might be disastrous for the Negro; it understood well enough that the return of self-determination to the Southern white would mean the reestablishment of white supremacy—class rule—in the South itself and the freedmen would soon be reduced to a near servile state. Unlike such pro-Southern journals as the *Missouri Republican,* the *Post-Dispatch* did not accept the position of the white supremacists that the Negro should remain in permanent subjection. Pulitzer's profound belief in equality placed the *Post-Dispatch* in a dilemma. Commenting on a migration of Negroes from the Delta states up the river to

The Radicals, moreover, were guilty of the sin of "imperialism" in their economic policies towards the South, pursuing a program of discrimination and exploitation for the benefit of special interests in the North—mainly the manufacturers of New England. The South was "a scraggy section," the paper said bitterly, because

> unlike New England and the North generally, the South has not enjoyed for twenty years the advantages of class legislation. On the contrary, the tariff laws, which have enriched the Yankee manufacturers, have absolutely impoverished the agricultural South. . . . There is no reason why the North should have all the fat unless the country acts upon the theory that the States participating in the rebellion are no better than so many conquered provinces. If none but the rich and the prosperous are to have the direction of public affairs there will never be a change of control in this country, for under this theory the North will continue to grow richer and the South poorer.[24]

Thus, as it entered the campaign of 1880, the *Post-Dispatch* defined what it believed were the pressing issues of the day—focused in and illustrated especially by the Republican policies towards the South. Under the heading THE SILENT REVOLUTION, in the fall of 1879 the paper declared portentiously:

> Next year will be the crisis. If the Republican party can elect its candidate, we will retain the name and form of our Republic, but that's all. It will be a sham Republic, as much so as our neighbor south of the Rio Grande. Only physical revolution would put the daring political desperadoes out of power if they succeed in 1880. If England can practically cease to be a monarchy without changing its form of government, we can cease to have *real* popular self-government under the name of a Republic.[25]

St. Louis and across Missouri into Kansas in the late seventies, the paper agreed that "it certainly points to a bad state of affairs in the home they are leaving and to an unfortunate relation between the planters and the negroes. The great majority of the planters no doubt treat the negroes fairly, but there is no getting over the fact that the negroes are in a state of dependence which is irksome to them, and which has grown odious in proportion as it has grown hopeless. The mere freedom of the slave has not wiped out the traces of . . . slavery. . . . The instinct which sends the negro to another land in which he will be his own master, till his own soil, raise his own crop and own his home, is not only a natural one, but a laudable one. . . . Certainly no one will urge that the negro should be kept in the South for the convenience of anybody. The convenience of the whole nation demands that the negro shall cease to be a shiftless, dependent inferior, and that whatsoever faculties he may have shall have room for the utmost development." *Post-Dispatch*, April 15, 1879.

[24] *Post-Dispatch*, Aug. 14, 1880.

[25] *Ibid.*, Oct. 27, 1879.

The chief political news in 1879 was the emergence of General Grant as a candidate for an unprecedented third term. The Stalwarts —despite *Post-Dispatch* claims to the contrary—had broken with Hayes and lost the reins of party control. Now they persuaded the old hero to bid for a return to power. Throughout 1879 Stalwart regional bosses like Logan, Conkling and Cameron gathered their forces for a showdown with such assorted opposition as John Sherman, Hayes' heir apparent, James G. Blaine, the party's "plumed knight," and the corporal's guard of liberal reformers led by Carl Schurz.[26]

The *Post-Dispatch* followed this internecine warfare in Republican ranks closely, looking upon Grant's attempt for a third term with mixed feelings. On the one hand, because he was the bête noir of the Liberals, the paper did not hide its contempt for him; but on the other, his candidacy—so the *Post-Dispatch* thought—would make the issues clear and, if he won renomination, would insure victory for the Democrats.[27]

When the general denied to a reporter in Hong Kong any intentions of running for office, the *Post-Dispatch* told its readers sourly that this "may possibly do for the Chinese, but for America it is too thin." [28] And it asked, WHY NOT GRANT?

> The lingering remnant of respectability in the Republican party is trying to feed itself with the fond delusion that there may be some escape from the ignominy of re-nominating Grant for a position in which decent Republicanism declared him a failure. . . . Instead of sympathizing with the distress of panic-stricken respectability at the approach of the monster, the world will simply say that Grantism is the legitimate result of Republicanism, and that, while Grant did a great deal to make Republicanism what it is, Republicanism did more to make Grant what he was. Grant is undoubtedly the worst specimen of a President that has been seen in any civilized republic, but the worse his official conduct was the more closely it was in accord with the party. . . . Personally, Grant would have been content to draw his salary, to pension his relatives on the country, to surround himself with his cronies and to let the people govern themselves under the law, but it was the need and greed of party, the pressure of party exigency, the policy of party managers, which made him an intolerable despot and drove him to excesses.[29]

[26] Clancy, pp. 26-51.
[27] *Post-Dispatch*, Feb. 12, 1880.
[28] *Ibid.*, Aug. 19, 1879.
[29] *Ibid.*, May 14, 1879.

Although the *Post-Dispatch* confidently predicted that if Grant were nominated the Democrats would win easily, it could not bring itself to be so cynical as really to favor his nomination; and, when Pulitzer's old Liberal friends among the Republicans called an anti-third term convention in St. Louis's Mercantile Library, the *Post-Dispatch* was sympathetic. The promoters of the convention—Preetorius of the *Westliche Post,* William A. Patrick, Schurz, and others —represented "a devotion to the traditions of the Republic," but the paper shook its head sadly that they were under the delusion that their anti-Grant movement would do much good. "The danger to the Republic is not in one man," it reminded them, but in "the base and desperate character" of the party. The small band of Republican Liberals in St. Louis were swamped in the state convention by Missouri's Stalwart machine, controlled by the efficient Chauncey I. Filley. He secured the state's delegates for Grant. This news the *Post-Dispatch* reported under A SORRY VICTORY.[30]

The Republican national convention opened in a barnlike structure in Chicago in the first week in June. Though strongly Democratic, the *Post-Dispatch* gave it full coverage; it sent a group of "special correspondents" to the scene, including Pulitzer himself, John Reavis, its political reporter, and John McEnnis to gather human interest material. It leased "special wires" directly from convention hall to provide immediate and complete information which it published in editions printed early and late to meet the demand for news.[31]

The stories filed from Chicago were published under large black extras on the front page. The headlines, the conventional one column in width and cascading far down the page, told the story. The top head, in heavy block type, supplied color rather than information and not infrequently revealed the paper's prejudices. The first dispatch, dated June 1, was appropriately headed CHICAGO's CIRCUS with eight subdecks. On June 3 an extra told St. Louisans under CRUMBLING AWAY, "Grant Losing Votes in Every Direction," and, for the first time, "Garfield Looming Up as a Dark Horse." WORSE AND WORSE had eleven subdecks—the nineteenth century equivalent of a streamer —carrying such information as "The Defeat of the Democratic Favorite [Grant] Grows Hourly More Probable" and "All the Committees against Useless G. by Large Majorities." On June 5, under THE CALDRON, ten decks announced "The Grant Boomers Routed, Horse, Foot and Dragoons" on a vital test vote, which meant "Bully Boy Blaine Gaining Ground all the While." Finally, on June 8 in a 6:30 extra came the climactic news. Under the largest type the paper pos-

---

30 *Ibid.,* March 12, 24, 1880, April 13, 1880, May 6, 1880.
31 *Ibid.,* May 29, 1880, May 31, 1880.

sessed, GARFIELD, the paper said "The Convention Absolutely Carried by Storm" and "Scenes of the Wildest Tumult," as "Grant's Column Dies Heroically in the Last Ditch." [32]

In keeping with the style of the day, the accounts themselves were written chronologically, with no attempt to give the important news in the first paragraphs. Thus, the edition which carried the story of Garfield's nomination on the thirty-sixth ballot began:

> At 10:30 the convention began to assemble, rather languidly, and, as usual, when Conkling and Garfield appeared they were cheered to the echo.

News of the key event, the nomination itself, was buried in the *third* column! Next day, Chester Arthur's selection as the vice-presidential candidate was not even noticed in the headlines, and mention of it in the story was deep in the second column. For all its progressiveness as a news-gatherer, the *Post-Dispatch* was old-fashioned in presentation.

The selection of the Garfield–Arthur ticket came as a surprise to the *Post-Dispatch*, as it did to the public generally.[33] Both men, however, were well known and the paper was at no loss for vigorous opinions, and, as befitted a new-style journal, they were by no means unfavorable. In fact, Garfield's selection was "a great, good, lucky piece of fortune to the Republican party." He was a man of "scholarly attainments, . . . oratorical talents . . . and intellectual force," attributes which particularly impressed Pulitzer. "He has beyond question a fine mind, and . . . originality of thought," "a man of genius." Most of all, Garfield's nomination was a wise tactic because "it will unite the entire Republican party. . . . The bitterness of feeling between Grant and Blaine will soon disappear in the revival of the common interests at stake." [34] With Garfield, the paper warned the over-confident Democrats, the Republicans would not be easy to defeat.

Nevertheless, the *Post-Dispatch* was confident because the Garfield–Arthur ticket had heavy liabilities. For all his intellectual capacities, according to a story headed GARFIELD'S PRICE, the tall, handsome Ohioan had been implicated while chairman of the House Committee on Appropriations in a number of scandals, including the Credit Mobilier and DeGolyer paving contract schemes. In short, his *"character is as dubious as his talents are unquestioned."* [35] As for Arthur, "suffice

[32] *Ibid.*, June 1 through June 8, 1880. Clancy, ch. 3, gives a detailed account of the proceedings.

[33] Republican insiders were aware of the Garfield threat, however, well before the convention. See Clancy, ch. 3.

[34] *Post-Dispatch,* June 8, 1880, June 9, 1880.

[35] *Ibid.*, June 8, 1880. Garfield's activities are discussed in detail in Clancy, pp. 222-31.

it to say that he is Conkling's man Friday, who never held another office than that of Collector of New York," from which Hayes had been forced to remove him. The Republican candidates were the worst examples of "Grantism," the paper declared, and it promised to expose their venal records in full during the campaign.[36]

If the *Post-Dispatch* followed developments in the Republican Party closely, it was always with the air of an outsider. The case was far otherwise with the Democracy. The paper claimed independence, to be sure, but Pulitzer was far from nonpartisan, and although he claimed to be a publisher of the new school, the obvious bias of his newspaper was apparent to all subscribers.

The Democratic Party of 1880—as it is today—was a jumble of incongruous factions, ranging from the traditional Democrats of the Solid South to the volatile inflationists of the Prairies, and from the impeccably conservative, patrician Bourbons of the Northeast and Midwest to the powerful and corrupt machines built upon thousands of immigrant votes in the cities. Also influential were the Liberals, who included, besides genteel reformers of the Tilden school, a group of newspapermen like Joseph Pulitzer. The significance of these journalists did not end with the fact they were Liberal Reformers, however, for they—especially Pulitzer—represented an increasingly significant element in American politics: the urban middle classes. Unorganized and individualistic, the small businessmen of the towns and cities proliferating across the land, especially in the Middle West, were nevertheless beginning to be heard. Their views were expressed by such new "independent" newspapers in both parties as the *Post-Dispatch*, published by middle class businessmen like themselves.[37]

In national politics their differences with the orthodox Liberals were only a matter of emphasis, but already—if Pulitzer was typical— the newspaper editors were beginning to stress certain aspects of the Liberal creed while neglecting others which their friends thought important. The *Post-Dispatch* was less interested in civil service reform than were the Tilden-type reformers, and it was more inclined to emphasize the evils of Republican economic policies. The reason for this, no doubt, lay in a difference of background. The genteel reformers sprang from old patrician families and thought the cure for "Grantism" lay in eliminating the uncouth Radical spoilsmen from

---

[36] *Post-Dispatch,* June 9, 1880.

[37] The *Globe-Democrat* performed somewhat the same function in Republican circles.

Several works discuss the composition of the parties in this period. Wilfred E. Binkley, *American Political Parties: Their Natural History* (New York, 1947), ch. 13; Goldman, *Rendezvous with Destiny,* chs. 2-3. See also, Merrill, *Bourbon Democracy,* who analyzes the Midwestern Democrats, and Josephson, *Politicos.*

power and returning government to responsible citizens—themselves; there was a touch of elitism in their outlook.[38] The egalitarian *Post-Dispatch* was less sanguine about the efficacy of this cure-all. It was more deeply concerned about the tendency of government to foster economic privilege. On local levels the paper already was developing a reputation for attacking privilege which was often in the hands of respectable old families, and in national politics it was beginning to attack the great monopolies fostered by Republican favoritism. Representing the ordinary businessman, the paper was becoming uneasy about the great railway combines. "It is easy enough . . . to see how all the railroads in the country are being grouped into a few great systems," it remarked on one occasion, "and how they will all soon be under the general management of a few great capitalists." [39] Its excoriation of the Western Union telegraph monopoly was more severe, no doubt because of the company's corner on the transmission of news:

> The Western Union is the greatest monopoly in the country. Its rates . . . never change. They were made high, and they remain high. Its stock pays an enormous dividend, and a few men are enriched at the expense of the many. Of course, they will never permit competition if they can prevent it.[40]

The *Post-Dispatch* vigorously attacked Democratic politicians who were known to be friends of monopoly. When Samuel Randall of Pennsylvania sought reelection as Speaker of the House of Representatives the paper snapped, "The Democratic party deserves defeat unless it adheres to principles. . . . Sam Randall is a trimmer and a trickster." [41]

However, Pulitzer and his fellow editors—Henry Watterson of the Louisville *Courier-Journal* and Manton Marble of the New York *World*—were loyal Democratic politicians, as much interested in winning nominations and elections as in reform and, beyond a general demand that the party attack "Grantism," they did not insist upon their particular views. Most important, the outlook of the old style and middle class reformers in Democratic ranks as yet had more in common than otherwise.[42] Coming from a border state, Pulitzer still laid greater stress upon Republican policies towards the South than any other single issue as the campaign got underway, and the genteel Liberals agreed that in economic matters the cure for monopoly was a

---

[38] Goldman, pp. 10-16.
[39] *Post-Dispatch*, Dec. 11, 1879.
[40] *Ibid.*, July 16, 1879.
[41] *Post and Dispatch*, Feb. 1, 1879.
[42] Mott, p. 458; Seitz, pp. 124-25.

return to laissez-faire. Abolish the Republican program of favoritism in Washington and equal opportunity would return. Thus, despite its growing dislike of the railroads, the *Post-Dispatch* opposed Representative John H. Reagan's proposal of national regulation, observing that "it is not at all probable that the American people will ever consent to . . . Federal ownership or control of railroads. Such a thing belongs only to such misruled countries as Germany and Russia." Besides, it thought, there were other, more reliable "influences and conditions" which "will regulate the railroads of this country." It argued that

> the railroads of this continent can never enjoy a complete monopoly, and can therefore never become very dangerous, for the reason that we have a magnificent system of water transportation that will always compel a healthy competition. The two great lines of travel and traffic from the Mississippi Valley run south and east. The Mississippi River and its tributaries run to the sea in one direction, and the chain of lakes reaches to the sea in the other. . . . The waterways of this country will never allow any general extortion on the part of the railroads. . . .[43]

Competition, then, was the cure. "Competition is the life of trade," the *Post-Dispatch* declared. "Without it monopoly reigns supreme." [44]

On one other issue the *Post-Dispatch* was uncompromisingly conservative, bespeaking the outlook, not only of Liberalism but of the urban middle classes. This was the money question, which by the late seventies was beginning to loom large in Democratic politics. When the Granger revolt failed to alleviate the deepening distress of the Middle Western farmers thousands of rural voters turned to inflation as a cure-all.[45] Located in the center of agrarian unrest, the *Post-Dispatch* nevertheless set its face against the rural demands. It was a city journal, devoted to the interests of the middling merchants of St. Louis who supposed that their prosperity would be damaged if rural customers got their way with the currency.

> The POST-DISPATCH is uncompromisingly for honest, hard money. It is against all efforts in the direction of inflation or repudiation. It does not believe in any paper money that is not

---

[43] *Post-Dispatch,* July 17, 1879.

[44] *Ibid.,* Dec. 11, 1879.

[45] Many besides agrarians were attracted to greenbacks. See a thorough discussion of the subject by Unger, *Greenback Era,* esp. chs. 2-3. See also, Buck, *Agrarian Crusade,* ch. 6; Clevenger, "Agrarian Politics," ch. 1; Leach, "Public Opinion and the Inflation Movement," *Missouri Historical Review,* XXIV (April 1930), 379-413.

redeemable in coin. It is utterly opposed to the idea that the general Government shall . . . have the ruinous power of making or changing at its will the amount of money in circulation, or make money out of rags.[46]

The paper was flint-hearted about this: a hard money policy might "make the rich richer and the poor poorer, but it can not be helped. . . ." [47]

Happily, bumper crops and rising prices in Europe for Midwestern wheat in 1879 brought temporary relief to the struggling farmer, and the pressure for greenback inflation subsided somewhat. The Midwestern Democrats, therefore, became less hospitable to the greenback "heresy" as the campaign of 1880 approached. The *Post-Dispatch* breathed a sigh of relief, noting with some exaggeration that "every Democratic platform this year is sound. There is not one—not one, we repeat—whether adopted in Ohio, Pennsylvania, Iowa, Wisconsin or Minnesota which does not clearly recognize gold and silver as the basis of paper money. . . ." [48]

The decline in enthusiasm for greenbacks, however, was accompanied by the first suggestions to remonetize silver and correct the "crime of '73." This movement appeared early in Missouri, always a hotbed of inflationism. Its leader was a Democratic congressman, Richard P. Bland.[49] The *Post-Dispatch* did not oppose this scheme as flatly as it did greenbacks. In fact, it announced itself as favoring "bimetallism," but only in the mildest sense.[50] The paper admitted there was a deficiency in the supply of money, and it thought the coinage of silver might correct the problem. However, it added significantly,

There is a vast difference between those who, as a principle, are in favor of a double standard and the coinage of silver equal to

[46] *Post-Dispatch*, June 6, 1879. See also, Unger, pp. 147-48. Pulitzer was evidently closer in viewpoint to the wholesale and retail merchants in St. Louis than to the manufacturers, who perhaps had somewhat greater sympathy for a managed currency. *Ibid.*, chs. 2-4, for an extended discussion of this subject.

[47] *Post and Dispatch*, Jan. 30, 1879.

[48] Josephson, p. 261; *Post-Dispatch*, Oct. 14, 1879. Ohio, for instance, did not so flatly reject the greenback idea, as the *Post-Dispatch* implied. See Merrill, pp. 128-29.

[49] See William Vincent Byars, *An American Commoner: The Life and Times of William Parks Bland* (Columbia, Mo., 1900). Byars was a St. Louis newspaperman who often wrote for the *Post-Dispatch* and later was on the staff of the New York *World*.

[50] *Post-Dispatch*, June 27, 1879. The Bourbon paper of St. Louis, the *Republican*, also was "bimetallist" in the same sense the *Post-Dispatch* was, although it spoke for a different constituency. Leach, "Public Opinion and the Inflation Movement," *Missouri Historical Review*, XXV (Oct. 1930), 116-25.

gold, and those who want unlimited coinage without the slightest reference to the ratio of value. . . .[51]

The Bland Act, calling for the recoinage of silver, received mild praise, but only because it was properly watered down in the Senate by Iowa's astute William B. Allison:

> The coinage of silver under the Bland bill is not unlimited. On the contrary it is doubly limited, first by the law itself, which makes $4,000,000 per month the maximum, and next by the capacity of the United States mints, for all of them together could not turn out more than 50,000,000 silver dollars per year. So far, therefore, the Bland bill has done no harm. On the contrary, as a silver producing country, it is in the interest of the United States not to demonetize or depreciate silver, but let it take the place of small bills as a circulation medium. It might become a very serious question if silver could be coined or silver certificates be issued to an unlimited extent, as the Bland bill originally contemplated, as the intrinsic, real value of a silver dollar is less than that of the gold dollar.[52]

Given these opinions, it was not surprising to find the *Post-Dispatch* seeking a Liberal-type reformer as a Democratic candidate for the presidency. But for a politician of Pulitzer's temperament candidates with principles alone were not sufficient. They must also be men like himself, endowed with a will to win. The proprietor of the *Post-Dispatch* had only contempt for the faint-hearted and the over-cautious. Consequently, although their views were similar, the paper vigorously opposed the renomination of Samuel J. Tilden, the most prominent and obvious choice. Ever since Tilden's pusillanimous acquiescence in the Electoral Commission's decision in 1877 Pulitzer had had little use for him. The *Post-Dispatch* early showed its contempt.

> The party owes nothing to Mr. Tilden. It elected him to the Presidency. He allowed the great office to be filched out of his hands. He was nominated as a bold leader. When the emergency arrived he led no more than a mouse. Eager in the pursuit

[51] *Post-Dispatch,* June 27, 1879. Western business interests and several newspapers which had utterly opposed greenbacks, including the Cincinnati *Commercial* and the Chicago *Tribune,* favored remonetization of silver, at least to a limited degree. A number of St. Louis merchants also were for remonetization. Silver, unlike greenbacks, was specie. Unger, pp. 328-45. Nevertheless, the *Post-Dispatch's* tepid endorsement of silver prompted the *Journal of Agriculture,* also published in St. Louis, to charge that it was "a gold-bug newspaper" which opposed the "poor, downtrodden and oppressed farmers of the land." Quoted in *Post-Dispatch,* March 5, 1880.

[52] *Ibid.,* Nov. 19, 1880.

of both the nomination and the election, he seemed to be deaf and dumb and dead when the great crime against the Republic was openly threatened. Professing to love the Constitution and free institutions, he tamely submitted to . . . their subversion without a word of protest. . . . Is this the quality and character the American Democracy admire? Is this the man to represent the free choice of five millions of voters—of five millions of men with blood in their veins? Is this the fit person to lead against Grant and his desperate gang? . . . . The party placed the Presidency into his hands once. He did not take it. That settled the matter.[53]

Who then? At first the *Post-Dispatch* looked with favor upon Senator Allen G. Thurman, who, although he had flirted with soft money, had proved he could carry Ohio. But, as has been seen, Thurman also committed the unpardonable sin of faint-heartedness when he virtually surrendered to President Hayes in the dispute over the riders to the appropriations bills. "Both Tilden and Thurman are now out of [the] question," decreed the *Post-Dispatch*.[54]

Then it turned to Thomas F. Bayard, the cultured and dignified senator from Delaware, who had long been a respected leader of the Democratic Party. He appealed strongly to Pulitzer as a man of intellect, steadfast determination, and sound money views. Moreover, in agreeable contrast with Thurman, Bayard refused to give ground in crossing swords with the Republicans in the "rider" controversy; he was firmly and gratifyingly partisan. But the gesture which evoked the *Post-Dispatch's* all-out support was Bayard's success in blocking a silver inflation measure. "The Democratic party should rejoice," the paper exclaimed. "At last it has found a leader who has shown the backbone and spirit of Old Hickory!"—surely an incongruous comparison! [55]

Confident that it had found the right man, the *Post-Dispatch* joined in launching a GREAT BAYARD BOOM late in 1879. For weeks it published inspired stories and editorials to "sell" the Delaware senator to Midwestern Democrats. But it did not get far among rural readers. "Can't the *Post-Dispatch* fall in love with a man more in

---

[53] *Post and Dispatch*, Feb. 12, 1879. See the rather unfriendly treatment of Tilden in Clancy, *Presidential Election of 1880*. See also, Barnard, esp. pp. 304-96, 474-77; and Merrill, esp. pp. 110-12.

[54] *Post-Dispatch*, June 6, 1879.

[55] *Ibid.*, June 18, 1879. See also, Charles Callan Tansill, *The Congressional Career of Thomas Francis Bayard, 1869-1885* (Washington, D.C., 1946), pp. 234-35. For a characterization of Bayard, see Allan Nevins, *Grover Cleveland: A Study in Courage (American Political Leaders)* (New York, 1933), p. 194. See also, Clancy, for a favorable view of Bayard and his candidacy.

sympathy with Western financial ideas?" the Louisiana, Missouri *Journal*, complained.[56] The drive suddenly ceased when Bayard overreached himself. He introduced a resolution in the Senate calling for the immediate withdrawal of all greenbacks from circulation. This raised such a storm of protest in the West that although the *Post-Dispatch* tried to defend him it soon saw the cause was hopeless. By the end of February 1880 Bayard's name was missing from the paper's list of presidential possibilities. Its explanation was frank and practical:

> There was a time when the POST-DISPATCH regarded Mr. Bayard as the most available man before the country. [But] His pronounced position on one or two questions before Congress and the revival of one of his [pro-Confederate] war speeches checked the movement in his direction. He is a great and pure man. . . and nothing would afford us more pleasure [than] to support him for President, but we want the Democrats to nominate a man who can win this time.[57]

Bayard's eclipse left Tilden once more the front-runner; in a desperate effort to head him off the *Post-Dispatch* turned to a slim hope, the chance that the aging Nestor of the Democracy, Horatio Seymour, might be persuaded to emerge from retirement to seek the Presidency. Pulitzer left John Cockerill in charge of the paper and journeyed himself to the Mohawk Valley of upper New York where the seventy-year-old Seymour lived the life of a country squire. There was a twofold purpose in Pulitzer's quest. Not only did he hope to find in Seymour a candidate with which to checkmate Tilden, but if he succeeded in obtaining Seymour's consent to run, it would furnish his newspaper with a newsbeat of national importance.[58]

Pulitzer failed to persuade Seymour to make the race, but he gave the interview full play in the *Post-Dispatch*. In the fashion of the time, the story was flowery and loosely constructed, with the significant information at the end, in chronological sequence rather than in the lead paragraph. Pulitzer described in fulsome detail all of the preliminaries before—at the end of the second column—he finally got to the point. He related that as he was being escorted to the door to take his departure he looked directly at Seymour and said,

> "I have always said that you were too good a patriot and too good a Democrat to decline the leadership. Have I said wrong?"

---

[56] Scattered references in *Post-Dispatch* from June 1879 to Feb. 1880. See especially the following: June 23, 1879, June 27, 1879, Oct. 15, 1879, Oct. 27, 1879, Nov. 11, 1879, Dec. 5, 1879, Dec. 11, 1879.

[57] *Ibid.*, Feb. 25, 1880.

[58] Reynolds, pp. 73-74.

This was almost as squarely as I dared to put the question. The Governor paused as he stood at the doorway and looked at me fixedly for a moment, and then pressed my hand and shook it cordially. I was satisfied with his silent reply, and I told him so. He only added, with a laugh, "You had better lay me on the shelf and get a younger man."

With exultation in my heart I rode down the Deerfield hills, content for the future in the knowledge that America's greatest living statesman would not refuse to take the political helm in the supreme hour of peril.[59]

Returned home, Pulitzer entered the fray to control the Missouri delegation to the national convention. In this struggle the *Post-Dispatch* served as Pulitzer's instrument much in the manner of an old-style political organ. It urged the supporters of all candidates opposed to Tilden to join forces. Pulitzer himself won a seat in the state convention at Moberly, and here he helped administer a sharp defeat to his arch-enemies, the publishers of the *Missouri Republican*, who favored Tilden, by securing an anti-Tilden delegation to the national convention at Cincinnati. Again, Pulitzer was chosen a delegate. Said the *Post-Dispatch*, "We are so well satisfied with the result that we propose to let it speak for itself, and not crow over it." But crowing was a *Post-Dispatch* habit, and the paper could not contain itself as it chortled, MISSOURI AGAINST TILDEN.[60]

In Cincinnati the restlessly ambitious Pulitzer joined forces on the convention's resolutions committee with Henry Watterson to help compose the party's platform. Understandably the *Post-Dispatch* approved of it in every particular.

The platform called for

home rule, honest money, consisting of gold and silver and paper convertible to coin on demand. The strict maintenance of the public faith, State and nation, [and] a tariff for revenue only.[61]

The drive to nominate Seymour had little chance of success and collapsed altogether when, as the paper told its readers under SEYMOUR SPEAKS, he announced his determination to turn down even a draft. Editorially, the *Post-Dispatch* declared "we are heart and soul for any man whose name has been mentioned . . . bar one. His initials are S. J. T." A day or two later Tilden obliged by writing

[59] *Post-Dispatch*, April 28, 1880.
[60] *Ibid.*, May 18, 1880, May 24, 1880, May 27, 1880.
[61] *Ibid.*, July 2, 1880. Later the *Post-Dispatch* quoted with obvious approval the remark of a Cincinnati paper that Pulitzer and Henry Watterson had phrased the tariff plank. But see Clancy, pp. 146-47, who does not mention Pulitzer at all.

the delegates an obscurely phrased communication which the majority preferred to interpret as another withdrawal.[62]

As in the case of the Republican convention, the *Post-Dispatch* sent special reporters—including Pulitzer, of course—to the scene, and their stories were transmitted by special wire to St. Louis. Again the one-column Gothic headlines told the tale: FROM THE FIELD; CHAOS REIGNS; and, finally, HAIL, HANCOCK![63]

Until the eve of the convention the *Post-Dispatch* had been strongly opposed to Winfield S. Hancock. Nominating a general, it had declared, would be "a stupendous mistake." Indeed,

> the power of ideas, the force of all traditions, the teaching of American history, the example of every Republic that has yet existed and perished, the admonition of Washington, the popular love of liberty, and jealousy of power, the instinct of the common sense and the general intelligence of the country, all agree in pointing against the military idea in a civic Republic. All point against the danger of a soldier in the place of the chief magistrate. . . .[64]

"If a soldier is needed for President," the paper added, "Grant fills the bill." [65]

But on June 24, the day of Hancock's choice by the convention, the *Post-Dispatch* said of him:

> Although a soldier all his life, he has ever been on the side of civil supremacy, *habeas corpus* and a strict construction of the Constitution. He was a gallant and faithful officer during the war, and his nomination puts a quietus to the attempt of Garfield and his followers to make the war and military service the paramount issue in the campaign. We will hear no more of tramping hosts and rallying around the banner in this campaign. . . .[66]

Within another week the conversion of the *Post-Dispatch* to Hancock was complete. It published a paean to THE RECORD OF A STATESMAN, saying, "No king in Europe has greater power than General Hancock had when under the Reconstruction laws he became Military Governor of Texas and Louisiana." Yet,

> Unprejudiced Republicans who sincerely object to military spirit and military candidates should look at General Hancock's

---

[62] *Post-Dispatch*, June 19, 1880, June 21, 1880. For interpretation of the reaction to Tilden's letter of withdrawal, see Clancy, pp. 123-26.
[63] *Post-Dispatch*, June 21, 22, 24, 1880.
[64] *Ibid.*, Oct. 28, 1879.
[65] *Ibid.*, Jan. 6, 1880.
[66] *Ibid.*, June 24, 1880.

record before they conclude that he is "only a soldier." It is a most extraordinary fact that there is no civil statesman in the land who ever expressed as earnestly and forcibly the true idea of the subserviency of the military to the civil law as did this soldier at the very time when he possessed the most absolute one-man power.[67]

Feature articles and news stories painted Hancock as a hero at Gettysburg and attractively presented WINFIELD AS A BOY.[68] The paper, in short, was loyally Democratic, accepting with enthusiasm a candidate it had labeled unfit until he was selected.

The *Post-Dispatch* now threw itself into the campaign. Pulitzer himself was away on the hustings during most of the time, but John Cockerill composed vigorous and readable editorials. Increasingly, as the campaign developed, the paper forgot its pledges of objectivity; the Republican candidate was castigated for everything from "hippodroming" when he appeared on the stump to the coarsest venality. Pieces with such headlines as GRABBER GARFIELD and A GRABBER'S RECORD detailed his unsavory connections with Credit Mobilier and the Washington paving scandals. Indeed, the charges against the Republican candidate were "so clear, so well founded . . . so thoroughly convincing, that there is nothing left but to believe them." The paper failed to understand how "the respectable element" in Republican ranks—such as the *Nation,* the Springfield *Republican,* and *Harper's Weekly*—could continue to support the ticket.[69]

For the most part, the *Post-Dispatch's* campaign was typical of Democratic journals generally—undistinguished except for its vigor.[70] Once, however, the paper exploded a bombshell heard from coast to coast. On August 7, under LIGHT AT LAST, it printed excerpts from a manuscript written by General John A. McDonald, tentatively titled, *The Secrets of the Whisky Ring Exposed.* The general, a St. Louisan, had not been able to find a publisher for his sensational book which charged that President Grant had had full knowledge of the operations of the Whisky Ring, a major scandal in which the principal figure was McDonald himself.[71] The *Post-Dispatch* gleefully published excerpts from McDonald's account and ran with them facsimile reproductions of letters from his files—in itself a journalistic feat—

---

[67] *Ibid.,* July 2, 1880.
[68] *Ibid.,* July 15, 1880.
[69] *Ibid.,* June 15, 1880, July 24, 1880, Sept. 10, 1880.
[70] Clancy, ch. 7.
[71] McDonald was convicted for his part in the fraud and served a prison term. The title of the book, when published somewhat later, was *Secrets of the Great Whiskey Ring, and Eighteen Months in the Penitentiary* (St. Louis, 1880).

which proved that Orville E. Babcock, Grant's private secretary, definitely had been a member of the ring.[72]

This exposure was a brilliant journalistic stroke. It landed the *Post-Dispatch* on the first pages of newspapers across the nation. The paper had carefully apprised newsdealers in advance of the impending sensation and had advised that "agents at a distance who can not reach us by mail can order any reasonable number of extras by telegraph at our expense." Within a few days it happily harvested the results, reprinting on page one the comments of journals everywhere.[73] This may have compensated Pulitzer for twinges of doubt in publishing McDonald's charges against the ex-President. The proprietor himself believed they were "maliciously false" when they were first advanced just a few weeks before in an interview story with a *Post-Dispatch* reporter. At that time he had apologized, saying "it is hardly necessary to state that the editor of this paper would never knowingly have permitted the coarse epithets about Gen. Grant to be printed." [74] But when the campaign quickened, Pulitzer's partisan ardor was aroused and now he viewed them in a different light. Above all, true or false, they were sensational and served to advertise his newspaper. A strain of irresponsibility was evident in Pulitzer's developing style of journalism.

Late in the summer, when it was becoming apparent the election would be close and might hinge upon preliminary balloting in the so-called "October states" of Ohio and Indiana, the party chieftains on both sides mobilized their orators and organizers for a trial of strength. Indiana was especially critical; in 1876 it had gone Democratic by a scant 5,000 votes and was essential to victory in 1880. Among the speakers called upon to stump these states for the Democracy was the proprietor of the *Post-Dispatch*. In the course of his tour Pulitzer stopped in Indianapolis where he delivered what he later remembered as "one of the best speeches" of his political career.[75] An enthusiastic audience heard his discourse on what was now be-

---

[72] *Post-Dispatch*, Aug. 7, 1880, Aug. 9, 1880.

[73] *Ibid.*, Aug. 11, 1880.

[74] *Ibid.*, June 29, 1880. Pulitzer believed, as most authorities have thought since, that for all his defects, Grant was a man of "personal integrity." David P. Dyer, a federal attorney involved in the prosecutions of the case, years later declared that no evidence implicating President Grant in the frauds had ever been turned up. (David P. Dyer, *Autobiography and Reminiscences* [St. Louis, 1922], p. 164.) Dyer believed the revelations against Babcock printed by the *Post-Dispatch* were more substantial. Dyer had been hot on Babcock's trail when, to save his secretary from conviction, Grant dismissed the prosecutor from the case. (*Ibid.*, ch. 10.) See also later authorities, who advise the exercise of great caution in utilizing McDonald's book. Louis A. Coolidge, *Ulysses S. Grant* (Boston, 1917), p. 478; and Josephson, p. 135.

[75] Joseph Pulitzer to Florence D. White, Oct. 17, 1903, Pulitzer Papers (CU).

coming his favorite theme, the dangers of class government under Republican rule. "Show me a land where the money power, the organized capital, privileges and monopolists, the railroads, telegraphs, banks, protected manufacturers are favored and fostered by the government and you have shown me imperialism," he shouted. "We want prosperity," he went on,

> but not at the expense of liberty. Poverty is not as great a danger to liberty as wealth, with its corrupting, demoralizing influence. . . . Let us have prosperity, but never at the expense of liberty, never at the expense of real self-government, and let us never have a government at Washington owing its retention to the power of the millionaires rather than to the will of the millions.[76]

Republican spellbinders turned this peroration to account. Just before the state went to the polls none other than Roscoe Conkling journeyed to Indianapolis where he answered Pulitzer's charges. It was true, this clever politician said, wealth was indeed on the side of the Republicans, but this only proved that they were the party of talent, brains and virtue, the party of successful men who had made the nation prosperous and great. Thus was the gospel of wealth enlisted in the cause of Republicanism.[77]

In a tone of outrage the *Post-Dispatch* claimed Conkling had deliberately "garbled" Pulitzer's address.

> The point of the matter is simply this: Mr. Conkling tries to make political capital out of the fact that most of the money and capital of the country is in Republican hands. This we admit. . . . He must be blind who does not see that nearly all the millionaires and monopolists, nearly all the organized corporations and privileges are in the hands of Republicans. The Democracy is comparatively the party of the poor and the lowly. If this is an injurious admission the Republicans may make the most of it.
>
> But he must also be blind who does not see that there is an open, direct and dangerous alliance between this growing and powerful money-aristocracy and the Republican office-holding army. . . . Thus we behold the distinct assertion . . . of the right to govern by a small class against the majority of the people. Every appeal made by Republican leaders . . . is made directly to arouse the money interests of the country on the theory that Hancock's election would ruin the business of the country. The most infamous appeal yet made . . . is the systematic effort . . .

[76] Reynolds, pp. 91-99; Silas Bent, *Newspaper Crusaders* (New York, 1939), p. 34; *Post-Dispatch*, Oct. 11, 1880.
[77] Reynolds, 98-99; *Post-Dispatch*, Oct. 11, 1880.

to arouse the fears of business men, and especially the manufacturers, on the distinct charge that Hancock's election would mean the repeal and the ruin of the tariff, the banking system, etc., etc. Never before did the monopolists, millionaires and stock brokers of the East contribute so much to the Republican campaign fund as this year. . . .

The growing money aristocracy of the country will yet be more dangerous to the Republic than the slaveholding aristocracy ever was. The war of the rebellion to openly destroy the Government by arms was not so dangerous to the real life of the Republic as the slow but steady growth of corruption, the increase of a fanatical, sectional, partisan spirit, and the rise of a powerful money aristocracy whose vital aim and interest it is to control the Government.[78]

More and more now the *Post-Dispatch* was dwelling on the dangers of monopoly.

The struggle for Indiana was not decided by speeches. Pulitzer and his fellow Democrats continued their barrage of words, but the Republicans used a far richer campaign chest to score a stunning upset. CHAOS! the *Post-Dispatch* cried in dismay, "The Democracy Knocked Blooming Silly." [79] But even in the midst of disaster Pulitzer did not lose his news sense; he wired various Democratic leaders for their reaction to the defeat and what this might mean for November. Senator McDonald replied with hollow bravado, "We will carry our State for Hancock." Next day, the *Post-Dispatch* took heart, headlining an election story ALREADY RALLIED, "Chances of Democratic Victory Strong as Ever—[But] Hard Work is Needed." Editorially, however, the paper was grim: "Let the fight go on." [80]

As Conkling's reply to Pulitzer reveals, the Republicans abandoned the bloody shirt during the last weeks of the campaign—it was ineffective against the hero of Gettysburg—and turned with startling success to exploiting the Democratic commitment to a tariff for revenue only. The alarm raised by Conkling that the Democratic proposal would ruin a slowly reviving prosperity by leaving the nation's industry unprotected from a flood of cheap European goods had much to do

---

[78] *Post-Dispatch,* Oct. 11, 1880.

[79] *Ibid.,* Oct. 13, 1880.

[80] *Ibid.* Another reason for Republican victory in Indiana, according to the *Post-Dispatch,* was the liberal use of bribery and "colonization" of voters from other states. Chauncey I. Filley, Republican boss of Missouri, it was charged, imported many Negroes from St. Louis. *Ibid.,* Oct. 15, 1880. See also, *Spectator,* April 21, 1883, and Clancy, p. 204. Pulitzer himself later recalled that the Republican war chest was "the vilest campaign fund of all." Joseph Pulitzer to Frank Cobb, July 18, 1908, Pulitzer Papers (LC).

with swinging Indiana into the Republican column. Businessmen of Pulitzer's own class were frightened. The *Post-Dispatch* was dismayed because the Democrats had been forced on the defensive, a position the aggressive Pulitzer never relished. It was angered by Hancock's evasiveness on the subject. "It is too late now for the Democrats to gain anything by preaching the sound doctrine of 'tariff for revenue only,'" the paper complained, "but the folly of putting a good clause in the platform and then running away from it in the most cowardly manner has been so thoroughly demonstrated that it will hardly be repeated four years hence." [81] Yet, the *Post-Dispatch* itself tried editorially to soften the plank:

"A tariff for revenue only" does not mean bitter opposition to protection. As we have to raise from $150,000,000 to $200,000,000 per annum by duties on imports, *any* tariff must of necessity "protect" home industries. . . . Anybody, therefore, who really believes that the Democratic plank . . . means free trade, is a most melancholy fool. *Free trade means, practically, no tariff at all.* . . . The Democratic plank favoring a "tariff for revenue only" means no more than the Republican plank. [82]

Despite these frantic last-minute efforts, the *Post-Dispatch* noted a dimming of Democratic chances. In the waning days of the campaign Pulitzer swung into one more speech-making tour, this time through the Eastern states, winding up in New York. At the end of the tour he sent to his newspaper a signed article which was published under the headline NEXT TUESDAY. A subdeck described the piece as "A Calm, Careful and Impartial Review" of election prospects in which Pulitzer gloomily predicted "the probability that Garfield will have the majority of the electoral votes." [83]

For a few brief hours election day the *Post-Dispatch* hoped its predictions might be wrong. A six o'clock extra noted "A Magnificent Majority for Hancock in New York City" and a "Close Vote" in Jersey, but on November 3 A DAY OF DISASTER recorded another dismal Democratic defeat. Still, the paper had its own triumph:

However disappointed some of our readers may be, they can not be surprised, for the result of the election does not vary one shadow from the forecast made by the POST-DISPATCH. . . . Hancock has a popular majority, but Garfield has a large majority of the electoral votes. [84]

[81] *Post-Dispatch*, Oct. 30, 1880.
[82] *Ibid.*, Oct. 29, 1880.
[83] *Ibid.*, Oct. 23, 1880, Oct. 28, 1880; Reynolds, p. 98.
[84] *Post-Dispatch*, Nov. 3, 1880. Garfield had a 10,000-vote majority.

The paper's penchant for "I told you so," always pronounced, was more unpopular than usual among Democratic organs which had observed the canon of party journalism that mention of possible defeat before an election was *verboten*. The St. Louis *Times* complained, indeed, that the *P-D's* traitorous prediction had contributed to the defeat. The *Post-Dispatch* replied indignantly that

> it is the duty of thick and thin party organs to deceive their followers under all circumstances [but] we do not find it inconsistent with our devotion to Democratic doctrine to tell the truth as it is given to us to understand it. We don't get paid for lying, and we are occasionally complimented for telling what we honestly believe to be true.[85]

Evidently the paper's course was popular with St. Louis readers because its circulation soared during election week to 23,000 copies daily, the highest point yet. Moreover, "as this circulation is mainly local we can safely say that the POST-DISPATCH has this week printed more papers within the city of St. Louis than any newspaper establishment here." [86] This lesson in the popularity of independent reporting among city readers was an important one to Joseph Pulitzer.

In a series of post-mortems the *Post-Dispatch* examined the causes for this sixth successive failure of the Democrats to capture the presidency. One was timid leadership. From the first this had been one of Pulitzer's severest criticisms. Too often the Democrats had the advantage "so far as arguments and right are concerned," only to lose because the Republicans were superior in "cunning, unscrupulousness, audacity, ability and aggressive tactics," traits the *Post-Dispatch* owner saw no reason to criticize. The trouble was, the paper said, scornfully, "Democratic leaders, though patriotic and pure, are too timid, too conservative, too sluggish and nerveless." [87] Ruefully it added,

> What Democratic leader is there upon whom the party looks with confidence or admiration? . . . There is the rub. The Democratic party is still a great historical party, but it has no leaders—none—not one worthy of the name. What it needs more than anything else is a Democratic Conkling.[88]

But most of all, insisted the *Post-Dispatch*, the Republicans had "all the organized capital, corporations and privileges, the monopolies and money interests of the country" in its ranks. The only consolation

---

85 *Ibid.*, Nov. 4, 1880. The *Republican* flatly told its readers late on election night that Hancock had won. *Ibid.*, Nov. 18, 1880.

86 *Ibid.*, Nov. 6, 1880.

87 *Ibid.*, May 16, 1879.

88 *Ibid.*, Nov. 18, 1880.

was that "the Democracy, though beaten, still comprises a large majority of the American people." [89]

Joseph Pulitzer told a mournful Democratic gathering in December:

I still adhere in all sincerity to my opinion that the Democratic party is the only party to save the country and restore it. In these days of monopolies, to resist the injurious effects of organized capital, a Democratic success becomes a strong necessity.[90]

By the end of the campaign, the *Post-Dispatch* had shifted its emphasis from an increasingly antiquated solicitude for the South—the mark of outworn Liberalism—to the pressing problems of middle class Americans in the new industrial age when great monopolies were threatening equal opportunity.

---

[89] *Ibid.*, Nov. 4, 1880.
[90] *Ibid.*, Dec. 28, 1880.

CHAPTER VII

The Turning Point

Active though he was in the national campaign, Pulitzer's ambition for a career in politics was centered chiefly in Missouri and St. Louis. It was here that he hoped to play a really significant role in influencing elections and particularly to win for himself a seat in Congress. By the same token, however, his activities in city and state politics in 1880 endangered most gravely the growing reputation of his little newspaper as a disinterested spokesman for the public weal. Indeed, had Pulitzer succeeded in satisfying his ambitions the *Post-Dispatch* might have become merely another political journal—the organ of a Democratic officeholder.

Like all the St. Louis dailies, the *Post-Dispatch* kept a watchful eye on Jefferson City, the seat of government in Missouri and known to disgruntled reporters as "the most unattractive, melancholy, miserable spot that ever enjoyed the honor of being the capital of any civilized State." [1] Tucked away in the center of a largely bucolic commonwealth, it was here that the legislature met in alternate years, dominated by rural politicians who had little sympathy for the problems of a rapidly growing St. Louis. Exasperated, the *Post-Dispatch* often complained that the lawmakers exhibited a "traditional, unpatriotic and unnatural jealousy of St. Louis." [2] Discord between urban and agricultural interests was a common characteristic in the Middle West where urbanization was growing apace. Metropolitan communities chafed at unsympathetic interference in their affairs by farm-dominated legislatures. It is true that in 1876 St. Louis to a great degree was emancipated from the excessive controls exercised in the antebellum period, but irritating powers of interference remained, which the city-bred *Post-Dispatch* declared were "utterly at variance with the spirit of local self-government." [3] Ill feeling between St. Louis and outstate Missouri was especially noticeable in the Democratic Party which since the end of Reconstruction in 1872 had dominated the state. The party was an unwieldy alliance of ex-Con-

---

[1] St. Louis *Post-Dispatch*, April 24, 1879.

[2] *Ibid.*, May 20, 1879.

[3] *Post and Dispatch*, Feb. 6, 1879. Soraghan, "History of St. Louis," pp. 30-31, 46, discusses the origins and extent of state interference with St. Louis's local government. Williams and Shoemaker, *Missouri*, II, 293-94. See also Arthur M. Schlesinger, "The City in American Civilization," in *Paths to the Present* (New York, 1949), pp. 210-33, for general observations on the theme of city vs. country.

141

federate farmers who hated "Black Republicanism" with a traditional, emotional intensity and the commercial and financial classes of the cities whose interests had kept them loyal to the Union but who opposed post-war Republican Reconstruction and tariff policies. The rural population, when they recovered the ballot in 1871, provided the Democrats with their great majorities, making Missouri the largest "normally" Democratic state in the nation, but a conservative oligarchy, many of whom were in St. Louis—the financiers, railroad magnates, franchise holders, merchant princes—controlled the party machinery. Employing superior financial resources and greater organizational skill, they had a firm grip on the central committee, enabling them to name the party's candidates for governor, the supreme court, and other state offices. These controls provided a convenient checkmate to the farmers' hold on the legislature. In 1880 the chairman of the central committee was John O'Day, a railroad attorney, the governor was John S. Phelps, a conservative Union Democrat, and the state supreme court was safely in the hands of judges who sympathized with corporate interests and special privilege.[4] Through the *Missouri Republican* and other party organs throughout the state, on election day the Bourbons rallied the party faithful with exhortations to defeat the "Black Republicans"—the "bloody shirt" in reverse—and as long as this appeal to the past was effective the oligarchs maintained a firm grasp on the state.[5] The system worked well; in the mid-seventies majorities ranged as high as 50,000 votes for handpicked Bourbon candidates; once in power, governors and judges blocked legislation considered inimical to corporate interests or rendered such proposals as were approved innocuous in operation.[6]

However, even while the Bourbons were perfecting their system, revolt was brewing. In the farmlands, as has been seen, when depression struck in the seventies thousands of harried farmers turned to demands for state action to save them from disaster. The Granger movement demanded state regulation of railroad rates and prohibition of unfair corporate practices. And when the Bourbons dragged their feet many abjured their Democratic allegiance and turned to a People's Party. A majority of the agrarians remained loyal to the old

---

[4] Clevenger, "Agrarian Politics," esp. ch. 1; and Williams and Shoemaker, ch. 13.

[5] Carl Schurz was especially bitter at Democratic strategy which lumped the Liberals indiscriminately with the Radical Republicans. He appealed to the farmers not to be hoodwinked by the Bourbon use of this technique. Williams and Shoemaker, II, 268-72.

[6] Only in one matter were the oligarchs unable to control the country wing. This was when the legislature met in joint session to name a United States senator. Here the farm element had free rein to choose its own favorite. Hence, whereas the governors of Missouri invariably were Union Democrats, the senators were ex-Confederates from outstate. Clevenger, pp. 3-7.

party, but they constituted a restless, unstable element who threatened to bolt the party's traces unless the Bourbons responded to their demands. To stem the rebellion, the Bourbons reluctantly agreed to a semblance of reform. A railway regulation bill was permitted to become law, but only after the railroad commission which it established was stripped of any real powers to enforce fair rates. The strategy worked; agitation for effective regulation declined, and the Granger movement faded into obscurity.[7]

But not all farmers were satisfied. The hardest pressed ones—generally small farmers on poor land—turned to inflation as a cure for agricultural depression. A Greenback Party sprang into being. To draw the sting of a renewed revolt, the Bourbons once more agreed to a meaningless concession. The Democratic platform of 1878 carried a plank which mildly endorsed the inflationists' demand for a modification of the Resumption Bill of 1875 and a tepid endorsement of demands for the recoinage of silver. This, together with a slackening of bad times in 1879, seemed to slow down the nagging drain on Democratic strength.[8]

In the meantime, however, the first indications of a revolt in a new and unexpected quarter began to appear. Depression was felt in St. Louis, too, and in searching for its causes members of the Merchants' Exchange became aware of discriminatory rates charged by the railroads, particularly in western Missouri, which seemed to favor Chicago. But it was when a merchants' committee discovered it was actually cheaper for a Missouri farmer only ninety miles from St. Louis to ship grain all the way to the lake city that St. Louis businessmen felt a chilling realization as to how much at the mercy of the railroads the local economy was becoming. A movement of protest began to develop.[9]

The *Post-Dispatch* gave voice to this rising urban protest. In an article entitled FACTS ABOUT FREIGHTS the paper declared:

> If one will take a walk up Main Street, and interview the men who do business there, he will find that over half of them are in a state of exasperation over the bad treatment they have received from some railroad. The complaint of merchants against railroads

---

[7] *Ibid.*, chs. 1-2; Williams and Shoemaker, II, chs. 11, 13. F. B. Munford, "A Century of Missouri Agriculture," *Missouri Historical Review*, XV (Jan. 1921), 287. For the national picture, see Buck, *The Granger Movement*, pp. 194-96.

[8] Clevenger, p. 8. For general histories of the greenback movement, see Unger; and Don C. Barrett, *The Greenbacks and Resumption of Specie Payments, 1862-1879*, Harvard Economic Studies, XXXVI (Cambridge, Mass., 1931).

[9] Clevenger, "Railroads in Missouri Politics, 1875-1887," *Missouri Historical Review*, XLIII (April 1949), 226-27; Clevenger, "Agrarian Politics," pp. 113-14.

is just as natural and just as chronic as the complaint of farmers about the weather.

. . . St. Louis merchants have long felt that they were not dealt fairly with by the railroads, not only in the way of freight charges, but in the promptness of shipments and in the matter of general courtesy. . . .

[The most serious complaint] is that there is a constant and unjust discrimination in freights made against St. Louis in the matter of freight charges. Here is the source of most of the unceasing wrangle that is going on here between the merchants and the freight lines. It is claimed . . . that St. Louis can never get a fair rate east as compared with Chicago. . . .[10]

The *Post-Dispatch* was a city paper, and its detestation of railroad monopolies was in no way influenced by sympathy for the farmer. Indeed, it spoke slightingly of "Granger persecutions" of business corporations, but this did not prevent it from expressing support for the new state railway commission in efforts to protect the city merchant. "We have three high-priced Railroad Commissioners," it declared, and "if they are good for anything they are good to see that the people of this State get a fair share from the railroads of this State in the fall business. . . ."[11] The paper went further, bursting out that the commission

should receive increased power and prestige. The power of railroads is constantly growing, and constantly growing, too, should be the check and control of the people over them. . . . Of course the railroads and demagogues and brainless twaddlers combined to cry "sinecure," and demand their [the commissioners'] abolition. There is no doubt but the railroads could afford to give a good deal to have them abolished. But the people can not afford to lose them.[12]

This spirited defense of the railroad board constituted the paper's first departure from its normal laissez-faire views. To a large extent, however, the change was more apparent than real. The *Post-Dispatch* was suspicious of the agrarians who controlled the board, and whenever specific suggestions for strengthening its powers were advanced it was usually unsympathetic. In any case, it continued to believe that competition was a better safeguard than governmental regulation. "The Mississippi River," it repeatedly observed, "is the only check we have against the railroads. It is the power that will compel them

10 *Post-Dispatch*, Aug. 4, 1879.
11 *Ibid.*, Aug. 28, 1880.
12 *Post and Dispatch*, Jan. 24, 1879.

to reasonable terms. . . . Without the river St. Louis would be at the mercy of a few gigantic and soulless railroad corporations. . . ." [13]

The *Post-Dispatch* showed no reluctance, however, in condemning special concessions for the hated monopolies, a policy which Bourbon politicians in Jefferson City habitually pursued. In a long editorial soon after its founding, it exposed the fact that although the state's railroads had been subsidized to $50,000,000 in public grants and enjoyed $16,000,000 in annual profits, they paid only a paltry $104,-000 in taxes. The *Post-Dispatch* demanded that the Board of Equalization rectify such inequities. [14] Favored treatment for other types of corporations was as vigorously condemned. "The Board of Equalization," it growled once,

> is just now engaged in the consideration of bank assessments, which . . . are reported to be outrageously low. . . . Corporations are never noted for their generous contributions to the public revenues, and we have no doubt the Equalizers will find a conspicuous need of reform. . . . [15]

For all its dislike of corporations, however, the paper's lack of sympathy for the farmer was constantly manifest. Thus, when a rural legislator introduced a bill to provide safeguards for farmers threatened with loss of their homes, the *Post-Dispatch* read the lawmakers a lecture. It declared that the state could not afford

> to interfere in bargains freely entered into between lenders and borrowers as it proposed to do in . . . the foreclosure bill. By the terms of this bill, no foreclosure for any default in interest or principal can take place without suit and judgment, and no sale can take place unless the property brings two-thirds of an appraised value. While giving the law credit for the best intentions, its results would be injurious to the State. A large amount of money has been loaned on mortgages in the State, because the brokers found this a good market for loans. If the law makes it a bad market, the brokers and lenders will simply seek another market. . . . This would be a serious calamity. . . . [16]

The *Post-Dispatch* considered the maintenance of unlimited opportunity for capital investment to be more important than succoring a distressed rural population. Agrarian proposals for economic legislation continued to be made, however, causing the *Post-Dispatch* to

---

[13] *Post-Dispatch,* Dec. 12, 1879.
[14] *Post and Dispatch,* Jan. 24, 1879.
[15] *Post-Dispatch,* April 2, 1879.
[16] *Ibid.,* April 4, 1879.

lose its temper. Missouri was lagging behind other states, it said, because

> the Legislature will no longer allow its citizens to make their own terms in the ordinary contracts of business, and at each recurring session . . . we are menaced with some new experiment in paternal government, the offspring of ignorance, or worse. One session all insurance contracts are threatened; at another session all capital loaned on mortgage is threatened; at a third session the rate of interest is fixed for us. . . . The government habitually and systematically meddles with those things which need no governmental intervention. . . .[17]

As the state campaign of 1880 approached, however, the most insistent issue in Missouri politics was the rural demand for greenback inflation. On this issue, reflecting the views of St. Louis merchants, the *Post-Dispatch* was adamant; indeed, it resembled all other St. Louis newspapers in its implacable opposition to greenbackism. Missouri journalism illustrated an urban-rural cleavage on the subject. Whereas country papers were infected with the greenback virus, every major St. Louis journal was strongly opposed; the *Globe-Democrat,* voice of middle class Republicanism; the *Missouri Republican,* the oligarchical organ; and the *Post-Dispatch,* spokesman for the middling classes of Democratic persuasion. "If greenbackism is an ugly word it represents a still more ugly thing," snarled the *Post-Dispatch* in an editorial which might have appeared in almost any St. Louis newspaper in 1879.[18] As the state campaign approached, it was this issue more than

---

17 *Ibid.,* May 5, 1879. The paper was equally firm, if somewhat more sympathetic, in insisting that the numerous counties in the state which had attempted to repudiate bonded debts must be required to pay. The debts had been incurred during the "railroad craze" following the war when rural communities throughout the Middle West had granted generous subsidies to promoters to build railroads in their districts. The *Post-Dispatch* was embarrassed; it was true, "these bonds, in nearly every instance, were issued to some railroad scheme which was never carried out except in a way to cheat and swindle," but the paper insisted on NO REPUDIATION! *Ibid.,* March 22, 1879, April 21, 1879, Sept. 17, 1879, July 30, 1880. For details of the controversy, see Clevenger, "Agrarian Politics," pp. 10-14; and Williams and Shoemaker, II, 371.

18 *Post-Dispatch,* July 22, 1879. Leach, *Missouri Historical Review,* XXIV (April 1930), 379-413; XXIV (July 1930), 568-85; XXV (Oct. 1930), 116-46, traces the course of the greenback movement in Missouri. There were, of course, greenback inflationists in St. Louis as in other cities, among both laboring and entrepreneurial elements. For a general treatment, see Unger, esp. chs. 2-3. See also, Chester McArthur Destler, *American Radicalism, 1865-1901: Essays and Documents* (Connecticut College Monographs, III) (New London, 1946), esp. chs. 1, 4. There were many types and degrees of inflationists, of course, and the *Post-Dispatch* itself, like other St. Louis journals, favored silver coinage so long as the gold standard was maintained. Nevertheless, at least as reflected by its major newspaper spokesmen, St. Louis's middle class merchants were generally hostile to greenbacks as an inflationary device.

any other, that tended to balance the paper's dislike of the oligarchs on the issues of monopoly and privilege.

In the months leading to the state nominating conventions, however, although Pulitzer felt deeply about these matters, they did not determine the course of the *Post-Dispatch;* Pulitzer's own activities and ambitions as a Democratic politician did that. This explains why, as the campaign moved into high gear, the paper pursued a deliberate policy of slurring over and muffling the great issues agitating the state. Pulitzer wanted victory for his party above all. And for a particular reason: he hoped to engineer the nomination and election of a candidate upon whom he himself could exercise influence.[19] To accomplish this purpose the *Post-Dispatch* went very far in the direction of the political journalism it professed to disdain.

The struggle for control of the Democratic Party centered on the selection of a gubernatorial nominee. Each major faction—the rural radicals and the Bourbons—had a candidate. At the outset the oligarchs favored John A. Hockaday, once attorney-general and now a lawyer for the Hannibal & St. Joseph Railroad, a favor-seeking corporation whose unsavory record of corruption was a state scandal. A Hockaday administration could be relied on to keep intact the privileges of corporations; thus, his candidacy would alienate the farmers. Unfortunately for him, Hockaday's record as attorney-general was questionable, and the *Post-Dispatch* used it to demolish his availability, partly because it, too, found him distasteful, but more because he would have split the party. The paper brought attention to rumors that he became an attorney for the Hannibal & St. Joseph with suspicious suddenness following his term as attorney-general, and it broadly hinted that this amounted to a bribe from the road for services rendered while he was in office. When Hockaday's supporters, including the *Republican,* accused the *Post-Dispatch* of unwarranted character assassination the paper replied pointedly:

> We said before and we say again, that there is no evidence that Mr. Hockaday . . . received a *bribe.* . . . But . . . there is no denial whatever that he did receive $20,000. . . . There is no denial that he did receive this sum very soon after his term as Attorney-general expired, and in the very case which under his administration was brought against the railroad. *These* are the facts which make an ugly impression. The entire vindication of Mr. Hockaday rests upon the difference between the words *bribe* and *fee.*[20]

Hockaday's candidacy rapidly withered after this, and the oligarchs found it necessary to look elsewhere for a candidate.

---

19 St. Louis *Spectator,* Jan. 15, 1881.
20 *Post-Dispatch,* March 30, 1880, March 31, 1880, April 6, 1880, June 22, 1882.

The candidate of the agrarian wing of the party was John S. Marmaduke, an ex-Confederate general with a substantial following outstate. For the past five years Marmaduke had been a state railway commissioner, and his campaign for a really stringent railway regulation law struck a warm response among hard-pressed farmers.[21] Pulitzer, besides being suspicious of rural radicals, opposed him for the same reason he had opposed Hockaday—a Marmaduke candidacy would injure the chances of victory. But the *Post-Dispatch's* handling of him was different. It borrowed from the party's conservatives a conspiracy of silence. A reader of the *Post-Dispatch* exclusively would scarcely have known that Marmaduke was a candidate at all, for it never mentioned his name. Nor did it discuss the basic economic issues behind his candidacy. This, of course, accorded ill with the paper's pledge "to tell the truth." The nearest it came to noticing the agrarian candidate was in a debate it had with the St. Louis *Times*. In A FAMILY TALK ABOUT CONFEDERACY the *Post-Dispatch* declared it to be essential that a Union veteran, not an ex-Confederate, should be the Democratic candidate for governor.

> Political parties should . . . do what is to their own best interest. Now, can any one deny that thousands . . . of semi-independent voters in Ohio, Indiana, and our immediate Republican neighbor States—yes, in Missouri, too—would look upon the nomination of a Confederate General in this State as a confirmation of the Republican charge that Democracy means Confederacy? Would it not be wiser for the party to disprove this charge wherever it can?[22]

This illiberal view contrasted sharply with the paper's condemnation of the "bloody shirt" in the national campaign. Until now, it had never expressed squeamishness about the election of an ex-Confederate. By such unbecoming policies did the *Post-Dispatch* seek to draw public attention away, not only from Marmaduke, but from the pressing issues he represented.[23]

The candidate Pulitzer quietly but assiduously worked for was Thomas T. Crittenden, a colorless, dignified and entirely "safe" member of an old Kentucky family who in 1860 had migrated to Missouri where he had fought for the Union cause. After the war he had settled in Warrensburg, located west of St. Louis, where he entered law practice with Francis M. Cockrell, United States senator and an

---

[21] Clevenger, "Agrarian Politics," p. 112.

[22] *Post-Dispatch*, July 9, 1880.

[23] This "conspiracy of silence" concerning especially the issues presented by the agrarian radicals was a characteristic conservative maneuver. Clevenger, "Agrarian Politics," pp. 111-12.

ex-Confederate. Crittenden seemed an ideal candidate to bridge over the differences in the party. Pulitzer was instrumental in obtaining the support of the St. Louis delegation for Crittenden over the strenuous opposition of the *Republican*.[24] In so doing, the owner of the *Post-Dispatch* hoped to become a power behind the throne in a Crittenden administration.

Though he had little love for them, Pulitzer now found himself in league with the Bourbons, for in their effort to defeat Marmaduke and the agrarians the oligarchs, led by the publishers of the *Missouri Republican,* climbed aboard the Crittenden bandwagon and made use of their control of the party machinery to steamroller his nomination through the state convention, where all debate on divisive issues which might split the party was carefully choked off. The only concession forced from the conservatives was the resignation of John O'Day, railroad lobbyist, from the state chairmanship of the party. But this was of little value to the agrarians for O'Day's successor was Griff Prather, a prominent St. Louis attorney closely associated with the publishers of the *Republican*.[25]

All of this political maneuvering was accomplished without a sign of protest from Joseph Pulitzer, who claimed to publish an independent newspaper. But the *Post-Dispatch* breathed a sigh of relief when it was all over and Crittenden was safely nominated: "Now let us have peace and furl the bloody shirt."[26]

The rural radicals, however, had been roughly used and were scarcely reconciled. The veneer of party unity maintained almost by main force during the convention meant little. This was quite apparent to Chauncey Filley, the wily boss of Missouri's hitherto ineffectual Republican Party. Filley's party was faction-ridden, too, with a Stalwart Grant wing led by himself and a Liberal group captained by Carl Schurz, Emil Preetorius and others. But Filley swallowed his convictions and consolidated the Republicans by arranging the nomination of David P. Dyer, a strong Liberal, for the governorship.[27] At the same time he paved the way for fusion of

---

[24] Thomas T. Crittenden to John F. Darby, Aug. 5, 1880, Thomas T. Crittenden Papers. Pulitzer's support, of course, was only one factor, and probably not the most important one, in Crittenden's victory. The ward bosses of the city's "Dark Lantern" cabal "delivered" the strongly Democratic wards. (*Post-Dispatch,* July 8, 1880, July 21, 1880; *Spectator,* Jan. 15, 1881; Williams and Shoemaker, II, 316. For a sketch of Crittenden, see McReynolds, *Missouri,* pp. 298, 300.) Crittenden was "available" since he had cannily stood for currency inflation as a Congressman, although he was a conservative on such matters as railway regulation.

[25] Clevenger, "Agrarian Politics," pp. 21-23.

[26] *Post-Dispatch,* Aug. 6, 1880.

[27] Dyer was a Liberal Republican who, the *Post-Dispatch* declared, was "so near being a Democrat that it is hardly fair to call him a Republican." *Ibid.,* Sept. 16, 1880. Dyer, *Autobiography,* p. 175.

his party with rural inflationists by conveniently neglecting to make any mention at all in the Republican platform of the burning green-back issue. He had little hope that ex-Confederates would vote Republican, since hatred of the Radicals ran deep, but he did seek a union with the Greenback Party, which was still attracting many unhappy rural Democrats. In a number of Congressional districts the Republicans quietly supported Greenback candidates.[28]

The *Post-Dispatch* suddenly took alarm. In an editorial entitled SERIOUS DANGER it warned its party to redouble its campaigning efforts or risk disaster in November. "We know that it is not the fashion for party organs to recognize and admit danger," it said, "but we do not believe in this. . . . Outside of the city of St. Louis the Congressional districts are in a very wretched condition. Seven seats are more or less in danger." [29] It urged the chairman of the Democratic committee to forego a vacation at Camp Prather, Arkansas, in order to concentrate on the shaky districts, but that complacent Bourbon politician saw no need to cut short his pleasures.

Despite its alarm over the Republican-Greenback fusion, the *Post-Dispatch* continued to avoid the basic issues which agitated the farmlands. Indeed, it scarcely took notice of the campaign at all, a strange course which its readers remarked on.[30] But there was method in this studied neglect; to discuss the issues, the party strategists agreed, would only expose the bitter disagreements among the Democrats, which might lose the election. When the *Post-Dispatch* did deign to notice the gubernatorial race it uttered platitudes. On election eve, for example, it commended Crittenden for his speeches, which "have everywhere been courteous and respectful," and the candidate was praised for being a "gentleman." [31]

The strategy worked; Crittenden was elected by a comfortable plurality. Nevertheless, the party lost ground, for Crittenden's majority was only 17,000 greater than the combined vote of the Republicans and Greenbackers, a decline of two-thirds from the lopsided Democratic majority of 1876.[32] A greater shock was the loss of five of the state's thirteen seats in the Congress to the Republican-Greenback coalition. For the first time since Reconstruction the hegemony of the Democrats in Missouri was seriously breached. The *Post-Dispatch* was outraged by the cynicism of Chauncey Filley in engineering "the shameful alliance with the lunatics who still cling to the barbarism

---

[28] Clevenger, "Agrarian Politics," p. 17.
[29] *Post-Dispatch*, Sept. 17, 1880.
[30] *Ibid.*, July 8, 1880.
[31] *Ibid.*, Nov. 1, 1880.
[32] Clevenger, "Agrarian Politics," pp. 19-20. The Democratic majority over all other parties was 37,000 in 1878 and 50,000 in 1876.

of Greenbackery," but it poured the vials of its wrath upon the Bourbon leadership in its own party for ignoring its warnings. Noting that in each of the five congressional districts where the fusionists had triumphed the margin of victory was 500 votes or less, the *Post-Dispatch* moaned that had Prather listened to it instead of the *Republican,* which, as a good political organ, had daily predicted victory, *"every one of these districts could have been saved."*[33] It neglected to add, however, just what Prather should have done to stem agrarian unrest. The truth was the paper itself should have accepted a share of the blame. Like all city politicians Pulitzer had subscribed to the mistaken strategy of ignoring the root causes of the farm revolt; like the business classes he represented he had no interest in the real reasons for agrarian unrest.

In the meantime, Pulitzer's ambitions for public office came to a climax in St. Louis. As he confessed, "I am passionately fond of politics. Yes, that is true . . . , perhaps too much so for my own pleasure." [34] In the late summer of 1880 he offered himself as a candidate for the Democratic nomination for Congress in the Second District, one of two districts assigned to St. Louis. The Second District was a cross-section of the city, embracing tough river wards along the levee, downtown business and middle class neighborhoods, and the select Eighteenth Ward, "the most respectable . . . in the city." It was also usually Democratic, with nomination insuring election.[35] Pulitzer prepared the ground by quietly obtaining the support of a small group of local politicians known as "the Dark Lantern." Apparently, upon payment of a "fee" this little knot of managers agreed to arrange the nomination.[36] When rumors of the deal gained currency "on all sides . . . the nomination of Pulitzer for

---

[33] *Post-Dispatch,* Nov. 8, 1880.

[34] Walter Stevens, "The New Journalism in Missouri," *Missouri Historical Review,* XIX (Jan. 1925), 330.

[35] *Post-Dispatch,* July 20, 1880.

[36] *Ibid.,* June 21, 1880, Aug. 12, 1880. There is some dispute whether Pulitzer actually paid a "fee" to be permitted to run. The St. Louis *Spectator,* Oct. 2, 1880, a relatively friendly organ, thought not, but a reminiscence some years later by a newspaper reporter claimed that Pulitzer had paid the Dark Lantern $6,000 for its support. *Reedy's Mirror,* Oct. 20, 1910. Still another recollection has it that Pulitzer paid $10,000. Undated memorandum, Collins Thompson Papers. In view of the fact that a "fee" was regarded as normal and required of all candidates by the Democratic machine abuilding in St. Louis, there is no reason to think an exception was made in Pulitzer's case. The amount, of course, is another question. In any case, when the *Post-Dispatch* began to crusade against this practice, it would have been extremely embarrassing for Pulitzer to have admitted making such a payment himself. See also, Thomas, *Print of My Remembrance,* p. 125; and Reynolds, "Joseph Pulitzer," pp. 98-99.

Congress was looked upon as a foregone conclusion; that he had secured the 'organization of the party.' " [37]

By 1880, if one hoped to go to Congress from the Second District it was more than advisable to play ball with the Dark Lantern. This group, an informal cabal of city committeemen, ward bosses, and small-time lawyer-politicians, had pooled their resources, establishing control of the local Democratic party. As yet there was no single "boss," but an unlettered blacksmith named Edward Butler, who, it was said, "slapped the First ward every time he struck his left pants pocket," was beginning to gain prominence. [38] According to one journal, already "as Butler goes so goes the First ward and a good many more." [39] In 1880, the riverfront boss was just catching hold as a more than ordinarily potent figure in local politics. Soon he would be known to every St. Louisan as the "Village Blacksmith," the notorious "boss of St. Louis" and the prototype of municipal bossism in the United States. Through the Dark Lantern Ed Butler was reaching out to other parts of the city.

Butler came to St. Louis in 1857 a penniless, illiterate, but shrewd and brawny Irish immigrant. He established a blacksmithy near the waterfront and within a few years, as the St. Louis agent of a patented horseshoe, he built up a thriving business shoeing the mules and horses for the city's car lines, and thereby developed close business relations with some of St. Louis's most powerful magnates. At the same time, he patiently fashioned a political machine in the teeming working class neighborhood of the First Ward. His popularity among the politicians at city hall grew with his ability to deliver votes, and by 1880, through his undercover connections with leaders in both parties he was corrupting city commissions and departments to obtain contracts and concessions for himself and his henchmen. Most of all, Butler quietly exerted his growing influence upon the municipal assembly to obtain or extend valuable franchises for his allies in the upper world of gentility and finance. Erastus Wells, St. Louis's pioneer street railway promoter, was—so it was rumored—the man behind Ed Butler in these early years. [40]

---

[37] *Missouri Republican*, Dec. 29, 1880.

[38] *Post-Dispatch*, April 2, 1881. See MS biography of David R. Francis by Walter B. Stevens in David R. Francis Papers.

[39] *The Hornet*, March 12, 1881.

[40] Material on Ed Butler, the boss of St. Louis, is voluminous. Publications consulted here were the following: Claude Wetmore, *The Battle Against Bribery* (St. Louis, 1904), ch. 2; Joseph McAuliffe, "From Blacksmith to Boss," *Leslie's Monthly Magazine*, LVIII (Oct. 1904), 635-39. Both Wetmore and McAuliffe were on the *Post-Dispatch* and well acquainted with Butler. See also, Zink, *City Bosses in the United States*, pp. 302-16; Cox, *Old and New St. Louis*, pp. 20-22; *Reedy's Mirror*, March 21, 1895, Jan. 17, 1901. See also, generalized sketch of a political boss in Bryce, *American Commonwealth*, II, 109.

Naturally enough, Pulitzer and his *Post-Dispatch* were somewhat embarrassed by the proprietor's deal with the Dark Lantern. Trying to maintain a pose of objectivity, the paper had nothing whatever to say about Pulitzer's candidacy, and it made light of rumors of "dark lanternism" in the Democratic party. It tried to be facetious:

> It is almost in the nature of a frightful charge that . . . the *Times* makes a startling assertion that Ed. Butler, the eminently respectable and famous boss horse-shoer, is at work for Tom Crittenden's nomination for Governor. We have taken no part in this matter and don't know how true the charge is; but, pray, Mr. *Times,* confess, wouldn't you like to have Ed. Butler on your side of the fence? If Butler is for Crittenden, all the better—for Crittenden.[41]

Another time the paper admitted hearing of a judge who had bought his nomination from the ring—even as Pulitzer was doing—but laughed it off as of no consequence.[42] Thus the *Post-Dispatch* stultified itself for the sake of its proprietor.

From this situation the *Post-Dispatch* was "rescued" by the *Missouri Republican*. "We hear of caucuses going on," it told its readers one morning. "The 'ring' manipulators, known as [the] Tammany or 'dark lantern' organization have agreed upon their candidate. He is said to be Hon. Joseph Pulitzer." It continued:

> But is Pulitzer sufficiently identified with the class of people who live and do business in the Second District to properly represent them in Congress? Is he a representative St. Louisan? . . . We think not. . . . The attitude of seeming to dictate is not an agreeable one, but if this is dictation, "Tammany" may make the most of it.[43]

In thus passing judgment the ponderous *Republican* spoke with a sense of outrage. Ever since it began publication, "the little *P-D*," as its rival patronizingly called it, had been attacking the older paper's claims to be the undisputed organ of the Democratic Party in city and state. Worse, the *Post-Dispatch* had administered stinging defeats to the venerable journal and had rubbed it in. Most of all, perhaps, the new paper had impudently attacked the local gas and

---

[41] *Post-Dispatch*, July 8, 1880. According to one reminiscence—clearly an unfriendly source—at the time he paid his "fee," Pulitzer had given Butler a *carte blanche* to insert in the *Post-Dispatch* any material he desired "to blacken the character of anybody or anything." Butler said he was "staggered" by the offer. (Undated memorandum, Collins Thompson Papers.) In view of Pulitzer's jealousy about his own paper, this seems unlikely.

[42] *Post-Dispatch*, Sept. 8, 1880.

[43] *Missouri Republican*, Aug. 12, 1880.

traction monopolies while simultaneously holding up the "best families" to public ridicule. Such insolence the *Republican* was determined to punish. As a first step in forestalling Pulitzer's nomination to Congress the old organ's managers persuaded Thomas Allen, St. Louis's leading railway magnate, to enter the race.

Now it was the turn of the *Post-Dispatch* to be outraged. The paper fairly erupted as Pulitzer saw his carefully laid plans for slipping into the nomination go glimmering. "It is the policy of this paper to be at all times fair and candid," it began evenly, and then lost its temper. "We do not seek a quarrel with the sordid, malevolent, and domineering managers of the *Republican*," but it was going too far to try to impose Allen, "a railroad king," upon the Democrats of St. Louis.

> The Democratic party is the foe of monopoly—it is the hereditary enemy of kings of every character and the jealous watcher over the Railway Kings who purchase legislation, corrupt official life and encroach upon the rights of the poor and the defenseless. Does anybody suppose for an instant that Mr. Allen, if sent to Congress, would sacrifice his personal interests to public good? Is it not reasonable to assume that . . . he would be found voting on the side of organized Capital, advocating the schemes of monopolists and in every way aiding the men who are acknowledged to be the insidious enemies of the Republic? [44]

The determination of organized capital in St. Louis, at the behest of the *Republican*, to defeat Pulitzer took concrete form just one day before the primary. The key was Ed Butler and his Dark Lantern. Although the riverfront boss had given his word to arrange Pulitzer's election and he and his henchmen had carefully worked to accomplish it, pressure from Butler's patrons among the oligarchy brought a last minute change of heart. The afternoon prior to the election one of Butler's lieutenants was seen, hat in hand, humbly asking admission to a meeting of business leaders in the offices of the Iron Mountain Railroad, which had been called to bend every effort to bring about Pulitzer's defeat. The threat to withdraw Butler's street railway shoeing business caused him to cave in. [45]

Hurriedly, the Village Blacksmith toured the Second District during the night with orders to allies and lieutenants to change their votes to Allen. At two in the morning the boss appeared at the *Republican* office and announced that he had "every damned one

[44] *Post-Dispatch*, Sept. 22, 1880.
[45] *Spectator*, Oct. 2, 1880; *Reedy's Mirror*, Nov. 3, 1898, Oct. 20, 1910; Reynolds, pp. 93-99.

of 'em switched." [46] Next day, as the *Post-Dispatch* wryly admitted, "there was no contest at all." Pulitzer received fewer than one thousand votes to his opponent's four thousand. In Butler's ward—the First—there was no other except the Allen ticket; so Butler, Turner, and their ilk visited the other wards, working with the bummer element to get out the vote. The "respectability" also did its bit, the paper claimed, as

> arrayed on Mr. Allen's side were all the great corporations. The Missouri Pacific ordered their men to quit work at three o'clock and provided them with carriages to take them to the polls, compelling them to vote for the Allen ticket. The same was the case with the Market and Olive street railroad lines. All the employes were forced to vote for Allen. The Transfer Company, the Bridge Company, the Elevator Company and the Gas Company did likewise. Every corporation and monopoly in the city was most active for Mr. Allen. . . .
>
> With "respectability;" with the "ring;" with the "machine;" with the "bummers;" with the railroads; with the corporations; with the monopolies; with nearly the entire press under direct money obligations to Mr. Allen passionately proclaiming innumerable dirty lies against his competitor . . . no wonder such an extraordinary vote was cast.[47]

Editorially the *Post-Dispatch* commented: "All is vanity—vanity of vanities, saith the editor as he contemplates politics," and then it added, significantly, "the nomination of Tom Allen was the very best thing that could possibly be done . . . for the POST-DISPATCH and its readers." [48] For the rest of his stay in St. Louis, at least, Pulitzer had learned his lesson: politics and independent journalism did not mix. He now decided to turn single-mindedly to journalism. This he made explicit a few weeks later when he told a gathering, "I am out of public life. The only suffrage I solicit you can extend to me by purchasing my newspaper daily." [49]

The effect on the *Post-Dispatch* was immediate. Only four days after the disastrous primary an article, headed SLOPS, signalized a

---

[46] *Reedy's Mirror*, Oct. 20, 1910.

[47] *Post-Dispatch*, Sept. 24, 1880. Although the results were overwhelmingly against Pulitzer everywhere, the power of Ed Butler in his own First Ward was apparent when it went 641-1 for Allen. Undated memorandum, Collins Thompson Papers.

[48] *Post-Dispatch*, Sept. 24, 1880.

[49] *Ibid.*, Dec. 28, 1880. In 1884, shortly after purchasing the New York *World*, Pulitzer sought election to Congress again in a Brooklyn constituency, although Seitz says he was "reluctant" to run. This time he was successful, only to learn again after a few months that politics and independent journalism did not mix. He resigned his seat. Seitz, *Joseph Pulitzer*, p. 152.

PULITZER'S *POST-DISPATCH*, 1878-1883

tone of new independence. The story reported that the board of health had strangely thrown out a low bid for a contract to haul away the city's garbage. Perhaps, the paper went on, the explanation lay in the fact that a higher bid had been submitted by a minor politician from the First Ward, a man named Jim Hardy, who was the brother-in-law of Ed Butler. Further investigation uncovered additional interesting information. The Village Blacksmith was found to be Hardy's "silent partner," and when the board of health threw out the embarrassing low bid it "temporarily" hired Hardy to continue hauling away refuse at even a higher fee than he himself had asked for. Then the board, as the law required, advertised for new bids, but in the meantime, the paper's reporters discovered, it quietly lobbied through the municipal assembly an act which virtually "fixed" the refuse contract in Hardy's hands by raising the bond required of all bidders to a point which would discourage future competition.[50]

Thus the *Post-Dispatch* launched a campaign to expose the creeping corruption of "dark lanternism" in local government. The facts, which had hitherto remained hidden, "occasioned considerable comment."[51] The paper hammered away at the board of health and its machinations. What lay behind them? The *Post-Dispatch* thought it knew: "It is a given fact . . . that the slop contract carries the First Ward" in the coming mayoral election.

> The only person who can be benefited by the solidification of the First Ward . . . is Henry Overstolz, the Mayor, and this fact, coupled with his silence on this outrageous job, has given rise to a number of ugly rumors which may seriously affect the spring election.[52]

The connections between the mayor and Ed Butler, it developed, were close. The paper pointed out that Overstolz was also zealously protecting Butler's interest in shoeing the police department's horses.[53]

In the weeks that followed the *Post-Dispatch* broadened its campaign into a full-bodied crusade to reform the local Democratic Party. Naturally, there were many St. Louisans who were suspicious of the paper's sudden independent air. It was altogether understandable that the old-line Democratic organ, the *Missouri Republican*, should have complained that "it was only a few months ago that the *P.-D.* was the recognized champion of the Dark Lantern Association. . . . And now this disorganizer and bolter . . . attempts to read lectures

---

[50] *Post-Dispatch*, Sept. 28, 1880, Sept. 29, 1880, Oct. 12, 1880, Oct. 20, 1880.
[51] *Ibid.*, Sept. 29, 1880.
[52] *Ibid.*, Dec. 27, 1880.
[53] *Ibid.*, Feb. 15, 1881.

156

on Democratic duty."[54] Even the relatively friendly *Spectator* suspected that Pulitzer's determination to uproot the ward bosses was a case of spite.[55] But another onlooker, Daniel M. Houser, Pulitzer's old friend and manager of the *Globe-Democrat,* welcomed the *Post-Dispatch* to the ranks of independent journals.[56] Whatever the motive, Pulitzer's newspaper was freed from the incubus of political "organship"; his withdrawal from active politics at last permitted the *Post-Dispatch* to fulfill its early promise as an aggressive, disinterested voice of "the honest merchant and quiet citizen" in attacking venality wherever it existed in St. Louis.[57]

The paper succinctly formulated its new platform in a manifesto labeled PLAIN POINTS, published soon after its emancipation. "We believe in party men, but not in party *slaves,"* it declared. In national and state politics, it continued, where parties represent "principles," the paper would be Democratic,

> but locally they [the voters] will, for the various city offices, vote for the *best men,* regardless of politics, because there is no political principle whatever involved in the question of who shall be Sheriff, Constable or member of the Legislature.
>
> The man who votes for the whole ticket without a scratch, no matter how unfit some candidate may be, is not a party man but a *party fool* and sets a premium upon rings and the fixing and foul huckstering of nominations.
>
> We say: . . . Examine your tickets before you cast them, and if you find any taint of rings or political rascals, scratch—scratch —scratch.[58]

The Democratic Party, which the *Post-Dispatch* proposed to reform, controlled the municipal government. Mayor Overstolz was a canny politician who had managed to receive the nomination of both parties in 1877, but during his four years in office he had moved into the Democratic camp.[59] He was known to be friendly with the

---

[54] *Republican*, Jan. 3, 1881.

[55] *Spectator*, April 9, 1881.

[56] Houser called on Pulitzer at the *Post-Dispatch* office to tell him "that was the line to follow." John Norris to Joseph Pulitzer, March 10, 1900. Pulitzer Papers (CU).

[57] A year after this, the *Post-Dispatch* offered the following advice to a Chicago newspaperman who was seeking public office: "Mr. PENN NIXON should stick to his pen. He is old enough to know that in journalistic circles it is held to be a violation of the code of ethics for a man with any sort of interest in a newspaper to hold public office." *Post-Dispatch*, Dec. 29, 1881.

[58] *Post-Dispatch*, Nov. 1, 1880. Looking on, the *Spectator* congratulated the *Post-Dispatch*, but twitted it mildly: "I am astonished most that the *Post-Dispatch* has been so long in making up its mind." *Spectator*, Oct. 9, 1880.

[59] Scharf, *History of St. Louis*, I, 712-16; St. Louis *Globe-Democrat*, Oct. 12, 1952, Oct. 19, 1952; *Post-Dispatch*, March 21, 1881.

gas and traction interests, the local oligarchy behind Butler. Consequently, it was scarcely surprising, as the spring campaign approached, that the mouthpiece for the oligarchy, the *Missouri Republican,* laid the groundwork for Overstolz' reelection. It forged still more tightly the combination that had so decisively put an end to Joseph Pulitzer's political career. "Let it be distinctly understood," charged the *Post-Dispatch,* "that the *Republican* has become the organ of the coarsest ring that ever ran the Democratic machine in this city." [60]

Representing the independent businessmen of St. Louis with clarity and force now, the *Post-Dispatch* launched into a campaign of exposure to destroy the growing power of bossism in Democratic ranks. [61] Its first foray was against Dark Lantern control of the "cabbage wards," gerrymandered districts on the edges of the city, where population was small. [62] These wards had equal representation in the party's city central committee and conventions with the large districts downtown. Thus, the politicians of the Dark Lantern, operating from neighborhood saloons, had little difficulty in naming the delegates they wanted by manipulating a mere handful of votes. This was, to use the words of the *Post-Dispatch,* "a rotten borough system on a small scale—rotten to the core. Representation in city committees and city conventions must be based on Democratic votes or people, not on cabbages or acres." [63] The paper also exposed machine control of the slum neighborhoods where the ukase of neighborhood bosses was absolute. A *Post-Dispatch* reporter was physically ejected from a vote-counting session in a Second Ward saloon by machine-selected judges. The paper seethed:

> We run a newspaper and don't care a straw who runs the machine of any party. But we can tell the distinguished gentlemen who constitute a majority of the Democratic City committee that they are doing their very best to make the election of the entire Republican ticket next spring an absolute necessity. [64]

---

[60] *Post-Dispatch,* Jan. 3, 1881.

[61] At the outset of its campaign the *Post-Dispatch* remarked, "It is rather a remarkable co-incidence that local movements to disestablish machine and ring rule are simultaneously progressing in New York, Philadelphia, Brooklyn and St. Louis." *Ibid.,* Dec. 30, 1880.

[62] The "cabbage wards" were carved out by the Radical Republican machine before it lost control of St. Louis in 1871, which gave control of the upper chamber of the assembly, the Council, to the Republicans. The Democrats, when they came to power, did not change the districting. Democratic politicians found it convenient to use these small wards to control their own party. *Ibid.,* March 17, 1881.

[63] The Eighteenth Ward, for example, which cast 2,087 Democratic votes in the most recent election, had no greater representation on the city committee than the Twenty-fifth, which cast 37 Democratic votes. *Ibid.,* Dec. 10, 1880.

[64] *Ibid.*

The campaign continued. A feature story with the eye-catching head, THE PUBLIC TEAT, detailed the apparatus of the ward "rings" who made up the Dark Lantern.[65] Frank Turner represented the most notorious ring of all on the city committee, as he

> stands in the committee for Ed. Butler. . . . Pat Sheehan, the market plaster[er] at Center Market, and James Lancaster, the plumber in the Water Department, are lieutenants in the Butler clique, and with Turner and a very few others make up a close corporation which controls the patronage of the ward. Whether Turner is dog and Butler tail or vice versa makes little difference. They wag together. . . .

Dark Lantern committeemen representing other wards were equally unappetising to the middle class *Post-Dispatch*. They included Dan Kerwin, a blacksmith, presently the city chairman; John Ernst, Theodore Schoenken and William Huber, all saloon-keepers; William Stanton, a teamster; "Big Mike" Reilly, a butcher; Andy Blong, a painter; and Peter Laurie, a carpenter at the gas works who was the kept man of the St. Louis Gas-light company. Only in two or three instances was this dismal roster relieved by an independent merchant.[66]

Other articles and editorials detailed the methods by which the ring maintained itself in power. With the approach of an election large numbers of hangers-on were placed temporarily on the city's rolls, and the polls on election days, in the bossed wards, were filled with "bummers" and "strikers" who stuffed the ballot boxes.[67]

The *Post-Dispatch* did not stop at exposure and censure. It undertook a campaign to arouse the independent citizenry to positive action. Late in December 1880 Pulitzer helped to organize a mass protest meeting which filled Armory Hall with "representative men, manufacturers and professional men." The Armory Hall Democrats, as they were called, enthusiastically greeted a parade of speakers among whom was Joseph Pulitzer, the only editor present. He provoked loud applause and shouts of laughter by his declaration, "The Chinese must go, Mr. Chairman!" and he warned, "I will not lend any support to any ticket which has not a pure record. Whenever I become convinced that the true interests of the party are not represented by the names upon its ticket, I am under no obligation to support it." [68]

The Armory Hall protestors established an organization and issued an ultimatum to the city committee to turn over to a new group com-

[65] See Bryce, *American Commonwealth*, II, 107-108, for generalized comments on the techniques of municipal political rings.

[66] *Post-Dispatch*, Feb. 8, 1881.

[67] *Ibid.*, Feb. 8, 1881, Feb. 28, 1881, March 11, 1881; Thomas, pp. 125-216.

[68] *Post-Dispatch*, Dec. 28, 1880.

plete control of the party for the duration of the mayoral campaign. In the face of this massive revolt the ring leaders appeared to give way, agreeing to set up a committee of seven, the majority of which would be reformers. But in the end the amateur politicians found their committee was little more than window dressing; the real power remained in the hands of the ward politicians.[69]

During the course of the struggle, which lasted for four months, the *Post-Dispatch* discerned the shadowy form of the franchise interests behind the city machine. Not only was the *Republican* constantly at the side of the ring, but James O. Broadhead, attorney for the Gaslight company, was a quiet adviser to Kerwin, Turner, and Butler. For them, the paper commented, it was a case of "rule or ruin." The gas monopoly was determined to bring about the renomination of the "safe" Henry Overstolz and prevent the Armory Hall reformers from naming an unfriendly merchant as the Democratic candidate.[70]

At the outset of the campaign the *Post-Dispatch* boomed Edward C. Simmons, a highly successful hardware merchant, for mayor. Although the paper admitted Simmons was not a politician, he was "a business man" who would "take hold and develop the interests of the city as he has managed his own business." [71]

Inexorably, however, the Dark Lantern, with the backing of the magnates, brushed aside the Armory Hall opposition in their determination to nominate Mayor Overstolz. As the inevitable neared, the *Post-Dispatch* exploded in frustration:

> Mr. EDWARD BUTLER, the Village Blacksmith, backed by his gang of strikers, has taken a contract to give Mr. OVERSTOLZ four more years of Mayoral glory. The scheme is to hold a City Convention in which the cabbage wards will have as much voice as the great populous wards in the heart of the city. The ticket made by this packed and unrepresentative body is to be called Democratic. . . .
>
> All municipal rings, the office-holders, the gas and street railway corporations, the ED BUTLERITES and the *Republican* grinders are expending their perspiration in an effort to re-elect Mayor OVERSTOLZ.[72]

If the ringsters go through with it, the *Post-Dispatch* warned, "we will consider it our duty . . . to repudiate the Convention and its

---

[69] *Ibid.,* Jan. 6, 1881, March 18, 1881.

[70] *Ibid.,* Jan. 6, 1881, March 18, 1881.

[71] *Ibid.,* Nov. 11, 1880, Feb. 22, 1881; *Spectator,* Dec. 4, 1880.

[72] *Post-Dispatch,* March 17, 1881. It was characteristic of the sudden change which came over the *Post-Dispatch* in local politics as the result of Pulitzer's defeat, that until late in 1880 the paper had had nothing but good words for Mayor Overstolz. See, for example, editorial of May 19, 1880.

work." [73] But the combine was not impressed, and on March 29 a three-column story, headed OVERSTOLZISM, recorded the failure of the merchants' revolt. "After a Hard Fight, Overstolz is Declared the Democratic Candidate," a subdeck announced. "The Cabbage Wards Assert Themselves Once More in Politics." [74] But the fight was close; the Overstolz forces, with all their built-in advantages, won by a scant three votes in the nominating convention. This proved, the *Post-Dispatch* declared, that it had "an influence in this community such as the ancient *Republican* never dreamed." [75]

The new independence of the *Post-Dispatch* now reached its grand climax. Instead of supinely accepting Overstolz' nomination— the usual course of a political newspaper—the paper carried out its threat of a bolt. The bitterness of the Armory Hall revolt had split the local Democrats and the *Post-Dispatch,* which was largely responsible for it, led the merchants into the ranks of the opposition.

Not that the choice was a clear one. William L. Ewing, the Republican candidate for mayor, was himself tainted with "ring" interests and the pervasive influence of the franchise-seekers. As speaker of the municipal House of Delegates, he had also established (as it turned out) amicable relations with the First Ward clique.[76] Moreover, the paper was frank to say that Ewing was a "small potato" and as an administrator Overstolz was "infinitely better qualified to fill the office of Mayor." [77] But Pulitzer was determined to encompass the defeat of his own party and cleanse it of bossism. The growing power of the twin influences which Pulitzer now considered the greatest dangers to local self-government—bossism and privilege—must be uprooted.

In the week between the nominating conventions and the city election the *Post-Dispatch* attacked "Overstolzism" with all its strength. Detailed articles revealed the mayor's activities in behalf of the gas and street railway interests, the influence of Ed Butler and the Dark Lantern in corrupting city government, and the ballot-stuffing proclivities of the machine. The campaign was highly effective. When it was all over an Overstolz supporter ruefully remarked that "the *Post-Dispatch* undoubtedly contributed very largely to the defeat of Mr. Overstolz. Its assaults were quick, sharp, and bitter, leaving no time to take breath between blows." [78]

---

[73] *Ibid.*, March 17, 1881.

[74] *Ibid.*, March 29, 1881.

[75] *Ibid.*

[76] Butler was seen in the lobbies of the Republican convention working for Ewing's nomination, *Ibid.*, March 24, 1881. For favorable sketches of Ewing, see Scharf, I, 716-18; and Cox, pp. 106-108.

[77] *Post-Dispatch,* Feb. 5, 1881, April 6, 1881.

[78] *Spectator,* April 9, 1881.

Overstolz was overwhelmed. In the final count the undistinguished Ewing had 24,000 votes to a meager 11,000 for his opponent. "Thanks, thanks," exclaimed the paper. "It was a very flattering vote of confidence in the POST-DISPATCH." [79] And for once, in taking full credit, Pulitzer's newspaper spoke truly. The merchants' revolt, which it had stimulated and to a large degree directed, was the key factor in smashing the Democratic hold on St. Louis for the first time since the ending of Reconstruction.

The influence of the *Post-Dispatch,* now fully independent, was clear for all to see. "We take it that our dearly beloved brethren of the *Republican* are now ready to concede the point that the city circulation of the POST-DISPATCH is already much larger than that of Old 1808," the paper crowed. The triumph was at least as much journalistic as it was political. During the paper's campaign an onlooker remarked:

> The growth of the *Post-Dispatch* seems to be wonderful. The paper will soon have a Perfection Press, the unfailing mark of great prosperity. Mr. Pulitzer was once deemed a good politician. I . . . think he is a better journalist than politician.[80]

Politically, however, it is difficult to say what the *Post-Dispatch* accomplished. True, the Democratic machine received a bad beating, but chameleonlike, Ed Butler was not long in recovering control of municipal garbage and shoeing contracts, and his machine continued to grow in power. The mayoral campaign of 1881 was really the beginning of a quarter-century struggle against the rising power of Butler, boss of St. Louis, and the local oligarchy behind him. It was a struggle carried on by the *Post-Dispatch,* speaking clearly now for "the honest merchant and quiet citizen."

---

[79] *Post-Dispatch,* April 6, 1881.
[80] *Hornet,* Dec. 11, 1880.

CHAPTER VIII

A Sensational Newspaper

Political independence was not the only consequence of Pulitzer's disappointment at the polls in 1880. Freed now from private political ambitions, he turned with single-minded devotion to journalism, and for the next two and a half years utilized lessons already learned and experimented with new ideas to perfect a brand of daily publication which, later in New York, would revolutionize metropolitan journalism. [1] His aim was to acquire mass circulation because, as he said later, "I want to talk to a nation, not to a select committee." [2] Moreover, to be truly independent of politicians and advertisers the *Post-Dispatch* needed a mass readership. This Joseph Pulitzer set out to obtain by appealing more and more to the tastes of the ordinary citizen.

More than ever the *Post-Dispatch* became a newspaper for local consumption. The mass audience Pulitzer sought was the people of St. Louis. Although the paper by no means ignored national or international events, experience and careful observation taught its owner that purveying local scandals, promoting local causes, and supplying his city readers with gossip and entertainment which in small towns was retailed across the back fence were the high road to success. The results were highly profitable; during the next two and a half years before Pulitzer left St. Louis the paper's circulation boomed.

The intensified tone of sensationalism was signaled one afternoon late in December 1880 by a two-column story under an arresting headline, A HELL FOR BOYS. The paper returned to a subject neglected in Pulitzer's pursuit of a political career: the insidious spread of the gambling underworld. City Editor Moore detailed John McEnnis to uncover a den operating in the fashionable West End which was catering to youths of the best families. [3] Three days later, New Year's Eve, Pulitzer marshaled his entire staff of local reporters to expose organized gambling in the city. The evidence they gathered by visiting every downtown joint was emblazoned on the first page of

---

[1] Will Irwin, "The American Newspaper, Part III," *Collier's Magazine*, XLVI (Feb. 18, 1911), 14.

[2] Creelman, "Joseph Pulitzer—Master Journalist," *Pearson's Magazine*, XXI (March 1909), 246. See similar comment noted in Alleyne Ireland, *Joseph Pulitzer* (New York, 1914), 68-69.

[3] St. Louis *Post-Dispatch*, Dec. 28, 1880; St. Louis *Spectator*, Jan. 1, 1881, Jan. 15, 1881.

the *Post-Dispatch* in a seven-column story under a heavy black head, IN FULL BLAST, and many subdecks reaching half-way down the page. The reporters discovered that upwards of four hundred St. Louisans had gambled away $10,000 on "the green baize tables" in no less than seventeen wide open establishments. So blatant were they, the paper declared, that "the gamblers themselves are beginning to think that they are conducting a legitimate business." [4]

The very next week the *Post-Dispatch* leveled its guns at a second institution, the garish variety theaters operating on the edges of the red light district. These forerunners of modern burlesque halls also were "raided" by the paper's entire reportorial force on a Sunday night, and the next day appeared another sensational exposure, THE ROAD TO RUIN. Subheads declared that "nearly a thousand boys" were seen in the balconies of these "man-traps baited with harlots and rot-gut whisky" watching "professional young women" exhibiting "the female form divine." The article continued:

> It is in the dramas these cheap houses produce that one of the most objectionable features is to be found. Without at least one, of impossible plot, with murder, robbery and all the crimes in the decalogue crowded in, the night's performance is not complete. There must be shooting and cutting in every act, heroes and heroines, desperadoes and dare deviltry generally. The plot must be thrilling and the dialogue profane and slangy. [5]

Although heretofore the paper had accepted paid notices from the variety theaters, it now piously announced that "we would not knowingly . . . permit an advertiser to perpetrate a fraud upon our patrons, nor would we sell our columns [to persons] seeking patronage for immoral institutions." [6] Under MORAL LESSONS it justified the new campaign:

> In making war on the gambling dens and Variety Halls we are not actuated by a desire to create a journalistic sensation. We fight . . . [these] shams and frauds because we believe it to be right. There is nothing Puritanical, close or illiberal about the POST-DISPATCH . . . but there are certain fixed principles of morality which it is the duty of every public journal to maintain. We believe that the prosperity and moral health of St. Louis could be advanced by the suppression of gambling and the regulation of Variety Shows. . . . [7]

---

[4] *Post-Dispatch*, Jan. 3, 1881.

[5] *Ibid.*, Jan. 10, 1881.

[6] *Ibid.*, Jan. 11, 1881.

[7] *Ibid.* Onlookers were a bit cynical about *Post-Dispatch* motives, although they agreed that the exposures were good journalism. See *Spectator*, Jan. 15, 1881, and the St. Louis *Criterion*, Oct. 1, 1882.

This was only the beginning. Each Sunday for weeks thereafter the *Post-Dispatch's* busy reporters uncovered additional vices which it played up under sensational headlines. One week the revived lotteries were the target, then fortune tellers fronting for abortionists, followed by "opium hells," DAGO DENS, CRAPS, and THE SOCIAL EVIL.[8] In some cases—as with the opium dens—there was a decided strain to make the stories live up to the lurid headlines, whereas in others the exposures were sensational enough. THE SOCIAL EVIL, according to the many subdecks, was spreading a blight through the business district, abetted by "eminently respectable" property owners "Who Profit by the Wages of Sin." A timid grand jury refused to reveal their names, but

> the reporters of the POST-DISPATCH have found little trouble in securing the matter which the grand jurors thought ought to be published, but were unwilling to send forth. . . . Below is given a list of the keepers of houses of ill-repute, with the names of owners, lessors or agents. . . . The list will give the people of St. Louis an idea of the extent of the social evil. . . . The territory from Chouteau to Case avenue, and from the river to Fourteenth street, embracing the heart of the city, is dotted thickly with plague spots. In some places whole blocks are given up to abodes of the depraved. In other places there are single houses— just enough to contaminate and ruin neighborhoods.[9]

The *Post-Dispatch* philosophized on its new policy with a statement which became the standard argument for sensational papers in the years to come:

> Our interest is a common one with society. We have learned that there must be exposure before wrong can be righted. There can be no reform without agitation. Since we commenced our crusade upon the evil-doers some weeks ago, we have had the satisfaction of seeing the lottery and policy shops restrained, the fortune-tellers restricted, the gamblers driven to cover, and several of the most noted resorts for the vicious closed completely. It was not until the POST-DISPATCH exposed the character of the EAGAN and CARROLL dance-houses that the authorities moved to their suppression. The City continues to license vice in its worst forms. The public will hardly believe that such dead-falls and dens of iniquity as we describe to-day, are licensed and protected by the municipality, yet such is the case. We propose to keep at the work

---

[8] *Post-Dispatch*, Jan. 17, 1881, Jan. 24, 1881, Jan. 31, 1881, Feb. 7, 1881, Feb. 14, 1881, Feb. 21, 1881, March 1, 1881.

[9] *Ibid.*, March 1, 1881.

of reform, and if necessary, we will cut deep. In the end the community will thank us, and this, together with the happy consciousness that we have performed a plain duty, will be all the reward that we will ask.[10]

Whatever else its purpose, a major aim of this type of "moral crusading" was to attract circulation. The paper's attacks on sin, its pious statements and the exaggerated tone of many of the campaigns betrayed this essential purpose. Genuine crusades attacked fundamental public problems and were characterized by Pulitzer's basic liberal philosophy. Sometimes it is true—as with the attack on gambling—even sensational exposures developed into genuine crusades, but the element of sensationalism for its own sake was never absent.

Moreover, moral crusading had its risks. It tended to rouse illiberal instincts in the community. When the *Post-Dispatch* inaugurated its campaign against the variety halls, it invited ministers and their flocks to join this "fight against Satan." It admonished the pastors that

> if . . . [they] will form an association having for its object the suppression of gambling-houses and low variety halls, where women are ruined and youth corrupted, they will render a valuable service to the POST-DISPATCH in its good work and benefit society more than if they preach sermons every day in the year. . . . If our great moral teachers will move in this matter they will find the POST-DISPATCH close by their side in the thickest of the fight.[11]

The paper got more than it bargained for. Together with a body of church women, the ministers responded by encouraging the local Sabbatarian society to launch a drive to close down all places of amusement on Sundays, the opera "as well as low dives and nasty theaters." The *Post-Dispatch* was embarrassed; it tried gently to head off "the dear ladies" with the discreet advice that they were distorting the purpose of the invitation.[12]

There were other risks. Indiscriminate sensationalism ran the danger of depriving law-abiding—if sleazy—individuals of their rights. In the case of the variety theaters, the *Post-Dispatch* admitted that they were "low but legal," and that the trouble lay rather with a faulty city ordinance which permitted them to flourish. Moreover,

---

[10] *Ibid.*, Feb. 14, 1881.
[11] *Ibid.*, Jan. 11, 1881.
[12] *Ibid.*, Jan. 31, 1881, Feb. 1, 1881, March 10, 1881, April 18, 1882, July 2, 1883. The forthright *Westliche Post* denounced "the hypocritical . . . praying sisters," as did the *Globe-Democrat. Ibid.*, Feb. 16, 1881, Feb. 2, 1881.

some were not really dens of "iniquity" but simply panderers to low tastes.[13]

Exposing sin, however, was popular. In the first two months of 1881 circulation rose from 9,300 copies daily to 12,000.[14] Henceforth, exposures of dens of vice—"fights against Satan"—became a steady diet for *Post-Dispatch* readers.

This was not the only reason for the rapid rise in readership during 1881. The paper launched into a systematic policy of publishing prying, gossip-mongering, frequently salacious "news" which a modern journal would ignore. It gave the *Post-Dispatch* a reputation for indecency which lingered well into the twentieth century. Delighting especially in the publication of scandals involving the "best classes" in the West End, the paper appealed to the equalitarian instincts of its readers, exposing for ordinary folk the fact that the pretentious, too, had feet of clay.

The St. Louis oligarchy, as has been seen, was peculiarly vulnerable to this sort of ridicule. Living in their iron-gated "places" and impregnated with Southern-gentleman exclusiveness, they were fair game for the style of "news" the *Post-Dispatch* now purveyed. Uncovering delicious bits of gossip, the paper played them up in column-length stories under such headlines as ST. LOUIS SWELLS, AN ADULTEROUS PAIR, DUPED AND DESERTED, DOES REV. MR. TUDOR TIPPLE?[15] In a ten-day period in 1883, the top heads on page one, introducing chiefly local scandals, were: LOVED THE COOK, A RIOT IN CHURCH, A WILY WIDOW, KISSING IN CHURCH, AN ADVENTURESS, DEACONS' DISAGREE, and MY DAUGHTER.[16]

The new approach to "society" was launched one warm June evening in 1881 when, with little to find in the way of substantial news, John McEnnis happened into Uhrig's Cave, a typical German-type summer theater, where he found a group of young swells ogling a line of chorus girls. One, it seemed, went so far as to send a note to a lovely creature in red tights. The alert reporter found out the young man's name and the next day the paper played up the incident—certainly scarcely newsworthy by any modern measure—under a headline, THE GIRL IN RED. Subdecks informed the reader: "The Story of A. B. Lansing's Mashedness," "A Sample Letter From a Nice Young Man," "How the Ladies at Uhrig's Cave Escape Paralysis."[17] There followed a pretty tale of how young Lansing had sent his note, a

---

[13] *Ibid.*, Jan. 11, 1881. Mayor Ewing sought to establish a distinction between proper and improper variety shows in a new ordinance aimed at outlawing only indecent performances. *The Hornet*, Dec. 24, 1881.

[14] Memorandum [1905], Pulitzer Papers (CU).

[15] *Post-Dispatch*, June 16, 1882, June 17, 1882, Aug. 18, 1882, Sept. 8, 1882.

[16] *Ibid.*, June 25-July 4, 1883.

[17] *Ibid.*, June 25, 1881.

verbatim publication of the very gushy epistle, and an account of the beauties of the girl in red tights. But the reporter had made a wrong identification, and the outraged Mr. Lansing sued the *Post-Dispatch* for libel. The paper apologized with the following editorial, written in the humorous style of the managing editor, John Cockerill:

Gentle reader, sitting on your cool doorstep this evening with a POST-DISPATCH in one hand and a fan in the other, what do you think of a young man who insists that a newspaper shall pay him $15,000 for simply saying that he sent a note to a pretty chorus-singer. . . . Egad, it strikes us that people have grown fastidious. . . . We have been incontinently sued. Yes, we are to be dragged before a tribunal by our highly esteemed young friend, A. B. LANSING. There was a large and fashionable audience at an uptown summer garden theater last Friday night. A young girl in red tights, as beautiful and irradiant as TITAN'S "Ariadne," was capering about the stage. . . . Anon a youthful GANYMEDE . . . was handed a note by a gentleman and requested to deliver it to the golden-haired nymph. . . . GANYMEDE, being requested to indicate the person who had given him the note to deliver, pointed out . . . Mr. LANSING. The POST-DISPATCH, with the good taste for which it is celebrated, printed the letter next day and related the episode in its own charming way. Mr. LANSING was surprised. He had written no note to the pretty princess. . . . Some young men might have been content to let the impression go out that they were slightly inoculated with Don Juanism and were devilish sly dogs. . . . Not so with A. B. . . . It was a case of mistaken identity. Next day we made an *amende* —full, ample, and somewhat tinctured with the oil of humiliation and sprinkled with the dust of regret. It is possible that our genial fellow-citizen, Mr. LANSING, would have been satisfied with this, but he had a friend, a guide, a counselor, who felt from the first that a terrible wrong had been done—a deep, ineffaceable wrong that called for some sort of enjoyable retribution. This person was J. WALLENSTEIN DRYDEN, by profession a barrister, a gentleman cast in a Puritanic mold and trained . . . to look upon all the affairs of life with a severe and solemn aspect. Mr. DRYDEN'S features are such as might belong to a person born amid the depressing scenes of the French Reign of Terror. . . . Mr. DRYDEN is seized and possessed of a great legal mind. . . . He made up his mind that something had to be done to check the encroachments of a licentious press. He called to us, breathing hard through his teeth. His complexion was that of the ashes of a five-cent cigar. . . . He indicated . . . that nothing short of an enormous libel suit would produce the necessary vindication.

For the life of us we can't see why a newspaper should be charged $15,000 for intimating that a young, unmarried man sent a gushy note to a charming damsel. . . . We do not charge that Mr. LANSING wrote the note. In fact it would have added to his literary reputation to have been suspected of authorship. . . . Counselor DRYDEN, in convincing us of the innocence of his client, assured us that he didn't think Mr. LANSING had sufficient intellect to write such a letter. . . . At the very worst it can only be said that we caused Mr. LANSING to appear ridiculous for a few hours. . . . We have certainly inflicted no permanent damage on him, for thousands of people now know him to be an innocent, steady-going youth who never heard of him before, and who would not have known him from his Satanic Majesty's off ox but for our little *faux pas*.[18]

Even more representative of the new style was the paper's handling of a similar incident, this one involving Miss Nellie Haseltine, known in Eastern watering places as well as in the Middle West as the "belle of St. Louis." Endowed with an ambitious mother, she had achieved nationwide notoriety a short while before at White Sulphur Springs in Virginia as the gay young fiancée of an elderly bachelor, Samuel Tilden.[19] In the summer of 1881 she became the subject of what the *Post-Dispatch* captioned A SOCIAL SCANDAL. As usual, the subdecks told the story, which ran to four columns: "The Belle of St. Louis Reported 'Mashed' on a Chorus Singer," "The Lady's Brother and Lover Thrash and Cowhide the Poor Troubadour," "A Retraction Forced From Him and Photographs and Billet-Doux Confiscated," "Mr. Fred. Paramore Makes an Official Statement of the Case." [20] This piece received greater prominence (for that day) than a story concerning President Garfield, lying mortally wounded from an assassin's bullet. From the standpoint of reader interest, however, the paper rated the story accurately; a boost in circulation of several hundred copies accompanied the Haseltine sensation.[21]

The *Post-Dispatch* pulled out all the stops for this affair. Prominent and flashy heads accompanied each installment; when the obviously

---

[18] *Ibid.*, June 29, 1881. The case was settled out of court. *Ibid.*, July 8, 1881.
[19] Cleveland Amory, *The Last Resorts* (New York, 1948), pp. 457-58.
[20] *Post-Dispatch*, Aug. 10, 1881.
[21] The paper's circulation enjoyed a rise of 700 copies when the story first broke. It is significant that the *Post-Dispatch* carefully noted this. *Ibid.*, Aug. 10, 1881, Sept. 10, 1881.

snooty Haseltines sought to blame a servant for their daughter's indiscretions, the paper sent a reporter to interview the maid, giving her side of the affair under WAS IT THE LAUNDRY MAID? When the offended chorus singer sued the family for administering a cowhiding, the head was $10,000 FLIRTATION; the matter of the authorship of a "mash" note was gaily discussed under WHO WROTE IT? And the climax of the story, a hushed-up, out-of-court settlement, was trumpeted to the public under the *Post-Dispatch's* biggest and blackest type, LOVE AND LUCRE. The subheads were just as sensational: "Amweg Happy and His Lawyers Merry Over Their Harvest," "Nellie's Papa Pays $1,000 and Costs For His Daughter's Flirtation," "How a Belle's Constant Desire for Notoriety Terminates." [22] Editorially, the *Post-Dispatch* drove the point home for its plebeian readers. An explanation by the flirtatious belle's suitor as to why he had thrashed the "uppity" Amweg prompted the remark: "One may imagine the thanks of the lower orders to whom this official statement was addressed for the brief glimpse given there of how the shoddy aristocracy avenges itself on its traducers." [23] And recalling the famous Tilden episode in the ambitious young lady's past, the paper concocted a special dispatch from Gramercy Park, New York, captioned COULD IT BE TRUE?, which read:

> When the news of the Uhrig's Cave sensation in St. Louis was brought out to Gramercy Park this morning Mr. Tilden was sitting with his feet in a mustard bath, eating apples. On hearing the story he rushed to the telephone and ordered his broker to sell every share of stock in his possession. He is converting his estate entirely into money, and will leave on the 8:10 train for the White Sulphur [where Miss Haseltine had retreated].[24]

These exploitations of the didoes of high society set the tone of the *Post-Dispatch* towards the city's West End select. Gone was the old respectful tone of St. Louis journals. Any indiscretion or pretension of the exclusive set was grist for headlines, illustrations, waggish copy, sarcastic editorials. Even the barest rumor or the slightest affair was likely to receive front page attention. A story which the paper itself labeled "Much Ado About Nothing," was accorded a full column. It concerned the rumor that two young bloods had been bounced from a high-toned club for outrageous conduct. The matter received typical *Post-Dispatch* treatment. The young men were disciplined

---

22 *Ibid.*, Aug. 11, 1881, Aug. 12, 1881, Aug. 19, 1881, Sept. 7, 1881.
23 *Ibid.*, Aug. 11, 1881.
24 *Ibid.*, Aug. 12, 1881.

for bringing chorus girls into the charmed circle of the West End Club. The crime was of so heinous a nature that full two weeks' suspension was adjudged against the offenders. It was not claimed . . . that anything wrong had been done; it was simply the shock to society that had been communicated by the atrocious introduction of chorus girls into the sacred precincts of the West End Club.[25]

Another thin event involved a prominent pastor who had unintentionally offended a lady on a streetcar. It received sensational play under ROCK AND RYE: "Rev. Dr. Geo. A. Lofton Goes Upon a Saintly Spree," "He is Said to Have Been Intoxicated and Grossly Insulted a Lady," "A Terrible Clerical Scandal Involving the Pastor of the Third Baptist Church," "Gen. Sherman Views the Reverend Gentleman's Escapade—A Shocking Story of a Divine." A close reading of the piece disclosed that the Reverend Lofton had been ill and on doctor's orders had taken an alcoholic stimulant, and on the streetcar he had inadvertently breathed into the face of a woman who sat next to him. She moved to another seat. This was all, but the *Post-Dispatch* parlayed it into a two and a half column article.[26] The paper sought to justify itself editorially:

As a newspaper we seek to deal impartially with all classes. The higher the position of a man the more society demands of him. It is a species of cruel unfairness in a newspaper to publish offenses of PAT. DONAHUE, the drayman, and cover up the open, public escapades of a rich man or a high exemplar. We seek to deal with all affairs of this kind without malice.[27]

Pastors were often the subject of sensations. A Catholic priest was suspended by the Bishop of St. Louis for a *Post-Dispatch* story based on sheer rumor. Frank Bigney, one of the paper's best sleuths, discovered the priest was suspected of fathering a child by "a young girl of much personal beauty." This was the celebrated "Gleason case," which reverberated in St. Louis newspaper circles for a long time as a particularly fine example of journalistic enterprise.[28] "What limits, in respect to such matters, ought newspapers to observe?" exclaimed a dismayed society magazine after a spicy *Post-Dispatch* story.[29] The

25 *Ibid.*, July 19, 1882.
26 *Ibid.*, May 16, 1882.
27 *Ibid.*
28 *Ibid.*, June 1, 1882; *The Journalist*, Nov. 13, 1886. The *Post-Dispatch* gained more than a thousand copies in circulation the day the Gleason story broke. *Post-Dispatch*, Feb. 15, 1883.
29 *Spectator*, Nov. 26, 1881.

same publication supplied its own answer a year later when booming *Post-Dispatch* circulation proved the sales value of scandals:

> Of course, the public which loudly condemns sensationalism ought not to like it, ought to put the seal of its condemnation on sensationalism by not reading the papers which engage in it. . . . But this is what they do not do, and the course of events clearly shows that if there is any guilt in sensationalism the public are more than guilty accomplices of it. . . . It is the sensational papers which are most widely read, which are crowded with advertising, which have a jaunty air of success about them, and which flourish . . . with an assurance which asserts that sensationalism is the coming card, and that the public like it.[30]

Even normal society news was handled with a new irreverence. The sacrosanct Veiled Prophet festivities, an annual pageant and ball staged by the city's elite, always was treated deferentially by the local press until Johnny Jennings discovered its innermost secret, the plan of the Veiled Prophet parade, which the *Post-Dispatch* triumphantly published on the front page. This got to be an annual feat by the *Post-Dispatch,* a tribute to the ingenuity of City Editor Moore who refused bribes of free tickets from the Veiled Prophet Association if he would desist.[31] The exclusive Home Circle and Imperial Clubs, *creme de la creme* of local society, including scions of old French families, also became the subject of *Post-Dispatch* gossip. A story captioned PARISIAN ROBES detailed the "worry and vexations" of a debutante and her mother when they attempted to smuggle expensive clothes from Europe for a coming-out party under the aegis of the Home Circle. "The picture is a sad one, and the young lady readers of the POST-DISPATCH can understand the horror of it," intoned the paper.[32]

But the *Post-Dispatch* by no means confined itself to West End gossip. The paper made use of wire stories, utilizing to the full scandalous divorces, infidelities and court cases wherever they occurred. Nor were the lower classes exempt. Many tales of sex and sin were prominently written up. DUPED AND DESERTED, "A Story of Man's Inhumanity to Woman," "How a Ruined and Discarded Girl Attempted Self-Destruction" was a frequent theme, as was RESCUED FROM RUIN, "A Denver Maiden Taken From a Disreputable House" "In This City and Returned Home With Her Father."[33] Altogether, the *Post-Dispatch* became more and more a scandal sheet.

---

[30] *Ibid.,* Jan. 27, 1883.
[31] *Ibid.,* Sept. 15, 1883, Sept. 6, 1884, Aug. 31, 1889.
[32] *Post-Dispatch,* March 15, 1882.
[33] *Ibid.,* Aug. 18, 1882, Aug. 23, 1882.

The *Post-Dispatch's* reputation as a lively newspaper was not due just to its use of social sensations. It exploited what might be called "normally" sensational items, lavishing considerable ingenuity upon them. Illustrations of murderers and their victims were used more and more, and Henry Moore, the resourceful city editor, acquired a reputation for his ability to get scoops. The Zou Watkins case was typical. Zou Watkins was a visitor in St. Louis who disappeared one night while mailing a letter. The *Post-Dispatch* ran a cut of her, carved from a likeness held by the police—in hopes, the paper said, that someone might recognize it. A few days later the body was discovered in the river. Moore received the information at 7:30 p.m., sent a reporter to investigate, and had an extra on the street at ten o'clock that night. "This was quick work," said the *Spectator* admiringly. The extra earned for the *Post-Dispatch* a boost of 5,000 in circulation for the day.[34]

Although the paper became more and more absorbed in local news, events of larger importance were not ignored; here, too, it displayed such enterprise that the *Spectator* exclaimed, "ideas certainly . . . flow with rapidity" from the *Post-Dispatch*.[35] For Pulitzer was a sophisticated man of the world, intellectually far more interested in affairs of importance than he was in scandal stories. Now and then he himself contributed signed articles on events and personalities of national significance encountered during frequent trips to the East.[36] The biggest event of 1881 was the assassination of President Garfield, which the *Post-Dispatch* went to great lengths to exploit and which paid important dividends in circulation. Like other journals all over the country, the *Post-Dispatch* received the news of Garfield's shooting incredulously, playing it up under its largest type: GARFIELD'S LIFE.[37] The paper's press groaned under the load of supplying "all the orders that are pouring in on us for extra papers," and it was far into the night before a record run of 31,000 copies—two and a half times the normal total—was printed. *Post-Dispatch* editors were dazed.[38]

For the rest of the hot summer the *Post-Dispatch* recorded the President's slow decline. His temperature could almost be gauged by the number of subdecks over the daily account. At first there was WHITE-WINGED HOPE for recovery, but soon it became evident that he

[34] *Ibid.*, May 27, 1882, May 30, 1882, June 5, 1882; *Spectator*, June 3, 1882.
[35] *Spectator*, Feb. 3, 1883.
[36] Reynolds, "Joseph Pulitzer," pp. 73-76.
[37] *Post-Dispatch*, July 2, 1881.
[38] *Ibid.*, July 2, 1881, July 22, 1881. Interestingly, the *Post-Dispatch* commented on how rapidly and mysteriously the news of the shooting spread: "Everywhere the rumor preceded the exact news. . . . The first dispatch from Washington had not been opened in the POST-DISPATCH office when a telephone inquiry about the President's health was received from East St. Louis." *Ibid.*, July 2, 1881.

was engaged in a grim BATTLE FOR LIFE.[39] The paper set itself to wring all possible news value from the story. In August reporters interviewed local physicians as to the President's chances and ran with the story a detailed drawing of his body, startling in that Victorian age, showing the position of the pistol ball, the wound and the vital organs.[40] More striking was the fearless—and sensational—interpretation of bulletins from the President's bedside. By late summer it was becoming apparant that the optimistic stream of statements from the White House was hiding the true situation. The *Post-Dispatch* became suspicious and began to make its own diagnoses from the published facts. "The Doctors' Bulletin and Talk, as Usual, Rose-Colored," declared one headline; editorially the paper commented:

> The condition of President GARFIELD is serious, if not critical. . . . Those who accept the predictions of the President's physicians and believe the hundred-times repeated tale of his certain recovery should remember that even great physicians may deliberately conclude to tell white lies to save a mortally wounded patient. It is well understood that the bulletins are watched and read by the President. . . .
>
> This of course is simply our own theory, but we believe there are numerous strong indications pointing to it.

The paper stressed particularly the Chief Executive's pulse, which was an abnormally high 104, indicating a "burning fever." [41] Becoming more and more critical of the doctors' "white lies," the *Post-Dispatch* in mid-August headlined its opinion: HE IS DYING, and Joseph Pulitzer rushed to Long Branch, New Jersey, where Garfield had been removed, to report firsthand.[42] In characteristically rasping tones Pulitzer told his readers that "the President could hardly have selected a worse time to come here. . . . When I say that it is as oppressively hot at Long Branch as any July day in St. Louis this will be plainly understood." [43] In signed dispatches under such heads as THE TRUTH TOLD, he attacked the cheerful official bulletins:

> There is no doubt about it. The President has chronic blood poisoning. Unless his blood can be cured he can not be saved. I said this over a week ago and I repeat it. . . . The physicians and bulletins and reporters have lied for days and weeks and months denying this fact. . . . Even the official bulletin this morning

---

[39] *Ibid.*, July 5, 1881, July 7, 1881.
[40] *Ibid.*, Aug. 3, 1881.
[41] *Ibid.*, Aug. 8, 1881.
[42] *Ibid.*, Aug. 11, 1881, Aug. 12, 1881.
[43] *Ibid.*, Sept. 7, 1881; Reynolds, pp. 74-75.

admits at last that blood poisoning exists when in a roundabout way it refers to the septic accidents which have for weeks complicated . . . the case. I suppose the abscess on the lung is one of these septic accidents. . . . The best sign of this morning is the absence of Dr. Bliss [the chief physician], who has gone to New York. But unfortunately he will be back soon. . . . The official bulletins are entirely untrustworthy, Dr. Bliss' particularly. Everybody here knows that he is a reckless liar.[44]

Five days later Garfield was dead. The edition which carried the sad news also published large cuts of both the martyred President and his successor, surmounted by a large shield and other national emblems. The paper sold as heavily as the issue that carried the shooting in July.[45] A long editorial, written by John Cockerill, appraised Garfield in dignified and friendly terms. In the same issue the paper defended itself from the charge of sensationalism for having desired "to prematurely dispose of the sufferer." Characteristically, the *Post-Dispatch* declared

we simply endeavored . . . as we always do, to tell the truth. In common with every good citizen we hoped and prayed for the restoration of the President, but we were not blinded by the bulletins of the physicians. . . . We went behind the bulletins. . . . Our predictions, we are sorry to say, have nearly all been verified.

There followed the bizarre trial of Guiteau. The most spectacular of the paper's efforts in this connection was published following his conviction. An issue carrying two dozen woodcuts was carefully "prepared by special artists" for the *Post-Dispatch,* portraying "every personage in the historic trial," together with scenes of the trial itself and various stages in the life of the defendant. It was the paper's first attempt to give a really comprehensive pictorial report of a news event of the kind that weeklies like *Frank Leslie's* had been doing for some years.[46] The results were highly gratifying; the *Post-Dispatch* gained 8,000 in sales for the day.[47] On the day of the execution the paper ran a two-column cut of the condemned man on page one, "as he appeared to-day on the scaffold." [48] Again the *Post-Dispatch* broke all records;

---

[44] *Post-Dispatch*, Sept. 8, 1881, Sept. 15, 1881. Oddly enough, editorials written in St. Louis by John Cockerill mildly defended the President's physicians.

[45] Exact figures are unavailable, but the *Post-Dispatch* mentions running its press until 7 p.m. *Ibid.*, Sept. 20, 1881.

[46] Mott, *American Journalism*, pp. 378-79.

[47] The paper's circulation jumped from 20,360 copies to 28,580. *Post-Dispatch,* Feb. 11, 1882.

[48] This, of course, was clearly impossible in a day long before phototelegraphic transmission of pictures. But the cut had terrific appeal. *Ibid.*, June 30, 1882.

its circulation reached the truly astounding figure of 45,720 copies.[49]

Before Guiteau's case ran its course in Washington, the attention of *Post-Dispatch* readers was suddenly captured by news which broke closer to home. In April 1882 the saga of the James Boys came to a climax in the sparsely settled border country on the other side of the state. The murder of Jesse and the subsequent surrender of his brother, Frank, electrified all Missourians. The James Boys had been terrorizing Western Missouri for years, but Robin Hood-like, their depredations had been committed against railroads, those accoutrements of advancing civilization, much to the delight of the borderlanders. The eastern part of the state, however, especially St. Louis, was angered by these raids, damaging as they were both to business and the reputation of Missouri. Editorially, the *Post-Dispatch,* representing the urban middle classes, was one with other St. Louis journals in vigorously condemning the James Boys. But in ex-Confederate outstate areas the brothers had become a symbol of the Lost Cause. Thus, the destruction of the gang aroused once again the old passions between rural Missouri and the growing city classes and threatened to split asunder the state's unwieldy Democratic majority.[50]

Late in the afternoon of April 3, 1882, the *Post-Dispatch* received a telegram from a reporter in Kansas City:

> Police Commissioner Craig has just received authentic information that Jesse James was killed near St. Joseph at 12 o'clock today. No particulars.

This bare intelligence was rushed onto the street in an extra edition under the simple heading, JESSE JAMES. That night Pulitzer and his editors busily assembled five cuts of the leading figures of the gang, which were published the next day with a jumble of confused reports from Kansas City under A DASTARD'S DEED. As usual, the subheads gave the report: "Cold-Blooded Treachery at Last Conquered Jesse James," "The Noted Border Bandit Shot Like a Dog From Behind" "By a Man Who Was Eating His Bread and Was His Friend," "By a Coward Traitor's Hand Missouri Vanquishes Jesse James," "Bob Ford Shoots Jesse Through the Head." [51]

---

[49] *Ibid.,* July 1, 1882. The *Globe-Democrat,* similarly exploiting the execution, reached a figure of more than 50,000 for the day.

[50] See William A. Settle, Jr., "The James Boys and Missouri Politics," *Missouri Historical Review,* XXXVI (July 1942), 412-29, for political repercussions of the James Boys issue. The best accounts of the James Boys story are by two one-time *Post-Dispatch* reporters: Robertus Love, *The Rise and Fall of Jesse James* (New York, 1926); and Homer Croy, *Jesse James Was My Neighbor* (New York, 1949). See also, Carl W. Breihan, *The Complete and Authentic Life of Jesse James* (New York, n.d.).

[51] *Post-Dispatch,* April 4, 1882.

During the next few days the *Post-Dispatch* published additional pictures of leading personalities in the murder story from woodcuts made specially for the paper, together with a diagram of the house where Jesse James was killed. One of the cuts was a portrait of Jesse's mother, the indomitable frontier woman, Zeralda Samuels. This was run with an exclusive interview obtained by a *Post-Dispatch* reporter when he boldly hired a hack to escort Mrs. Samuels and James's distraught widow from the railroad station when they arrived at Independence. It was a scoop envied by all other papers.[52]

Editorially the paper's course was equally sensational. It charged Governor Crittenden with complicity in a despicable crime—the line followed by the rural papers. The Governor had offered a large reward for Jesse James, dead or alive. In part, no doubt, Pulitzer reacted on the basis of principle—even a criminal should have the right to a trial —but he was also well aware of the publicity that would accrue to his paper if he joined in the hue and cry against Crittenden. Also, by 1882, Pulitzer had conceived a bitter dislike of him, and the James assassination was a good club to beat him with.

> It must not be thought for one moment that we have a particle of kindly sentiment for the late Mr. JAMES. He was a murdering, thieving bandit and a shame and injury to the State. We have no sort of patience with the weak-minded people who regard him as a hero or sympathize with his family on account of his fate. We simply claim that, as a criminal, he was entitled to be adjudged and dealt with under the laws. . . . The State has been disgraced by the brutal and barbarous manner of his taking off. In the estimation of civilized States we have suffered more by this piece of Executive Assassination than we ever did on account of the JAMES brothers.[53]

Suspecting Pulitzer's sincerity in working his paper up to such a frenzy that before long it was demanding the impeachment of "His Leniency," [54] the Cincinnati *Commercial* cynically commented that "the St. Louis *Post-Dispatch* has broken out afresh on St. James. We suppose its weeping and wailing must be popular. Ink and tears, type and pocket handkerchiefs go together." [55]

The *Post-Dispatch* almost as violently attacked the pro-James partisans outstate. Particularly it assailed Major John N. Edwards,

---

[52] *Ibid.*, April 5, 1882, April 8, 1882.

[53] *Ibid.*, April 10, 1882.

[54] *Ibid.*, April 10, 1882, April 12, 1882, April 13, 1882.

[55] Crittenden dismissed *Post-Dispatch* charges as "for sensational purposes only." *Ibid.*, April 12, 1882, April 13, 1882. See also, Crittenden's own defense in H. H. Crittenden, *The Crittenden Memoirs* (New York, 1936).

editor of the Sedalia *Democrat* and spokesman of the extremist ex-Confederates who called on "the surviving comrades of the bandits to turn themselves loose on the FORDS." [56] To him the *Post-Dispatch* paid its respects, concluding:

> Of course the Sedalia *Democrat's* wrath is bound to hurt the State. The Democratic party will be held responsible for the *Democrat's* wild utterances. It will be claimed that Maj. ED-WARDS has voiced the true sentiment of the Confederate Democracy of our "robber-ridden State". . . .

> Between CRITTENDEN and EDWARDS, both law-defying in the extreme, between assassinating a bandit and assassinating the remnants of the reputation of this State, Missouri will soon have a very peculiar name.[57]

This spectacular course continued unabated for the entire month of April and, more sporadically, on into the summer and fall. It was climaxed by the surrender of Jesse's brother, Frank, an event, however, in which the paper was badly scooped.[58] The James saga, together with the sensational methods applied to reporting it, brought the paper enjoyable dividends in circulation. In April 1882 it achieved its greatest sustained advance, a boost in readership from 20,000 to 26,600 copies daily.[59]

National and regional events of this sort provided a stimulus to circulation, but the *Post-Dispatch* carefully noted that, in general, news from distant places failed to attract St. Louisans. This must have been something of a disappointment to Joseph Pulitzer, who personally reported the Star Route trials in Washington and Conkling's fight for reelection to the Senate in New York. In addition, in 1882 the *Post-Dispatch* leased a special wire to connect it with New York to supplement Associated Press dispatches. The paper boasted that it received daily 3,000 to 4,000 words of foreign and national news.[60] Yet, as the first big war story carried by the *Post-Dispatch* showed, most significant news had little appeal despite the lengths to which the paper went in reporting it. In 1882, under SHOT AND SHELL, it published news from London that the British fleet was bombarding Alexandria, beginning a struggle by Great Britain to establish a pro-

---

[56] *Post-Dispatch*, April 14, 1882. For Major Edwards' inflammatory course as the spokesman of the James partisans, see Love, pp. 293-99.

[57] *Post-Dispatch*, April 14, 1882.

[58] Frank O'Neil of the *Republican* was the go-between in arranging Frank James' surrender. Soon after—characteristic of Joseph Pulitzer—O'Neil was persuaded to come to the *Post-Dispatch*.

[59] Memorandum [1906], Pulitzer Papers (CU).

[60] *Post-Dispatch*, Dec. 4, 1882, Dec. 14, 1882.

tectorate over Egypt and gain control of the Suez Canal. So important did Pulitzer consider the news that the paper ran a three-column map of the theater of war—the Nile Estuary and Suez—which, it proudly said, "has been engraved especially for the POST-DIS-PATCH." [61] Throughout the summer and fall large headlines carried the news of the war: IN FLAMES, "The City of Alexandria Given Over to Pillage," "Fire Devastating the Egyptian Port—The Bedouins Looting," "A Night of Horror and a Fight for Life," "Massacre of Europeans by the Alexandrians," "British Sailors and Marines Landed From the Fleet." [62] In September the paper reported under its heaviest type that the Egyptian defenses had collapsed. Next day the *Post-Dispatch* commented disgustedly:

> The Battle of Tel-e-Kebir was the most important to us of any that had occurred since the Franco-Prussian war, for it involved a nation to which we are allied by blood, language and commerce. The fate of 25,000 English troops . . . depended on the turn of this struggle and yet it created less sensation in St. Louis than an ordinary item of local news. [63]

Pulitzer's constant concern over what sort of news attracted circulation was often reflected in editorial comment. A lengthy editorial in 1882 noted the findings of the New York *Sun*—a journal Pulitzer greatly admired—on this point. At the end of it the *Post-Dispatch* remarked:

> As an afternoon paper having large street sales, the POST-DISPATCH is also largely affected by the character of its news specialties. Of course our floating readers are not moved by the same springs that touch those of the metropolis. As a rule political events do not affect our sales favorably. Next to the assassination of President GARFIELD our greatest increase has been by a local hanging. Our people are not easily worked up by a sporting event, but they take considerable interest in a "social sensation." [64]

The paper's bearish attitude towards sporting news changed shortly after this. The reason was clear: such events in 1882 and 1883 began

---

[61] *Ibid.*, July 11, 1882.

[62] *Ibid.*, July 13, 1882.

[63] *Ibid.*, Sept. 14, 1882.

[64] The *Sun* observed that in its experience elections were great circulation getters. Riots, fires, crime also produced gains, but only if they were local. It, too, observed that foreign news, even the Franco-Prussian War, produced little interest among New York readers. The *Sun* concluded that "our home politics are the most profitable news theme, and that next to politics athletic sports seem to command the interest of the greatest number of occasional newspaper readers." *Ibid.*, June 21, 1882.

to interest St. Louisans. Hitherto, at best there had been only a weekly catch-all sporting column, and even this was dropped in 1881. The only exception had been the opening of the racing season each spring at the Cote Brilliante race track in the western part of the city, at which time the *Post-Dispatch* published racing extras with the latest results telegraphed to the office. But racing was not so much a sporting, as a social, affair which the *Post-Dispatch* exploited by paying much attention to who appeared with whom and what the ladies wore at the track.

Boxing news also was played up, but again more because of extraneous attributes than for its attractions as a sporting event. At the time, pugilism was not quite proper and was outlawed in many states, including Missouri. Thus, boxing matches were in the same class as cockfights and dog matches, which the paper also ferreted out and played up as sensational items. Of prizefighting news, the paper had this to say:

> It may appear to some of our readers that we are having a little too much prize-ring literature in our paper. The same thought occurs to us. Still we endeavor at all times to keep up with the news procession. Prizefighting is coarse and demoralizing and . . . vulgar; still some of the people like to read about them, and we endeavor to supply the demand as best we can. It is distasteful to us to print "Society News" and vulgar intelligence of various kinds, but in our journalistic capacity we follow ST. PAUL'S advice and endeavor to be all things to all grown-up men. When there are prizefights hovering around the horizon our lady-readers will have to excuse us.[65]

The first illustration used in connection with a sporting event was a large cut of the Sullivan-Ryan match in New Orleans in 1882. An unkind bystander thought it could as well have been used to picture "a county fair, or an escape from a penitentiary," indicating the primitive quality of newspaper illustration from woodcuts, but the *Post-Dispatch* was finding them profitable.[66]

The increasing space devoted to baseball in the *Post-Dispatch* after 1882 was the best index to the paper's revised opinion of sports as a circulation-getter. Baseball had no other recommendation than its growing popularity as "the only field sport that interests the masses." [67] Only recently the paper had observed that in St. Louis "no one appears to think much of base ball. Probably the day of the sphere

---

[65] *Ibid.*, Feb. 8, 1882.
[66] *Ibid.; Hornet*, Feb. 18, 1882.
[67] *Spectator*, Nov. 17, 1883.

has passed." [68] But early in 1881, a picturesque German brewmaster, Chris Von Der Ahe, with the help of Al Spink, the comatose Brown Stockings; that summer the sport revived. The *Post-Dispatch* did not react immediately to this change of affairs, in part because games played at refurbished Sportsman's Park on Grand Avenue started at four in the afternoon, too late for the paper's last edition. But the large crowds of rabid fans soon brought out its enterprise. In the spring of 1883, when, under the leadership of a rookie from Dubuque named Comiskey, it became evident that the Brown Stockings were in the fight for the championship of the new American Association, the *Post-Dispatch* took to publishing late sporting extras carrying the latest scores direct from the ball park and lengthy writeups much like today's sports copy. It estimated there were 30,000 fans in St. Louis who

> read base ball scores with more interest than they do the pro-
> ceedings of the Phoenix Park assassin trials. . . . Even the ladies
> are enthusiasts on the subject, and the presence of 1,500 of the
> fair creatures in the grandstand on Thursday [shows it]. They
> are perhaps a little obscure in the technicalities of the game, and
> apt to confound the left fielder and the pitcher, but, bless their
> dear hearts, they are loyal to St. Louis. . . . A glance at the
> audience on any fine day . . . will reveal the presence of represen-
> tation of all respectable classes. Telegraph operators, printers who
> work at night, men of leisure . . . , men of capital, bank clerks
> who get away at 3 p.m., real estate men who can steal the declin-
> ing hours of the afternoon, and employes of the theaters, police-
> men and firemen on their day off . . . clerks in a position to leave
> their stores with a notice to the bookkeeper that they will not be
> back to-day; call-board operators who need recreation after the
> experience of the noon hour . . . workingmen with lame hands;
> butchers, bakers and candlestick makers; mechanics out on strike;
> lawyers in droves, an occasional Circuit judge, city officials . . .
> and last, but not least, doctors.[69]

With such a potential readership, it was hardly surprising that a trade magazine noted late in 1883 that "the *Post-Dispatch* has latterly given considerable space to sporting matters, and in Saunders [Sanders]

[68] *Post Dispatch*, May 8, 1880. The most authoritative work on the history of baseball in St. Louis is Lieb, *St. Louis Cardinals*. See also, Harold Seymour, "St. Louis and the Union Baseball War," *Missouri Historical Review*, LI (April 1957), 257-69.

[69] *Post-Dispatch*, May 19, 1883, May 8, 1966. Al Spink is credited with naming Sportsman's Park. It remained the scene of major league baseball in St. Louis from Spink's day to the spring of 1966 when the Cardinals moved to a new municipal stadium.

and Magner they have two brilliant writers, who are aggressive according to the rule of their force. . . ." [70]

The new emphasis on sporting events was not the only aspect of a
general growth in the paper's coverage of local news. Borrowing from
the *Globe-Democrat*, it established a regular railroad column in 1882.
A Merchants' Exchange column, which had appeared irregularly before, now also became a daily feature when George Kelley, an experienced reporter of commercial news, was hired. [71] At about the same
time a column of religious news made its appearance in the large
Saturday edition. It was written by Gay Waters, pastor of the Fourth
Christian Church, and telegraph editor of the *Post-Dispatch*. [72] In part,
the proliferation of news features reflected enlarged space; by 1883,
although the daily was still eight to ten pages, the Saturday was often
sixteen. In order to emphasize the newsiness of the paper, the editors
also experimented sporadically with a more modern makeup, clearing the first page of advertisements on several occasions. [73]

The exploitation of news—searching for the kinds of news that
would attract wide readership and presenting it in eye-catching fashion—was not the only preoccupation of *Post-Dispatch* editors between
1881 and 1883. Building on the lessons of the first two years, they
continued to liven the paper's "miscellany" with feature columns and
entertainment matter which also were designed to have wide popular
appeal. Here, too, more and more emphasis was placed on the local
scene. Whereas in 1881 the *Post-Dispatch* still prided itself on its
exchange page, filled with human interest items clipped from other
journals, in 1882 this feature was gone. [74] In its place were articles
written by the paper's own staff and invariably upon St. Louis subjects. Moreover, they were usually handled in the paper's new style
of sensationalism: entertaining, sometimes more than a bit spicy and
often startling, articles which revealed, frequently in a garish light,
aspects of the city's life little known to the paper's readers.

Articles with a touch of raciness, like one headed SOILED DOVES, were
common. "Nearly Three Hundred of Them Gathered Under One

---

[70] *American Journalist*, Oct. 1883.

[71] *Gould's St. Louis Directory*, 1881, p. 604. Kelley remained as *Post-Dispatch*
Commercial Editor for many years. His brother, James, became Livestock Reporter.

[72] *Gould's St. Louis Directory*, 1884, p. 1,148; *Post-Dispatch*, July 7, 1883; *American
Journalist*, Oct. 1883.

[73] Clearing the front page of ads usually happened if an important news story
was published, or in the summer, when advertising was light, especially during
1881 and 1882. It was not done frequently enough, however, to establish a definite
trend. Late in 1890 ads finally disappeared from the front page.

[74] In 1881 the paper remarked that "we give the second [exchange] page a great
deal of editorial attention. Everything that appears there is culled with great care"
from other journals. *Post-Dispatch*, Aug. 4, 1881.

Roof," said the subheads. "A Visit to the House of the Good Shepherd," "How the Work of Reforming Fallen Women is Done."[75] Another, also aimed at the prurient curiosities of conventional readers, was captioned ARTISTS' MODELS. The handling of this subject was characteristic of the new style:

> The demand in St. Louis studios for models, male or female, is scarcely as active as the supply. Artists are flooded with applications . . . from young men and women who are anxious to pose for a dollar a sitting. . . . A sentiment of false shame was developed in the higher circles here about a year ago when it became known that studies from the nude female figure were in progress at Washington University. The pressure brought to bear upon Chancellor Eliot . . . was so great that he vetoed the pursuit of further study in that direction. . . .
>
> A full length picture was recently taken here by a well-known artist who studied from the nude. . . . The figure, a young, fair-haired, blue-eyed German girl of shapely proportions, was admirably adapted for the subject. She was accompanied to the studio daily by a relative, and it may be said that prudish sentimentality did not in this instance interfere with the artist's work. Studies from the nude are as necessary to an artist as to a physician, and they are conducted without the shadow of a suggestion of indelicacy. Highly respectable women and young girls in this city offer their services in this regard. . . . Some very deserving men and women have sat in St. Louis studios from time to time, among them the widow of an army officer and the daughter of a deceased merchant. . . .[76]

Another feature story often run was a type that pulled at the heartstrings of a sentimental age. Of this kind was a story headed BE A GOOD GIRL, which began:

> The doorkeeper of the jail rapped his large key against the iron door yesterday to warn the visitors that the hour had expired. The last of the friends of prisoners had passed out, when a little girl plainly but comfortably dressed presented a pass to Doorkeeper King and was admitted to the screen. William Erb, the doomed wife-killer, walked across the stone floor to the wire screen, where the child awaited him. The girl was Erb's daughter. . . .
>
> Kneeling on one knee, Erb listened to the child's prattle, absently looking at the little face. Then he straightened up,

---

[75] *Ibid.*, March 15, 1882.
[76] *Ibid.*, April 12, 1881.

saw it was growing dark, and gently told his little girl to go home and to "be a good little girl."

As the child walked up the iron steps to the outer gate, Erb pressed his face against the screen and watched his daughter as the large door was swung behind her.[77]

SHE LOVED HIM, another story was headed, "Although He Wore a Convict's Suit," "How an Imprisoned Tenor Desolated a Female Heart at Chester, Ill." [78] Human interest items like this were frequent, as was one captioned A SAD STORY, which told how a country youth, a stranger to the hardness of the city, sought vainly for days to find work and, finally, in despair, broke a street lamp in order to be sent to the workhouse for food and shelter.[79] Contrasts between social groups and the blindness of the respectable classes were highlighted: ENVIRONED BY VICE, "The Y.M.C.A. Block Completely Given Over to Sin," "Eight Dens and Forty Inmates on the Block," "The Association Evinces the Utmost Apathy, and Will Do Nothing—Interviews with Officers, Etc." [80]

Many articles simply appealed to conventional middle class interests. HOW TO SUCCEED, "A Singular Contribution to the Literature of Money-Making," "Mr. E. C. Simmons Tells What He Knows About Getting On in the World," "A Receipt Whereby Every Man May Become His Own Capitalist—Some Breezy Views on the Whys and Wherefores of Commercial Success" by one of the city's successful merchants.[81] Or—and the slightly risqué touch was typical—SKIN BEAUTIFYING: "The Enormous Demand of St. Louis Ladies for Complexion Treatment," "Over Two Thousand Complexions, Treated in Fifteen Months," " 'Bosom Beautifiers'—Method of Treating the Skin of the Face," "A St. Louis Dermatologist Who Has Speedily Won Wealth and Retired." [82] Prying into the private lives of the rich was a frequent theme, shown by such features as a list of millionaires in St. Louis and A RELIGIOUS ROSTER of the elite.[83]

The most significant feature articles, however, were those which gave readers a look at the hardships of the poor. There were many of these in 1882 and 1883. Partly, the paper—perhaps stealing a march on Scripps' *Chronicle*—was seeking to appeal to the working classes in its effort to increase circulation, but to a large extent it simply desired to startle St. Louisans, most of whom were of a type scarcely

[77] *Ibid.*, Dec. 17, 1881.
[78] *Ibid.*, June 19, 1882.
[79] *Ibid.*, Dec. 14, 1881.
[80] *Ibid.*, June 1, 1882.
[81] *Ibid.*, Feb. 18, 1883.
[82] *Ibid.*, July 29, 1882.
[83] *Ibid.*, Feb. 12, 1881, March 26, 1881.

aware of the seamier sides of city life. FIGHTING FOR FOOD headlined a story that described working conditions in the city. It was subdecked: "The War of the Wage Earning Class for Subsistence," "$472 the Annual Wages of Workingmen and Their Expenses $469," "They Only Spend $2 to $25 per Year for 'Recreation,'" "Out of the Above Earnings Families of Five Persons Must Live." [84] The story began:

> People who attend fashionable churches and who never had a struggle in life shudder at the increase of crime without ever thinking how much of it is the result of misery. Men grow disgusted with labor when the result of it is only such that by assiduous attention they can only acquire board and clothing.

Written by reporters who themselves had come from the lower classes, these articles portrayed the plight of the poor with sympathy. Another of this kind was an exposure of child labor in St. Louis industry. TINY TOILERS it was headed, and subdecked: "Little Girls Who Work in St. Louis Factories," "A Tour Through the Tobacco, Match and Other Factories," "A Sad Picture of the Lives of Poor Juvenile Workers," "Over 3,000 Under Ten Years of Age Toiling Eleven Hours a Day," "The Poisoned Atmosphere the Children Work in for $3 a Week." [85] The lead paragraph was typical and set the tone for the piece:

> Young ladies who would not wear a $400 sealskin more than one season may read the statement of the horrors of child-labor as published in the POST-DISPATCH, shudder over them and then pass them by as colored impossibilities. Girls who put in part of the week attending a fashionable school, and their Saturdays and Sundays in matinees, pleasure trips and a round of amusements, never know that thousands of children of their own age work ten hours for six days every week for a miserable pittance of $2 or $3. Yet it is a fact that at least 3,000 children, half of them girls, and many of them not more than 8 years of age, are working as hard and as long as any man to keep themselves alive.

The article then took the reader on a round of St. Louis factories and drew a pathetic picture of "the wan and weary faces" of "the little toilers" who, "almost as soon as they were able to toddle," were driven "into the struggle for life." The story pulled no punches in its recitation, but it was also careful to note that "in anything that is written . . . there is no intention to reflect upon the owners or superintendents," who, after all, gave the children their opportunities to gain a livelihood.

---

[84] *Ibid.*, March 1, 1882.
[85] *Ibid.*, March 3, 1882.

Indeed, in keeping with the middle class attitudes of the proprietor, the working classes who were depicted with such sympathy in feature articles were either ignored or lectured to on the editorial page. There were no clarion calls for reform of child labor, and whereas an exposure captioned A STRUGGLE FOR LIFE described the working conditions endured by employees in a white lead factory where many died young of "lead colic," in the same issue an editorial admonished the men— who were contemplating a strike—to stick to "moral suasion" and to foreswear "force and threats." [86]

Another type of story depicted the squalor of the lowest classes. One concerned THE HAUNTS OF VICE, "Sights of Filth, Bestiality, Sin and Crime," "What Can Be Seen in a Big Christian City" "While Preachers and Congregations Talk of the Heathen and Pagans," "Let Them Read and Mark and Then Go Into the Dens and Slums of Ignorance, Uncleanliness and Degradation Right at Their Doors." [87] This article introduced the reader to sickening scenes in Clabber Alley, the toughest neighborhood in the city. In one tumbledown tenement which the police dubbed "castle thunder," the reporter came across "a repelling sight":

In a large room . . . upon a filth-begrimed floor, reclined in beastly drunkenness several negro men and women and three white women, the latter in a half-nude condition. . . . Their intoxicant had consisted of stale beer which had been "canned" from beer kegs standing on the outside of saloons after having been used. . . . One of the white women, whose face was partially destroyed by a disease, and otherwise presented a . . . disgusting sight, with the utmost sang froid requested a "chaw of tobacco". . . . Stretched in one corner of the room, upon a bed of straw saturated with filth, lay a white child whom the above mentioned woman claimed as her own. Emaciated with disease and probably hunger, the little thing moaned feebly, its pitiful wails failing, however, to reach the stony heart of its mother, in whom the voice of nature was dead. The vile creature was asked her name, and replied with an imbecile grin, that a good many years ago it had been Nellie May, but now was simply "Limping Lizzie."

Outside, in mud six inches deep, hogs were wallowing, chickens cackling, and children paddling about. A bit further on, a fight was going on between "Blinky Mag," a white woman, and "Tough Annie," a Negress, "over the possession of a drunken white man who had

---

[86] *Ibid.*, March 8, 1882.

[87] *Ibid.*, April 26, 1882. See a vivid portrayal of similar scenes in St. Louis slum districts a few years later by Dreiser, *Book About Myself*, p. 219 *passim*.

been 'steered' into the alley for purposes of robbery." At the end of the alley was a "low dive of a saloon" where a gang of Negro roustabouts were brawling. Similarly depraved scenes were found in "Wild Cat Chute," where "a repulsive-looking Italian woman" named "The Queen" held sway. In all these places of indescribable filth "negro families were huddled together like so many cattle in a pen."

When winter came the *Post-Dispatch* frequently ran articles describing in vivid detail "How the Sick and Destitute are Neglected by the City." POOR HUMANITY depicted "Centers of Poverty Visited by a Post-Dispatch Reporter," where there was "Less of Misery" than last year, "But Still Enough and to Spare." [88] The paper described the policies of church-supported organizations which extended aid to the hardest-hit families—but only if they showed themselves worthy of Christian charity:

> No disreputable or suspicious characters receive assistance, and if poor or destitute people are found in disreputable localities, they are told that they must move out before aid can be extended. For instance, no one living on Almond street, no matter how deserving, can obtain a loaf of bread from the [Provident] Association. . . . They must move out. [89]

The *Post-Dispatch* editorial columns apparently saw nothing to criticize in this and, in fact, expressed doubts about the efficacy of charity at all. Commenting on a decline in donations to the city's relief agencies, the paper declared it was time to ask them

> just what they have accomplished. The loss of over $5,000 in resources for the city's charity does not seem to have had any bad effect. In fact, the more pauperism is studied the more clearly is it seen that poverty adjusts itself to relief much more readily than relief can . . . adjust itself to poverty. [90]

The classical economics of the editorial page, however, comfortable as they might be for the middle classes, were not permitted to blight the search of the editors for material with which to shock the reader or appeal to his sympathies. When a number of poor Irish in Kerry Patch were to be evicted by an absentee landlady, the *Post-Dispatch* uttered no protest, but it sent a reporter to interview the unfortunate. He found, for example,

> a little old woman, whose face, though covered with wrinkles and seamed all over with indelible traces which a bitter and long-continued fight with poverty had left there, was intelligent

---

[88] *Post-Dispatch*, Nov. 30, 1882, Dec. 9, 1882.
[89] *Ibid.*, Jan. 31, 1882.
[90] *Ibid.*, March 2, 1882.

and kindly withal. An open-hearted Irish invitation to enter was at once extended [and the reporter stepped into a rude shanty] . . . the only occupants of which were a pair of goats chained to a stake in the floor and munching a quantity of calico rugs. The old woman opened another door which admitted into a small chamber used as a reception room, sleeping apartment and kitchen. Everything was quite cleanly.[91]

The effects of such pieces on the paper's readers cannot, of course, be measured. Certainly there was no crusade on the part of the *Post-Dispatch* demanding welfare measures; in fact, the tenor of its laissez-faire views was opposed to any such suggestion. The paper's motive was mainly to stimulate circulation by publishing stories of sensational impact about the city of St. Louis and to present them in an arresting style calculated to attract the attention of the ordinary householder. Nevertheless, perhaps it would not be too much to suggest that articles of this type in the *Post-Dispatch* must have stirred the consciences of many a St. Louisan, and, contrary to Pulitzer's apparent intention, these vivid word pictures may have helped to stimulate sentiment for social amelioration that in time would bear fruit.

In its efforts to reach the largest mass of readers, the *Post-Dispatch* not only localized and livened up its feature articles but applied the same policies to gossip and humor columns. The "letters" from out-of-town correspondents like "Ida Clare" in Boston were gradually relegated to a filler status and replaced by a *Post-Dispatch* column retailing local gossip. Written in a light, personal vein for readers living an impersonal city existence, this feature contained trivial observations about prominent persons, civic events, and politics. Possibly the *Post-Dispatch* picked up the idea from the New York *Star,* whose comment about its own feature was reprinted in the *Post-Dispatch:*

> There is an increasing demand for more of the personal element in journalism. People tire of the impersonal "we". . . . The success of our "Man About Town" shows that . . . [this] feeling exists in this country. It is the first thing read in the Sunday *Star.* It is more talked about and commented on than any other feature. . . . It has a freshness, a directness and a piquancy which the impersonal style could not give.[92]

The first *Post-Dispatch* gossip column appeared in a large Saturday edition late in 1882. Called "Saturday Chat," it proved so popular it was soon joined by a second column, published in the daily edition

---

[91] *Ibid.,* Jan. 20, 1883.
[92] *Ibid.,* Dec. 21, 1882.

and entitled "Gossip on the Streets."[93] Typical of their light and breezy tone was the following, written by a reporter loitering in the rotunda of the busy Southern Hotel one summer evening:

> More than ever it [the rotunda] has become the exchange where, after business hours, all classes of prominent St. Louisans meet . . . each evening, before setting out for the clubs, places of amusement, or toward the home-comforts of dressing gown and slippers. . . . If you want to see a prominent professional or commercial gentleman . . . go to the Southern Hotel, take a cane-bottomed chair and wait until he comes in; it won't be long. All manner of topics are discussed by the strolling or lounging groups that woo the evening breezes on the sidewalk. . . .
> EDWIN HARRISON, dressed in a light blue suit of serge, looking very cool, comes in for a chat with A. B. PENDLETON and they stroll off to a club together. . . . JOHN S. MARMA-DUKE is engaged in a conversation with several prominent Missourians, in a quiet corner. It is supposed they are talking politics.[94]

The entertainment features of the paper were enhanced still further early in 1883 when the immensely clever Johnny Jennings returned from the *Globe-Democrat* and began a column labeled "Officer Magoogin, the Talking Policeman."[95] In inaugurating this feature the *Post-Dispatch* availed itself of a new style, dialect humor, which a few journalists like Opie Read, Bill Nye, and Joel Chandler Harris had begun to popularize elsewhere.[96] Jennings created a voluble good-natured policeman whose opinions on many subjects were expressed in picturesque Irish brogue to Fopiano, a taciturn Italian vendor whose peanut stand was located in the business district. Characteristic of Jennings' style was the dialogue between Officer Magoogin and Fopiano concerning a local election:

> "Fopi," said Officer Magoogin this morning, as he pulled up alongside the Italian's peanut tray, and with a Land League smile on his face and a gleam of Democratic triumph in his eye began to toy with a handful of the inviting goobers, "I've bin kapin' me mouth shut all along, afeart I'd say annything, but, be heavens, the election is too near at hand to hould me tongue anny more an' I musht express me sintiments for the occasion, if it breaks the heart av uv'ry frind I've got an' bushts up the intoire Ightal-

---

[93] *Ibid.*, Dec. 16, 1882, Jan. 31, 1883. Other names were given this column at various times, such as "The Lounger" and "In the Corridors."
[94] *Ibid.*, June 6, 1883.
[95] The first one appeared Feb. 1, 1883.
[96] Mott, pp. 483-85.

yun colony in Wildcat Chute. Fopi, me b'y, how do ye wote?"

"Me no vote-a at all," said the peanut merchant. "De banan' an' de ap' cost-a too much to neglet-a de biz for-a de vut."

"There now, that'll do," said the valiant officer. "Yer talkin' loike an insean man. I wouldn't give foive cints fur yer loife aff ye shpoke that way in the foorth Ward to-morry fwhin wan av the sthroikers offer'd ye a Dimmycratic ticket. Fwhy, man aloive, they'd massacry ye an' scatter yer bananies an' paynuts to the foor winds. Be sinsible, Fopi, fwhile ye have yer wits about ye an' go to the polls an' wote the sthrait ticket if it's the lasht act av yer cheroobic existence. That's no more'n the angel Gabriel himself 'ould do aff the election was on the aiv av the Judgement Day an' the divil himself was a Dimmycratic candidhate."

"You make-a me sick," said the Italian, turning sadly towards the charcoal furnace and leaving Magoogin standing lonely but quite content at the peanut tray.

"Faix'n I'll make ye sicker, ye yalley-faced macaroni aiter," the officer shouted, "an' I'll tell ye now fur the foinal toime that anless yer up brave an' airly to-morry mornin' wid a Dimmycratic ticket in yer hand an' pit the same in the box afore me own eyes, the way I'll know yer not decavin' me, I'll close up yer Shtand undher the salune law an' rin ye in fur thryin' to incoite a riot by refusin' to wote in accordance wid the requesht av a respecc'able majority av the citizens av the ward. . . . Wote the Dimmycratic ticket aff ye lose your immortal sowl in the sthruggle. That's the advice I give ye, Fopi, an' be very careful that ye don't forget it.[97]

The Magoogin papers became "very generally read and . . . furnished a vast deal of amusement" to St. Louisans, although "Mr. Jennings occasionally gets in an expression that would hardly pass muster." [98] So successful was his column that two or three others from time to time were attempted, and the paper reprinted similar features from other newspapers, particularly Joel Harris' "Uncle Remus" in the Atlanta *Constitution* and George W. Peck's "Peck's Bad Boy." [99] Jennings' Talking Policeman was run in the *Post-Dispatch* off and on for several years, and, according to one commentator, had much to do with the popularity of Pulitzer's newspaper.[100]

---

[97] *Post-Dispatch*, April 2, 1883.

[98] *Spectator*, Feb. 17, 1883.

[99] Opie Read's "Arkansaw Traveler" was another favorite often reprinted in the *Post-Dispatch*. Pulitzer later employed Read on the New York *World*.

[100] In 1900 a compilation of Jennings' columns was published under the title of *The Widow Magoogin* (New York, 1900). By this time Jennings was writing a column, by the same name for the *World*, the New York *Mercury*, and other

The *Post-Dispatch*, indeed, became well known for its broad humor, not only in feature columns but on the editorial page. John Cockerill's pieces, even those dealing with serious subjects, were enlivened by barbs of wit. "It is a fact," said the Moberly *Chronicle* one day that

the St. Louis *Post-Dispatch* is too witty for any use. The whole editorial page is continually on the broad grin. Not an article or an item—grave or gay, lively or severe—is found without something to make the poor reader laugh.[101]

Cockerill's Mark Twainish style was particularly evident in short paragraphs where his remarks on every conceivable subject produced laughs from even casual readers. Preachers were a special object of his pen:

In his last Sunday sermon the Irreverend Mr. Talmage said: "If from the mound of my grave more people can get into the kingdom of heaven than are helped there through my life, I am willing to die." Let's try the experiment, anyhow.[102]

Or this on Henry Ward Beecher:

Mr. Beecher seems to think Col. Ingersoll would make a very good Christian if he would keep his mouth shut. Mr. Beecher would be a better Christian if he didn't keep the door shut quite so much.[103]

When he heard about a series in the New York *Graphic* on "types of American beauty," Cockerill remarked about the first example that

her particular type of beauty has points of difference from the recognized American ideal. Her face is beefy, her jaws massive and muscular, her nose avate and pendulous, her eyes slightly crossed, her forehead low and her hair thin. If she is a type of American beauty, then it is no wonder that the current of emigration is being directed toward Australia. . . . It is to be hoped that no St. Louis girl will permit her face to appear in this collection, because . . . the blow to her good looks would be something she could never recover from.[104]

---

journals. At that time *Reedy's Mirror* remarked: "The good lady [Widow Magoogin], relict of a policeman, Mike Magoogin, who was the precursor of Dooley by not less than sixteen years, and made most of the early fame of the St. Louis *Post-Dispatch* . . . was discovered and invented by Mr. John J. Jennings. In these days Mr. Jennings was the star reporter in St. Louis." It was Reedy's opinion that Jennings' column was "more veritistic than Dooley's." *Reedy's Mirror*, June 28, 1900.

[101] Reprinted in *Post-Dispatch*, Sept. 11, 1880.
[102] *Ibid.*, Dec. 22, 1880.
[103] *Ibid.*, May 10, 1880.
[104] *Ibid.*, Oct. 12, 1880.

On Mark Twain himself:

> As a rule MARK TWAIN has a new book in press about once a year. . . . This country is getting very weary of Mr. SAMUEL L. CLEMENS. He was a second-class pilot on the Western rivers and went into humor because the pay was better and the work not so exhausting. His style is bad, his matter is bad and his humor was worn out three years ago. His later books are simply a rehash of the earlier ones. . . . As a matter of fact Mr. SAM'L L. CLEMENS is a standing monument to the success which will always attend literary dishonesty.[105]

The sheer readability of the *Post-Dispatch* after 1880, its liveliness, its habit of constantly widening its news and entertainment horizons, and its use of sensational techniques, all on a sustained daily basis, attracted to it the mass circulation which Pulitzer was so determined to have. But the ultimate secret of its startling success was its energetic organization and the manner in which Pulitzer fired it with enthusiasm. Once it decided to concentrate on local news, the paper enlarged its staff of reporters. Where there were a mere half-dozen early in 1881, there were at least twice that in 1883, excluding editors and special writers, and within a few more years the *Post-Dispatch* boasted the largest local staff in the city.[106] Invariably, Pulitzer chose young men, often those who showed promise on other papers, and persuaded them to come to his newspaper. "It is generally admitted that the *Post-Dispatch* has a superb force of reporters," exclaimed the *Spectator* in 1882.[107] Generally—not always—they were sons of policemen, clerks, and other lower middle or working class families; but even so, many of them possessed a better than average education, and all of them exhibited drive and inventiveness.[108] Typical of the new reporters was John F. Magner, a waspish, red-headed Irishman who had been a teacher of English and Greek at Christian Brothers College before Pulitzer noticed him as a resourceful writer on the *Globe-Democrat*.[109] Walter B. Stevens, who had proved himself a keen competitor as city editor of the defunct *Times-Journal,* was educated at the University of Michigan. Another addition was William J. Thornton, a cultivated Englishman whose urbane manner gave him

---

[105] *Ibid.,* Sept. 10, 1881.

[106] *Ibid.,* Jan. 3, 1881; *American Journalist,* Sept., 1883; *Journalist,* June 18, 1892. In 1884 the paper had twenty-four reporters and a total staff of perhaps twice that. *Journalist,* Dec. 13, 1884; *American Journalist,* May, 1884.

[107] *Spectator,* May 13, 1882.

[108] See scattered references in Kelsoe, *St. Louis Reference Record.*

[109] *Who Was Who in America, 1897-1942,* p. 767; *Spectator,* Oct. 30, 1880, Jan. 22, 1881.

an entrée to important sources of news.[110]   George S. Johns, one of the last of Pulitzer's appointees before he left St. Louis, was a graduate of Princeton College in New Jersey. He caught the publisher's eye as editor of a small paper in nearby St. Charles. Pulitzer subjected him to a grilling, as he did so many others:

> What are you doing? What have you done? Where do you come from? What do you like to do best? Why? . . . I want to know what you can do. Do your best in the next two weeks and send me everything you write.[111]

There were others, it is true, who conformed to the average, men who by wits and spirit alone discovered many a story. William Hobbs, the fire and railroad reporter, was unable to write a complete sentence grammatically, but his innumerable contacts, his gregariousness and his endless drive—the *Post-Dispatch* noticed he had not missed a fire in twelve years—made him a valuable man in a newspaper office. When Pulitzer decided to add a railroad column to his paper, he got Billy Hobbs from the *Globe-Democrat*.[112]   And Cliff Sanders, who displayed a "brazen assurance [which] defies adjectives and beggars description," though he had scarcely a grade school education, was hired to be Jefferson City correspondent. Sanders had shown his aggressiveness in 1877 when he threatened to return a frightened woman to her burning hotel room if she did not furnish him with information for his paper as they were descending the fire ladder.[113]

But Hobbs and Sanders were exceptions. Pulitzer, who had an enormous respect and ambition for his chosen field, hoped even then to see the time when journalism would rank as a profession equal with medicine and the law. "A new profession," he called it in an editorial in 1880:

> It is a fact that few men now can become successful journalists who are not ballasted with a good education. The prejudice against the callow graduate is just as strong as it ever was, but when the graduate has worn off his callowness he can distance the rest in the race. There is a greater demand for general information and

---

[110] *Gould's St. Louis Directory*, 1880, p. 990; 1881, pp. 1,071, 1,103; *Spectator*, March 26, 1881; *Hornet*, Dec. 11, 1880; *Post-Dispatch*, Sept. 9, 1879. Stevens ultimately became Washington correspondent for the *Globe-Democrat*.

[111] Orrick Johns, *Time of Our Lives*, p. 63. Johns became for many years editorial editor of the *Post-Dispatch*.

[112] *Spectator*, Nov. 17, 1883, Sept. 3, 1892; *Post-Dispatch*, Aug. 16, 1881, Sept. 26, 1881; *American Journalist*, May, 1883, Oct., 1883; *Gould's St. Louis Directory*, 1884, p. 528.

[113] *Spectator*, Dec. 23, 1882; *Gould's St. Louis Directory*, 1883, p. 950; *Hornet*, Feb. 19, 1881; *Journalist*, July 14, 1888. Sanders later became assistant city editor and editor of other local journals.

knowledge in a newspaper office than there is in any other place anywhere and when the college man can give this he generally can get money in return. . . . Nevertheless, the talk about schools of journalism, with which Eastern colleges occasionally divert themselves, will not amount to anything in our day. Men still must rise from the ranks and learn their business from the bottom to the top . . . and no lecture delivered by the sagest professor will ever teach a young man how to do up a fire or a funeral, or follow a convention so that his copy can go into the printer's hands as the motion to adjourn is being carried.[114]

In addition to Hobbs, who launched the new railroad column, other specialists were hired, among them David Reid, who built up the sporting department.[115] John Henton Carter, a one-time river pilot, friend of Mark Twain, and a literary figure of sorts himself, replaced the elderly Captain Ryland as the river reporter. This branch of news, still important to St. Louisans, took on new life. Carter was better known to contemporaries by the pseudonym of "Commodore Rollingpin," which he used in the publication of a humorous almanac for river men.[116] The society department, which also had been languishing, was enlivened by the employment of Mrs. Hannah Daviess Pittman, member of an old Kentucky family of aristocratic pretensions and one of St. Louis's most remarkable feminine journalists. A mature, billowy woman, she was the real founder of the *Post-Dispatch's* society department, remaining for many years the society editor. She, too, acquired ephemeral literary fame as a composer of light operettas and short stories celebrating particularly Southerners of "gentle birth." She achieved a more genuine reputation as a genealogical historian with her still useful compilation, *Americans of Gentle Birth and Their Ancestry*.[117]

---

114 *Post-Dispatch*, Sept. 18, 1880. John Dillon was a bit more old-fashioned. He especially saw little use in schools of journalism. Journalists are born, not made, he said. Sara Lockwood Williams, *Twenty Years of Journalism: A History of the School of Journalism of the University of Missouri, Columbia, Missouri; U.S.A.* (Columbia, Mo., 1929), pp. 14-15.

115 *Spectator*, Nov. 17, 1883; *The Whip*, May 9, 1885.

116 *Hornet*, March 19, 1881; *Post-Dispatch*, May 12, 1882. Among other of Commodore Rollingpin's many local color stories are "The Mississippi Bedouins," "The Ozark Post Office," "The Man at the Wheel," "The Log of Commodore Rollingpin," "Out Here in Old Missoury." Carter at various times was river editor for several St. Louis papers and a special writer for the New York *World*. Alexander N. De Menil, "A Century of Missouri Literature," *Missouri Historical Review*, XV (Oct., 1920), 100-101.

117 *Spectator*, Aug. 25, 1883, May 9, 1885, Feb. 6, 1886, Nov. 15, 1890; interview with Harry Duhring, Nov. 9, 1950; De Menil, p. 109; Johnson, *Notable Women of St. Louis: 1914*, pp. 185-87.

To acquire such a staff and especially to attract men from other papers—even the *Globe-Democrat*—the *Post-Dispatch* had to offer unusual advantages. Because of Pulitzer's enlightened views and his shrewd business understanding, these were abundant. Besides the better hours afforded by employment on afternoon journals—morning papers required night work regularly—the *Post-Dispatch* offered substantially higher pay than any other paper in St. Louis.[118] A survey conducted by the *American Journalist,* a trade publication, listed St. Louis newspapers as paying reporters an average of $19.25 for a seven-day week, while New York's papers, the next highest city, averaged only $17.25. Why was St. Louis's average the highest, the *American Journalist* asked, and answered: because the *Post-Dispatch* "pays its reporters the highest salaries paid by any newspaper in the world," an average of $23.00 per week. Without the *Post-Dispatch,* the St. Louis average would have dropped to $18.08.[119] Individual reporters of the highest caliber earned as much as $35 weekly on Pulitzer's paper.[120] Moreover, the pay of men taken sick was continued, a contrast with other journals.[121] But the most unusual inducement, one about which Pulitzer was exceedingly proud, was a paid two-week vacation each summer for each employee. Elsewhere, one reporter remarked, "even a day off is a rarity." [122] The *Post-Dispatch* practice "is an example that is sadly needed in other offices," commented

---

[118] First, of course, the *Post-Dispatch* had to overcome—as it did—the lowly reputation of afternoon journalism. As late as the 1890's, however, many reporters still felt the prestige of working on a morning journal compensated for the less attractive hours. Many felt an evening paper was "scrappy and kicked together." (Dreiser, p. 99.) In 1884 one St. Louis reporter commented that "there is no great field except on morning newspapers." William V. Byars to James Byars, Dec. 7, 1884, William Vincent Byars Papers.

[119] *American Journalist,* Jan. 1884. This paper's survey listed the average salaries for reporters for a seven-day week as the following: St. Louis, $19.25; New York, $17.25; Chicago, $17.00; Philadelphia, $16.85; San Francisco, $16.00; New Orleans, $15.50; Cincinnati, $15.25; Boston, $14.90; Baltimore, $14.50. The average on St. Louis papers was: *Post-Dispatch,* $23.00; *Globe-Democrat,* $19.50; *Republican,* $19.25; *Chronicle,* $15.50. The editors of the *American Journalist,* a St. Louis publication, admitted that their poll was far from foolproof; the response to their questionnaire was by no means complete.

[120] *Spectator,* Dec. 1, 1883. Figures as to individual salaries for this period are difficult to obtain. In 1887 John Jennings was offered $40 weekly to return to the *Post-Dispatch.* Henry Moore to Joseph Pulitzer, Sept. 29, 1887, Pulitzer Papers (CU).

[121] *Spectator,* Nov. 13, 1880.

[122] *Journalist,* Aug. 2, 1884, June 11, 1887; Kelsoe to Byars, June 19, 1897, William Vincent Byars Papers; Florence White to George Johns, Oct. 28, 1902, Pulitzer Papers (CU). The *Republican* later in a partial way granted seven to ten days a year to editors.

another.[123] Not long after leaving St. Louis Pulitzer discussed his liberal policies in practical terms:

A paper cannot make itself, can it? I believe in engaging the best talent and paying for it the highest price. Indeed, I believe that such a policy, in the fierce struggle of competition that rages, is the only one that can possibly bring lasting success. You can't get good men without paying for them. Without good men you cannot get good work, and without good work no paper can prosper largely.[124]

That such a policy succeeded for the *Post-Dispatch* was evident to all. Exclaiming upon a *Post-Dispatch* scoop, the *Spectator* observed that this was "such, indeed, as could only be expected from the best paid reportorial force in St. Louis." [125]

For editors and managers, of course, salaries and other perquisites were much higher than those for reporters. Precise figures for the period of Pulitzer's stay in St. Louis are unavailable, but one managing editor in the eighties was known to have received $3,600, then considered a munificent sum.[126] A city editor's pay, however, was far less; John Magner, who took charge of the local staff in 1884, received only $30 a week.[127] For one or two there were additional rewards. As has been seen, Steigers, the rough and ready advertising manager, received commissions for new business he secured for the paper, and in 1881 John Cockerill, whom Pulitzer particularly valued, received substantial stock interest in the *Post-Dispatch*. This afforded him dividends of $2,500 and $2,700 for 1882 and 1883.[128]

The proprietor's reasons for paying his men well, as he himself phrased it, were largely practical. Yet, as one of his chief editors remarked later, "Mr. Pulitzer loved his profession, loved his newspaper, and loved his men." [129] He was genuinely solicitous of them and their welfare, as he often showed, from his top editors to employees in the back room. Beginning either before he left St. Louis or shortly after, he established the habit of sending each a turkey on Christmas, and when a reporter was married he was likely to receive a gift from Pulitzer. A year after he went to New York Pulitzer instructed Busi-

---

[123] *Journalist,* June 11, 1887.
[124] *Ibid.,* Oct. 23, 1886.
[125] *Spectator,* Sept. 6, 1884.
[126] He was Henry Moore, by then the managing editor. *Ibid.,* July 14, 1888.
[127] Henry Moore to Joseph Pulitzer, Jan. 22, 1887, Pulitzer Papers (CU).
[128] Ignatz Kappner to Joseph Pulitzer, Nov. 29, 1886, Pulitzer Papers (CU).
[129] Charles Chapin, *Charles Chapin's Story: Written in Sing Sing Prison* (New York, 1920), p. 211. Chapin was one of the legendary city editors of modern journalism, a product of Pulitzer's sensational school. While he made his name chiefly as the hard-driving editor of the New York *Evening World,* he got his start in the nineties on the *Post-Dispatch.*

ness Manager Kappner to pay one hundred dollars monthly to the widow of John McGuffin, his old associate.[130] Even the compositors upstairs and the newsboys on the street were not neglected. Long afterwards, when the typesetters received their annual turkeys at Christmas, the official publication of the trade remarked:

> With the exception of the Post-Dispatch, nothing happened on the daily papers of St. Louis that would lead an outsider to imagine that the proprietors thought any more of their faithful employes than was absolutely necessary.[131]

Pulitzer was especially solicitous of the women compositors and was contemptuous of other journals who paid female printers low wages. He was forever inquiring after the well-being of his own. As one woman remembered:

> Mr. Pulitzer was a fine man and very considerate of all of us, just like a father. He used to advise us to keep to ourselves and not to mingle with the printers. He never allowed the printers to call us by our first names. He often used to tell us how he had come to this country as a poor boy and how one of his first jobs had been as a waiter in a restaurant. He liked to say, "You can do just as I did—start at the bottom of the ladder and go up." [132]

A Christmas dinner for newsboys became an annual event, the first occurring in 1881. One boy, showing some perturbation for the lack of manners displayed by his hungry comrades at the first dinner, told the proprietor, "Some of dose fellers acts like dey never was in company before. Deir behavior is scanderlous." But they were sufficiently appreciative to give Mr. Pulitzer three rousing cheers at the *Post-Dispatch* office.[133]

Although there was a touch of paternalism about the showers of gifts, and even now Pulitzer was exhibiting some jealousy of his ultimate authority (a tendency which became an obsession later), he continued to maintain an easy, democratic atmosphere in the *Post-Dispatch* office. He was open and friendly, "simple, kindly and un-critical," and "he takes a point from an office boy as quickly as from any king of the profession." [134] When John Cockerill organized a local press club, Pulitzer was a charter member, the only publisher to join. But the club soon folded because of the hostile attitude of other

---

130 Ignatz Kappner to Mrs. J. M. McGuffin, Aug. 18, 1884, Pulitzer Papers (CU).
131 *The Typographical Journal*, XVI (Jan. 15, 1900), 68.
132 *Reynolds*, "Joseph Pulitzer," p. 76; *Post-Dispatch,* Jan. 29, 1880.
133 *Post-Dispatch*, Dec. 26, 1881.
134 *Spectator*, May 26, 1883.

employers.[135] Pulitzer was forever encouraging his men, as when, on one occasion, he rewarded John Magner, "one of the best reporters in the West," with a gold watch and Florence White with a week's pay for exceptional work.[136] All this inculcated a spirit of intense loyalty and comradeship on the *Post-Dispatch*.

The only important difficulty Pulitzer encountered with his employees occurred in the spring of 1881 when the local printers' union, stirring in a general revival of the labor movement, sought to unionize the *Post-Dispatch* compositors. The affair, which brought strong reactions from the paper, throws light on Pulitzer's essentially middle class views as an employer, which were reenforced by his determination to be master in his own house. St. Louis Typographical Local No. 8 was the oldest trades union in Missouri, having been chartered in 1856. Before 1881 it had scored some successes in newspaper offices, especially in gaining the recognition of the powerful *Globe-Democrat*.[137] But neither the *Post-Dispatch* nor the *Republican* would recognize its jurisdiction. Therefore, in March 1881, backed by the pro-labor *Chronicle* and the trades union assembly, Local 8 launched a campaign to boost wages and force from these papers recognition as the employees' bargaining agent. A committee of three "utter strangers" outraged Pulitzer by presenting him their demands. He refused. A month later, when the *Post-Dispatch* was swamped with reporting a local election, "a committee, representing eight or ten printers employed by the POST-DISPATCH, entered the editorial room" with an "insolent and dictatorial" request for union recognition. Again they were refused, and the disaffected printers were peremptorily dismissed. Then the *Post-Dispatch* published a defiant editorial:

> There is superhuman activity just now in the ranks of the gentlemen who band themselves together under the name of Trades Unions to direct and control the business of men who have brains, energy and skill enough to start factories, build up newspapers and conduct enterprises which contribute to the prosperity of communities. . . .
>
> The POST-DISPATCH enjoys the hostility of the so-called labor conspirators because it refuses to be dictated to by a Typographical Union. It declines to be told who it shall and shall not employ. It refuses to be instructed as to how to measure its type,

---

[135] *Post-Dispatch*, Feb. 18, 1882, Dec. 23, 1882; *Hornet*, June 4, 1881, Feb. 11, 1882, Feb. 25, 1882; *Journalist*, Nov. 3, 1888, March 23, 1889; St. Louis *Life*, Feb. 8, 1890. The hostility, especially of the *Republican's* proprietors, who feared it might turn into a reporters' union, doomed the club.

[136] *Post-Dispatch*, Aug. 10, 1882; *Spectator*, Aug. 5, 1882.

[137] *Post-Dispatch*, April 27, 1881; *Typographical Journal*, XXXIV (May 1909), 514.

feed its presses and to be limited to the number of apprentices it shall take into office training. In other words, the POST-DIS-PATCH, while paying wages that are satisfactory to its employes, joins the leading newspapers of the country in resisting the inquisitorial, supercilious and vexatious tyranny of the Typographical Union. . . .[138]

At the same time, the paper triumphantly issued a statement signed by a great majority of the compositors who said they were satisfied with their employer and rejected the claim "of any Trades Union . . . to dictate rules for our guidance or to interfere in the pleasant relations existing between our employees and ourselves." And it paid its respects to Scripps' *Chronicle*, "a little, one-eyed, starveling penny-sheet," for fomenting labor troubles in the offices of its competitors.[139]

Retaliating, the local trades assembly promoted a boycott among the business establishments that advertised in the *Post-Dispatch*. Pulitzer countered by raising wages to union levels while still refusing to recognize its jurisdiction. The move undermined the position of the printers, and the pressure on the *Post-Dispatch* subsided. But before it did, the paper loosed another editorial barrage:

> The POST-DISPATCH believes in the right of trained artisans and skilled mechanics to organize for their own good, but the right to manage the internal affairs of this office, employ and discharge and to direct when and how labor shall be performed, is one that the proprietor reserves to himself. The doctrine laid down by the Union that it is justified in resorting to "Boycotting" measures to enforce recognition is the most dangerous and pernicious one ever advanced in this free country. It is simply one form of mob law, and if enforced may in time attack every business interest in St. Louis. It practically amounts to this, that a newspaper is expected to take out license, not from the established authorities as is the case in despotic Russia, but from an irresponsible lot of unknown men who assume no risks and share no losses. The POST-DISPATCH has resisted as a matter of principle.[140]

Except for this incident, which apparently left no scars, until late in 1882 the *Post-Dispatch* encountered few other problems in its skyrocketing progress. The modest gains in circulation during the

---

[138] *Post-Dispatch*, April 4, 1881, May 12, 1881.

[139] *Ibid.*, April 5, 1881, April 16, 1881.

[140] *Ibid.*, April 9, 1881, May 12, 1881. The *Republican* lost its fight to remain nonunion, however, in 1884, and the *Post-Dispatch* surrendered a year later. *Inland Printer*, II (Dec. 1884), 122; *The Boycotter*, Jan. 2, 1885. *The Boycotter* later became the *Union Printer*.

paper's first two years after 1880 were obscured by a burst of popularity which brought to it the mass readership Pulitzer so ardently desired. In January 1881 circulation stood at 9,300; seven months later, on August 1, a notarized statement declared that sales had reached a daily average of 15,030 copies.[141] Less than a month later another notarized statement showed a jump of another thousand readers. "Although daily newspapers, as a rule, expect to lose readers in the summer season," it chortled, "it has been the good fortune of the POST-DISPATCH to maintain a steady increase . . . since the opening of hot weather. This is something absolutely unusual." [142] Of course, the Garfield assassination accounted for much of the boost, but it was remarkable that the paper kept its new readers and added to them. In January 1882, in another of its triumphant notarized statements, the *Post-Dispatch* disclosed that its circulation had more than doubled in a year's time and now stood at a daily average of 20,320 copies.[143] "The annals of journalism contain no record of such a steady, rapid and unprecedented advance," Pulitzer declared.

Supplementing the efforts of the editorial and news departments, John McGuffin, the "keen, far seeing newspaper manager" whose "methods were original with himself," continued to perfect the efficiency of the paper's circulation system, the rudiments of which he himself had established in 1880.[144] He stimulated readership by promoting contests such as one for the best poem submitted by a youthful citizen of St. Louis. Another was designed to increase the eagerness of the small newsboys in hawking the *Post-Dispatch* on the streets. Prizes were offered which "excited the liveliest interest. . . . [They] included a fine stem-winding gold watch, a suit of clothes, a silver watch, a handsome pair of opera glasses, a number of hats, half a dozen pairs of shoes, knives and other juvenile treasures calculated to stir the juvenile envy." With the stimulus of such booty, the boys outdid themselves, one selling 6,000 copies, several more than 3,000.[145] Consequently, when the rival *Republican* sought to force the carriers to drop the sale of the *Post-Dispatch* on pain of losing their *Republican* routes, the maneuver backfired; most of the carriers preferred the evening paper.[146]

In September 1881 the *Post-Dispatch* intensified its bitter circulation war with the *Republican* by once more reducing the price of the

---

141 Memorandum [1906], Pulitzer Papers (CU); *Post-Dispatch,* Aug. 1, 1881.
142 *Post-Dispatch,* Aug. 20, 1881.
143 *Ibid.,* Jan. 12, 1882.
144 *American Journalist,* Aug., 1884.
145 *Post-Dispatch,* April 2, 1881.
146 *Ibid.,* July 30, 1881, Aug. 4, 1881.

paper to regular subscribers from 20 cents to 15 cents weekly compared with the 30-cent price of the morning journals.[147] This "is part of our nefarious scheme to extend the circulation and the usefulness of the paper," the *Post-Dispatch* remarked, and, indeed, "without this low rate that paper would not have half the circulation it has to-day," said the *Spectator*.[148]

Another McGuffin measure was to expand the branch system he had first set up in 1880. The original three or four branches established to facilitate new subscriptions, want ads, and distribution of papers to carriers in the residential areas were increased to a dozen scattered over all parts of the city.[149] He also sought to tap the new communities springing up on the western edges of the city, as well as the "country towns" on the east side of the river. St. Louis had been known as a center virtually without satellites except for those in Illinois, but by 1883 "fashionable suburbs" like Kirkwood, Normandy, and Ferguson were appearing in St. Louis County. In these, as in East St. Louis, Belleville, Collinsville, and Edwardsville on the East Side, an efficient delivery system was established. An agent was employed in each community to meet trains and distribute papers directly to residences. As a result, for example, the *Post-Dispatch* built up a circulation of more than 600 copies in East St. Louis and 450 in Belleville, or "more than the *Globe-Democrat* and *Republican* together."[150]

Altogether, early in 1881, the *Post-Dispatch* was beginning to challenge the morning giants who, until now, had always dominated the newspaper field.

> It has got to be a very silly saying that an afternoon paper can have no political influence [the *Spectator* commented]. There are many commercial and working men who go to their labors early in the morning and do not see a paper until they go home in the evening. These are the readers of afternoon papers, and especially when . . . [they] are conducted with striking ability, such as . . . belongs to the *Post-Dispatch*.[151]

By this time the *Post-Dispatch*, nettled by condescending *Republican* references to "the little *P-D*," claimed its daily readership to be 15,000

---

[147] The morning papers, however, published a Sunday issue.

[148] *Post-Dispatch*, Sept. 1, 1881, Sept. 2, 1881, July 15, 1882; *Spectator*, Sept. 22, 1883.

[149] *Post-Dispatch*, July 20, 1882, Aug. 17, 1882.

[150] *Ibid.*, Jan. 12, 1882, July 6, 1883. Much, of course, depended on train schedules. This was especially true in towns some distance from St. Louis. In 1881 the paper established a tidy circulation in Wellsville, about sixty miles from the city, when a favorable rail schedule was arranged. *Ibid.*, Jan. 31, 1881.

[151] *Spectator*, April 9, 1881.

larger in St. Louis than its rival's and not far behind even the *Globe-Democrat's*. Within another twelve months, while admitting that the morning papers still had "the largest general circulation," the paper declared that "in the city of St. Louis the circulation of the POST-DISPATCH is more than twice as large as that of the *Republican*."[152]

By late 1882 the circulation of the *Post-Dispatch* stood at a daily average of 22,300 copies.[153] Of this, about three-quarters was distributed in the city, either in street sales or delivered by carrier in residential districts.[154] In readership the *Post-Dispatch* had arrived.

Mass circulation brought increasing financial prosperity. The paper developed prestige as an advertising medium as evidenced by growing volume, rising rates and a shift in the kind of advertising it attracted. "It has long been truthfully remarked," the paper commented,

> that advertising patronage is the last thing that goes to a newspaper, and about the last thing to leave it. In other words, it is necessary for a newspaper to have circulation before it can command advertising. Once secured, advertising can be held long after the newspaper has lost its hold upon the reading public, for advertisers are creatures of habit. . . .[155]

This preceded a happy announcement that for the first time the paper was beginning to gain valuable types of advertising which had hitherto eluded it. The *Post-Dispatch* had been making desperate efforts to break the monopoly of the morning papers on real estate advertising, and at last its growing popularity in St. Louis had convinced realtors that it was a good vehicle for their notices. "They seek the attention of St. Louis people, and they recognize the fact that no paper is so

---

[152] *Post-Dispatch*, March 19, 1881, July 25, 1881, May 31, 1882.

[153] There are discrepancies in the figures, depending on the source, varying as much as 3,000. For example, the notarized statement of the *Post-Dispatch* on Jan. 12, 1882, was 20,320 copies, but a memorandum in the Pulitzer Papers places the circulation average for the *entire* month of January at 17,000 daily average. The statement above is based on the memorandum. The highest monthly average for 1882 was in April when, due to the James Boys story, sales reached an abnormal 26,600. The paper did not reach this figure on a sustained basis until late in 1883. (Memorandum [1906], Pulitzer Papers [CU].) According to a private diary kept by A. G. Lincoln, longtime circulation manager of the paper, the average daily circulation of the *Post-Dispatch* for the entire year of 1881 was 13,791; for 1882 it was 20,866. N. W. Ayer published the following figures for 1882; *Post-Dispatch*, 22,010; *Globe-Democrat*, 29,369 daily and 24,000 Sunday; *Republican*, 25,000 daily, 28,000 Sunday. *American Newspaper Annual* (Philadelphia, 1882).

[154] This is based on an analysis of distribution the paper published in 1881. At that time the paper's circulation was listed roughly as follows: mail and rail, about 5,500 copies; newsboy and office sales, about 5,500; and carrier delivery, 9,000. *Post-Dispatch*, Sept. 24, 1881.

[155] *Post-Dispatch*, March 19, 1881.

generally received in the city as the POST-DISPATCH." However, since advertising habits were difficult to change, the wealthy *Globe-Democrat* remained the leader in advertising patronage for many years.[156] Even the *Republican* was still endowed with great prestige and was difficult to overhaul. Nevertheless, by 1883 the *Post-Dispatch* noted with glee that its volume of advertising on the days of publication—excluding the all-important Sunday *Republican*—was now greater.[157]

As the *Post-Dispatch* attracted more lucrative forms of advertising, it lost interest in its old standby, legal advertising. Since 1878 when it inherited the city printing contract from the *Evening Dispatch,* the *Post-Dispatch* had run pages of legal ads; in its early days these had constituted a necessary source of income. But because the contract was won by competitive bidding, income from it was low; legal ads were almost a mark of indigency among newspaper men. Consequently, in 1883, when the *Republican* underbid the *Post-Dispatch* and took over legal printing, the latter scornfully remarked that

> we experience no sentiment of sorrow as the time draws near for the abrogation of our legal advertising contract. We have passed the point where that sort of thing is beneficial to us, and we can afford to leave that species of business to the newspapers that were established in 1808, and which are now driven by adversity to grab everything that is in sight.[158]

The growing reputation of the *Post-Dispatch* among St. Louis businessmen was capitalized upon by Billy Steigers in 1881 when he raised the rates on display ads by twenty percent, a policy which he continued year after year.[159] By 1883 the paper was boasting that its rates exceeded the *Republican's*.[160] In want ads, too, the *Post-Dispatch* exhibited increasing business. Until 1883 it continued the policy of running Help Wanted notices free of charge, but by then it felt

---

[156] *Ibid.,* March 26, 1881. As late as the nineties, the *Globe-Democrat* was still the premier paper in St. Louis, commanding the highest advertising rates and far the greatest volume of advertising. See Addison Archer, *American Journalism from the Practical Side* (New York, 1897), p. 228.

[157] On one occasion, as a straw in the wind, the *Post-Dispatch* noted that the *Globe-Democrat* carried 74 columns of ads, the *Republican*, 45, and itself, 47. The paper compared its own Saturday with the Sundays of its rivals. *Post-Dispatch,* April, 2, 1883.

[158] *Ibid.,* Feb. 28, 1883.

[159] Said Steigers in 1900: "We find the raising of rates at this present time just as hard to accomplish as when we had but little circulation years ago, when I was raising rates every year." William C. Steigers to Joseph Pulitzer, March 17, 1900; Pulitzer Papers (CU); *Post-Dispatch,* April 30, 1881.

[160] *Ibid.,* March 1, 1883.

sufficiently secure once more to institute a nominal fee.[161] At the same time, McGuffin established "telephone offices" in various parts of the city, chiefly at drugstores, to enable customers to call in their want ad requests without taking the trouble of a trip downtown to the paper's main office.[162] This was a remarkable innovation. Consequently, the *Post-Dispatch's* want volume doubled in three years, from 27,740 ads in 1880 to 50,070 in 1883.[163]

So rapidly did business grow that late in 1881, only two and a half years after it had established itself on Fifth Street, the *Post-Dispatch* announced plans to construct a new building. The need for it was underlined when swelling circulation made necessary the purchase of a much larger press, ordered from the Richard Hoe Company, a piece of complicated machinery costing $25,000—a purchase that itself was evidence of financial prosperity. The new press, said the paper proudly, would print 20,000 copies per hour—more than double the capacity of the present machinery—and would automatically cut, fold, paste, and even count the copies as they rolled under the stereotype cylinders. It would be the last word in Hoe presses.[164] The manufacturers promised early delivery, none too soon for the *Post-Dispatch,* as the following editorial indicates:

> Occasional complaints reach us from our patrons in the remote sections of the city in regard to our carrier service. People who insist on being served early are compelled to put up with an edition . . . that does not contain all the news. The constant growth of our circulation embarrasses us very much. We have added nearly two thousand names to the carriers' lists within two months, and the capacity of our present press has about been reached. Our first edition we are required to put to press at precisely 2 o'clock. Our second edition goes to press at 3 o'clock. A half hour afterwards we stop and add later telegraphic material and the closing markets. Of course we can't print news until we get it, and carriers having extensive far-away routes will insist on taking out early editions. In a short time, however, all this will be remedied.[165]

---

[161] *Ibid.,* Nov. 14, 1882.

[162] *Ibid.,* June 29, 1882.

[163] Memorandum (1905), Pulitzer Papers (CU).

[164] *Post-Dispatch,* March 19, 1881, Aug. 18, 1881. This was the first press ever fitted with an automatic counting device, the latest gadget in the series of rapid developments in the manufacture of mass production newspaper machinery. So rapid was this development that within a year after the *Post-Dispatch* had installed its new presses an even more wondrous press was ordered by the *Globe-Democrat*. *Ibid.,* June 6, 1882.

[165] *Ibid.,* July 27, 1881.

As circulation continued to climb, the paper decided one new press was insufficient, and a second one of similar design was ordered.[166] These additions convinced Pulitzer more than ever that now was the time to construct an entirely new building, one fitted expressly to the needs of a journalistic enterprise, replacing the converted residence on Fifth Street.

When completed in December at a cost of $30,000, the new building, located on Market Street just off Fifth, was in the midst of a business district which was moving slowly westward. It was a four-story affair, unimposing against the Olympic Theater across the street and the massive Southern Hotel nearby. The facade was tastelessly ornate in keeping with the time, surmounted by a huge sign with the paper's name and a newsboy painted on it. The dark interior was entered by two doors at opposite ends of the building on the front sidewalk. Downstairs was the business office with a want ad counter placed conveniently at the front and flanked by private offices for the business manager and the cashier. The editorial and newsrooms were upstairs, reached by a narrow stairway at one side. Partitions separated the managing editor's and publisher's offices from the local room where the city editor presided. The compositors with their heavy typecases were in an ell at the rear, and the ponderous presses were set up in the basement. Altogether, the newspaper boasted in its usual superlatives, the new home was "one of the most complete and most practically arranged newspaper establishments in the United States." But within half a dozen years it would be abandoned as a dingy, inadequate structure.[167]

On January 12, 1882, the *Post-Dispatch* held an open house and published an anniversary edition reviewing the achievements of the past three years. Always aware of the value of public relations and uncritically proud of his accomplishments as a businessman, Pulitzer emphasized the financial independence of the *Post-Dispatch* as much as he did the new physical plant. His enterprise, he declared, "has no bonds, notes or mortgages. In spite of the enormous outlay involved in the acquirement of the new building, new presses, boiler, engine, general machinery, etc., it has paid a ten per cent dividend on its capital of $250,000. . . ."[168] Addressing himself to the business community, as was his habit, Pulitzer knew that such boasting would not

---

[166] *Ibid.,* Sept. 28, 1881.

[167] *Ibid.,* Jan. 12, 1882, March 24, 1882, Oct. 14, 1882, Oct. 16, 1882; *Globe-Democrat,* Oct. 14, 1882; interview with H. M. Duhring, Dec. 29, 1950, and Richard J. Collins, March 20, 1951. By 1885 St. Louis managers already were writing to Pulitzer, now in New York, urging the necessity for a new building. Charles Gibson to Joseph Pulitzer, Oct. 11, 1885, Pulitzer Papers (CU).

[168] *Post-Dispatch,* Jan. 12, 1882.

seem lacking in taste. After all, the *Post-Dispatch* was a marvelous example of the American success story, and Pulitzer was talking the language of the class in society he understood best.

And yet, it would be unfair to conclude that Pulitzer's justifiable pride in his accomplishment was merely that of a successful business-man. Imbued with the ideals of a refugee from caste-ridden Europe and publishing a newspaper which sought to instruct the people of a self-governing community, the proprietor realized that only if his *Post-Dispatch* was independent could he hope to make it a crusading newspaper, dedicated to the public interest. Hence his happiness at achieving a mass circulation, hence his pride in being completely free of any sort of financial obligation. In June 1882, when the second press arrived, Pulitzer again remarked that the new machinery was totally paid for. "Best of all," the *Post-Dispatch* declared,

> we have no debts. From the very commencement the cardinal principle of the paper and the chief ambition of its owner and conductor has been to achieve and maintain an absolute inde-pendence, financially, politically, personally and morally. This is our happy condition, and it is on this account that we are able to address ourselves to all public questions with a freedom not common to modern American journals. We have absolutely no master, and no friend but the great public.[169]

[169] *Ibid.,* June 1, 1882.

CHAPTER IX

The Uncertain Trumpet

The "ideal newspaper editor," said Joseph Pulitzer in his new mood of thorough independence, should be "shrouded in judicial impartiality. He is to have no associations, or political ties that will warp his judgment of public men or measures, no social entanglements to crowd out the news because it may be offensive to Mrs. Snobb or Miss Toady or to her favorite biped poodle." And as for a truly independent journal, it must be "agreeable to none except those who lead an honest life, agreeable to every citizen, agreeable to the injured, the oppressed, the downtrodden, the law-abiding, but it must be true and just above all." [1]

This spirit, buttressed by the rapidly increasing circulation which the *Post-Dispatch* attracted after 1880 was noticeable in the paper's approach to national and state, as well as local, politics. The excessive partisanship which—despite protests to the contrary—had marked his paper's first months of publication, disappeared. "The POST-DISPATCH is not the paper of any one party," he emphasized in a scornful reply to an attack by a Democratic organ.

> Whatever its doctrines and convictions, it is perfectly independent and absolutely free and untrammeled. We do not claim to speak any more in behalf of the Democratic party than of the Republican party. The only party we belong to is the independent party of the POST-DISPATCH, which knows no difference in politics, creed, sect, color or station. [2]

"We prize our independence above all things," the paper added. "The POST-DISPATCH belongs to its proprietor and knows no boss." [3]

To be sure, the *Post-Dispatch* intended to "keep on preaching sound Democratic doctrine—unrestricted trade, local self-government, opposition to monopolies and Federal centralization." [4] But—the Cockerill touch—"it is not essential to the success of pure Democratic principles that we should worship every man who sticks a feather in his hair, paints his navel and prances around as a Great Democratic Chief-

[1] *Post-Dispatch*, June 5, 1882.
[2] *Ibid.*, Sept. 8, 1882.
[3] *Ibid.*, July 23, 1881.
[4] *Ibid.*, July 13, 1882.

tain." [5] In short, the *Post-Dispatch* intended, more clearly than ever, to approach public matters on the basis of issues rather than partisan advantage.

For the paper now, "Monopolies and the tyranny of wealth are the greatest dangers our republican institutions have to face." [6] In this "great Republic," once dedicated to the ideal of "labor," plutocracy had triumphed, and "money is the only test of merit, the only sceptor of power.

> This drift of politics has within the last twenty years legislated an aggregate wealth of $670,000,000 into the personal possession of eleven railway magnates, who, with their allied capitalists and corporations, are to-day the real rulers of this country, and are running it for the benefit of the few against the many, to accumulate its wealth in the hands of soulless and perpetual corporations, thus as effectually preventing its equitable distribution as did the feudal system and its castled barons. [7]

The *Post Dispatch* warned, "This is a condition of things that cannot last . . . among such a people as ours. They will not tolerate the statesmanship which creates such disparity in the conditions of life which so aggrandizes the few with Government favors while aggravating the hard struggle of the many for bare existence and dooming their posterity to hopeless vassalage. . . ."

Unfortunately, neither party was blameless for this state of affairs:

> If we are to judge the principles of a party by the performances of its representatives it would be difficult to tell now just what Democracy is. . . . About two-thirds of the Democrats in Congress belong to the big corporations, the tariff-robbing rings and other institutions known to be inimical to Democracy and the true spirit of our Government. [8]

The Tweedledee and Tweedledum condition of parties might have been avoided, said the paper with asperity, "if the business men of this country"—men of Pulitzer's own class—"had made their voices heard and their wishes felt in politics, and had exercised that influence which legitimately belongs to them." But most business men

> avoid politics as if there were some contamination in it, and the result is that men are elected to Congress not because anybody knows what their views are on the practical business interests

---

[5] *Ibid.*, July 23, 1881.
[6] *Ibid.*, Oct. 16, 1882.
[7] *Ibid.*, Aug. 12, 1882.
[8] *Ibid.*, July 13, 1882.

involved in legislation, but because some of them call themselves Democrats and others call themselves Republicans.[9]

The paper resolved to educate its constituents in politics and to campaign for those proper principles which would permit the ordinary individual—for Pulitzer the small competitive business man—to survive and flourish.

In national politics the *Post-Dispatch* continued to adhere to the Democratic Party, for, despite its deficiencies, it "has stood between the Republic and the centralizing tendencies of the party in power more than once." [10] The paper happily reported the Democratic congressional sweep in November 1882, and most particularly did it hail Cleveland's triumph for the governorship of New York. With a spark of the old partisan spirit, still aroused in Pulitzer by the heat of a contest in spite of all his resolutions, the paper captioned its editorial page with the slogan: "A Very Strong Ticket for 1884; For President, GROVER CLEVELAND, of New York; For Vice-President, JOSEPH H. McDONALD, of Indiana." [11]

What defeated the Republicans so decisively, the *Post-Dispatch* thought, were the failure to reduce taxes in view of a treasury surplus, the high tariff, and, in general, the influence of "monopolists and great subsidized interests" [12] on Republican policy. A prime example was the Standard Oil Company, which had been "organized by railroad capitalists to obtain a monopoly of the great Pennsylvania oil product," and which, although it had made $40,000,000 in ten years, paid

---

[9] *Ibid.*, Jan. 3, 1883.

[10] *Ibid.*, April 7, 1882.

[11] *Ibid.*, Nov. 7, 1882, Nov. 8, 1882. This was the beginning of Pulitzer's highly effective campaign, when he transferred it to the New York *World*, to obtain the Democratic nomination for Cleveland. But it was typical of the new note of independence that the *Post-Dispatch* was highly critical of Cleveland in one of his first acts as governor. This occurred when Cleveland vetoed an act establishing a mandatory five-cent fare on New York's elevated railroads: "No one doubts the honesty of CLEVELAND's motives in coming to the rescue of the railroads . . . but his best friends cannot ignore the fact that, while his veto message presented a strong argument against a violation of its contract by the State, it was his duty as Governor to protect the State against such frauds in carrying out a contract as amounts to a violation of it on the part of the railroad companies. Popular opinion will forgive many errors in the conduct of public men, but it never forgives the mistakes that arise from overscrupulousness and weighing of grains of dust and arguing technicalities in controversies in which the rights of the people are antagonized by corporations that are notoriously fraudulent. . . . Governor CLEVELAND has been caught on the wrong side of this controversy, and though his reputation for honesty does not suffer, his political availability is greatly impaired." *Ibid.*, March 8, 1883. See Seitz, *Joseph Pulitzer*, pp. 148-49, and John L. Heaton, *The Story of a Page* (New York, 1913), ch. 3, for accounts of Pulitzer's campaign for Cleveland in 1884 as publisher of the *World*.

[12] *Post-Dispatch*, Nov. 16, 1882.

taxes of only about $4,000 annually. This monopoly, the *Post-Dispatch* declared, was

> a specimen of the *fungi* that grow up in the crevices of our rickety and rotten legislation in regard to corporations and no argument can longer reconcile the people to such legislation. The fact that the growth and development of these monstrous devilfish concerns has been mainly during the period of Republican supremacy has at last . . . caused the overthrow of that party, because the people began to regard it as closely allied with the corporations against the interests of the people. The latter demand such a reconstruction of our laws as will protect the individual from the predatory powers with which we have endowed these colossal aggregations of capital.[13]

Despite its detestation of monopoly, however, the *Post-Dispatch* repeated vehemently its rejection of socialistic solutions. It stoutly opposed any expansion of government. Thus, when the Chicago *Tribune* and other journals suggested that the government should nationalize the new Western Union monopoly fashioned by Jay Gould, the *Post-Dispatch* warned that this was DANGEROUS GROUND. Although Western Union had shown "shameless greed in watering its stock to about eight times its original cost and exacting tolls from the public to pay dividends on all these millions of watered stock," the idea of nationalization

> we regard as a proposition more dangerous even than the telegraph monopoly. Telegraphing is a private business, like banking, railroading or manufactures. It is *not* the function of the government of the United States . . . to carry on this or any other business like it.[14]

By 1882, however, the *Post-Dispatch* had begun to edge towards some sort of federal intervention to maintain competition. Gingerly and somewhat vaguely it approached the problem, hinting at antitrust legislation based on old common law principles which would involve no risk of erecting regulatory agencies. "When we talk about railway regulation in the United States," it commented in discussing what it considered the most threatening of all monopolies,

> we do not mean state ownership . . . but laws that will prevent their franchises from being converted into agencies of monopoly combination and extortion. But all this can be had through the exercise of wholesome police powers to which common carriers

---

[13] *Ibid.*, Nov. 28, 1882.
[14] *Ibid.*, Jan. 25, 1881.

have always been subject. Our Government has all it can do to manage the Post-office, the Army, the Navy, the Civil Service and the Diplomatic Service in the administration of national affairs. If it should go into the transportation business we cannot see why it should not also go into the laundry business.[15]

More congenial to the paper's tastes were its unrestrained attacks on governmental policies of favoritism which, it held, had created vast corporate monopolies that were choking freedom of opportunity. The Republicans had fashioned a Hamiltonian system of privilege which included "enormous grants of the people's property" to railroads in the West, "enormously profitable concessions of special privileges" and, above all, policies of taxation which fostered special interests and placed undue burdens on ordinary business enterprise.[16] The consequence of a high tariff protecting monopoly goods, and of internal excises upon competitive articles of trade was that "we have created a vast and complicated system of business interests built upon taxation, depending upon tax robbery for prosperity, and powerful enough to prevent any proper reduction and to perpetuate the insidious and delusive system at the expense of labor and the more legitimate industries of the country." [17]

Some taxation, of course, was necessary, but no matter how drastically levies might be reduced, the *Post-Dispatch* complained, under the present revenue laws a disproportionate share of the load would continue to fall upon businesses—including small ones like Pulitzer's —that were engaged in competitive enterprise. What was needed was a tax on privilege itself. This prompted the paper to espouse a radical proposal. Early in 1883 it began to agitate for the adoption of an income tax, which would be "the fairest tax we ever levied," for by tapping incomes from investments and other intangibles it would require the "money-archy" to shoulder its share of the load. At the same time, an income tax would enable the government to reduce its tariffs and excises, "relieving our industries of a great many burdens which now weigh heavily upon them." [18] Enthusiastically, therefore, the *Post-Dispatch* endorsed the Plumb bill which called for a five percent levy on income derived from securities.[19]

In taking up the income tax the *Post-Dispatch* broke with the old

---

[15] *Ibid.*, Dec. 6, 1882.
[16] *Ibid.*, Aug. 12, 1882.
[17] *Ibid.*, Sept. 13, 1882.
[18] A levy on incomes was also a plank in the agrarian platform as early as 1878 in Missouri. Buck, *The Agrarian Crusade*, p. 198; Clevenger, "Agrarian Politics," p. 55; Williams and Shoemaker, *Missouri*, II, 307.
[19] *Post-Dispatch*, Sept. 13, 1882, Feb. 16, 1883.

Liberals. The gulf between them was widening on other issues as well. Civil service reform, which for the Liberals almost assumed the status of a cure-all, the *Post-Dispatch* came to view with a skepticism bordering on cynicism. Pulitzer disliked the implicit assumption of many impeccable Liberals that only an elite should conduct the affairs of government.[20] The ordinary individual, he believed, was quite capable of handling public matters. His paper scoffed at Charles W. Eliot, the president of Harvard, who thought the issue so important that he advocated a civil service party which would draw millions of right-minded citizens to its standard. In its plebeian way the *Post-Dispatch* observed that far from being a nation-saving matter, the so-called "people's reform [is] not at all pressing" and "the people are not at all urgent" in their demands for it.[21] And when, at length, President Arthur signed the Pendleton Act an editorial commented deprecatingly:

> Before the civil service bill was passed we all wanted it, and doubted very much whether the country could get along without it. Now that we have it in our reach we do not think so much of it, and there is a general disposition to doubt its efficacy as a panacea.[22]

As a former politician, moreover, Pulitzer had a higher appreciation of the arts of practical politics and the values of a spoils system, for the paper remarked of the civil service reformers:

> These gentlemen are just now learning the painful lesson that it is not as easy to run the public service as it is to stand by and criticize those who are running it. . . . [Besides,] the people are getting tired of sentimental parties of all kinds, and sentimental politicians are finding their occupations growing as obsolete as that of the lecturer.

The paper added that civil service reformism was in the same class of "sentimental politics" as women's rights, a cause which was also "something of a bore."

Although it devoted much space to national issues, after 1880 the *Post-Dispatch* became more absorbed than ever in regional and local affairs. This tendency had been observable earlier, but now it be-

---

[20] Goldman, *Rendezvous with Destiny,* p. 19, emphasizes the elitist outlook of many civil service reformers. See also, Ari Hoogenboom, *Outlawing the Spoils: A History of the Civil Service Reform Movement, 1865-1883* (Urbana, Ill., 1961), for a careful appraisal of the entire movement. This study confirms Goldman's observations but goes much beyond them in examining the motives of the reformers.
[21] *Post-Dispatch,* June 16, 1882.
[22] *Ibid.,* May 10, 1883.

came a dominant characteristic. In part, of course, there was no presidential contest to focus interest upon larger problems, but to a great extent Pulitzer's concentration on Missouri and St. Louis resulted from his maturing conviction that a successful afternoon newspaper must be concerned with subjects of immediate interest to its constituents.

The political question the *Post-Dispatch* considered the most pressing in American life was being debated in the legislature at Jefferson City; this was whether the vast power of corporate wealth could be brought under reasonable control by government. Late in 1881, when a new break in grain prices once more plunged agriculture into depression, Missouri's agrarians returned to the Granger demands for railway and anti-monopoly legislation. As before, many farmers joined the ever-present third party—still called Greenback, although inflation for the moment had lost popularity—but the principal struggle took place in the ranks of the Democratic Party. Its top-heavy majorities of the seventies were gradually declining as traditional loyalties subsided, but it continued to dominate the state.[23]

The forces of privilege were as difficult to dislodge after 1880 as they had been earlier, but now the farmers seemed to be gaining the support of a growing body of businessmen in St. Louis who also were becoming alarmed about the effect of corporate monopoly upon trade. As we have seen, an urban revolt had taken root in the late seventies and now was developing into a movement of substantial proportions. The growing strength of the reform forces, consequently, should have presaged the passage of stronger anti-railroad and anti-monopoly legislation, but unfortunately important issues kept arising between city and country which weakened and divided the reformers. Freed from Pulitzer's old absorption in politics, the *Post-Dispatch* after 1880 expressed more clearly than ever the views of the urban middle classes, and it, too, revealed a deep-seated conflict in the outlook of St. Louis businessmen: a fear of the growth of corporate power and privilege, but at the same time, in the face of agrarian demands for increased governmental intervention in economic life, a rising concern for the sacredness of property and a deepening distrust of rural politicians.

The emancipation of the *Post-Dispatch* from Democratic partisanship in state politics—matching developments that had already taken place in St. Louis—occurred early in 1881. Pulitzer labored hard for Thomas Crittenden in the gubernatorial campaign, hoping to have an important voice in shaping the policies of the new administration,

---

[23] See Clevenger, "Agrarian Politics," esp. early chapters; and Williams and Shoemaker, II.

but almost immediately after attaining office Crittenden turned to the *Missouri Republican* and the Dark Lantern for advice and support.[24]

The first intimation of Pulitzer's fall from favor occurred when, at the behest of the *Republican,* Crittenden, a dignified, bumbling man, appointed a John T. Williams to the newly created post of state insurance commissioner. Williams had been connected with a fraudulent local insurance scheme exposed by the *Post-Dispatch* in 1879 and the paper suspected his appointment was desired by interests anxious to prevent rigid enforcement of the new laws governing insurance companies.[25] About the same time, the governor named to the St. Louis police board two men in league with the local machine and also backed by the *Republican.* Surprised and angered, the *Post-Dispatch* asked, WHO ARE THEY? [26] Realizing its loss of influence, it adopted a tone of contempt when Crittenden also selected a member of the Knapp family, publishers of the *Republican,* for a state job. It sneered that "the amount of dust that has to be licked off a Governor's shoes in an exchange for an office . . . would actually appall the St. Louis Street Cleaning Department." [27] The old quarrel was renewed, and soon the *Post-Dispatch* was saying:

> We begin to sympathize with Gov. CRITTENDEN. He has unintentionally secured the indorsement of the St. Louis *Republican,* and judging by the fate of Governors who have gone before, this means ignominious political death at the end of his term.[28]

Although the break between Pulitzer and Crittenden at first was scarcely more than a personal matter compounded by the bitter rivalry between the *Post-Dispatch* and *Republican,* it saved Pulitzer's newspaper from the dangers of "organship." The *Post-Dispatch* was now free to pursue an independent way in state politics, and its emancipation became more and more evident as it turned to causes dear to the hearts of St. Louisans.

The paper's independence was first shown in the renewal of its campaign to suppress organized gambling in the city, during which it exposed the influence of the gamblers on the local Democratic machine and through it, on Crittenden's policies in Jefferson City.[29] Crittenden's appointment of Morgan Boland, a "small politician," as head of the board, gave the *Post-Dispatch* an opportunity to at-

[24] St. Louis *Spectator,* Jan. 15, 1881.
[25] *Ibid. Post-Dispatch,* Jan. 13, 1881, Jan. 15, 1881.
[26] *Post-Dispatch,* Jan. 12, 1881, Jan. 13, 1881.
[27] *Ibid.,* Jan. 20, 1881.
[28] *Ibid.,* Jan. 29, 1881.
[29] Soraghan, "History of St. Louis," pp. 30-31, 46. St. Louis frequently went Republican, whereas the state administration was invariably Democratic.

tack the governor, which it did with startling venom, and condemn state control of local police.[30] Because the local machine was becoming permeated by corrupt influences, represented by the Ed Butler type of ward politicians, the new police board was expected to play ball with the gambling interests.

The governor, who meant well, was taken aback by the assault on his appointees, both by the *Post-Dispatch* and the *Globe-Democrat;* after a few weeks he abruptly dismissed the board.[31] A new panel of commissioners, this time well known merchants, was selected. The *Post-Dispatch* was pleased, remarking, "they are all good men and the Governor did the right thing at last." [32] The merchant-policemen inaugurated a vigorous program of law enforcement, as the newspapers demanded, but the gamblers, protected by ward boss influence, were difficult to suppress. In fact, Butler's lieutenants were reported to be in secret partnership with Bob Pate, the gambling king, and there were frequent rumors of payoffs to police officials.[33]

However, after a long crusade by the *Post-Dispatch* and unremitting efforts by the police board, Pate and other underworld chieftains were brought to trial and convicted. But just as the law was about to take its course, St. Louisans were dumbfounded to learn that the governor, no doubt at the behest of the local organization, had pardoned them. WHAT DID THEY PAY? the *Post-Dispatch* thundered in large headlines, as it turned its guns full upon Crittenden.[34] It pilloried the governor in the most unrestrained fashion, accusing "His Leniency" of being in league with the St. Louis gambling ring and paying off political debts with pardons. This should cause "every decent citizen to hang his head in shame," the *Post-Dispatch* spluttered in its attacks upon the "pig-headed dolt." [35] And in a signed statement Joseph Pulitzer himself demanded: "Impeach THOMAS T. CRITTENDEN for high crimes and misdemeanors." [36] This personal assault reached its climax when the paper ran a portrait of the governor on page one with a legend inscribed across

---

[30] *Post-Dispatch,* Feb. 10, 1881.

[31] Crittenden in the beginning, at least, although he appointed machine politicians to the police board, was sincerely determined to stamp out gambling in St. Louis. He issued explicit orders to this effect to the new board members. *Ibid.,* Jan. 22, 1881.

[32] *Post-Dispatch,* March 11, 1881.

[33] Frank Turner, a Butler lieutenant, was reported to be receiving a cut of Pate's takings from his gambling house. *Ibid.,* July 7, 1882; *Spectator,* Nov. 12, 1881.

[34] *Post-Dispatch,* June 26, 1882. At this time the paper was also in full cry against the governor over the James Boys.

[35] *Ibid.,* June 26, 1882, June 27, 1882.

[36] *Ibid.,* July 15, 1882, July 21, 1882.

his forehead, "Bob Pate's Governor." Cutlines beneath labeled Crittenden THE MAN WHO DISGRACES MISSOURI.[37]

Public reaction to this excessive exhibition of sensationalism chastened the *Post-Pispatch* a bit. The *Republican* voiced the sentiments of many when it commented that the picture was "shocking to the general sense of fair play" and "disgraceful to the journalistic profession." [38]

More fundamentally, the *Post-Dispatch* demanded that the Missouri legislature "repeal . . . the law which deprives the tax-payers of St. Louis the control of their police." It continued:

> If the voters of a city are competent to choose their municipal law-makers the executive officers of their city government, the judges of their courts, and to participate in the election of the executive, legislative and judicial functionaries of the State, how can they be unfit to elect the administration of their own local Police Department, which they alone support, and whose successful management concerns them more nearly than any one else? The fact is that the metropolitan police system is a departure from the fundamental principle of our republican government; it is a denial of the capacity of the people for self-government in local affairs, and as an experiment in opposition to the whole tendency of our institutions it has not worked well.[39]

The need for reform was underlined when, following the Pate pardon, in the summer of 1882 the merchants resigned from the police board in disgust. Once more Crittenden turned to the local Democratic organization, more potent than ever now, to appoint Dan Kerwin, a front man for Ed Butler, as the new police board president. The *Post-Dispatch* declared, "We have a Police Board now which was organized by the Governor to build up the Democratic rings in St. Louis." [40] What this portended was soon clear when Kerwin handed over the police department's horseshoeing contract to Butler at a fat fee, a transaction the paper exposed under A NEAT JOB.[41]

Turning the police board over to "the Village Blacksmith school of politics," as the *Post-Dispatch* expressed it, was only a part of a wider conspiracy by the Democratic forces to buttress their hold on

37 *Ibid.,* Aug. 3, 1882, Aug. 4, 1882. Actually, Pate was pardoned twice.
38 *Missouri Republican,* Aug. 5, 1882; *Post-Dispatch,* Aug. 8, 1882.
39 *Post-Dispatch,* July 11, 1882, July 19, 1882.
40 *Ibid.,* July 22, 1882.
41 *Ibid.,* Aug. 3, 1882.

Missouri. Locally, in the spring of 1881 the Butlerites sought to use the Democratic control of the state government to euchre the city from the Republicans who had won the mayoral election, while the Bourbon state organization needed larger majorities in St. Louis to cope with agrarian dissidents who threatened to upset conservative domination in Jefferson City. A plan was concocted which would have virtually repealed the city charter of 1876, permitting the state's Democratic officials to "tinker . . . at will" with St. Louis.[42] This scheme, exposed by the *Post-Dispatch,* was too ambitious to be successful. Crittenden's move to turn the police over to Democratic uses in 1882 was more practical, as the subsequent primary election showed. According to an indignant article in the *Post-Dispatch,* Kerwin stationed policemen outside many polling places and they, "by a series of petty annoyances that few respectable men could withstand," helped to secure a majority for regular candidates.[43] This was the start of twenty-five years of police interference in local elections which made St. Louis notorious in the annals of municipal politics.[44]

With this success, Democratic efforts became bolder. A flood of bills was submitted to the legislature, one proposing to transfer the fire department from municipal to state jurisdiction and another the election of all municipal officials whose salaries exceeded $1,800.[45] "The Democratic State Central committee has come forward with an indorsement of the scheme to shear the Mayor of St. Louis of his appointing power," fumed the *Post-Dispatch.* "This is Democratic Greed and Folly combined."

> Let the statesmen who propose to violate the principle of local self-government be thorough and consistent. Nearly every statesman at Jefferson City has an act to regulate some feature of our city government. Let them pool their issues. . . . It would be more satisfactory to have local self-government abolished at one fell swoop than to have it hacked to death by encroachments here and there.[46]

Thanks, at least in part, to the alertness of the *Post-Dispatch,* most of these proposals failed, but one fatal bill was pushed through

42 *Ibid.,* April 15, 1881.
43 Even the *Republican* objected when strong-arm methods by the police were responsible for the defeat of one of its favored candidates. *Ibid.,* July 22, 1882, July 24, 1882, July 25, 1882.
44 St. Louis *Globe-Democrat,* Oct. 19, 1952.
45 *Post-Dispatch,* Jan. 27, 1883, Jan. 29, 1883.
46 *Ibid.,* Jan. 27, 1883.

which virtually won the battle. It gave to the Recorder of Voters, an appointee of the governor, complete control of city elections, including absolute authority over the registration of voters, appointment of all clerks and judges, and the custody of the ballots.[47] The man selected by Crittenden for the post was Clarence Hoblitzelle, son-in-law of a publisher of the *Missouri Republican*.[48] The Democrats now had a firm grasp on local elections; Republicans railed. David P. Dyer, candidate for governor in 1880, later described the act as "a partisan measure of the vilest and most reprehensible character," which all but disfranchised the St. Louis Republican vote.[49] The independent *Post-Dispatch* also bitterly denounced the law, and although it did not then suspect the honesty of Hoblitzelle (who was later to perpetrate some of "the grossest frauds" in the city's history), it foresaw that "little groups of bummers, thugs, repeaters and pothouse ruffians" would now control elections.[50] "That is why the *Republican* supports a bill to extend the power of Mr. HOBLITZELLE," it remarked acidly. The *Post-Dispatch's* fight to save the city thus ended in failure.[51] Its dislike of outstate politicians who helped to put over the registration law became more intense than ever.

The paper's vigorous nonpartisanship extended into outstate politics where similar plans were afoot. Smarting from congressional defeats in 1880 at the hands of the Republican-Greenback coalition, the Missouri Democrats were determined to prevent a recurrence by gerrymandering the state's congressional districts.[52] A bill was introduced which divided St. Louis neatly into two districts, each with a narrow but definite Democratic majority, and carved up the rest of the state into a collection of safe districts except for one or

---

[47] *Ibid.*, March 21, 1883.

[48] *Ibid.*, March 9, 1883.

[49] *Autobiography*, pp. 175-77.

[50] Hoblitzelle was the Recorder at the time of the ballot rigging, both in 1884, when thousands of Cleveland votes were manufactured, and in 1885, when David R. Francis, later governor, was literally counted in as mayor of St. Louis. A number of court cases grew out of the former, in which much corruption was revealed. One address, a bawdy house, registered 38 male voters! The Recorder became known as "Dirty Dog" Hoblitzelle after Francis was "elected." Dyer, p. 181; *The Whip*, July 4, 1885, July 25, 1885, Aug. 1, 1885.

[51] *Post-Dispatch*, March 10, 1883. As Democratic strength continued to decline in the eighties and nineties; as the local machine grew stronger and bolder in St. Louis, Democrats continued more and more to interfere with local government until the Republican administrations virtually lost control of municipal government. Thus what some believed to be a normal, if narrow, Republican majority in the city was more and more neutralized in state politics by fraudulent vote counts and rigged elections. See article by Charles Nagel in *Reedy's Mirror*, Aug. 29, 1901.

[52] The occasion was the award to Missouri of an additional representative as a result of the census of 1880. *Post-Dispatch*, March 28, 1882.

two outstate which were irretrievably Republican.[53] The network of party papers led by the *Republican,* the Democratic organ, beat the drums for the measure, and "the little statesmen from the sage-brush districts," as the *Post-Dispatch* contemptuously referred to the rural politicians, pushed it through. The *Republican* justified the apportionment on the ground that the Democratic majority was overwhelming anyhow, a contention the *Post-Dispatch* refuted by citing recent election statistics.[54] Rural organs were blunter: "Meet gerrymander with gerrymander. Give blow for blow. When power is possessed use it. . . . Make no excuses. Explain nothing. Have but one object in view—fourteen Democratic Congressmen from Missouri."[55] The *Post-Dispatch* conducted a vigorous campaign against the gerrymander. "The mere idea of openly trying to disfranchise 189,000 voters—not to allow them a single representative— . . . is unfair and undemocratic, and will re-act on its imbecile authors." It warned heatedly that "the people of this State are not in a humor to put up with party blunders."[56]

The *Post-Dispatch* held the rural politicians accountable for this excess of partisanship, and no longer bothered to conceal its dislike for the "stalwart ex-Confederate sentiment which now sways and directs the policy of the party of this State."[57] It became shorter tempered than ever with appeals to the threadbare memories of the war indulged in by country politicians. No longer were there passionate editorials defending the right of Southerners to elect whomever they desired. "Here in Missouri we have just a shade too much of the old Confederate spirit in our politics," the paper observed in commenting on a veterans' encampment at Sedalia, "and the holding of these annual conventions will necessarily have the effect of stimulating the old sentiment and cementing more closely the element that controls the Democratic party."[58] It viewed sourly Senator Francis M. Cockrell's candidacy for reelection: "a third-class lawyer" who was "a fair representative of three elements in this State that combined form an overwhelming majority—mediocrity, hypocrisy, and Confederacy."[59] Yet, significantly, when the *Republican* put up Thomas Allen, the favorite of the St. Louis Bourbons, who only recently had defeated Pulitzer for Congress, the *Post-Dispatch* re-

[53] *Ibid.,* May 1, 1882, May 3, 1882.
[54] *Ibid.,* March 29, 1882.
[55] *Ibid.,* April 20, 1882.
[56] *Ibid.,* April 1, 1882.
[57] *Ibid.,* April 21, 1882.
[58] *Ibid.,* Aug. 15, 1882.
[59] *Ibid.,* Nov. 12, 1880.

marked that, although "Democratic policy should be to give a denial to the Republican charge that Democracy means Confederacy":

> Still the Democratic party of Missouri deserves credit for one thing. It was generally understood that a very big bar'l was ready to be opened [for ALLEN] to encompass the defeat of Mr. COCKRELL. Had the Missouri Senatorship been purchasable Mr. COCKRELL would not have been chosen. However mediocre he may be in intellect, he is not corrupt. On the contrary, he is poor and honest. He is not the tool of the rich corporations and powerful monopolies who already own a majority of the Senate. . . . After all the only great issue in the politics of the future is whether the monopolies, corporations and the money aristocracy shall govern the country. . . . If his [COCKRELL'S] election is no triumph to the mental status of the State, it speaks well for its morals. It shows that in Missouri, at least, the Senatorship cannot yet be purchased.[60]

The paper's contemptuous attitude towards outstate politicians was not improved by the rise of the prohibition movement. In 1882, triggered by the success of rural forces in Kansas and Iowa in enacting legislation against the manufacture and sale of alcoholic beverages, dry forces in Missouri launched a drive for a prohibition amendment.[61] A close connection existed between prohibition and agrarianism, illustrated by a statewide temperance meeting at Excelsior Springs which was addressed by H. Martin Williams, a leading greenbacker. In Cockerill's humorous style the *Post-Dispatch* lampooned "the oratorical tornado":

> H. MARTIN is one of those speakers to whom a thousand years are as one mild day, and, unmindful of the approach of train time, he unfortunately dwelt on the bright side of the drunkard's life first. . . . The gayety of the gilded saloon, the wit and soul, the fun and frolic that enliven the meetings of festive youth, are said to have been depicted with captivating power. None of his hearers had ever witnessed real scenes half so fascinating and seductive. They began to wish that he had meant what he said in his opening request that they should go with him into the haunts of Pleasure. . . . Brother WILLIAMS was forced to leave

---

[60] *Ibid.*, Jan. 6, 1881.

[61] The *Post-Dispatch* closely followed events in Kansas and Iowa. See issues of March 25, 1882, June 28, 1882. See also, Arthur Meier Schlesinger, *The Rise of the City, 1878-1898 (A History of American Life*, X) (New York, 1933), pp. 353-60, for a general discussion of the temperance movement.

the temperance side of the picture unfinished. The demoralizing effect is said to have been deplorable.[62]

But prohibition was no laughing matter. The Missouri Temperance Alliance, led by a Baptist minister, John A. Brooks, had become powerful in outstate Missouri, forcing from scores of delegates to the state Democratic convention a pledge to work for prohibition. A struggle ensued between country and city representatives when the convention met. MEET THE ISSUE, the *Post-Dispatch* urged the St. Louis delegation, declaring that because of its "deep, sincere interest in . . . local self-government," it wanted "to see the Democracy save the State from this wild plunge into despotic fanaticism." [63] Frantically the practical politicians sought to keep the party together by arranging a meaningless straddle which the *Post-Dispatch* denounced.

> A dominant party in the leading State west of the Mississippi and the greatest Democratic State in the Union, might, if it had the courage of its opinions, have placed itself in the lead of public thought on the greatest, most vital question of State government now agitating the active public mind. But we regret to say that after parroting over the old stereotyped phrases, and some sound doctrine . . . about civil service reform and centralization and monopolies, the deliverance of the Missouri Democrats on the Prohibition question is a miserable abortion and a disgrace. . . . It is laboriously constructed to mean acquiescence in Prohibition where Prohibition is strongest, and Anti-Prohibition where sound policy, the rights of property and the old Anglo-Saxon regard for individual liberty and responsibility are stronger than a domineering fanaticism.[64]

The *Post-Dispatch* conducted a vigorous campaign to defeat prohibition candidates in the fall elections. Its arguments voiced the city's concern. The prohibitionists would damage the prosperity of St. Louis, and without compensation (to the city) they would destroy $30,000,000 worth of property.[65] In a lengthy editorial, OMNIPOTENT MAJORITIES, the *Post-Dispatch* elaborated this theme:

> In this country all property rights rest upon . . . the basis of voluntary sale and fair purchase, and the primary object of all our constitutions is to protect these property rights and the liberty of the citizen. The Constitution of Missouri especially provides that private property shall neither be taken *nor damaged* for the

---

62 *Post-Dispatch*, June 23, 1882.
63 *Ibid.*, July 22, 1882.
64 *Ibid.*, July 27, 1882.
65 *Ibid.*, July 31, 1882.

benefit of the public without compensation to the injured owner. Nevertheless, in spite of our written constitutions, there is a restive reformatory spirit among us which insists that the rule of the majority should be as omnipotent in the United States as the legislative power of Parliament in England, and that all the rights of property and of personal liberty which it is the office of our written constitutions to protect shall be set at naught whenever the majority decides that such a course will improve public morals or promote the general welfare. . . .

Where is this sort of thing to stop? If all the injuries that individuals of perverted tastes and morals inflict upon themselves are to be visited upon the property, the industries and personal liberty of other people by this sort of legislation, what property will be safe? [66]

Although the threat to property and prosperity perhaps chiefly worried the *Post-Dispatch,* the paper was also alarmed at the attempt to invade private lives. Prohibition would jeopardize individual right, the paper maintained in an editorial entitled PERSONAL LIBERTY:

Not only eternal vigilance, but vigorous resistance is required to curb the tendency of majorities, as well as of autocrats and oligarchies, towards governing too much—towards making their own tastes, customs, sanitary creeds, moral hobbies and religious spasms the measure of other people's duties, imposed by law and enforced with penalties destructive of . . . property rights and personal freedom.[67]

In resisting prohibition, the *Post-Dispatch* displayed particular solicitude for the rights of the large German population to whom beer-drinking was an ingrained habit, and for the rights of the working classes "in a large city" to whom "the saloon is about the only place [in] which a poor man in his working clothes is welcomed. . . ."

To the moralist and reformer the beer saloon presents a spectacle of idle men, wasting their time and their money in drinking. To the tired workmen, the beer saloon, with its saw-dust carpet, its clean tables, and its daily papers, is as attractive a haven of rest as the club of the millionaires. . . . The prohibitionists and Sabbatarians who propose to shut out the enjoyment of life from all but the rich, would do well to provide a better substitute for the saloons before abolishing them, and to recognize that even the poor wage-worker may have some social needs.[68]

---

[66] *Ibid.,* Aug. 22, 1882.
[67] *Ibid.,* July 22, 1882.
[68] *Ibid.,* July 22, 1882, June 27, 1883.

Whatever the influence of the *Post-Dispatch*—and it was read largely by those already converted—the fall elections administered a sharp rebuke to prohibition. Dry candidates even in outstate Missouri were defeated, and a crowning psychological blow was sustained in nearby Kansas, where an anti-prohibition Democrat was elected governor. This in a state where people "were supposed to prefer the devil to a Democrat," chortled the *Post-Dispatch*.[69] Prohibitionists fought a rear-guard action in the legislature the following January, attempting to get their proposal before the people in a referendum. Surprisingly, this time they had the support of the *Post-Dispatch,* but it was insincere, almost a journalistic stunt. The paper's purpose was plain; confident now that the proposition would be rejected "by a majority of 100,000 at least," it called upon the legislature to TRUST THE PEOPLE.[70] The lawmakers, however, including every one of the representatives from St. Louis, timidly preferred not to take chances. They tabled the measure.[71]

The chief significance of the prohibition struggle was that it strained relations between city and country at a time when issues of corporate control, in which St. Louis merchants and farmers had a common interest, were rising to the surface. Certainly this was true of the *Post-Dispatch,* whose distrust and contempt for rural politicians already was great.

The old Granger law regulating railroads had been a disappointment; in the early eighties a renewed demand for really stringent controls became the battle-cry of the farmers, supported now by many St. Louis businessmen. The opposition, too, was an assortment: rural party regulars in control of county organizations, the growing Ed Butler machine in St. Louis, and the forces of privilege in St. Louis and elsewhere who represented the railroads, traction, gas, and other interests.[72] In this struggle, which began to move toward a showdown in 1882, the *Post-Dispatch* spoke for the increasingly large group of St. Louis businessmen who feared the railroad combines which seemed to be enveloping the city. But the *Post-Dispatch* drew back when the time came to drive through effective legislation. Indeed, between agrarians calling for stronger government regulation

---

[69] *Ibid.,* Nov. 10, 1882, Nov. 20, 1882, Nov. 22, 1882.

[70] *Ibid.,* Dec. 1, 1882.

[71] *Ibid.,* Feb. 22, 1883, March 2, 1883.

[72] Clevenger, "Agrarian Politics," pp. 1-6, discusses some of the elements in the Missouri Democratic Party. The *Post-Dispatch* mentions the rural county Democratic organs as part of the statewide regular organization. *Post-Dispatch,* June 27, 1882. A later editor referred to "the country press" as part of "the old machine crowd of editors." Frank O'Neil to Joseph Pulitzer, Nov. 8, 1907, Pulitzer Papers (CU).

and the privilege-greedy Bourbons, the paper threaded an erratic course.

The matter of railroad control in Missouri was becoming a pressing issue with the rise of Jay Gould's railway empire. Beginning with his purchase of the Wabash in 1879, the *Post-Dispatch* watched with mounting concern his steady absorption of the state's lines west and southwest from St. Louis. The headlines told the story: MERGED; IRON MOUNTAIN; AN ANXIOUS QUERY; and ONCE MORE TO THE BREACH, as one after another Gould took over the Katy, Missouri Pacific, Iron Mountain, Frisco, the Hannibal & St. Joe.[73] All but the last terminated in St. Louis. The comings and goings of Jay Gould and his party became front page news as local papers competed for interviews with the inscrutable financier.[74]

ENOUGH! ENOUGH! cried the *Post-Dispatch* during the course of Gould's buildup:

> We cannot agree with the general sentiment of satisfaction and sanguine expectation in regard to Mr. Jay Gould's extraordinary railroad investments in this State. . . . One Wall Street stock opera-tor can, with the motion of his little finger . . . control the four principal trunk lines of this State—four railroads running through almost every county, affecting the value of almost every farm in the State and the interest of nearly every business man in this city. . . .
> How will this enormous accumulation of power in the hands of this man Gould affect the destiny of St. Louis?[75]

Gould also branched out into other activities, acquiring "controlling interests in stock yards, in the great iron and steel manufacturing companies [in Carondelet], in the Mississippi Barge Line, in mining property . . . [in] Western Missouri. . . . He thus controls over $120,-000,000 worth of property in this State, which . . . makes him the arbiter of business competition between men and localities, and to a great extent the arbiter between parties and political aspirants."[76]

---

[73] *Post-Dispatch*, Nov. 30, 1880, Dec. 13, 1880, Jan. 5, 1882, Jan. 26, 1882. An excellent treatment of Gould's railway operations is Julius Grodinsky, *Jay Gould: His Business Career, 1867-1892* (Philadelphia, 1957). See esp. chs. 10, 13. See also, Robert E. Riegel, "The Missouri Pacific, 1879-1900," *Missouri Historical Review*, XVIII (Jan. 1924), 173-95; and V. V. Masterson, *The Katy Railroad and the Last Frontier* (Norman, Okla., 1952), chs. 25-30.

[74] Stevens, "New Journalism in Missouri," *Missouri Historical Review*, XVIII (July 1924), 560. *Post-Dispatch*, May 1, 1883. The *Post-Dispatch* scored a great triumph when City Editor Moore gained an interview.

[75] *Post-Dispatch*, Dec. 14, 1880.

[76] *Ibid.*

Dread of Gould's political influence grew rapidly, and the *Post-Dispatch* gave worried voice to it:

> How will he use this vast power through his grand army of employes may be inferred from his own recent statement that his pigeon-holes were full of letters from politicians and eminent men suing for his favor. "I take little interest in politics," said he, "and when I am forced to do so, it is because I must protect the enterprises in which I am embarked and the interests of the stockholders embarked with me." How he protects the latter is told in thousands of fleecing . . . operations by which his control of so many lines has enabled him to grow fabulously rich on the ruin of tens of thousands of capitalists and the plunder of millions of producers. His attorneys and dependents figure in every primary and are on hand to play his quiet tune in every convention. His secret influence over State officers and Legislatures lurks in the background of every public question. . . . It is charged that he controls our [State] Supreme Court nominations. . . . Our Governor is known to be his friend and ally, and the time is rapidly approaching, no doubt, when the road to every form of political advancement in Missouri will lie through the favor of JAY GOULD.
>
> Do the people of Missouri realize how thoroughly their institutions . . . are menaced by the erection of this vast fabric of One-man power in their midst? [77]

The paper was peppered with articles which, it said, "Business Men Should Read," stories of small producers squeezed out by "the methods of the great monopoly corporations of the present day." [78]

Especially was the *Post-Dispatch* concerned about "the vexed question of freightage . . . in which the [St. Louis] mercantile community is deeply interested," and well it might, for in 1882 Gould added to his existing holdings by acquiring a controlling interest in the St. Louis bridge connecting the city with the East. Largely blaming Gould, the paper wailed that the railroads were giving "this city the go-by for the benefit of Chicago and New England," and "even its own lines are beginning to take advantage of its mercantile good nature." [79] Exposure stories, such as one headed HAMPERED TRADE, provided chapter and verse to the charges of Gould's discriminatory policies.[80] The

[77] *Ibid.*
[78] *Ibid.*
[79] *Ibid.*, Nov. 3, 1882.
[80] *Ibid.*, Nov. 4, 1882. To what degree Gould actually discriminated against St. Louis is a matter of point of view. It is illogical to believe that he would have willfully damaged the trade of a city which was at the very center of his railroad

Post-Dispatch both represented and aroused the merchant community of St. Louis to the seeming peril.[81]

The solution? In keeping with its basic philosophy, the paper turned to the Missouri constitution which contained an antitrust clause placed there by the Granger revolt in 1875. Although it had been a dead letter ever since, the *Post-Dispatch* sought to use it to force Gould to divest himself of one or more of his roads and to resurrect competition—always a *Post-Dispatch* aim. In a blistering editorial it charged that Gould was "in direct violation of the explicit prohibition in the Constitution" by being, at the same time, president of the Wabash and the Missouri Pacific roads which it claimed were "parallel lines . . . competing lines," as were other Gould-controlled roads.[82]

In certain moods the paper also seemed favorable to increased regulation. In a vigorous editorial in 1883 it hailed a decision by the United States Supreme Court which upheld the power of the Illinois legislature to impose rates on the Burlington Railroad despite a charter giving the company the right to set its own rates. The *Post-Dispatch* thought the decision not only excellent but remarkable, since the Court was usually "very careful to leave every possible loop-hole for the benefit of the great corporations." "It will be a cold day for this country," it concluded, if the railroads "by any process obtain immunity from public control in their dealings with the people." [83]

In common with the agrarians, too, the *Post-Dispatch,* during the

---

interest. In fact, in 1879, after acquiring the Wabash, Gould fought to improve St. Louis's trading position. (See Grodinsky, pp. 200-202). Nevertheless, there were obvious burdens imposed on the city, such as, for example, the tolls on all shipments coming over the Mississippi bridge from and to the East—whether the tolls, from a stockholder's point of view, were justified or not. In any case, as his grasp on the transportation facilities serving St. Louis reached monopoly proportions, it was all too clear that this Wall Street operator was in a *position* to determine the fortunes of many local shippers. It was not so much, perhaps, what Gould actually *did* as what he was *capable* of doing which caused anxiety among the class of small merchants—and large ones, too—for whom Pulitzer spoke. In a larger sense, Gould's empire was a symbol of the vast, impersonal corporations developing in the industrial age which were so repugnant to the businessmen whose views were voiced by the *Post-Dispatch.* See Grodinsky, esp. chs. 10, 13, and 20, for a thorough discussion of Gould's policies relative to his St. Louis-based roads. See perceptive observations in Unger, ch. 6, as to the role of railroads, banks, etc., as symbols of a new economy which the farmers of this period did not understand. Undoubtedly the same remarks may be applied to the St. Louis merchants and to the *Post-Dispatch.*

[81] Clevenger, "Railroads in Missouri Politics, 1875-1887," *Missouri Historical Review*, XLIII (April 1949), 227-28.

[82] *Post-Dispatch*, Sept. 5, 1882.

[83] *Ibid.*, May 9, 1883. The Court declared that, despite the original contract, no legislature could bind a subsequent legislature in matters concerning the public interest.

campaign of 1882, attacked the state administration for what it termed a pro-railroad policy. It used this issue with peculiar bitterness in obvious efforts to destroy the political future of its arch-enemy, Thomas Crittenden. In a series of excited and violent attacks it accused the governor of permitting Gould to remain "above the law." [84] But in darkly hinting that Gould had somehow been the man who secured the Democratic nomination for Crittenden in 1880, the *Post-Dispatch* was guilty of a lamentable lack of sincerity. Pulitzer, who himself had worked unremittingly in Crittenden's behalf, had never before mentioned this claim. Obviously, the paper was indulging in reckless charges, as it frequently did when Pulitzer's ire was aroused. Moreover, these attacks on Crittenden would have rung more truly if the paper's own course had been consistent. Despite its cries against Gould and his Bourbon allies, the *Post-Dispatch* heartily welcomed the reelection of John O'Day, the well-known railway lobbyist, in 1882 as chairman of the state Democratic committee. The paper could not have been misled about O'Day, for he himself told a *Post-Dispatch* reporter that he saw nothing wrong with Gould's activities and "I should not like to see him attacked." The choice of O'Day, the paper must have known, would help maintain the Bourbons in power and most certainly would vitiate the drive to bring the railroads under effective controls.[85]

In sharp contrast with 1880, the *Post-Dispatch* was a nonpartisan sheet in the state campaign of 1882. It stuck to issues, particularly conducting a running attack upon what it considered Gould candidates—notably James Burnes across the state who was running for Congress. Never did it endorse the Democratic Party; and, in fact, it went out of its way to praise a convention of Republican bolters for attacking Crittenden's "notorious disregard . . . of the statutory provisions of the State against the consolidation of railroad corporations." [86] The fall elections, however, were a sweeping triumph for the Democrats. The Republican-Greenback fusion, so successful in 1880, was swamped this time, and the greenbackers were all but obliterated.[87]

---

84 *Ibid.*, Sept. 5, 1882.

85 The paper's approval of O'Day was in part because it considered him "a General of rare executive ability" in winning elections, an attribute Pulitzer, the ex-politician, admired. Too, O'Day's reelection as state chairman eliminated Griff Prather, an associate of the hated *Republican*. *Post-Dispatch*, Aug. 14, 1882, Sept. 4, 1882, Sept. 13, 1882.

86 *Ibid.*, Sept. 21, 1882.

87 The Republican-Greenback coalition was not so well executed as in 1880. "Boss" Filley, the Republican leader, had a revolt on his hands when many in his party who abhorred the greenbackers, refused to go along. However, although the Democrats had a majority of about 70,000 votes in 1882, the *Post-Dispatch* pointed

The Democratic triumph set the stage for a struggle at Jefferson City within the ranks of the victors, for the reform forces had made important gains. Back in the Democratic fold, the agrarians were determined to challenge the supremacy of the Bourbons.[88] At the capital in January 1883, a "farmers' club," or "caucus," composed of fifty-five legislators, was formed under the leadership of John S. Marmaduke, the popular leader of the ex-Confederates.[89] This hard core group resolved to push through the legislature bills to stiffen railway legislation, eliminate tax favoritism, control monopolies, and institute a state inspection system of the sale of grain at St. Louis elevators. Many in the growing number of St. Louis businessmen who feared Gould were prepared to back them, although there were some who had misgivings about parts of the farmers' program and were uneasy about how far they might go. The monopolists prepared to do battle as "lobbyists fairly crowded the hotels . . . smoothing the lapels of [legislative] members' coats." Especially was this true of the "convivial, agreeable and interesting" railroad attorneys who swarmed to the capital.[90] The Bourbon politicians, too, with a friendly governor, control of the state committee, and the backing of the *Republican,* girded for a trial of strength. *Republican* editor Hyde frantically sought to line up votes which would give the Bourbons control of the legislative machinery, and he partly succeeded. T. P. Bashaw, a party regular, was made speaker of the lower house.[91]

The most important bill framed by the farmers' caucus was one strengthening the authority of the state railway commission, somewhat on the model of the Illinois regulatory law of 1873.[92] Despite the governor's admonition that additional legislation would frighten away capital and inhibit further railroad construction, the agrarians proposed a law which would make the state commission—not private shippers as formerly—the complainant in enforcement cases. Also the commission was to be empowered to set schedules of maximum

---

out that, considering their troubles, the Republicans had done rather well. The Democratic dominance actually was continuing to decline. *Ibid.,* Dec. 5, 1882. See Clevenger, "Railroads in Missouri Politics," p. 123; and Williams and Shoemaker, II, 318.

[88] Clevenger points out that there were 150,000 Grangers in the seventies but never more than 35,000 greenbackers. The remainder had returned to the Democratic fold but constituted a rebellious element. Clevenger, "Railroads in Missouri Politics," p. 113.

[89] *Post-Dispatch,* March 2, 1883. Besides being a railroad commissioner, Marmaduke was president of the Ex-Confederate Association of Missouri. The "Farmers' Club" was patterned on a device of Illinois rural legislators in the 1870's. Buck, *Granger Movement,* pp. 143-44.

[90] *Post-Dispatch,* March 9, 1883.

[91] *Ibid.,* Jan. 4, 1883, April 4, 1883.

[92] Buck, *Granger Movement,* pp. 149-58.

rates.[93] Under this proposal railway regulation rates in Missouri for the first time would become a reality; not only the farmers, but numerous St. Louis merchants favored it.

Although the bill cleared the house of representatives, it failed in the more conservative senate. Party and administration pressures were partially responsible, as were the efforts of the ingratiating and indefatigable lobbyists. Senators from the poor districts of Southern Missouri were persuaded that too stringent a law might discourage railroad building in their areas.[94] Also important, perhaps, was a segment of St. Louis merchants which was uneasy about the farmers' caucus. The caucus was too much a secret clique, too militant, inclined to be prohibitionist, and it was pushing other measures unpalatable to St. Louis. From the first, the *Post-Dispatch* contemptuously referred to caucus members as "moss backs" disdained by "people with brains." It sneered at their provincialisms, especially their refusal to appropriate funds to encourage immigration into the state, accusing them of wanting "to build a fence eighteen feet high . . . around the State of Missouri." [95] The paper complained that they wasted the time of the assembly with bills to increase the bounty on wolf scalps while opposing a measure to increase the efficiency of the courts by providing circuit judges with stenographers. Too often, it commented bitterly, "the Missouri legislature sits in Jefferson City, and sits on St. Louis." [96]

Primarily, however, it was the *Post-Dispatch's* fear that the agrarians' proposals might dangerously infringe on the rights of property that finally turned it against the railroad bill. "There is no restriction nor limitation whatever on the action of the Commissioners, no appeal from their authority," it pointed out. "All the managers, pool commissioners and others will not have a word to say" in establishing rates. The paper continued, availing itself of conservative arguments:

> Now, of course, while we all want to get the railroads down and jump on them, it is only proper to remark that there are several counties in the State that have no railroads, and before confiscating all the railroad property in the State and stopping railroad

93 *Post-Dispatch*, March 12, 1883; Clevenger, "Agrarian Politics," pp. 116-17. A more drastic farmers' bill would have arbitrarily set rail rates by legislative enactment. *Post-Dispatch*, March 12, 1883.
94 Most of the railway mileage in 1880 was north of the Missouri River. *Post-Dispatch*, Feb. 10, 1883. See also Williams and Shoemaker, II, 366-71.
95 The *Post-Dispatch* especially took umbrage at evidences of nativism in rural Missouri, a point about which Pulitzer was especially sensitive. It accused the Jefferson City *Tribune* of attempting "to . . . wave the banner of Nativism in Missouri politics, and, not satisfied with Native Americanism . . . to draw the line against Americans who had the misfortune to be born outside Missouri!" *Post-Dispatch*, July 20, 1882, Feb. 8, 1883.
96 *Ibid.*, Feb. 10, 1883.

building forever, it might be advisable to wait until the railroad system is complete. We frankly say that we can think of no better plan than that . . . [contained in this bill] for utterly destroying the value of the railroad property in Missouri.[97]

Missouri should not "prevent railroad building or . . . confiscate railroad property," the paper insisted time and again, adding—in disregard of its previous views—that "no fault has been found with the existing regulations, and no complaint has been made that they do not sufficiently protect the public."[98] This apparent change in tune was a welling up in Pulitzer of his essential conservatism in matters touching the sanctity of private property together with his profound distrust of the farm radicals. The *Post-Dispatch* preferred other ways of getting at the problem, such as the antitrust approach.

At the same time, however, the *Post-Dispatch* vigorously supported the efforts of the farmers' caucus to bring about a revision of state taxing policies to eliminate favoritism to railway corporations. It denounced "the outrageous discrimination made by the State Board of Equalization in favor of the railroad property of Missouri" and strongly approved a bill to plug loopholes in the tax laws to prevent further evasion. But the Bourbons prevented action, prompting the paper to agree with the Kansas City *Times* that

> No State in the Union was ever more . . . completely under corporation control than Democratic Missouri is to-day. . . . Affairs have been so managed that the railroads have been allowed to stand one year in arrears for taxes during the last ten years, while all other taxpayers were forced to pay promptly. . . . The Democratic party may sweep the Union in 1884 by putting itself at the head of the great anti-monopoly uprising which overthrew the Republican party in Pennsylvania, New York and California. But if it does, it will have to make for itself . . . a record very different from that which it is now making in Missouri.[99]

The paper also favored other types of monopoly-control legislation, although most of them failed of adoption. The measure that attracted the chief support of the *Post-Dispatch* was one designed to strengthen oil inspection. Complaints had been raised, especially by "solid merchants" in St. Louis, that the Waters Pierce Company, which

---

[97] *Ibid.*, March 12, 1883.

[98] *Ibid.*, March 21, 1883. Contempt for the existing law was expressed by the paper as recently as July 1, 1882.

[99] *Ibid.* No law got through the legislature, but the popular outcry over the administration's favoritism forced from the Board of Equalization a promise—which was unkept—to revise its policies. *Ibid.*, Feb. 20, 1883, March 7, 1883, May 24, 1883.

controlled oil marketing west of the Mississippi for the Standard Oil monopoly, was engaging in the questionable practice of mislabeling coal oil and selling it to unsuspecting retailers and consumers. The *Post-Dispatch* itself had more than once exposed this practice, and a St. Louis grand jury had recommended remedial legislation.[100] Therefore, when a rural member of the state assembly introduced a proposal to tighten the inspection system and close other loopholes in the existing law, the paper strongly approved.—The bill was emasculated in the senate.[101]

The *Post-Dispatch* displayed an uncertain attitude toward another rural inspection proposal, illustrating again the paper's difficulties in steering a course between the agrarians and the Bourbons. In this case, a farm leader introduced a measure to establish public supervision of the St. Louis grain market. Beginning with the Granger revolt of the seventies, this had been a major demand of Western farmers. They complained that in the trading centers they were helpless victims of elevator monopolies which arbitrarily downgraded wheat and unaccountably "lost" many bushels in the warehouses. In Illinois in the seventies, the Grangers had succeeded in imposing state inspection and regulation on the warehouses, but in Missouri a similar outcry was stilled for a time by the St. Louis grain merchants, who averted state controls by establishing an inspection system administered by the Merchants' Exchange.[102] In the early eighties, however, cries again filled the air that St. Louis elevators were cheating rural shippers, and demands for state inspection again became insistent. Private controls were ineffective, argued the farmers. By now, agrarian hostility towards the Merchants' Exchange was increasing for other reasons, as well. A decline in farm income, the agrarians believed, was partly attributable to the operations of the commission merchants in buying and selling grain "on 'Change." The farmers charged that this was depressing prices and draining off much of the profit that legitimately belonged to the hardworking producers.[103] Thus, along with the growing pressure for state inspection of elevators there also

---

[100] *Post and Dispatch*, March 4, 1879; *Post-Dispatch*, Dec. 10, 1881.

[101] *Post-Dispatch*, Feb. 2, 1883, Feb. 6, 1883, Feb. 21, 1883, March 19, 1883.

[102] *Ibid.*, March 24, 1879, May 14, 1881, July 7, 1882, July 27, 1882; Clevenger, "Agrarian Politics," pp. 62-63; Buck, *Granger Movement*, pp. 130-31. The inspection system in Illinois did not extend to Peoria or East St. Louis, but primarily to Chicago. East St. Louis was considered part of the St. Louis trading area and, informally, was left under the control of St. Louis authorities.

[103] Clevenger, "Agrarian Politics," pp. 62-63. The Sedalia *Democrat* declared that "there is no form of gambling so vicious and demoralizing as stock gambling and operations in grain, cotton and pork 'futures.'" *Post-Dispatch*, July 7, 1882, Nov. 24, 1882.

developed among the agrarians a determination to outlaw option trading—or, in common parlance—"grain gambling." [104]

Since the grain trade was "the largest and most sensitive industry" in St. Louis, agitation of this sort naturally was a source of concern to the business community.[105] The *Post-Dispatch,* attune to the interests of the merchants, was also worried; but like merchants in the grain trade, it was not unfriendly to agrarian demands at first. In fact, it sharply attacked what it termed the high-handed policies of the elevators, who were leagued in a tight monopolistic "pool," declaring that they were endangering the standing of St. Louis as a trading center by causing many rural shippers to send their grain to the Chicago market where state laws had eliminated unsavory warehouse practices.[106]

In the summer of 1882, with complaints from country shippers "pouring in" and mutterings increasing "on 'Change," over the loss of trade, the *Post-Dispatch* launched a campaign of exposure against the warehouse combine. A series of articles spelled out in detail examples of short-weighting, arbitrary reductions in grade, and other forms of sharp practice. The elevator men growled that their business was a private affair and none of the paper's concern. The *Post-Dispatch* replied defiantly that the warehousemen "are finding out there is one paper that will publish facts, no matter who is hurt" by them, and furthermore,

> The theory expressed . . . that the elevator business is a private partnership which the newspapers have no right to "dabble with" is one which will not stand a moment's investigation. Both in law and in fact the elevators are public corporations chartered by the State to serve a public purpose and subject to the same legal restrictions and supervision as the railway corporations. . . . The public welfare is distinctly connected with their management as they are . . . a factor in . . . grain transportation and are in a position to do much good or harm, according as they are managed. If they are managed with proper regard to the public interest they are a great benefit to the community in which they exist and to the agricultural interests on which they depend. If they are managed as private partnership with no other consideration than squeezing all the profit that can be made out of them, they do incalculable harm to every interest except to the small ring of capitalists who have obtained control of them. Any pretense that

---

[104] This, too, was a grievance dating from Granger days. Buck, *Agrarian Crusade,* p. 63.

[105] *Post-Dispatch,* May 24, 1879.

[106] *Ibid.,* July 27, 1882, Dec. 14, 1882.

the elevator question is not a public question . . . is a challenge to the law-making power of the State to place the rights of the people in a position where they will not be questioned. . . . We advise the elevator men, as well for their own interests as for the interests of the public, to take a more correct view of the situation. . . .[107]

This radical language, reminiscent of the agrarians, reflected the sentiments of a group "on 'Change" also favoring state inspection as the only sound solution; only in this way could St. Louis retain its business and hope to compete with Chicago.[108] The *Post-Dispatch*, however, had difficulty making up its mind. On the one hand, it disliked the elevator monopoly for inhibiting legitimate trading and endangering the city's position as a grain center, but still it could not bring itself to advocate what more conservative merchants called "political inspection." It was sympathetic with the fear of many that agrarian inspectors might impose regulations damaging to the city's trade.

In January 1883 the farmers' caucus in Jefferson City brought the matter to a head when it introduced a bill providing for state supervision modeled on the Illinois law. The railroad commission was to be given the added duties of establishing reasonable prices and policing warehouse activities.[109] A countermeasure, the Carroll Bill, was supported by the majority of the Merchants' Exchange. It called for a plan similar in every respect to the farmers' bill, but with the proviso that administration would remain in the hands of the Exchange.[110] The *Post-Dispatch* took no clear stand on the controversy during the debates, but it was relieved when the agrarian bill finally went down to defeat. "The idea of putting the grain interest into the hands of the Railroad Commissioners was born in the Farmers' Caucus, which several members have been led to remark is a most unpatriotic body," it said, adding, "It is the farmer alone who arrogates to himself all that is wise and patriotic in legislation." [111]

The paper might have reacted more favorably to state inspection if the caucus had not submitted a second bill at the same time, this one outlawing trading in futures, or option trading, on the Exchange. The proposal—according to business interests—would have gravely

---

107 *Ibid.*, Aug. 4, 1882, Dec. 14, 1882.

108 *Ibid.*, July 27, 1882.

109 *Ibid.*, Jan. 18, 1883, March 8, 1883.

110 *Ibid.*, March 8, 1883.

111 John Carroll was a St. Louis ward chieftain who frequently introduced bills desired by local business interests. Like other members of the growing Ed Butler machine, he was a defender of railroad and other special interests. *Ibid.*, April 9, 1883. Wetmore, *Battle Against Bribery*, p. 151.

damaged the city as a grain mart. This aroused in the *Post-Dispatch* all of its suspicions of the agrarian bloc. The paper itself had often condemned commission merchants who engaged in "corners" and other irresponsible transactions "on 'Change," on the ground that they hampered legitimate business. It attacked them as practising "commercial keno." [112] Nevertheless, it could not see how a law framed to eliminate excessive speculation would not also inevitably damage legitimate trading. "The element of gambling enters so largely into all the operations of trade that it is hard to draw the line so as to cut off gambling without obstructing business." [113] It was the farmers' anti-option bill that brought all the paper's fears into focus. "The Granger Legislators of . . . Missouri seem to have one of their periodical spasms of virtue," it exploded.

> This fight against option dealing, or grain gambling . . . is not
> a new one. . . . We have fought it out years ago. Years ago some
> of the millers of St. Louis who could not understand that there
> was anything new under the sun . . . attempted to hold out for
> the sample-bag system of selling grain. . . . [Such individuals] have
> no business walking around in a live city or getting in the way
> of the progress of a great State.[114]

Although most of the reform bills debated in the legislature emanated from agrarian sources and were concerned mostly with maintaining a fair market, there was another type of proposal introduced into the proceedings in 1883. In the wake of the industrialization that followed the Civil War, growing humanitarian and labor elements in centers such as St. Louis and Kansas City began to press for legislation to protect the working classes from exploitation by employers.[115] The first modest achievement of this sort in Missouri was an act creating a bureau of labor statistics.[116] Established in the late seventies, it was empowered merely to gather data and publish annual reports. These

---

112 *Post-Dispatch*, Sept. 21, 1882, Nov. 29, 1882.

113 *Ibid.*, Nov. 29, 1882.

114 *Ibid.*, Feb. 24, 1883, Feb. 27, 1883.

115 The labor movement in Missouri, centered chiefly in St. Louis, was beginning to show some strength by 1882. It placed a Workingman's Party in the field which stood for enactment of factory and mine inspection by the state, safety laws, an eight-hour law, prohibition of child labor and modification of the "fellow servant" rule of common law. Major party candidates, courting the labor vote, were beginning to promise to work for one or more of these aims in speeches in workingmen's districts in the city. *Ibid.*, Sept. 22, 1882, Oct. 6, 1882. For a short sketch of the labor movement in Missouri, see Williams and Shoemaker, II, 377-79. See also, a less satisfactory article, Lee Meriwether, "A Century of Labor in Missouri," *Missouri Historical Review*, XV (Oct. 1920), 163-75.

116 *Post-Dispatch*, Oct. 31, 1879; *The Typographical Journal*, XXXIX (Nov. 1911), 527.

reports made interesting reading, and the *Post-Dispatch* frequently made use of them to print stories of incredible exploitation of labor by lead and iron mining companies in the remote Ozark country, most of which were owned by St. Louis capitalists.[117] No doubt these reports, together with publicity given to deplorable conditions of labor in St. Louis factories which the *Post-Dispatch* itself dug up, stimulated a movement to put teeth into the powers of the labor bureau. In 1883 a legislator from St. Louis introduced a number of labor reform bills, one empowering the bureau to make periodic inspections and to enforce safe and healthful standards of employment in factories and mines.[118]

Despite its utilization of the bureau's reports and its own frequent exposures of the same sort, editorially the *Post-Dispatch* had never been in sympathy with the bureau, whose work it once described as a species of "official bumptiousness." [119] It was the paper's position, often asserted by Pulitzer in connection with his own enterprise, that businessmen should not be restricted in their relations with their employees. Consequently, when a group of St. Louis manufacturers descended on the legislature to fight the proposal to enlarge the powers of the labor bureau, the *Post-Dispatch* gave them vigorous assistance. The bill, the paper declared,

> provides such minute and offensive regulations for the conduct and management of factories and workshops that if it were strictly enforced it would do a great deal towards preventing the establishment of any new factories in the State and thus do more harm to the cause of labor which it ostensibly aims to protect, than to capital, which it attempts to restrain and regulate. If the Legislature will wisely keep its hands off from the industrial and manufacturing interests of the State for a couple of years it will do all that the people ask from it in this matter.[120]

Once more, "the people" Pulitzer had in mind were the great body of middle class businessmen in St. Louis. The opposition was effective. Some weeks later the paper announced its approval of a watered down version of the bill, "since the features so strenuously

---

[117] The paper gave considerable play to reports by the bureau, which detailed such practices as payments in scrip good only in company stores, outrageous charges for rental of company houses, and long hours of work at low pay. The publication of the report brought hot denials from St. Louis managers of the mines. *Post-Dispatch*, Oct. 30, 1879, Nov. 1, 1879, Nov. 3, 1879, April 9, 1881, June 10, 1881, June 13, 1881.
[118] *Ibid.*, Dec. 22, 1882, March 22, 1883.
[119] *Ibid.*, Nov. 1, 1879.
[120] *Ibid.*, Feb. 20, 1883.

objected to by the leading manufacturers of St. Louis have been stricken out." [121]

The paper reacted quite differently, however, to another labor reform measure, this time aimed especially at the great corporations the *Post-Dispatch* so cordially disliked. The bill, introduced by a legislator from Kansas City, sought to amend the old "fellow servant" rule of the common law which still prevailed in Missouri's courts. According to it, an employer was not liable if an employee were injured because of the negligence of a co-worker. The key to the paper's views lay in the fact that the chief beneficiaries of the old principle were the railroads which were so bitterly resented by the middle classes on other grounds. The *Post-Dispatch* already had shown sympathy for workers on the Gould lines because of the low wages and long hours they endured, and now it vigorously supported the new proposal. It tangled with the pro-corporation journal, the *Republican,* over the matter, pointing out "the defeat of Mr. GAGE'S bill will leave Missouri far behind many of her sister States and all of the most advanced European powers in making just provisions for the safety of laborers engaged in the dangerous and complexly organized industries of our time." [122]

Thus, in the struggle of the reformers in Missouri in the early 1880s to secure legislation limiting monopolies, the *Post-Dispatch* pursued an uneven course. It saw clearly enough the dangers of uncontrolled corporate growth and, indeed, was a firebrand in awakening the citizenry of St. Louis to the necessity for action. But like the middle class businessmen and merchants it represented, it was still too greatly inhibited by old Liberal doctrines—that government is the source of tyranny and property right is the touchstone of liberty —to provide sustained leadership. This, together with a profound distrust of the agrarians, prevented the paper from grasping wholeheartedly the solution of governmental regulation to protect the community from over-powerful corporate entities. Nevertheless, by vigorously informing its middle class constituency of the issues and the vital necessity of some sort of reform, the *Post-Dispatch* played an important role in these early days of progressive politics in Missouri.

---

[121] Representative Carroll was a key figure in jettisoning the strong provisions of the bill. (*Ibid.,* Feb. 23, 1883, March 6, 1883.) Country representatives saw no purpose in the bill at all, since to them it would constitute an unnecessary additional governmental expense. (*Ibid.,* March 6, 1883.) In the late eighties, however, the powers of the bureau were strengthened somewhat, and the system of paying miners in scrip good only in company stores was checked. See Lee Meriwether, *My Yesteryears: An Autobiography* (Webster Groves, Mo., 1942), pp. 118-19.

[122] *Post-Dispatch,* March 22, 1883, March 24, 1883. The bill did not pass until the reform movement of the nineties. *Ibid.,* April 12, 1883; Meriwether, pp. 129-30.

CHAPTER X

An Urban Crusader

In the summer of 1880 St. Louis suffered a humiliating blow. The Federal census revealed that it had been outdistanced by Chicago in their keen rivalry for supremacy. Thus was punctured the "Great Illusion," borne of the fraudulent count which had inflated St. Louis's population figures in 1870 and nourished the hope that it was destined to be the Future Great City of Middle America.[1] Throughout the seventies, St. Louisans were lulled into a complacent belief that little change in time-honored ways was necessary to win the race.[2] There were voices, to be sure, which warned that all was not well; at the end of the decade the brash little *Post-Dispatch* had scolded the community for its unprogressive ways, but even it was unprepared for the census catastrophe. For, according to the new census, St. Louis had gained only 15,000 while Chicago had grown by nearly 200,000. St. Louis's population was now 324,000 to Chicago's 500,000.[3] The paper joined in a general cry for a recount, denouncing the census as an "outrage" and a "monster fraud." When the government agreed to one, the *Post-Dispatch* exhorted its readers to give the matter their fullest cooperation:

> Go among those of your neighbors who are apt to obstruct the enumerators and explain to them how vital it is that this should be a thorough and complete return. Tell them what a census really means. . . . Foreign [outside the state] capital and foreign trade will not seek a waning market.[4]

But even the recount failed to improve matters much; the city gained only 25,000 new names. "It is more than Cincinnati or Baltimore claim, anyhow," muttered the *Post-Dispatch,* but nothing could hide the unpleasant truth that St. Louis had irretrievably lost to Chicago.[5]

---

[1] See such panegyrics as L. U. Reavis, *Saint Louis: The Future Great City of the World and Its Impending Triumph* (St. Louis, 1881); and Snider, *The St. Louis Movement,* pp. 76-94. Of the census of 1870, one journal commented later, "at least 50,000 more names than we had citizens [were added to the rolls], and two very slick canvassers were suspected of having made a handsome sum by turning in bogus names." As a result, "for ten years we had labored under the delusion that we were larger than Chicago." St Louis *Spectator,* Jan. 25, 1890.

[2] See Belcher, *The Economic Rivalry Between St. Louis and Chicago,* ch. 11.

[3] *Post-Dispatch,* July 7, 1880.

[4] *Ibid.,* Nov. 6, 1880.

[5] *Ibid.,* Nov. 16, 1880.

Not that the newspaper was disposed to gloss over the truth. "We know now that we have less than Chicago," it said,

> and we know where we stand relatively to the other great cities of the country. We know exactly what we have to do to outstrip them in the grand race for commercial supremacy. We have learned that blowing neither makes us rich nor great; that our future growth depends on the encouragement we give to capital; that we must induce an increase of our manufactures, and that our municipal affairs must be conducted with more liberality and public spirit.
>
> The danger to St. Louis is her confidence in her natural resources. While these are great, they have proven delusive. Chicago has relied upon energy, and has shot ahead with the most dazzling rapidity. St. Louis has relied upon its natural advantages and has crept along at the conservative snail's pace. . . . We are destined to be the Future Great, but a revolution in our methods must come. Our business men of brains, pluck and energy must rise above the fogy elements which surround them and reach out with that greatness of spirit which constitutes the true genius of American affairs.[6]

The reaction of the *Post-Dispatch,* thus, was a demand for an all-out attack on the forces and habits hampering the growth of St. Louis. In this it reflected the views of reformers in the business community who were also shocked by the census. In 1881 they joined the *Post-Dispatch* in the Armory Hall revolt against the "bummer" machine which was taking over the local Democratic Party. At the same time, their organizations, the Mercantile, Commercial, and other clubs, pushed programs of economic and civic reform on a broad front.[7] Under a news head, WAKING UP, the *Post-Dispatch* gave great prominence to the movement.[8] A reporter interviewed one of its leaders, who declared:

> Our sources of revenue have been neglected in the past. Poor steamboat companies have been burdened with wharfage dues while rich streetcar corporations have torn up our streets without paying a cent to the city treasury. Our system of property valuation is at fault. There are many defects in our government. . . . The trouble is here that we have suffered ourselves to be deceived by the windy statements and publications of our wealth and importance. . . .[9]

---

[6] *Ibid.,* July 28, 1880.
[7] Cox, *Old and New St. Louis*, p. 24.
[8] *Post-Dispatch,* Aug. 20, 1880.
[9] *Ibid.,* Aug. 19, 1881.

Fully endorsing these criticisms, the *Post-Dispatch* became the spokesman of this businessmen's reform movement.[10] "There is no disguising the fact that St. Louis is a great, big, overgrown provincial town," it commented.

> Our streets are wearing out, our police force is too small, our fire department needs strengthening and we are generally being choked and strangled by a hoggish Charter which seems to have been cut out for Jefferson City instead of a metropolis. As soon as the citizens of St. Louis can be made to realize the true condition of things we propose to ask, "What are you going to do about it?" [11]

In the cause of local reform, between 1881 and 1883 the *Post-Dispatch* reached maturity as a crusading journal. The fundamental aims of the paper were middle class—to foster the development of St. Louis as a business center and as an attractive place of residence for the average citizen. Grappling with urban issues was congenial to Pulitzer's experience and tastes, and his paper entered wholeheartedly into the drive for civic regeneration. Here, in the arena of local affairs the *Post-Dispatch* was not deflected from its fight for reform by fears of agrarian attacks on prosperity or property; it felt free to go all-out in one campaign after another to improve municipal services, clean out corruption and curb the monopolies which held back community growth.

In the accomplishment of these purposes the *Post-Dispatch* fashioned the crusade into an effective instrument of local reform. The devices of sensational journalism, utilized in news stories and articles to stimulate circulation, were applied systematically to public crusades: startling headlines and relentless and numerous exposures, together with sustained editorial barrages hammering the issues home, were shaped into intensive campaigns lasting for weeks, months, and even years. The *Post-Dispatch* developed what Pulitzer later called "a red thread of continuous policy" in maintaining at high pitch and with stubborn persistency campaigns in the public interest.[12] By 1883 the paper had become the most dynamic voice of reform in the city.

One of the most important matters facing local businessmen was the alarming deterioration of public facilities and services. The shock

---

[10] On more than one occasion the *Globe-Democrat* joined in. It was not generally a crusading paper, but on some issues in local reform it was at least as effective as its evening contemporary.

[11] *Post-Dispatch*, Aug. 19, 1881.

[12] Charles G. Ross and Carlos F. Hurd, *The Story of the St. Louis Post-Dispatch* (St. Louis, 1949), p. 2.

of St. Louis's loss to Chicago awakened them—the *Post-Dispatch* included—to the needs of the new urban age. The paper's own attitude towards local government hitherto had been largely negative.[13] Taking its cue from the Commercial Club, however, a new note was introduced into its editorials. The paper now began to criticize the city charter which had been framed in 1876 under the influence of real estate and corporate interests, precisely to impose rigid limitations on municipal taxing powers.[14] What was needed, the *Post-Dispatch* recognized, was more funds, not fewer, if services were to be improved.

"Under the limited levy fixed by the Charter," it complained, "the city is running behind and wearing out."

> We have $270,000 less this year than we had last. . . . The burden of maintaining the Jail, the Poor-house, Insane Asylum and other highly necessary institutions falls upon our depleted treasury. . . . Our water-works need strengthening; the police force needs enlargement; the Fire Department is going to pieces and the streets are falling into such a condition that it will take years to put them in order. Unless the tax duplicate is increased at once it will be necessary to raise revenue from an increase of licenses and by holding charity fairs. Banks, real estate dealers and big corporations will have to pay a little more for the privileges they enjoy. . . . Revenue must be had, and if something radical isn't done soon the city will go to seed.[15]

The *Post-Dispatch* snorted at the *Republican's* insistence that taxes must be kept down. This organ of special interests, the *Post-Dispatch* remarked, "says that the city must be rescued from the slough into which it is sliding by cutting down municipal expenses." Where, it asked, could costs be cut? [16]

The most critical situation was the deterioration of the streets; on this subject the change in the paper's attitude towards local government was striking.[17] Whereas in 1879 it strongly opposed altering the constitutional limitations on municipal taxing powers and especially opposed the imposition of special assessments advocated by Street

---

13 *Post-Dispatch,* June 18, 1881.

14 Barclay, *The Movement for Municipal Home Rule,* p. 56; *Post-Dispatch,* Aug. 22, 1881.

15 *Post-Dispatch,* Aug. 22, 1881.

16 *Ibid.,* Aug. 31, 1881, Sept. 5, 1881, Sept. 6, 1881.

17 See Schlesinger and Fox, eds., *The Rise of the City,* pp. 87-89; and Blake McKelvey, *The Urbanization of America, 1860-1915* (New Brunswick, N.J., 1963), pp. 88-89, for general discussions of the subject. Such cities as Chicago, Cincinnati, Louisville, Philadelphia, Minneapolis were also reconstructing streets. *Post-Dispatch,* March 25, 1882, Aug. 16, 1882, May 10, 1883.

Commissioner Turner to finance the resurfacing of the busiest thoroughfares, in 1881 its viewpoint was drastically different. Now it hailed with satisfaction the news that "at last" General Turner was "taking steps looking to the paving of some of our principal streets with granite," and it noted approvingly that many businessmen were "willing to pay for granite block paving in view of the poverty of the city. They are tired of mud and chuckholes and the semi-annual ripping-up . . . [of] our rotten wood thoroughfares." [18] "We will never have a solid city," the paper concluded positively, "until the streets are packed with granite blocks." [19]

Warming to the subject, in the winter of 1881-1882 the *Post-Dispatch* opened a campaign for street improvement. "This is a topic difficult to handle with calmness," it exclaimed:

A few thoroughfares in the center of the city are in a passable condition; the balance of the town has been neglected, until the alleged streets are simply so many miles of torn-out and washed-out soft roadbed covered with limestone mud to a depth varying from two to ten inches. At places where the heavy traffic is frequent, about the railroad depots, the elevators and the great mills and factories, the streets have been worn into holes two and three feet deep, where wagons are mired and carrying brought to a stop. . . . The tribute which the bad streets exact from the industries of this city . . . can be estimated only in millions. . . . Why are the streets of St. Louis worse than those of any other city in America? [20]

The problem, however, in view of the limitations imposed by the "cast-iron rules of taxation" in the city charter, was not simple. A way must be found to finance granite paving, a material costing $100,000 a mile to lay. With much fanfare the *Post-Dispatch* presented a three-point program to plug tax loopholes produced by years of slipshod administration and favoritism.

First, it reopened—this time with a greater sense of public purpose—the spectacular crusade of 1879 against tax dodging. It pointed out that tax assessments on the personal property of wealthy citizens had declined by $4,500,000 in the last five years, although "nobody doubts that St. Louis has grown wealthier and its citizens richer since 1876." It charged that at least $35,000,000 in undeclared personal income deprived the city of $910,000 in annual revenues. Characteristically, the paper named names:

18 *Post-Dispatch*, Sept. 15, 1881, Sept. 17, 1881.
19 *Ibid.*, Dec. 29, 1881.
20 *Ibid.*, Feb. 18, 1882.

To show how lenient people are in estimating the value of their own property . . . Moses Fraley, the banker, and James Richardson, the wholesale druggist, were lately reported as saying that they would willingly donate $1,000 each toward a fund for street reconstruction, if other public spirited people would follow their example. An examination of the last returns of the personal property of these gentlemen will show that they have escaped the chance to be liberal when it was within their grasp.

Fraley, the paper went on, declared himself as possessing only $2,270 in personalty, and Richardson only $1,110, although he seemed "good natured enough to donate nearly the whole value of his personal estate . . . for street improvement." [21]

Second, the *Post-Dispatch* demanded that the practice of low assessments on real estate owned by wealthy citizens and corporations be revised. Assessments in St. Louis had risen only $12,000,000 in four years, although market values of real property had risen twenty to forty percent. Again the paper printed scandalous examples of favoritism. The building which housed Scruggs, Vandervoort & Company, a leading dry goods establishment, was assessed at a mere $210,000, although it rented for $24,000 annually, and the *Republican* building had received a light $60,000 valuation. These were compared with heavy assessments placed on humble enterprises like one owned by a Mr. Jungling on Eleventh Street, whose small business was listed at its true market value.[22]

The third drain on municipal income, the paper complained, was the army of "drones" and "barnacles" on the city's payroll. Asserting that there was a useless multiplication of jobs held by "ward bummers," it charged that there was monumental "waste" of the community's resources at city hall. "Remove the barnacles and sinecures in the city government," it demanded, "and there will be from $200,000 to $300,000 saved for the streets." [23] For weeks the *Post-Dispatch* advocated consolidations of departments to reduce the payroll, but the results were disappointing. A number of bills embodying the paper's demands were approved by the Council, but the ward politicians in the House of Delegates killed most of them.[24] Indeed, the results of this campaign, generally, were meager. There was no improvement in tax returns by the wealthy, nor a revision of assessments.

---

[21] *Ibid.*
[22] *Ibid.*, March 1, 1882.
[23] *Ibid.*, Feb. 20, 1882.
[24] *Ibid.*, April 25, 1882.

The business reformers had to fall back on the solution originally suggested by General Turner: special levies on property directly abutting streets to be paved. This would require petitions from a majority of owners on each street asking for enabling legislation by the municipal assembly.[25] On the basis of this procedure the Commercial Club, early in 1882, drew up a comprehensive program calling for granite paving of downtown streets and asphalting of principal thoroughfares in the residential districts.[26]

The success of the plan, of course, depended on the voluntary support of property holders, especially of the businessmen downtown. The *Post-Dispatch* dedicated its energies to arousing this group. "The man who owns property in St. Louis and is not willing to pay for good streets should be induced to sell out and move to a quieter, less ambitious town," it declared.[27] Appealing directly to the business community, the paper asserted that they should

> realize better than any other class how vital good streets are to trade, to the habitability of the town, to its growth and future.... A street solidly paved benefits the whole town, but it is most valuable for the property it bounds. The iron-clad charter prevents a thoroughly fair distribution of the burden of street paving, but we must make the fairest distribution that we can under the foolish laws with which the city's growth is hampered and confined. Let the property pay for the streets. That is the only solution of the difficulty.[28]

Day after day the *Post-Dispatch* pushed THE GRANITE BOOM until it became "the only topic of conversation on the streets . . . and the sentiment is almost universal that something must be done and done quickly." [29] Again and again it urged the Merchants' Exchange, the largest commercial body in the city, to endorse the Commercial Club's plan by calling a mass meeting of businessmen. Early in April this brought results, when five thousand persons crowded "on 'Change" to voice "enthusiastic" approval of the program.[30]

The *Post-Dispatch* was not alone in aiding the merchant reformers. In fact, "all the newspapers in the city are in accord now on the question of street paving. If the public mind is hammered at for a while longer," the *Post-Dispatch* added, "beautiful, solidly paved

---

25 *Ibid.*, March 23, 1882.
26 *Ibid.*
27 *Ibid.*, April 1, 1882.
28 *Ibid.*, April 3, 1882.
29 *Ibid.*, March 25, 1882.
30 *Ibid.*, April 4, 1882.

streets will begin to roll out." [31] And for a time, the crusade seemed to sweep everyone before it. Businessmen on Second Street, Washington Avenue, Olive, and Pine circulated petitions and called meetings to drum the matter through. Even residents on some of the outlying streets indicated willingness to be taxed to pay for asphalt paving.

Yet, as the *Post-Dispatch* was aware, sullen and powerful opposition lurked beneath the surface. "Whether the plan will be carried out nobody can say," it cautioned. "Bills of this kind must pass both houses of the Municipal Assembly," and it warned that certain interests had strong influence, especially in the House of Delegates.[32] Among these were the "macadam rings" who made fortunes supplying the city with crushed limestone, corporations like the railroads and streetcar lines which lacked public spirit, and particularly real estate speculators, organized into a Real Estate Protective Association, who owned large tracts of land in the newer residential districts.[33] Consequently, the petitions began to stall. The *Post-Dispatch* fumed when the petition of Second Street merchants was blocked by a large property holder. "The RUMSEYS are simply representative of a class of obstructionists who, while prospering themselves, wouldn't give five dollars to aid the general advancement." [34] When a petition on Walnut Street was similarly blocked, the paper reminded merchants there that if their thoroughfare were properly paved "it would carry more traffic than any street in the southern section of the city. It is traffic that makes business, and it is business that makes property valuable." [35]

The paper's sharpest denunciations were reserved for the Real Estate Association, which accused the reform movement of being "in its essential nature agrarian." "Sensible, thinking people," the association said, "know that all civilization, all enlightenment, all religions, all human happiness . . . are founded upon the rights of property." [36] The *Post-Dispatch,* whose respect for property rights was second to none, nevertheless, like the reformers it spoke for, was developing a sense of community, and its reaction to such obstructionism was bitter. "After years of ineffectual attempts to reconstruct the worn-out and miserable streets," it said, the real estate men were determined to wreck the one plan which might succeed.

---

[31] *Ibid.,* April 5, 1882. The *Republican,* however, was only lukewarm on the subject as the *Post-Dispatch* had occasion to note. *Ibid.,* Aug. 25, 1882.
[32] *Ibid.,* March 27, 1882.
[33] *Spectator,* Dec. 30, 1882.
[34] *Post-Dispatch,* April 12, 1882.
[35] *Ibid.,* Sept. 1, 1882.
[36] *Ibid.,* Nov. 1, 1882, Nov. 2, 1882.

They do not propose any substitute or alternative; they admit that if the present plan is defeated there is no other possibility of securing street reconstruction, and that the prosperity of St. Louis must continue to suffer in the future as it has in the past, if their opposition is successful. Yet they would rather see the whole city suffer than contribute a dollar more of their share towards removing one of the great difficulties which impede its progress.[37]

Despite all it could do, however, the "Real Estate Obstructive Association," as the *Post-Dispatch* called it, was unable to stem the street improvement crusade. The need for better paving was too obvious. During the rainy autumn of 1882 the streets once more were converted "into finely graduated courses of soup and pudding," a situation that lasted an entire month. "Of all the drawbacks . . . to our growth this is the most serious, and unless a plain and practical remedy is applied very soon . . . it will soon be beyond our power to remedy it," the *Post-Dispatch* snapped.[38] In December the municipal assembly approved the first of a stream of petitions which, by March 1883, assured the success of the Commercial Club's plan.[39]

The Real Estate Association made a final attempt to block street construction by trying to slip a bill through the legislature prohibiting special taxes. The *Post-Dispatch* discovered the maneuver. "The game of the St. Louis Obstructionists . . . has been nipped," it cried triumphantly. "The eyes of the members [of the legislature] have been opened and the bill will not pass." [40]

Street improvement was only one phase of a general campaign to rejuvenate municipal services. In 1881 the *Post-Dispatch* opened simultaneous crusades to improve the efficiency of the fire and police departments. "Our Fire Department seems to consider that its only object is to get up a wild, dangerous race through the streets to a fire and that, once arrived at the conflagration, it has done all that can be legitimately expected of it," the paper commented sourly. The chief, it added, "belongs to the bluff, hearty era of volunteer fire companies" whose methods were more conducive to camaraderie than fire fight-

---

[37] *Ibid.*, Nov. 1, 1882.

[38] *Ibid.*, Nov. 10, 1882, Dec. 27, 1882.

[39] *Ibid.*, May 4, 1883, May 15, 1883.

[40] *Ibid.*, March 17, 1883, March 19, 1883. In June the state supreme court approved the levies, killing any judicial objections. (*Ibid.*, June 30, 1883.) The next year the *Spectator* remarked of the paving program that already the pace of business had been immensely quickened. One business man said: "The amount of travel on Olive Street now, compared to three years ago or even last year, is almost incredibly greater. Property has advanced immensely. Why, I was recently offered $1,500 a front foot for one hundred feet; but it is not for sale, I prefer to hold." *Spectator,* Sept. 27, 1884.

ing.[41] "Every business man in St. Louis is beginning to feel the effect of the constant failure of our Fire Department to . . . combat . . . 'the fire fiend.' " [42] The *Post-Dispatch* resolved to build "a small fire" of its own under the department.[43]

The problem was twofold. In part, the *Post-Dispatch* charged, the city was to blame for starving the department of funds with which to purchase equipment and hire additional manpower. "We understand this thoroughly," the paper said. "We do not spend enough money [on fire fighting]. But at the same time,

> the fact is apparent . . . that we don't get enough for the money we do spend. There is a marked lack of discipline and a thorough want of method throughout. Our Chief is lacking in executive ability. The style in which our fires are handled shows that very plainly. . . . Our aim is to arouse the citizens of St. Louis to a sense of the real conditions of things. If our Fire Department is too weak it must be strengthened. The insurance companies have no alternative but to either withdraw from business here or to put up their rates. It may not be a popular thing . . . to point out the weakness of our Fire Department, but *something must be done,* and nothing can be done by suppressing the truth.[44]

Businessmen welcomed the *Post-Dispatch* campaign, and several severe fires seemed to bear out the paper's charges of "Terrible Mismanagement." When an especially devastating blaze destroyed a two-block white lead factory on Clark Avenue, a company official wrote the paper: "I am sure there are many business men whose views are expressed in this matter [by the *Post-Dispatch*]." [45]

There followed a series of articles exposing A DEMORALIZED DEPARTMENT and INCOMPETENCE.[46] Public pressure became so insistent that the mayor agreed to an investigation, but the hearings whitewashed the fire chief and only revealed that "the Fire Department and the Municipal Government are pitted against the tax-payer and property-owner." [47] But in the end, the paper's campaign bore fruit. The publicity prompted St. Louis underwriters to issue a report sharply criti-

---

[41] *Post-Dispatch*, Aug. 25, 1881, Aug. 30, 1881. St. Louis established a municipal fire department in 1857. In 1881 the fire chief was H. Clay Sexton, an old-time chief of a volunteer company. Apparently he was popular but bumbling. Scharf, *History of St. Louis*, II, 800-804. See Schlesinger and Fox, pp. 105-106, for a general discussion of this urban problem.

[42] *Post-Dispatch*, Sept. 26, 1881.

[43] *Ibid.*, Sept. 2, 1881. See McKelvey, p. 105.

[44] *Ibid.*, Aug. 26, 1881.

[45] *Ibid.*, Sept. 22, 1881, Oct. 1, 1881.

[46] *Ibid.*, Sept. 26, 1881, Oct. 6, 1881, Oct. 14, 1881.

[47] *Ibid.*, Oct. 19, 1881.

cizing the fire department and ordering a twenty percent hike in insurance rates.[48] This so stirred the business community that other papers were converted to reform, and such a din was raised that the municipal assembly increased funds for fire fighting and instructed the mayor to reorganize the department.[49] The *Post-Dispatch* could claim substantial credit for leading the way to the cleanup.

A *Post-Dispatch* campaign for increased efficiency in the Police Department and the courts accompanied the fire department crusade. In 1881 the paper awakened to a rapidly increasing crime rate in St. Louis.[50] The growth of industrialization was attracting to the city from Europe and the South a polyglot population, many poverty-stricken and brutalized by persecutions.[51] In St. Louis they settled in slum neighborhoods which became notorious for vice and hoodlumism. One of the better known—"Kerry Patch"—was just north of the downtown district; there resided a brawny, brawling element who "hate policemen as the poor tenant in Ireland hates the process-server. They regard brass buttons and the insignia of authority with absolute abhorrence." [52] The alleys and decayed streets along the waterfront and in the business district harbored an even rougher class, "low bred negroes, river roustabouts and drifters, having no respect, whatsoever, for law and fairness, who would, when the opportunity presented itself, attack a lone policeman in great numbers. . . ." [53] St. Louis, in short, was infested with what the middle class *Post-Dispatch* called "the vicious classes." "The police know . . . well . . . of the existence of certain gangs of hoodlums, which gather . . . purely for the purpose of insulting passers-by," the *Post-Dispatch* said.

> So well is this known that these localities are avoided as though smitten by the plague. [Passing along the streets at night in these neighborhoods] is an invitation to the plug-uglies to insult and beat the pedestrian. . . . The time has come to put down these lawless gangs and the police must do it. . . . What the tax-payers of this city are paying for is protection, but what they are getting

48 *Ibid.*, Oct. 31, 1881, Nov. 9, 1881.
49 *Ibid.*, Nov. 2, 1881, Nov. 4, 1881.
50 *Ibid.*, March 26, 1881, Aug. 26, 1881. See Schlesinger and Fox, pp. 115-17; and McKelvey, pp. 93-95.
51 As a river city, St. Louis always had had a tough floating population. See Richard C. Wade, *The Urban Frontier: The Rise of Western Cities, 1790-1830* (Harvard Historical Monographs, XLI) (Cambridge, Mass., 1959), pp. 120-21.
52 *Post-Dispatch*, Feb. 6, 1882; J. Elbert Jones, *A Review of Famous Crimes Solved by St. Louis Policemen* (St. Louis [1916]), p. 43. See also, remarks on Kerry Patch in Putzel, *Man in the Mirror*, pp. 12-13.
53 Jones, *Review of Famous Crimes*, pp. 44-45; Putzel, *op.cit.*, pp. 12-13. The downtown district, including the Patch, was known to police as "the bloody third."

is an average of more than one murder and twelve cutting and slugging experiences a week—all from the hoodlums, who have their well-known headquarters. If the police cannot do anything . . . let them stand back and the citizens will protect themselves. . . . When we understand that we are thrown upon our resources it will take about two weeks to make the town . . . quiet and peaceable.[54]

In part, the police force, like the fire department, was undermanned. The city had only "three policemen to the square mile. This is startling when we consider that we have about two hoodlums to the square yard." [55] Moreover, although the police chief, elderly James McDonough, was a man of integrity, he was accustomed to enforcing the law in a simpler community. The *Post-Dispatch* called for his dismissal, which was carried out by the governor in the summer of 1881, although McDonough's successor was scarcely better. Chief Kennett's claim to the job was political influence.[56] But the worst roadblock in the opinion of the *Post-Dispatch* was the laxity of the courts. "Another brutal, cowardly murderer has heard the doors of our City Jail clang close behind him with the blessed assurance that in a year or two they will open again and loose him once more upon society," it remarked one afternoon.

The lawyers of the desperado are already at work on his defense, while the Circuit Attorney is away summering in the mountains. . . . In other words, the State is idle while the criminal is at work. . . . Now, with crime rampant in this town, with the jail full of caught desperadoes and the city at the mercy of the desperado at large, our legal officers take their leisure. . . . The people of St. Louis cannot be expected to submit to these roughs much longer. A brutal murder was committed yesterday. . . . Tomorrow it may be the reader of this article, for no man can say who will be the next victim. It is idle to believe we will stand this sort of thing. Patience ceases to be a virtue with twenty-six cases of murder in the first degree on the docket.[57]

The *Post-Dispatch* launched a crusade to tighten the creaking wheels of justice. Noting that the number of murders in St. Louis in 1881

---

[54] *Post-Dispatch*, Sept. 5, 1881.
[55] *Ibid.*, Dec. 26, 1881.
[56] *Ibid.*, June 9, 1881; Jones, *Review of Famous Crimes*, pp. 23-25. McDonough was first appointed chief in 1861. He had headed a private detective bureau in the forties and fifties.
[57] *Post-Dispatch*, Aug. 27, 1881.

equaled Chicago's, its headlines read like a modern journal's tabulation of automobile fatalities. NO. 27, NO. 28, NO. 29, it recorded day after day while editorially urging "wide awake store-keepers" to "keep in stock twenty foot lengths of good, stout well-rope. There is no telling how soon we may have a demand for this commodity." [58] These hints at vigilantism were accompanied by strident editorials from Pulitzer's own pen. STOP MURDERING! the paper exclaimed.

> This sort of thing must be stopped. Murdering must be made odious in St. Louis. The corrupt Four Courts must be purified. The thievish shysters who cluster there . . . must be driven out. The first great duty of society is self-protection. Order and security are necessary at whatever cost. We kill mad-dogs for the protection of the community and we must kill human mad-dogs for the same reason. A Committee of Safety must be organized at once to employ able attorneys to assist in the prosecution of murderers, to collect testimony, to war upon the shysters and generally uphold the courts in the administration of justice. There is no need of mob violence—certainly not as yet. A stern, unyielding determination upon the part of our citizens to have the law enforced . . . will put a stop to this reign of bloodshed. There must be an end to the supineness and indifference . . . of our citizens.[59]

"We complain bitterly that murder is not adequately punished in St. Louis," the *Post-Dispatch* said in noting that there had not been a single hanging since 1875.[60] "If the law fails to make examples, other criminals trust that they will have equally good luck. As long as crime is not punished it will flourish." [61] Attacks upon the courts finally produced action. "There will be five hangings . . . within the next three weeks," said the *Post-Dispatch* triumphantly when several executions were ordered without further delay. "Good news for Christmas!" [62]

The paper's campaign to increase the efficiency of stern justice strikes the modern observer as unenlightened. Governed by prevailing middle class moralism, its drive boiled down to making a horrid example of law-breakers. It went very far in this direction, becoming at times highly critical of technicalities which stood in the way of punishment. On several occasions Judge Laughlin of Criminal Court was unmercifully criticized for permitting accused persons to escape the penalties

---

58 *Ibid.*, Aug. 29, 1881, Nov. 5, 1881, Nov. 9, 1881, Dec. 29, 1881.
59 *Ibid.*, Nov. 9, 1881.
60 *Ibid.*, Dec. 24, 1881.
61 *Ibid.*, Aug. 10, 1881.
62 *Ibid.*, Dec. 23, 1881.

of justice. The *Republican* called this "wholesale and indiscriminate abuse of courts and judges." The *Post-Dispatch* replied:

> It occasionally happens that the imbecility and knavery of the courts demand attention at the hands of the press. If a Judge places himself notoriously on the side of the criminal classes . . . he certainly brings as much contempt upon the law as the newspaper that calls attention to his conduct. So far as this journal is concerned we propose to criticize public officials, from the President down to the city lamp-lighters, when in our judgment the cause of public morality, decency and order is to be advantaged thereby.[63]

Of much greater significance, for it led the paper into the modern, urban problem of corrupt influence by the organized underworld in municipal affairs, was the paper's long crusade against gambling, reopened early in 1881. The drive which the *Post-Dispatch* had conducted in 1879, before Pulitzer's energies were drawn off into politics, had only managed to suppress lotteries. This time the paper was determined to suppress all forms of gambling. In the new campaign the *Post-Dispatch* perfected to a fine point its style of crusading, a combination of exposure and editorial attack. The campaign lasted nearly two years before success was finally achieved. The paper's

> main objection to gamblers is not gambling. . . . The great evil is that the very existence of gambling hells . . . means of necessity corruption and demoralization—means the hiring and buying of lawyers and officials, detectives and even thugs and assassins, if necessary. They can only exist by the corruption of the authorities, and this is their greatest evil.[64]

In the interval between 1879 and 1881 the gambling interest had entrenched itself more firmly than ever in the community. Bob Pate, the broad-faced "boss" whose establishment on Fourth Street flourished nightly, had organized a syndicate of leading gamblers to apply clandestine pressure on city government, and it had gained influence in almost every agency of local law enforcement and politics.[65] As before, the *Post-Dispatch* was joined especially by the *Globe-Democrat*, as well as—at various times and with varying degrees of enthusiasm—the *Republican*, the German-language press, and the weeklies.[66]

---

[63] *Ibid.*, June 13, 1882.

[64] *Ibid.*, April 24, 1882.

[65] *Ibid.*, March 28, 1881. See also, Soraghan, "History of St. Louis," p. 32.

[66] Stevens, "New Journalism in Missouri," *Missouri Historical Review*, XVIII (Jan. 1924), 199-202. The editor of the *Republican* remarked that "in the case of the gambling houses it was evident that I and the community . . . must either

As has been seen, the *Post-Dispatch* opened its new crusade against the gambling dens with a mass "raid" by its reporters on New Year's Eve. Accompanying its many-headlined exposure was a vigorous editorial:

> We do not say that gamblers pay for immunity here, but it will be interesting to note the policy that will be pursued by the authorities now that they can no longer plead ignorance. We have taken the trouble to give names of proprietors . . . where gambling is openly and defiantly carried on. What will the police do about it? [67]

The police reacted, but in suspiciously ineffective ways. After much newspaper prodding a raid was conducted which netted 145 persons, but only four were picked up in dens operated by the syndicate. The *Post-Dispatch* and *Globe-Democrat* printed rumors that payoffs from a syndicate slush fund had been used to bribe officers on the raiding squad. Four policemen were arrested and indicted.[68] Additional hints of a tie-up between the gamblers and ward politicians in the Butler "ring" were unearthed from time to time, especially when Morgan Boland was appointed president of the police board.[69] Boland's plans for "controlling" gambling were revealed by the *Post-Dispatch* when it heard that, although he told "the sports" that fixed games would not be tolerated, Pate's "square" gambling would be winked at.[70] WHERE'S THE POLICE? the paper thundered day after day as it listed in boldface type the casinos—members of the syndicate—which were "running in full blast." [71]

Public opinion, meanwhile, was becoming aroused by the *Post-Dispatch* and *Globe-Democrat* crusade. And when even the *Republican* expressed disgust with Boland, Governor Crittenden replaced him with Samuel Cupples, the hardware merchant, and a panel of respected citizens. At the same time, Charles P. Johnson, Pulitzer's old friend, pushed through the Missouri legislature a law strengthening the anti-

---

govern them or be governed by them, [therefore] I started in to close them and succeeded." William V. Byars to James Byars, May 2, 1887. William Vincent Byars Papers. The *Republican*, however, was inconsistent. Only the *Post-Dispatch* and *Globe-Democrat* conducted genuine crusades.

[67] *Post-Dispatch*, Jan. 3, 1881.

[68] *Ibid.*, Feb. 2, 1881, Feb. 3, 1881. They were subsequently tried but acquitted.

[69] In his booklet on Pulitzer's career in St. Louis, George Johns asserts that "Pate had the resignations of the members of the Police Board in his pocket, to be mailed to the Governor when their action displeased him." This is an overstatement. George S. Johns, *Joseph Pulitzer*, p. 82.

[70] *Post-Dispatch*, Feb. 2, 1881.

[71] *Ibid.*, Feb. 18 through March 7, 1881; *Hornet*, Feb. 19, 1881.

gambling laws. Hitherto, gambling was a mere misdemeanor, but under the new Johnson Act, conducting a gambling den or a lottery was classed as a felony punishable by heavy fine and imprisonment.[72] When he introduced the bill, Johnson told a *Post-Dispatch* reporter that he was determined "to strike such a blow at the influence of the gamblers in this city as to drive them from interference with the politics of St. Louis." [73]

At first the new law had slight effect. But after a brief interval, Pate, relying on political friends, cautiously resumed his activities, as did the remainder of the syndicate.[74] By now, as efforts to enforce the act proved unavailing, a large segment of the public, including many businessmen, began to have second thoughts about the efficacy of the Johnson Act. Petitions were signed by several thousand citizens calling for suspension of the Johnson Law where "square gambling" was concerned, and the *Republican* and other publications declared that the law was too drastic, and thus unenforceable.[75] Besides, a closed-down city might dampen the enthusiasm of visitors coming to St. Louis for Fair Week.[76] The *Post-Dispatch* mercilessly condemned the "shallow pated" citizens who thought gambling "a necessary evil, that the present law is severe and brutally impolitic, and that it ought, therefore, to be ignored. . . .

> It is true that the gambling instinct is very strongly implanted in man. So is the whisky appetite, the inclination to steal and a hundred other passions. . . . A city that will undertake to pander to all the vices that are recognized as ineradicable will be likely to attract attention. It will be what is called a "live" town, and sons of Belial will journey many miles . . . to enjoy its festivities. . . . It might be questioned, however, whether this would be the right road to municipal grandeur. The theory that some particular gambler should be allowed to carry on business and pocket the pennies of the fools who are determined to "gamble anyhow," because he has established a reputation for "square" gambling, is extremely beautiful. . . . As a matter of fact, professional gamblers are a dangerous class in any large community. If they are pros-

---

[72] *Post-Dispatch*, March 28, 1881.

[73] *Ibid.*

[74] Pate rigged a new gambling device which was designed to get around the Johnson Act by being attached to a legal horse track in Illinois. He also added the precaution of selling his establishment to his brother, Henry Pate. *Ibid.*, June 15, 1881, Aug. 25, 1881; *Hornet*, June 18, 1881, Sept. 3, 1881.

[75] More than 4,000 persons signed the petitions. *Post-Dispatch*, Oct. 28, 1881.

[76] *The Hornet* declared the Johnson Law a dead letter because the penalties were too severe. Everybody gambles, it added, including respectable merchants "on 'Change." *Hornet*, Nov. 12, 1881.

perous they are certain to assert themselves in politics—always seeking to elevate to power men who are decidedly lax in morals and inclined to look leniently upon vice—and if they are not prosperous they are likely to stimulate all sorts of small crimes in an effort to be so.[77]

The blue-ribbon merchant reformers on the police board shared the *Post-Dispatch's* determination to enforce the Johnson Act and turned down the petitions. But they met with constant frustration. When a grand jury convened in October 1881 it was misled—deliberately, the *Post-Dispatch* charged—by an assistant district attorney who belonged to the local machine.[78] And friends of the gamblers hidden in the police department continued to impede the effectiveness of raiding, particularly under the new chief, Ferdinand Kennett, whose evasiveness and foot-dragging earned him the bitter hostility of the *Post-Dispatch*.

The efforts of the reformers slowly began to take effect, however, which caused the gamblers and their allies to turn to desperate methods. A well-known prostitute named Frankie Howard was detained in the city jail incommunicado while police sought to force from her an "admission" that she had been led to ruin by Charles P. Johnson, the crusading attorney. Wrathfully, the *Post-Dispatch* accused Chief Kennett of reprehensible conduct. Attacks by both the *Post-Dispatch* and *Globe-Democrat* on him and others involved in the game of besmirching Johnson brought suits for libel not only from the angry police chief but from the knot of politicians who were seeking to besmirch Johnson's name. The *Post-Dispatch* gaily recorded these under AND STILL THEY COME.[79] Each time a suit was filed, Pulitzer, without waiting for a process server, hurried off to the Four Courts to put up bond, a defiant gesture his newspaper was careful to publicize. He thrived on this guerrilla warfare; he enjoyed the spotlight—it was good publicity—and it aroused his combative temper. His *Post-Dispatch* only stepped up its crusade.[80]

At length, in December 1881, the untouchable Bob Pate and other members of the syndicate were indicted under the Johnson Act. Upon their arraignment the *Post-Dispatch* acted to forestall another favorite

---

[77] *Post-Dispatch*, Aug. 31, 1881.

[78] *Ibid.*, Nov. 2, 1881, Nov. 4, 1881. The miscreant assistant attorney was E. A. Noonan, later on, a scandalously corrupt and bibulous mayor of St. Louis. His administration, 1889-1893, was "strewn . . . with disgraceful acts." *Spectator*, Nov. 19, 1892.

[79] *Post-Dispatch*, Nov. 10, 1881, Nov. 19, 1881. The paper eventually won all these suits. *Ibid.*, Jan. 7, 1882, Jan. 21, 1882, March 21, 1882.

[80] In later years on the New York *World*, Pulitzer is said to have become obsessively fearful of libel suits and ruined his eyes scanning the paper to make sure all articles were accurate. See McDougall, *This is the Life!*, p. 103. There is little evidence that this was the case in St. Louis.

dodge. It exposed the practice of permitting defendants in gambling cases to put up ridiculously low bonds which, when the time came for trial, were simply forfeited. Prosecution thus was avoided at small cost to the defendants. What was worse—the bonds usually were never collected. A *Post-Dispatch* reporter digging into the records found that Pate alone owed more than $9,000 in forfeited bonds. Obviously, as the paper pointed out, there was collusion between machine-minded officials in the courts and the gamblers.[81]

Apparently this revelation struck close to home. The same day the *Post-Dispatch* headlined DEMANDS THAT THE BONDS OF THE PATES BE RAISED IN CRIMINAL COURT, Pulitzer was waylaid by a "burly, rough-looking man" just as Pulitzer was coming from lunch. Reacting quickly, he threw his assailant against a store window and rushed to his office, where he wrote an excited account under the headline, WHO HIRED HIM?[82] Dramatically, the *Post-Dispatch* declared that this "mysterious and cowardly assault [was] an outrage upon the whole press of the city."

The paper also took full advantage of the crusade to further its reputation for sensationalism. Particularly spectacular were some of the newsbeats scored by the hardworking staff of reporters and its resourceful City Editor, Henry Moore. Early in the campaign Moore was called to testify before the grand jury. Next day, he published in full the questions put to him in the secret session. The court was so angered at this violation of judicial ethics that the city editor was threatened with a citation for contempt, although, as the *Hornet* shrewdly observed, "the grand jury . . . ought to fly at higher game. . . . It would be a deal more sensational to jug . . . Mr. Pulitzer."[83] Moore, however, did not scare easily. Towards the end of the campaign, he resorted to even more venturesome exploits as he encouraged his reporters to gain access to the secret records of the grand jury. These provided the *Post-Dispatch* with a new series of daily articles of the most sensational sort. Again Moore was threatened with prosecution, which an admiring journal commented was something "that all newspapermen covet."[84]

As the pressures mounted the paper's temper rose with them. Its crusading zeal became extreme and at times disturbingly irresponsible. Headlines too frequently were misleading, and editorial tirades lacked restraint. There was a resort to invective and "trial by newspaper." The *Post-Dispatch* grew impatient with the harassed reformers on the

81 *Post-Dispatch*, March 11, 15, 21, 24, 1882.
82 *Ibid.,* March 24, 1882.
83 *Hornet,* Nov. 12, 1881.
84 *Spectator,* Nov. 3, 1883.

police board who were doing their best against great odds. At first it merely criticized them for ineptitude, but soon was attacking their personal characters.[85] Gratuitously alluding to Samuel Cupples' prominence as a layman in the Methodist Church, the paper sneered that "our pious Police President" should have used his influence with the Almighty to enforce the laws, and it ran an illustration of a brand of playing cards he sold in his hardware establishment which, it said, was "popular with all classes of gamblers." It taunted:

> Mr. CUPPLES does not advertise his Eagle Cards in the St. Louis newspapers, where his benevolence and general piety are known and appreciated, but it occurs to us that it is our duty to lend a helping hand to a Christian gentleman who is exerting himself at all times to put down Vice and gives Virtue a few gratuitous points in the game.[86]

Onlookers were not impressed with such aspersions and sometime later, when the board members resigned, the *Spectator* expressed the opinion that the *Post-Dispatch* should apologize. "It would be an act of justice, such as the *Post-Dispatch* has not dealt out with a lavish hand to the retiring commissioners." [87]

There was greater danger in the paper's diatribes against Henry D. Laughlin, judge of the criminal court, who held the Johnson Act unconstitutional and freed Bob Pate. The *Post-Dispatch* exploded, declaring that an inferior court had no business questioning the validity of a legislative act.

> It is painful to read Judge LAUGHLIN'S decision. . . . For never was an important law trampled into the dust by a more miserable subterfuge. Never was a law more plain, direct and simple. Never was the emphatic intent of the law-makers more shamefully mocked and defied by so flimsy a technicality.[88]

Inflammatory editorials in both the *Globe-Democrat* and *Post-Dispatch* goaded the judge into challenging an editor of the former to a duel.[89] Admittedly there was reason for the newspapers' criticisms, for Laughlin's decision illustrated—or seemed to—the alarming influence of the gamblers even in the courts of law, but the *Post-Dispatch*

---

[85] The paper justifiably criticized the commissioners for permitting themselves to be used as a sounding board for the attacks on Johnson. *Post-Dispatch,* Nov. 15, 1881.

[86] *Ibid.,* April 4, 1882.

[87] *Spectator,* July 1, 1882. *The Hornet* insisted that the board was "irreproachable." *Hornet,* Nov. 19, 1881.

[88] *Post-Dispatch,* May 2, 1882.

[89] *Ibid.,* May 3, 1882, May 23, 1882.

was uncomfortably aware that the violence of its attacks tended to bring the processes of law into disrepute. Consequently, when the state supreme court overruled the St. Louis judge and reinstated the case against Pate, the paper sought to excuse its own course. While admitting it had shown "considerable severity," in criticising Laughlin's "official acts," it contended it had done so only because

> we honestly believed them to be in contravention of law and the interests of society. . . . It is not for the sake of sensationalism that we directed attention to Judge LAUGHLIN'S singular and unaccountable acts. . . . We did what we considered to be our imperative public duty and we defy any right-thinking man . . . to say that we were without justification.[90]

The vigor and persistency of the newspaper campaign finally achieved results. In the summer of 1882 Pate at long last was brought to trial and sentenced to six months in jail. Then, however, came the pardon from Governor Crittenden, which St. Louis received with "incredulity." [91] The *Post-Dispatch's* lack of restraint in assailing the governor for this action, which exceeded anything it had shown before, created an atmosphere of such extreme intolerance in St. Louis that a fair handling of the case was impossible. Indeed, the violence of the attack so stirred the public—as the *Post-Dispatch* itself crowed—that Pate was "frightened by the storm of popular indignation." The din of newspaper criticism quickly forced a second trial, and Pate was convicted again. Not without reason, the "boss gambler" complained to a reporter, "I am going into jail as a result of the abuse the newspapers heaped upon Gov. Crittenden when he pardoned the gamblers. I saw then that the consequences . . . would fall on me." [92] Perhaps because he recognized that the state of public opinion prevented a fair hearing, Crittenden pardoned Pate a second time, which elicited a renewed volley of editorials.

Nevertheless, the back of the gambling nuisance was broken. So aroused was public opinion that Pate did not dare reopen his business. Gambling was suppressed, at least temporarily, chiefly because of the long and intensive campaign by the *Post-Dispatch* and *Globe-Democrat*, and although gambling was only scotched, not killed, the paper could still say in 1883 that St. Louis at last was "free from one of the curses of other great cities." [93]

---

90 *Ibid.*, May 23, 1882.

91 *Ibid.*, June 26, 1882.

92 *Ibid.*, July 11, 1882, July 18, 1882.

93 *Ibid.*, May 24, 1883. In November 1883, after Pulitzer left St. Louis, another scandal shook the police board, proof that the problem lay just beneath the surface. Moreover, as Ed Butler's machine waxed in potency, the corrupt influence of

A second source polluting public order also had reached serious proportions by 1881. This was the "saloon interest," which had succeeded in rendering meaningless ordinances controlling the liquor traffic. Two thousand saloons infested the city, many in respectable residential neighborhoods, where they were foci of disorder and crime. This gave rise to agitation for more effective regulation, especially among "the best elements of society." It was an urban middle class movement, not to be confused with contemporary rural demands for outright prohibition, and the *Post-Dispatch* joined the campaign with enthusiasm.[94] Defending itself against prohibitionist charges that it was "a hireling of the liquor interest," the paper declared,

> we are in favor of temperance and the enforcement of laws designed to regulate and control the liquor traffic. We care more for good government than we do for the interests of brewers and saloon-keepers. We sympathize thoroughly with the people who are honestly moved to do all they can to suppress drunkenness, and we recognize the crime, demoralization and distress that result from alcohol. . . . The good intentions of the advocates of Prohibition we recognize. . . . We are not in sympathy with the liquor traffic. Our sympathies are arrayed on the side of good, clean government.[95]

The *Post-Dispatch* particularly attacked the Saloon-keepers' Protective Association, organized in 1882, for attempting to manipulate elections in St. Louis in order to "nullify wholesome and just laws for the regulation of their business." [96] The liquor interest "has no business in politics," the paper burst out in exposing its practices undermining local ordinances.[97]

Not until the November elections had safely disposed of prohibition, however, did the *Post-Dispatch* launch into an all-out crusade. Early in 1883 the Commercial Club laid before the legislature a bill authorizing urban communities to raise the charge for liquor licenses from

---

organized gambling became all but ineradicable. The gambling menace was not finally broken until the famous crusade to clean up St. Louis by Joseph W. Folk in the early twentieth century. See *Spectator*, Nov. 3, 1883; *The Whip*, June 6, 1885; Clevenger, "Agrarian Politics," pp. 114-15; Wetmore, *Battle Against Bribery;* Louis G. Geiger, *Joseph W. Folk of Missouri* (University of Missouri, *Studies*, XXV, No. 2) (Columbia, Mo., 1953), chs. 3-4.

94 The prohibitionist movement in St. Louis—as distinguished from the movement for regulation of saloons—was venerable but weak. It stemmed from the settlement of New Englanders in the city. The chief prohibitionist sentiment, however, was outstate. *Post-Dispatch*, April 19, 1883. See also Schlesinger and Fox, pp. 355-60; and McKelvey, pp. 94-95.

95 *Post-Dispatch*, Aug. 3, 1882.

96 *Ibid.*, Aug. 15, 1882.

97 *Ibid.*, Sept. 15, 1882, Sept. 29, 1882.

$120 to $1,000 annually.[98] This proposal, which acquired the popular name of "high license," was designed to eliminate from half to three-quarters of the worst saloons in St. Louis. The *Post-Dispatch* strongly endorsed it, declaring that it would "close out the little 'boozing kens' which are the abiding places of the vicious classes, and would place the [liquor] traffic in the hands of responsible people." [99] Under such headlines as THE GROGGERIES MUST GO and DEBAUCHING MINORS the paper vividly depicted the evils of "the low groggeries and small dispensatories of kill-me-quick."

> The city is full of dens in which liquor is not only sold freely to minors, [the paper continued] but in which boys of twelve . . . are bribed to become drunkards. The best residence neighborhoods of the city are polluted by bar-rooms, with a pool-table in a back room, and the boys of the neighborhood are encouraged to play with the temptation of a drink to be given away with each game.[100]

The bill was strenuously opposed by the Saloon-keepers' Association, working closely with the local Democratic machine. Ed Butler himself hurried to Jefferson City to lobby against it.[101] But, aided by prohibitionist legislators who looked upon the bill as better than nothing, the Downing Bill—as the Commercial Club's proposal was called—was approved and signed into law. Unfortunately, it was loosely drawn; rural prohibitionists attached a Sunday closing clause to it, which stored up trouble for the future.[102] The greatest immediate drawback, however, was a provision apparently requiring enabling legislation by local government before the law could take effect, and in St. Louis's municipal assembly the liquor influence was so strong, especially in the House of Delegates (the lower house) that some years later a man reportedly emptied the hall by shouting, "Mister, your saloon is on fire." [103] In the spring elections of 1883, despite frantic urging by the *Post-Dispatch* to bring out the "respectable" vote, the saloonists increased their strength. Consequently, when the high license proposal came before the assembly the chances for passage appeared dim.[104]

---

98 *Ibid.*, Jan. 24, 1883, Feb. 6, 1883.

99 *Ibid.*, Jan. 25, 1883.

100 *Ibid.*, March 1, 1883.

101 *Ibid.*, Feb. 15, 1883.

102 *Ibid.*, March 15, 1883, March 26, 1883. At the same time the Missouri legislature was considering high license, the Illinois and Ohio legislatures approved similar measures. In each case, high license was passed following the defeat of a prohibition proposal. *Ibid.*, April 20, 1883, June 9, 1883.

103 Wetmore and Steffens, "Tweed Days in St. Louis," *McClure's Magazine*, XIX (Oct. 1902), 579.

104 *Post-Dispatch*, April 4, 1883.

Nevertheless, the *Post-Dispatch* pressed hard for the measure. WHO RUNS THE CITY? it wanted to know.

> There is not much public spirit in St. Louis, and public opinion here does not take that . . . aggressive stand which holds public servants strictly to the line of duty. This matter, however, is so intimately connected with important considerations of morality and good order that it will be more closely watched by a great many citizens who are anxious to know whether this city is really run by the low grog shops whose abolition is sought.[105]

The paper's campaign had some effect because the Council (the upper house) by a vote of seven to three passed a watered-down bill setting a fee of $500 for establishments selling hard liquors, although it retained the old $120 charge for beer saloons.[106] The *Post-Dispatch* believed the bill was better than nothing, and supported it. After considerable pressure and publicity the House of Delegates was prevailed on to pass the measure.

The *Post-Dispatch,* however, was not impressed by the conversion of the House of Delegates. "The suddenness with which the hitherto hostile interest of saloon-keeping has acquiesced in the high license business suggests the presence of a colored citizen on the wood pile," and such, indeed, was the case. For one thing, the saloonkeepers expected to make use of the retention of the $120 beer license as a blind behind which many planned to sell hard liquors surreptitiously.[107] The saloonkeepers also saw in the Sunday closing clause an opportunity to make the entire high license plan appear odious. In an interview with a *Post-Dispatch* reporter the counsel for the Saloonkeepers' Association pointed confidently to the provision and observed that the act "could not be enforced in a town where 100,000 people drink beer in public every Sunday. . . . The beer gardens are too popular." [108]

The *Post-Dispatch* agreed, and it was dismayed when Governor Crittenden played into the hands of the saloon men by announcing that Sunday closing would be enforced to the letter. The paper accused the governor of all but wrecking the high license drive. "To close up the beer gardens and beer saloons of St. Louis would be to . . .

---

[105] *Ibid.,* June 13, 1883.
[106] *Ibid.,* June 30, 1883. The Council was elected at large, while the delegates were chosen by wards; it was in the wards that the saloon interest was especially strong. *Ibid.,* June 14, 1883.
[107] *Ibid.,* July 7, 1883.
[108] *Ibid.,* July 9, 1883.

make Sunday a day of imprisonment," it said angrily, "instead of a refreshing holiday to nearly half of her working people. . . .

So far as the DOWNING law is a new law it is entitled to respect and obedience, and an earnest effort should be made to enforce it. But the real friends of high license and strict regulation as antidotes to the prohibition mania, should beware of making the DOWNING law a mere pack-horse for Sabbatarian fanaticism.[109]

As the paper foresaw, the net result of bickering over Sunday closing was to draw public attention away from the original purpose of the act and render it unworkable. And when Governor Crittenden was persuaded by his St. Louis friends to appoint Dan Kerwin and other politicians aligned with Ed Butler to the police board, the saloon interest was placed beyond reach. Kerwin had no intention of enforcing the Downing Act, which became a dead letter. The saloonkeepers triumphed, the consequence of the rising potency of machine politics and discouragement among the opponents of the liquor traffic.[110]

As might have been expected from the history of reform in other cities, the efforts of the *Post-Dispatch* and middle class elements in St. Louis to secure improvements through municipal action were mixed. More successful was the backing the paper gave to a campaign for civic betterment by a purely private association.

Early in 1883 the Mercantile Club launched a project to construct an exposition building, an idea already adopted elsewhere, including Louisville, Cincinnati, and Chicago, to house displays of science and art and whose concert hall would be the scene of musical and lecture programs.[111] The aim, however, was only incidentally cultural. "All the Merchants [are] Enthusiastically in Favor of the Enterprise," the *Post-Dispatch* headlined a story one day, because "An Exposition in the heart of the city will bring . . . [thousands] in contact with our fine stores and shops." [112]

The *Post-Dispatch* quickly got behind the Mercantile Club's efforts to raise $500,000 in popular subscriptions, chiefly from the business community. Columns of feature articles pushed THE EXPOSITION BOOM and vigorous editorials drummed up enthusiasm as the paper whipped up interest and harassed the laggards. Declaring that "the retail

---

[109] *Ibid.*, July 10, 1883.
[110] *Ibid.*, July 9, 1883.
[111] *Ibid.*, Jan. 30, 1883; Cox, *Old and New St. Louis*, pp. 20, 85.
[112] *Post-Dispatch*, Jan. 31, 1883, Feb. 5, 1883. The paper pointed out that the Cincinnati Exposition, just then in progress, was drawing as many as six thousand persons per day to the city. "If this can be done by a comparatively small and uncultured city like Cincinnati, what might not be done in St. Louis." *Ibid.*, Feb. 1, 1883.

merchants, manufacturers and other small capitalists, who have always shown public spirit and enterprise," had subscribed heavily, the *Post-Dispatch* castigated "the great capitalists and real estate owners" for their failure to support the project. "Up to Saturday night the subscriptions for the Exposition reported from the street railroads were $000,000; from the steam railroads $000,000. We trust they will do better this week." [113] In publishing the lists of subscribers, the *Post-Dispatch* reiterated, "our big capitalists are not doing as well . . . as the average retail merchant and manufacturer. But this was to have been expected." [114] The campaign, it said, was

> winnowing out the frauds and pretenders who assume the role of "prominent citizens" and claim recognition as leaders in helping the city, but who are conspicuously absent when a test is made of the value of their professions.[115]

Despite foot dragging by the corporations, the campaign was a notable success, for which Samuel Kennard, chairman of the drive, gave the *Post-Dispatch* full credit.[116] In 1884 the exposition building was completed in Missouri Park between Thirteenth and Fourteenth Streets and for many years exhibitions and musical concerts there drew large crowds; it became one of the city's chief attractions.[117]

The paper got behind many movements to improve the cultural facilities of the city. This was particularly true of education, where Pulitzer's motives were higher minded. All his life he set great store by education and in the campaign to improve the city after 1880 his *Post-Dispatch* strongly backed a movement to convert the public school library into an institution serving the entire community.[118] Observing that "many other cities" already possessed public libraries, the paper justified the importance of one for St. Louis in characteristically practical terms:

> A free public library is as much an essential feature of a modern city as a free public park or a system of free public schools. It is

---

[113] *Ibid.*, Feb. 19, 1883. *Post-Dispatch* personnel contributed $6,000. Pulitzer himself subscribed $5,000.

[114] *Ibid.*, Feb. 17, 1883.

[115] *Ibid.*, Feb. 21, 1883.

[116] *Ibid.*, Feb. 7, 1883.

[117] Cox, *Old and New St. Louis,* pp. 85-86. Band concerts conducted by such famous figures as Patrick S. Gilmore and John Philip Sousa played to packed houses every fall for years during the eighties and nineties.

[118] Pulitzer's many benefactions in later life were usually for the purpose of establishing or strengthening cultural institutions. His most famous gift provided for the Columbia University School of Journalism and the establishment of the annual Pulitzer Prizes. Pulitzer also developed a habit of showering his editors with books on intellectual subjects at Christmas time.

not merely an aid to learning, it is a stay to good morals, a check on crime, a help to prosperity. . . .[119]

As for the public school system, the *Post-Dispatch* took a constant interest in its expansion, its curriculum and teaching methods, and particularly in preventing its exploitation or distortion by interests which would corrupt its democratic purposes. Although occasionally, in its restless search for sensations, the paper descended to a busy-bodying interference with pedagogical practices, in general its attitude was one of disinterested determination to protect the role of education in the community.[120]

In the very first year of publication the *Post-Dispatch* entered a controversy similar to many occurring elsewhere in this period when a large foreign-born population was becoming typical of urban growth. This involved a nativist objection to required instruction of German in the public schools. Such a policy stemmed from a compromise arranged some years before, when, to persuade the large, German-speaking community to send its children to public instead of the many parochial schools, administrators agreed to require the teaching of German in the first six grades.[121] As a citizen of foreign birth himself, Joseph Pulitzer was especially sensitive to any tendencies toward nativism in the English segment of St. Louis and Missouri. At the same time, he believed deeply that the foreign-born should become Americanized, and viewed the public schools as important in promoting this process. His *Post-Dispatch,* therefore, pursued a middle course between extremists of both sides. Turning to the *Westliche Post,* spokesman for the German minority, the paper said tartly:

> The subject should be considered with candor and without prejudice. Especially should there be no appeal to the prejudices of birth or race. . . . Germans should claim their rights and present their case not as Germans, but as *Americans.*[122]

---

[119] *Post-Dispatch*, Dec. 11, 1882. The Public School Library was finally converted into a genuine public library in 1894. Cox., *Old and New St. Louis*, p. 123. See Schlesinger and Fox, pp. 175-78, and McKelvey, pp. 220-23, for accounts of the urban public library movement during this period.

[120] The paper carried on crusades now and then against what seemed to it unfortunate or ridiculous "hobbies" imposed upon the pupils by the school administrators, such as the practice of making children stand for minutes at a time to recite—a policy which the *Post-Dispatch* claimed produced curvature of the spine—and the cramped posture demanded during writing drill. To the *Post-Dispatch* these were "Crooked Hobbies." *Post-Dispatch*, Feb. 28, 1883, March 17, 1883. See Schlesinger and Fox, p. 169, who mention teaching fads as a common complaint of the time.

[121] *Post-Dispatch*, Sept. 22, 1879.

[122] *Ibid.*, Sept. 19, 1879; Schlesinger and Fox, pp. 169-71.

Replying to the *Republican,* whose objections to teaching German on the point of economy, the *Post-Dispatch* suspected, cloaked an illiberal hostility to the German population, the paper reminded it that it should remember

> the time when St. Louis swarmed with German schools, in which the tuition was given in German by German teachers to German children, and in which thousands of future citizens were growing up a body separate and apart from the rest, with no community of language, idea, aspiration or feeling. . . . The strongest influence on the juvenile mind is the influence of association, custom and fashion; and as the tone of thought in the public schools is not German, but American, the German children are only too anxious to keep in line with the public sentiment of their little world. They resent being called German, they Anglicize their German names and are, in every respect, what our system of education should aim to make them—thorough Americans. Now, it may seem to the *Republican* that $60,000 a year is too much for this gain, but it should tolerate differences of opinion on this point. The Germans themselves pay part of the expense.[123]

The *Post-Dispatch* also insisted on the expansion of the school system, even if it meant an increase in taxes. "The high school education should not be the privilege of the few," it said in support of a recommendation that this institution be enlarged, "but the possession of the many, and it is . . . a positive loss and detriment to the city, that the high school accommodation stands in the way of our development of education." [124]

The main task of the *Post-Dispatch* after 1880 was to protect the schools from the influence of ward politicians and the machinations of textbook monopolists. According to the paper, the school board was becoming progressively corrupted by the encroachment of "ward

---

[123] *Post-Dispatch,* Sept. 22, 1879. A short time later the *Post-Dispatch* remarked: "After all the stupid appeals to ignorance and national prejudice [on both sides] German will be continued in the public schools. . . ." (*Ibid.,* Oct. 8, 1879.) The issue flared up again in 1883 when a representative of Irish extraction introduced a bill into the legislature calling for abolition of German instruction by state enactment. It failed of passage, much to the satisfaction of the *Post-Dispatch,* which opposed it on the additional ground that such a law would violate the principle of local self-government. (*Ibid.,* Jan. 23, 1883, Feb. 21, 1883.) In the late eighties, however, required German instruction was finally dropped, and by then, for reasons of economy, it said, the *Post-Dispatch* favored the action. In 1893 there were still more than 20,000 pupils enrolled in parochial schools. Cox, *Old and New St. Louis,* p. 122.

[124] *Post-Dispatch,* June 15, 1883. The high school was established in 1850. By 1881 the building had become badly overcrowded, having 450 students. Scharf, I, 852.

bummers" and called upon its fellow citizens to defeat them. The board, it said, "should be composed of men of character," but

> it is unfortunately true that . . . small and mediocre ward bimbashees, who have ulterior political objects, have crawled into the place and are peddling "influence" where it will do them most good. Little rings are formed in the Board for the dispensation of patronage and it is more than hinted that when rival text-book agents appear . . . actual bribery is among the possibilities. . . . There are at least a half dozen men in the present Board who would hardly be trusted by the voters in a private capacity, and yet they are permitted to handle public funds and direct the most important branch of our municipal government. Let every good citizen resolve at once to lend himself to the good work of reforming the School Board.[125]

The paper itself went to work with a will to "reform the board." In the fall of 1881 it vigorously backed a slate of public-spirited businessmen in a race against a group of machine candidates. Declaring that "men of character, regardless of politics, should be supported," among those it campaigned for was William Scudder, head of a shipping line and a Republican, who was running in a strongly Democratic ward. When victory crowned its efforts, the paper congratulated itself: "The POST-DISPATCH . . . asked the people to send SCUDDER, BUSCH and PLATE to the School Board. The returns show that our kind of advice was acted on." It added that this should be a salutary lesson for the "little Democratic managers" in the wards as to the effectiveness of independent journalism.[126]

Unfortunately, this successful campaign did not allay rumors of corruption. As Lincoln Steffens observed a generation later in a survey of Missouri politics, bribery is a two-way affair, involving "the 'contemptible bribe-taker' and the very 'respectable' bribe-giver," the office-holder and the business interest desiring a special privilege.[127] The latter had not been eliminated by the defeat of the ward bummers. The *Post-Dispatch* discovered that book companies competing for lucrative contracts had long been the main source of disruption and corruption in the proceedings of the board. It revealed that William T. Harris, St. Louis's famous school superintendent, had resigned "in disgust" in 1880 because a bitter quarrel between Appleton's and

---

[125] *Post-Dispatch*, Oct. 19, 1881.

[126] *Ibid.*, Oct. 19, 21, 24, 25, 26, 1881.

[127] Lincoln Steffens, "Enemies of the Republic: The Political Leaders Who Are Selling Out the State of Missouri, and the Leading Business Men Who Are Buying It—Business as Treason—Corruption as Revolution," *McClure's Magazine*, XXII (April 1904), 590.

McGuffey's had divided the school directors so irreconcilably that little could be accomplished. And following Harris's resignation "gentle allegations of perjury, corruption, lying, lechery, fraud and dishonesty" were flung back and forth by the adherents of each company as they fought over the choice of a new superintendent.[128]

Although City Editor Moore delightedly exploited the juicy charges of immorality with front page stories—embellished with additional information dug up by his own reporters—editorially the *Post-Dispatch* was not amused. And when several of the largest book companies formed a publishers' trust the paper took genuine alarm:

> We regard this as one of the most insolent and dangerous monopolies now threatening the public welfare. . . . Its danger lies in its power of levying on the cause of public education a tax heavier than the whole present expense of carrying on the public schools.[129]

"The book fight in the public schools has to be fought sooner or later," the *Post-Dispatch* remarked when it returned to the subject early in 1883, "and this is as good a time as any." It printed anew the charges of bribery which book agents made against each other as well as board members, hoping to raise a public outcry against this powerful interest.[130] The campaign, however, was fruitless. The *Post-Dispatch* was about "two weeks too late" in inaugurating its campaign, according to the *Spectator,* which added that the paper's efforts should have been aimed at the legislature instead of the local school board. "The Syndicate have fixed things at Jefferson City so that the county adoption system will hold for seven years longer. This means absolute control by the Syndicate . . . and not even the patient Post-Dispatch can break it. . . ."[131]

The *Post-Dispatch's* hostility to monopolists—to the "capitalists" as it somewhat vaguely termed them—reflected the fear and dislike of small and competitive business for powerful interests, both local and national, which threatened to stifle their prosperity. This was compounded by the apparent indifference of the monopolists for the welfare of St. Louis. The *Post-Dispatch* was convinced that they were primarily responsible for the failure of the city to keep pace with Chicago. The paper believed the community must do all in its power

128 *Post-Dispatch,* Sept. 17, 1881.
129 *Ibid.,* March 28, 1883.
130 *Ibid.,* May 15, 1883, May 19, 1883.
131 *Spectator,* March 31, 1883. The Missouri law provided that book companies could make contracts with entire counties. The monopoly could more easily negotiate with the comparatively few counties than with the myriad of local school boards. *Ibid.,* March 3, 1883. See McKelvey, ch. 12, for a general discussion of developments in urban education.

to protect the welfare of the ordinary merchant and resident upon whose public spirit the future of the city depended. Consequently, after 1880 the *Post-Dispatch* launched into a ceaseless war—almost a vendetta—against privilege, especially local privilege. Some monopolies were old, and the paper had attacked them before; others were new and loomed up menacingly. Some the paper had encountered in Missouri politics but had failed to come to grips with them because of its fear of the agrarians, but in St. Louis the *Post-Dispatch* asked no quarter in its fight to break their grip on the community. In this many-sided struggle, the paper's goal in general was the old one of restoring competition, but gradually in some cases it began to come to the conclusion that this solution was impracticable and that governmental regulation, or even ownership—a concept it had always viewed with distaste—might be necessary. However reluctantly, the paper's liberal philosophy was beginning to be modified by a recognition that government—at least on local levels—might be a useful instrument in protecting the community. Discernible, too, in the *Post-Dispatch's* outlook was a growing belief that in an urban society property rights were not so absolute after all.

In grappling with the powerful monopolists, the *Post-Dispatch* battled almost alone. It had only occasional help from the *Globe-Democrat*, whose outlook was generally conservative, while the *Missouri Republican,* because it was the mouthpiece of the elite, invariably lined up on the side of the monopolists. Only the German-language *Westliche Post* sided with the *Post-Dispatch* with any consistency, but unfortunately its influence was largely confined to a minority group.

"The most disgraceful and treacherous of all the monopolies" was the venerable St. Louis Gas-light Company, mentioned earlier, which, through court action in 1879, had recovered its old monopoly of the distribution of gas in the southern two-thirds of the city. Upon regaining its franchise the company had resumed its callous ways, restoring charges which made St. Louisans pay the highest rates in the nation, and resorting again to slipshod maintenance which made its rotting mains a danger to the community.[132] It even had the effrontery to sue the municipality for $500,000, alleging damages because the receiver had reduced rates when the city operated the works in the seventies, although the *Post-Dispatch* pointed out that the reduction—

---

132 *Post-Dispatch*, March 12, 1881, April 28, 1883. Philadelphians were charged $1.50 per thousand feet, while St. Louisans paid $2.50. Consumers in Cincinnati paid $1.60, and in Baltimore, $1.60. *Ibid.*, April 25, 1883.

which had not affected profits—had been achieved through efficient management by municipal officials.[133]

Seconding the *Westliche Post,* and on guard as always for the interests of the consumer, the *Post-Dispatch* declared war on the revived monopoly. The bitterness of the paper's campaign to unseat Mayor Overstolz in the spring election of 1881 was heightened by its discovery that "His Honor," whose connections with the local oligarchy were close, was trying to push through the municipal assembly a proposal to extend the exclusive franchise of the St. Louis Company twenty years beyond the expiration date of its present charter, which was due to expire on January 1, 1890. To attract public support, the proposal was billed as another "compromise," a generous offer by the company to help the community finance its street reconstruction program by paying into the city treasury a portion—a small portion, as it turned out—of its profits in return for renewal of its charter.[134] The *Post-Dispatch* condemned the proposition as a sly trick of monopolists posing as "pure and noble capitalists," interested only in the welfare of St. Louis, when in reality they were seeking for a song to continue an arrangement which "binds and chains the city like a galley slave." "Let it be distinctly understood," continued the paper,

> that when the clock strikes midnight . . . the last day of 1889 . . . *the franchise of this monopoly dies.* Of course it retains its property and can take up its gas pipes and sell them. But after that day *it cannot use the streets of St. Louis, for the soil belongs to St. Louis.*[135]

The monopolists had influence in both parties, however, and despite the defeat of Overstolz, the new mayor, Republican William L. Ewing, appeared as determined as his predecessor to push the "compromise" through. There was reason for urgency, although the present charter still had nine years to run; a line on the editorial page of the *Post-Dispatch* told why: "Mr. EDISON claims to have made an incandescent loop out of bamboo which now renders his Electric lamp perfect." [136] Jubilantly, the paper observed:

> The fact is, the days of the gas monopoly are numbered. The electric light is by no means what it should be, but it is on the way to perfection, and the next five years will see it in common use in lighting streets, hotels, large stores and manufacturing establishments. By the time that the charter of the St. Louis Gas

133 *Ibid.,* March 12, 1881, April 28, 1883.
134 *Ibid.,* March 10, 1881.
135 *Ibid.,* March 2, 1881.
136 *Ibid.,* April 18, 1881.

Company expires [1890] two-thirds of the private dwellings of St. Louis will be lighted by electricity.[137]

Experiments with electric lighting in St. Louis were already taking place. In 1878 Tony Faust tried the new illumination in his restaurant on Fifth Street, and in 1881 one or two hotels had begun to use it to light their great lobbies.[138] In North St. Louis a streetcar line had just installed a huge arc lamp atop a hundred-foot water tower, which at night cast a pale glow over a large area.[139] The embattled gas company gave notice of resisting this innovation by taking legal action against one of the hotels,[140] but the handwriting was on the wall. A group of local promoters organized a company to sell electricity in St. Louis and applied to the city for a charter. Believing strongly in the virtues of competition, the *Post-Dispatch* welcomed the project, but it warned:

> the gentlemen who are proposing to light the city . . . with electricity must prepare themselves for a terrible conflict with the old Gas companies. . . . The gas rings will make unrelenting war upon anybody who threatens to interfere with their fat privileges. If St. Louis is to keep abreast of the times she will be compelled to march over the prostrate bodies of those monopolies.[141]

The paper redoubled its attacks upon the "compromise" and succeeded in arousing the business community to form a citizens' committee to help in the crusade.[142] After months of twisting and turning under the blaze of *Post-Dispatch* publicity and mounting public pressure, the municipal assembly early in 1882 buried the measure.[143] Before the end of the struggle, however, the paper uncovered some of the tactics utilized by the "franchise-grabbers." Most sensational was

---

137 *Ibid.*, May 11, 1881. See Schlesinger and Fox, pp. 98-102, for a general discussion of the development and spread of electric lighting in America's cities during this period.

138 *Post-Dispatch*, May 20, 1881; *Hornet*, May 7, 1881.

139 *Post-Dispatch*, May 21, 1881, June 11, 1881, June 21, 1881. In later years a politician who voted to approve the installation on the water tower gained local fame—and perhaps votes—for shouting to his audience, "Who put the light on the water tower?" The crowd would shout back, "You did, Julius!" *Globe-Democrat*, Oct. 14, 1952; Hurd, "St. Louis: Boundary Bound," pp. 254-55. Hurd was a long-time *Post-Dispatch* reporter.

140 *Hornet*, May 7, 1881.

141 *Post-Dispatch*, June 22, 1881, June 23, 1881.

142 *Ibid.*, Aug. 31, 1881.

143 *Ibid.*, Jan. 11, 1882. The bill passed the Council but failed in the House of Delegates. One publication charged that it was neither altruism nor *Post-Dispatch* crusading which caused the delegates to kill the bill. Rather, it was lack of "sugar"—bribes—that was responsible. Already the boodling practices for which the Democratic machine was to become notorious were exhibiting themselves. *Hornet*, Jan. 14, 1882.

an admission by the publisher of a defunct journal that he had been paid $3,000 to refrain from criticizing the St. Louis company. He also asserted that another paper—unnamed—had accepted $5,000 for the same purpose. Pointing to its own record of unwavering opposition to "the big gas companies," the *Post-Dispatch* declared that "neither corporations nor private individuals are able to purchase the silence or the advocacy of the POST-DISPATCH. Not a line of our editorial space has ever been sold to a human being or cause." But, it continued:

> There is at least one newspaper in this city whose record . . . is by no means so clear. . . . It has been so servile in its devotion to the interests of the Gas Company and all other rich corporations that we can safely trust the public to locate the concern that received . . . the interesting sum of $5,000 for keeping its mouth shut when the city was being shorn by the Gas Ring.[144]

The *Post-Dispatch* was not surprised that the *Republican* maintained a discreet silence, which prompted it to comment:

> The corruption of the press is the greatest danger to American liberty to-day. There is nothing that . . . is fraught with such peril to the future of the Republic. Venal newspapers are a thousand times worse than corrupt politicians. Whenever the rich corporations can buy the press as they buy legislators and judges the days of the Republic are counted.[145]

The maneuverings of the gas company were defeated, but meanwhile consumers like the *Post-Dispatch* still suffered under a monopoly with eight years to run. Late in 1882, however, a new competitor appeared, the St. Louis Heat and Power Furnishing Company, a water gas concern which—unlike the infant electric light industry—promised immediate relief.[146] The promoters of the new enterprise first invaded the domain of the Laclede Gas Company north of Washington Avenue, forcing the latter to slash its rates from $2.25 to $1.50 per thousand feet, an illustration of how much consumers were being overcharged.[147] The grasping old St. Louis Company, however, refused to budge, retaining its rate of $2.50 and threatening to sue the water gas company if it tried to come south of Washington Avenue. "Agitate, agitate, agitate," the *Post-Dispatch* urged its readers as it attacked the "unjust

---

[144] *Post-Dispatch,* Oct. 14, 1881.

[145] *Ibid.,* Oct. 15, 1881. The *Globe-Democrat* wanted it "distinctly understood" that it would never be a party to such a dishonest practice. *Globe-Democrat,* Oct. 18, 1881.

[146] *Post-Dispatch,* Nov. 16, 1882. Water gas could be produced more cheaply than the conventional coal gas.

[147] *Ibid.,* April 9, 1883.

discrimination against property, business and progress" maintained by the monopoly.[148] Once more the paper demanded that the city cancel the St. Louis Company's franchise on the plea that

> the streets of the city are the public property of all the citizens, to be enjoyed by them equally; the franchises, liberties and privileges of doing business in the city are open to all citizens on the same terms, and any attempt to give to one corporation privileges from which other persons are excluded is void from the start. The city does not possess the right to say that one corporation . . . shall sell gas in any one district and that no other company shall compete.[149]

The paper's solution of open competition seemed about to take place. "A gladsome sight greeted the belated loiterer about the corner of Sixth and Washington avenue last night," it said. "It was the invasion of the Two Dollar-and-a-Half Gas Company by the One Dollar-and-a Half [Water] Gas Company."[150] The "gas war" now flared up in the bailiwick of the old monopoly.

Then a second water gas company made its appearance and began to rip up the streets. This was too much of a good thing, and the *Post-Dispatch* took alarm. It began to dawn on the paper that the streets could not be used as a battlefield by irresponsible competitors without causing disfigurement; moreover, the city was in danger of becoming entangled in endless lawsuits.[151] The heaven of open competition had its limits. Most of all, an insistent rumor began to be heard that the promoters of the water gas companies were not in earnest, but were stalking horses for the monopolists. In applying for charters to sell water gas they were really planning "to sell out to the old St. Louis Gas Company at a round figure." [152] Thus, the devious old company would get its way after all by purchasing water gas franchises extending beyond 1890.

These revelations produced a remarkable change in the *Post-Dispatch's* outlook. Almost overnight it abandoned its belief in unlimited competition as a cure-all and endorsed the idea of municipal ownership of the gas works. It seemed the only way out. "Cheap gas is not to be obtained by the multiplication of gas companies," it now de-

---

[148] *Ibid.*, April 10, 1883.
[149] *Ibid.*, April 13, 1883.
[150] *Ibid.*
[151] *Ibid.*, April 27, 1883.
[152] *Ibid.*, April 28, 1883. Some of the backers of the water gas project had unsavory reputations. One man, Monheimer, was a New Yorker whose record in connection with the Tweed Ring in New York a number of years before was certainly not reassuring. *Ibid.*, Nov. 22, 1880.

clared, "all of which . . . sell cheap for awhile and then commence the same old process of extortion; but it is and will be accomplished by the city taking possession of the works and holding on to them.

The city cannot grant the right to use the streets to any of the companies now asking it from the Municipal Assembly, without thereby giving the right . . . to the old and the new . . . to come together and cut the city out of the immense advantage it has when the old company's charter expires. . . . An ordinance should be introduced at once to condemn the remnant of the term of the old company and take possession of its works. Upon the verdict being rendered the city takes possession . . . and then we will have cheap gas.[153]

Sentiment for so drastic a solution, however, was weak. Indeed, the *Post-Dispatch* itself, arriving at such a conclusion so suddenly, seemed startled at its own audacity. In any case, it did not push the proposal with very great energy. Utilizing their political influence and strong legal position, the gas monopolies managed to hang on to their exclusive privileges until 1890 when an electric lighting company was given a share of the illumination business.[154]

Public transportation was controlled by the old horse-drawn street-car corporations, against whom the *Post-Dispatch* also had inveighed from its earliest days of publication. Displaying an arrogance characteristic of monopolies, the car lines gave poor service. Especially odious were the "bob-tail" cars operated by some of the busiest lines. These diminutive vehicles, descendants of the stagecoach, were cramped for space, usually unkempt, and their drivers were forced to double as conductors. They were cheap to operate, but patrons resented them, as the humorous complaints of Officer Magoogin attest. "It's a burnin' shame that payple has to roide in thim little sawed-off cars," observed the talking policeman, as he recounted a ride on a bob-tail with his "Cass avenoo gerl" to hear "Gertrude Nailson" in a downtown theater:

We rid down in Cass avenoo car No. 11 that had a few panes av glass out, and a bit av zinc nailed over the broken change-makin' hole in the dure. Every toime anybody wanted tin cints changed

---

[153] *Ibid.*, May 11, 1883.

[154] The *Post-Dispatch* never ceased its opposition to the gas company, however, and between 1884 and 1890 was chiefly responsible for a reduction in gas rates. In 1889 the stockholders of the Laclede Company, which, since 1873 had held a monopoly of gas distribution north of Washington Avenue, bought control of the old St. Louis Company. Because of persistent *Post-Dispatch* crusading, the newly consolidated corporation was forced to halve its rate to consumers from $2.50 to $1.25 per thousand feet. *Two Anniversaries: The World, 1883-1903; The St. Louis Post-Dispatch, 1878-1903* (New York, 1903), pp. 42-43; Cox, p. 114; *Spectator*, Jan. 14, 1888.

he had to open the dure an' hould an argymint wid the dhriver, an' fwhile this was goin' on the wind kom peltin' through so shtrong it'd take the breath away from a dhrunken man. We moight as well have sat on the roof av the car or on the horse's back for all the gud sittin' insoide did us. . . . Comin' in there was a man [who] got into our two-be-four car wid three big valaises that he poiled up agin Bedalia's shins an' there was the same throuble about passin' fares an' purthecktin' her tinder corns. . . . We had a terrible an' distressful toime, an' fwhat I'd loike to know how if there isn't some ould bloo law or cansoled statoot that moight be dhragged out to the loight for the suppression av thim disgraceful bob-tails.[155]

Such inconveniences were merely annoying. More serious were other irresponsible practices by the car companies which, according to the *Post-Dispatch,* gravely impaired the political morality of the community and endangered its future growth. Under COSTLY CORRUPTION the paper exposed how, in 1869, the owners of the local traction lines had used a large fund to gain from the legislature a law that freed them altogether from obligations contained in their original charters from the city. No longer were they required to keep in repair the streets they used, or to pay more than a nominal fee of twenty-five dollars per car in lieu of municipal taxes, and, above all, they were even relieved of submitting reports of earnings. In short, the paper said grimly, "the city was robbed of its rights." [156]

At the same time, the paper charged, these corporations were still extracting generous franchises from the city by means of liberal bribes to members of the municipal assembly. "The Cass Avenue Railway, for instance," it commented, "which could afford to bribe the Council, could not afford to pay the city anything; [and] the city was tricked in the building of the bridge at Twelfth and Fourteenth streets." [157] "Why should the House of Delegates be in so great a hurry to part with such a franchise [as one on Lindell Avenue] before its real value is ascertained?" the paper asked suspiciously on another occasion.[158] So worked up did the *Post-Dispatch* become that early in 1883 it began to seek governmental regulation: "We insist that these profitable lines should give the people of St. Louis better accomodations," it declared, and continued:

The people have a right to demand that they shall not be compelled to act as conductors on bob-tail cars. . . . They have a

155 *Post-Dispatch,* Feb. 7, 1883.
156 *Ibid.,* May 14, 1881, March 23, 1882.
157 *Ibid.,* April 14, 1883.
158 *Ibid.,* Feb. 5, 1883.

right to demand that the cars shall be furnished at the hours they are most needed, and that the people who pay for a seat shall have a seat. They have a right to demand that the cars shall be kept clean and decent, and finally that the horse car companies shall report to the State Commissioners as the steam railroads do.[159]

The right to impose some sort of regulation "is a recognition of the fact that the city has something to do with the prosperity of these semi-public corporations," the paper added, suggesting that the city should have a right to share proportionately in the growing profits of these increasingly profitable concerns.[160] Once more the *Post-Dispatch*, in grappling with local utilities, seemed to be modifying its old faith in unlimited competition. Reluctantly, perhaps, but quite definitely, it was beginning to change its philosophy of liberalism.

What most disturbed the *Post-Dispatch,* however, was that the horse-drawn car corporations, with their stranglehold on the community, were hampering the normal growth of the city. This was a theme the paper had dwelt on earlier. Sprawling over an ever wider area, St. Louis was in constantly greater need of improved transit facilities. Yet, utilizing their exclusive franchises, the horse-car lines continued to block expansion.[161] As before, the Fifth Street Line, monopolizing the southern approach to the downtown district, effectively prevented South St. Louis and Carondelet from enjoying direct communication with the center of the city, and the residents of North St. Louis were similarly discriminated against.[162] The chief victims, however, were the growing neighborhoods on the western edges of the city; not a car line from downtown provided unbroken service beyond Grand Avenue in 1881.[163] Thus, the citizens of Cote Brilliante, finding it necessary to transfer from one line to another, spent three hundred dollars yearly on carfare. "It is due them in justice and equity," the *Post-Dispatch* told its readers, to put an end to this "flagrant outrage" by authorizing direct communication.[164] Forest Park, a handsome acreage west of Kingshighway, was "like some foreign territory beyond the seas" to most St. Louisans. Consequently, the *Post-Dispatch* vigorously supported demands by the Mercantile Club that track be extended to the park.[165] But the railway combine was difficult to budge.

159 *Ibid.,* Feb. 17, 1883.
160 *Ibid.,* May 29, 1883.
161 See Cox, pp. 23, 72-75, for the history of public transit in St. Louis in this period. See also, Schlesinger and Fox, pp. 90-93; and McKelvey, for a general discussion of the development of urban transit. *Post-Dispatch,* Feb. 16, 1881.
162 *Post-Dispatch,* Jan. 20, 1882.
163 Cox, p. 73.
164 *Post-Dispatch,* Nov. 11, 1880.
165 *Ibid.,* Jan. 18, 1881, Feb. 21, 1883.

It had, for example, persuaded the local police to close down a line of "Herdic" coaches competing against it for a time between Fifth Street and Grand Avenue.[166]

Meanwhile, the horse-car interests also resisted fiercely the introduction of rapid transit already in use elsewhere. The paper itself at first was unsure about one new mode of transportation. It had heard that cable cars, which had been tried out in San Francisco, "cannot be stopped quick enough to prevent accidents." But the news in 1882 that Chicago had installed a successful cable line caused it to change its mind. The *Post-Dispatch* became a vigorous supporter of a plan to construct a cable system on Olive Street.[167] It also enthusiastically backed an elevated railroad scheme, urging approval of a franchise applied for in 1881 by a group of local and out-of-town promoters. "A city with an area of sixty-three square miles can be but illy served by the old methods of locomotion," it declared,

> and the problem now is to make it possible for a man to reside in the extreme limits of the city and carry on business conveniently in the quarter set apart to affairs. The day that all sections of St. Louis are brought into close communication by means of an elevated road will witness a vast increase of business and a rapid appreciation of real estate.[168]

A barrage of special articles and editorials followed as the *Post-Dispatch* launched into a spectacular crusade booming RAPID TRANSIT as essential to FUTURE ST. LOUIS. "In populous towns the centers of business . . . become so noisy and crowded that people naturally fly to the suburbs as a relief," it pointed out, but in St. Louis this expedient "is . . . shut out by the difficulty of reaching the place of employment in anything like a reasonable time. . . . Business needs require that the principal points in a city should be so connected as to be easily reached." [169] Noting that many local residents spent as much as three-quarters of an hour reaching the center of the city, the paper declared flatly, "Horse[s] can no longer supply the demand and are really an impediment to business." [170]

The horse-car monopolists, who had "grown rich and . . . are daily

---

166 *Ibid.*, Sept. 10, 1881, Jan. 26, 1882, April 3, 1882; *Hornet*, Sept. 10, 1881, Jan. 28, 1882. Herdics were small, horse-drawn busses which ran free of tracks. They were popular at first because they proceeded more rapidly than the cars on rails, but they acquired unpopularity when they wore deep ruts in the streets and the rides in them were far from smooth.

167 *Post-Dispatch*, June 3, 1882, Feb. 16, 1883. A cable car line was installed on Olive Street the next year, 1884. Cox, p. 73.

168 *Post-Dispatch*, May 25, 1881.

169 *Ibid.*, May 26, 1881.

170 *Ibid.*, June 18, 1884.

growing richer," naturally were "not anxious to have competition," the *Post-Dispatch* commented sourly, continuing that "their big, well-paid lawyers are very busy" organizing public opinion against the elevated scheme.[171] The monopolists, in fact, cleverly exploited the conservative fears of many citizens by pointing to the prospect of noise, dirt, and sparks which *were sure to accompany* such rapid transit. Frightened property holders on Olive, a proposed route for the elevated, met in mass protest, declaring in a petition that an elevated line would damage property values along the right-of-way. The *Globe-Democrat* also was unsure about this project, and the *Republican*, expressing the views of the monopolists, was bitterly opposed.[172] The outcry thus raised against the enterprise was successful; the council—where the old monopolies were strongest—shelved the proposal.[173]

Late in 1882 the matter was revived when a new group, composed primarily of New Yorkers, sought permission to build an elevated road west on Walnut to Forest Park.[174] Once more the *Post-Dispatch* supported the project, contending again that commercial property would be enhanced by rapid transit. It sought to refute the arguments of the conservatives, claiming that, far from depressing values along the right-of-way, the elevated would make property more valuable. However, although the *Post-Dispatch* persuaded "a number of merchants and businessmen" to support the project, it was dismayed to learn that more than three thousand residents on Walnut and adjacent streets were opposed on the ground that, if approved, "foreign capitalists" would exploit the city. Throwing up its hands, the *Post-Dispatch* printed a sarcastic editorial, ST. LOUIS ENDANGERED:

> The idea of an Elevated Railway in St. Louis is highly preposterous. None of the men who built up the city . . . ever rode on an Elevated Railway. . . . The City has done without an Elevated Railway since the days of PIERRE LIGUESTE [the founder], and it can get along without one for the next century. . . . The introduction of electric lights and telephones here by outsiders is an interference with the peace and quiet of the city. It may be all very well for Chicago to have these modern institutions and be in a perpetual fret and ferment, but St. Louis was intended by nature to be a quiet, old-fashioned place. . . . We are

---

171 *Ibid.,* June 20, 1881.

172 *Ibid.,* June 1, 1881, June 20, 1881, June 24, 1881, July 29, 1881; *Hornet,* May 7, 1881. A huge real estate deal also was attached to the scheme, which the *Globe-Democrat* very much objected to. *Globe-Democrat,* June 20, 1881.

173 George Tansey, himself the head of a transfer monopoly, led the move to defeat the bill in the council. *Post-Dispatch,* June 25, 1881.

174 *Ibid.,* Dec. 28, 1880.

a charming provincial town now and all efforts to metropolitanize us should be resisted. In fact we need a Chinese Wall around the place to protect us against the designs of rapacious outsiders.[175]

Playing upon provincial fears, the local oligarchy successfully blocked the introduction of an elevated railroad, but these same capitalists seemed not at all disturbed by another "rapacious outsider," Jay Gould, whose steam railway empire, by 1882, all but enveloped St. Louis. Allying with Gould, these local interests profited from the iron grip of the railways with subsidiary monopolies of their own. This interlocking network of special privilege was the most pervasive monopoly of all, and although the *Post-Dispatch* was too fearful of the agrarians to favor effective state regulation, in St. Louis itself it fought with all its energy this threat to the city's prosperity. Its aim was to arouse the business community to collective action, either to force a reduction in rates or, better, to revive competition by finding alternative means of transportation.

Most notorious of the railroad devices holding the city in thrall was the bridge monopoly which, long before Gould grasped it in 1881, had levied tribute upon St. Louis's commerce with the eastern half of the nation. It was the outgrowth of an old ferry monopoly fashioned early in the nineteenth century. In 1829 a man named Samuel Wiggins obtained from the Illinois legislature the exclusive privilege of transporting goods and persons across the mile-wide Mississippi to St. Louis on the west bank. In the 1850s, when rail lines began to crowd the Illinois bank, they were forced to submit to the Wiggins monopoly to gain a share of St. Louis's commerce. The arrangement developed whereby the railroads, building their terminals on the east bank, turned their freight over to the St. Louis Transfer Company, employed by the ferry, for delivery in St. Louis—a monopoly that was exceedingly lucrative. The beneficiaries were its stockholders, who, in time, were numbered among the elite on Lucas Place.[176]

So firmly fixed was the arrangement that in 1874, when James Eads' great bridge doomed the ferry, the transfer monopoly was scarcely disturbed. Having no desire to incur the expense of erecting new terminals in St. Louis, the railroads simply continued to make out bills of lading to East St. Louis where, as before, the transfer company hauled the freight to St. Louis. The only change was that the transfer company, seeing the shape of things to come, deserted the ferry to cart freight over the new bridge. Maintenance of the old monopoly prompted Officer Magoogin to remark to Fopiano, his Italian friend,

---

[175] *Ibid.*, Feb. 2, 1883.
[176] Wallace, "The Wiggins Ferry Monopoly," *Missouri Historical Review*, XLII (Oct. 1947), 1-10.

This is a fooney town, Fopi. . . . You can shkaircely foind it on a railroad map that'll have Aist St. Louis marked down as big as a roundhouse, an' Chicago as prominent as a three-cint shtamp in the corner av wan av those leetle love-letthers that dhry goods clerks an' Wesht Ind gerls sind tu aich other.[177]

Gradually the railroads were permitted to haul trains directly into the city, but this was scarcely a help, for the company levied a charge of five dollars per car on freight over the bridge.[178] Together, in short, the transfer and bridge monopolies constituted a heavy drain on St. Louis business. The *Post-Dispatch* estimated that they made from one-half to three-quarters of a million dollars annually from their tolls on the city's commerce.[179]

Nevertheless, it was not until after Jay Gould purchased control of the bridge in the summer of 1881 that local businessmen took alarm. Gould, they feared, might raise the bridge tolls—popularly called an "arbitrary"—to new levels or he might even bar rival lines from access to St. Louis altogether.[180]

Aroused, local businessmen plunged into a long campaign to break the arbitrary, a struggle directed by the *Post-Dispatch*. It lasted well into the next century, before success was finally achieved. This was one of the most notable crusades in the paper's history, and because it so well suited Pulitzer's philosophy, it was conducted with brilliant and sustained aggressiveness.[181]

The paper's first target in opening the crusade in 1881 was the transfer company, which had fallen far behind in the delivery of goods to St. Louis merchants from east side terminals. "Thousands of dollars are lost to the city . . . every day now," the *Post-Dispatch* complained. "Early in the fall, when the natural increase of business manifested itself, the Transfer people were unequal to the demands on

---

[177] *Post-Dispatch*, Feb. 6, 1883.

[178] Travelers on passenger trains were charged twenty-five cents each.

[179] *Ibid.*, Oct. 25, 1881, Nov. 9, 1882, Dec. 15, 1882; Wallace, pp. 12-16.

[180] *Hornet*, July 30, 1881. Although some papers, notably the *Republican*, viewed Gould as "sort of a patron saint," a number of weekly publications, in addition to the *Post-Dispatch*, very early showed alarm. Grodinsky, *Jay Gould*, pp. 338-40. *The Hornet* published a striking lithographic cartoon showing Gould straddling the Mississippi with Eads' Bridge at his feet. *Hornet*, May 20, 1882. *Post-Dispatch*, Jan. 27, 1882.

[181] Eventually, the *Post-Dispatch* took the case to the United States Supreme Court where in 1912, under the Sherman Anti-Trust Act, the bridge monopoly was dissolved. For the later history of the campaign against the arbitrary, see Orrick Johns, *Time of Our Lives*, pp. 142-43; and Robert R. Bowie, ed., *Government Regulation of Business: Cases from the National Reporter System* (Brooklyn, 1949), pp. 311-20.

them, and when the horse malady [epizooty] reached the city they went entirely to pieces." But,

> having a monopoly of the business, they refuse to allow the merchants to handle their own freight when they furnish their own teams. St. Louis is too much of a city to be at the mercy of a corporation of this character and the railroads owe it to themselves to see to it that this system is either changed or broken up.[182]

Knowing the railroads would not act, the *Post-Dispatch* turned to the business community, arousing it with a hard-hitting series of articles exposing the transfer company's highhanded and inefficient ways, under such heads as "Good Reading for Merchants to Digest," and editorials calling for collective action.[183] Efforts to defend the monopoly by the *Republican* brought the withering retort that

> it is just as natural for the *Republican* to stand by the Transfer Company as it is for sparks to fly upward. . . . The Chestnut street concern is the recognized organ of all corporations and monopolies and is the flexible tool of the money powers from ragpicking to railroad managing.[184]

Not satisfied with words, the paper circulated a petition for a mass meeting declaring, "We know that we reflect the sentiments of the business men of St. Louis in saying that, whatever may be the causes for this blockade, some effective . . . remedy must be found." [185] When they met, the merchants appointed a committee to investigate the possibilities of breaking the bridge monopoly by constructing a second bridge over the river, an idea the *Post-Dispatch* heartily espoused. "Our great bridge, while something of an ornament, is to some extent an impediment to our commerce," it observed. "The fact is, we have outgrown our bridge, and another one seems to be a necessity." [186]

The determination of the merchants produced an immediate effect on the transfer company; it frantically pressed into service every team of horses it could hire and within four weeks the situation was cleared up. The *Post-Dispatch* preened itself: "A newspaper coal dropped on the back of a monopoly sometimes produces pleasant results." [187]

This was the opening gun. In 1882 the *Post-Dispatch* opened a general assault on the bridge monopoly. Numerous examples of the

---

182 *Post-Dispatch*, Oct. 20, 1881.
183 *Ibid.*, Oct. 25, 1881.
184 *Ibid.*, Oct. 22, 1881.
185 *Ibid.*, Oct. 24, 1881.
186 *Ibid.*, Oct. 26, 1881, Oct. 28, 1881.
187 *Ibid.*, Oct. 28, 1881, Nov. 24, 1881.

adverse effect of the arbitrary received prominent publicity, such as a letter received by a local stove manufacturer from a customer in Petersburg, Illinois, canceling further orders. "Of course we won't find fault with you," the message ran, "you have treated us well, we like your goods and we like to trade with you, but you can't blame us if we can save from $5 to $7 in freight charges by buying elsewhere." In the same issue a grain merchant told the paper he saved $25,000 annually by maintaining a flour mill in Alton to supply his eastern trade.[188] As a result of the arbitrary, the *Post-Dispatch* declared, not only was Chicago forging ahead of St. Louis in Southern Illinois, but Cincinnati was offering "keen competition" in Indiana and Kentucky.[189]

In pursuance of another call made by the *Post-Dispatch,* a second meeting of local businessmen was held at the St. Louis Club, this time to organize a sustained program of action. The paper hailed the establishment of a freight bureau, composed of more than a hundred merchants, as "a great public movement, by which St. Louis must stand or fall." [190] The bureau drew up a series of proposals, including a demand that the railroads abolish the arbitrary by merging the bridge tolls with the general mileage rate and applying it to all shipments passing over the bridge, not merely to those destined for St. Louis. In addition, it requested the roads to transfer their terminals to St. Louis, and it appointed a standing committee to explore alternatives to the bridge route. Once more there was talk about a second bridge, but this time more emphasis was placed on developing river traffic to New Orleans.[191] Indeed, the greatest success of the freight bureau was its negotiation of an agreement with a New Orleans steamship firm to carry St. Louis wheat to Liverpool.[192] The *Post-Dispatch,* whose favorite solution to monopoly was always the reestablishment of competition, applauded the work of the bureau:

> The one circumstance which if rightly utilized will remove all doubt of the complete success of the movement to secure cheap

[188] *Ibid.,* Nov. 4, 1882, Nov. 11, 1882.
[189] *Ibid.,* Nov. 16, 1882.
[190] *Ibid.,* Nov. 9, 1892, Nov. 13, 1882.
[191] *Ibid.,* Nov. 22, 1882. The idea of constructing a second bridge across the Mississippi to destroy the arbitrary, a project consistently supported by the *Post-Dispatch,* came to fruition in 1890 when the Merchants' Bridge was built. The hopes of its backers were frustrated, however, when local businessmen and politicians, ostensible supporters of the new bridge, secretly negotiated a deal whereby the new bridge, when completed, was sold to the old bridge monopoly. Such was the power of monopoly in St. Louis. See Orrick Johns, *Time of Our Lives!,* p. 143; and Cox, p. 64, for this episode.
[192] *Post-Dispatch,* Feb. 20, 1883, March 21, 1883.

and uniform rates for St. Louis is our possession of a choice of two methods of transportation for our imports and exports. During the current year the railroads have taken a larger share of our export grain and flour than has gone by river; last year these proportions were reversed. . . . St. Louis possesses in the river a permanent and effective check and regulator upon exorbitant [railroad] rates.[193]

There were problems to be overcome before the Father of Waters could be fully utilized, however. River traffic, too, had fallen into the hands of the monopolists, among them the ubiquitous Jay Gould. In order to choke off the threat of the Mississippi to his growing rail combine, he had bought and consolidated several barge lines plying between St. Louis and New Orleans.[194] If this could not be broken, the *Post-Dispatch* commented grimly, the contract with the trans-oceanic line would "be about as serviceable . . . to St. Louis as a railway from Jericho to the moon." [195]

More serious was the problem of improving the navigability of the river. Undisciplined by levees or dykes for much of its length below St. Louis, the Mississippi often capriciously changed direction, and in many places its channel was scarcely the height of a man.[196] The paper enthusiastically supported a campaign to obtain from the federal government an appropriation for deepening and straightening the river—notwithstanding its unwavering opposition to paternalistic government so far as other segments of the economy were concerned. Despite the machinations of "the great railroad and corporation interests . . . [who] seize upon every opportunity to defeat schemes of Western river improvement," and myopic legislators who made "a general grab-game" of it, an appropriation of five million dollars was approved by the Congress.[197] The project accomplished little, however, for the members of the Mississippi Improvement Commission, set up to direct operations, fell into bitter disagreement over engineering methods.[198] In 1883 the *Post-Dispatch* and the St. Louis merchants

---

[193] *Ibid.*, Nov. 16, 1882, Feb. 20, 1883.

[194] *Ibid.*, Aug. 16, 1881, Aug. 17, 1881; Grodinsky, pp. 340-41, 408.

[195] *Post-Dispatch*, Feb. 26, 1883, Feb. 28, 1883.

[196] *Ibid.*, Nov. 26, 1879, Dec. 18, 1879, Feb. 27, 1883.

[197] The appropriation was passed as an item in a notorious pork barrel rivers and harbors bill. President Arthur vetoed it, but it was passed over his veto. *Ibid.*, Feb. 7, 1882, Aug. 2, 1882.

[198] James Eads, whose dedication to river improvement was complete, but whose single-minded zeal must have made him difficult to work with, disagreed violently with other members of the commission, thus disrupting the entire program. *Ibid.*, Feb. 27, 1883, April 16, 1883.

tried again. Looking for a really substantial grant, this time the Merchants' Exchange called for a national convention to be held in Washington to impress upon Congress the importance of river improvement.[199] Catching a vision of a program integrating the entire Mississippi Valley, the *Post-Dispatch* declared:

> Let us have a convention of representative men from the length and breadth of the valley. . . . The day of Goose Creek and Minnow Run is over. The old flag and an appropriation is a slogan which must be silenced. . . . The petty interests and petty jealousies must give way to a broad statesmanship which will admit the paramount importance of Mississippi river improvement.[200]

But the *Post-Dispatch's* hopes of using the river as a makeweight against the railroad domination were dashed. Because the patchwork of regions occupying the valley could not be made to work together, and as continued railroad competition proved to be insurmountable, the temporary increase in the volume of trade sent down the river in 1880 and 1881 proved to be false dawn.[201] The hold of the bridge monopoly on St. Louis's economy was unbroken, but the battle was just begun, and, in time, under *Post-Dispatch* leadership, it would prove successful.[202]

In the meantime, the paper challenged other phases of the interlocking network of monopoly connecting local interests with the railroads. Among these was a campaign against the coal exchange for maintaining an artificially high price on fuel coming across the big bridge from the coal fields of southern Illinois. This crusade consisted of a series of exposures in the winter of 1881-82 under such arresting headlines as THE COAL MANIPULATORS, POOL PLUNDERERS, and CROOKED COAL. The paper revealed how, in 1879, after a period of declining prices, a number of large coal dealers established a tight combine to limit the supply on the St. Louis market. Through a secret agreement with the railroads traversing the coal fields across

---

[199] The idea of a national convention did not originate with the *Post-Dispatch*, although its campaign helped put it over. The *Spectator* claimed to be the originator. *Spectator*, June 30, 1883.

[200] *Post-Dispatch*, July 11, 1883.

[201] The national river improvement convention met in Washington in 1884, but broke up amid quarrels among the delegates. Dorsey, *Road to the Sea*, p. 268. A reduction in railroad rates helped to bring about a decline in river traffic. The rate reduction was produced by fierce rate wars among eastern rail lines, not by the efforts of St. Louis merchants. Grodinsky, p. 408.

[202] The *Post-Dispatch* continued its fight in behalf of the river trade and river improvement. See Ross and Hurd, *Story of Post-Dispatch*, p. 20; and later, Richard G. Baumhoff, *The Dammed Missouri Valley* (New York, 1951).

the river, the monopolists were able to reduce shipments to an amount barely sufficient to meet the city's day-to-day needs. The scheme worked; coal prices rose from five to seven and a half cents per bushel. To maintain the monopoly, the rail lines were persuaded to refuse to provide cars for operators who insisted on mining too much coal and to nonsyndicate dealers in St. Louis. This arrangement, declared the *Post-Dispatch*, "is simply . . . a conspiracy to throttle the coal market," and to deprive the city's industries and homeowners of fuel in order to raise prices.[203]

A final target of *Post-Dispatch* wrath in the struggle against the railroad interests was the Union Depot Company, owned originally by a group of local capitalists who also had sold out to Jay Gould. In this case the paper's campaign was a coordinated exposure-editorial assault upon the monopoly for its failure to provide decent terminal accomodations for passengers arriving in St. Louis. The station was a string of dingy, leaky sheds on Twelfth Street where passengers scrambled for trains without benefit of porters or guides. A favorite *Post-Dispatch* device was to interview travelers. "Oh, the horrid snow! Oh, this nasty depot!" exclaimed a pretty young lady one winter day when slush cascaded from the roof and spattered her clothes.[204] Typically the paper said, "A NEW DEPOT is What is Desired by the Great Mercantile Fraternity." [205]

In editorial after editorial the *Post-Dispatch* castigated the arrogance and perfidy of the Depot Company in dealing with the public. It charged that the company was under obligation—virtually amounting to a contract—to the city to put up an adequate passenger terminal. But, although it hammered away for months along this line, there was remarkably little effect on the company's officials. The reason was not hard to find. To a badgering reporter a spokesman for the monopoly roared his contempt for the *Post-Dispatch* in particular and the public in general:

> No, I won't give you a particle of information. What business is it of yours? What does it matter to the POST-DISPATCH? It's none of your business, it's none of the POST-DISPATCH'S business and it's none of the people's business. What does your miserable paper mean in attacking the Union Depot? . . . . This company is independent of the city of St. Louis and is under no obligation to it. . . . If you don't like this depot you needn't

---

[203] *Post-Dispatch*, Oct. 31, 1881, Nov. 1, 1881, Nov. 2, 1881, Nov. 25, 1881, Nov. 26, 1881, Feb. 24, 1882, Feb. 28, 1882.
[204] *Ibid.*, Nov. 26, 1880.
[205] *Ibid.*, Nov. 30, 1880.

use it. If the people of St. Louis don't like it they can go to East St. Louis and take their trains there. . . . It's none of your business.[206]

The *Post-Dispatch's* defiance of this monopolist's views, expressed the same day, was characteristic:

If Mr. Thompson's intellect were proportionate to his personal charms he would understand that it is poor business for the servant of a monopoly to rail and snarl and snap at a dignified newspaper, especially when the newspaper has right and justice on its side. Thompson . . . has furnished some excellent backing and justification for the POST-DISPATCH in its warfare on the Union Depot.[207]

The paper's efforts between 1880 and 1883 to break the monopolies oppressing St. Louis produced negligible results, but its determination to carry on the struggle was symptomatic of the times. The fight of the growing cities—of the middle classes in those cities and their newspapers—to free themselves from great corporations having little sense of public responsibility had only just begun.

---

[206] *Ibid.,* Dec. 4, 1880. The *Post-Dispatch* also gave great play to William H. Vanderbilt's famous remark, "The public be damned." It paid its respects to Vanderbilt in a number of lengthy editorials, including the following: "It would be well for the great corporations and their allied monopolies if they could only be induced to entertain a suspicion that their power over politicians may be once too often flaunted in the face of an indignant public. . . . The fact that a few colossal aggregations of capital in possession of all the transportation of our vast domains have combined to put down all competition, to maintain each other in violating laws, and to exact from overawed or corrupted officials the privilege of charging 'all the traffic will bear,' or of discriminating as they please in the exercise of an autocratic power over every interest and every industry of this country, is cause for alarm and for counteracting organization upon the part of the people. And sooner or later the power of the people to uphold their Constitution, to enforce their laws and to exact a strict loyalty from their public servants will assert itself. The only danger is that the final provocation may urge them too far!" *Ibid.,* Nov. 2, 1882.

[207] *Ibid.,* Dec. 4, 1880. A new and impressive passenger terminal was finally built in 1894 on Market Street. The ornate structure with its high towers was acclaimed a building of great beauty. It still stands as a monument of the period. (Cox, pp. 66-67.) Credit for forcing the Union Depot Company to build a satisfactory terminal in great part belonged to the *Post-Dispatch* and *Globe-Democrat,* both of which fought unceasingly to obtain it. *Spectator,* Nov. 5, 1887, St. Louis *Life,* May 7, 1890.

CHAPTER XI

To the National Stage

A principal reason why the *Post-Dispatch,* despite its vigorous assaults, made little progress toward freeing St. Louis from the monopolies was the undiminished influence of the oligarchs in local politics. As we have seen, the Republican mayor elected in 1881 when the businessmen's revolt unseated Henry Overstolz was no improvement on his predecessor in resisting the pressures of the gas and streetcar interests. And in Democratic ranks, although the reformers enjoyed a brief hour of success, the monopolists soon recovered their customary influence. Their agent, Ed Butler, the shrewd Irish riverfront ward leader, was fast becoming the boss of St. Louis. By 1882, he was no longer merely one of the Dark Lantern cabal of ward bosses; through his connections with the local oligarchs he was coming to dominate the Democratic organization. "The 'Village Blacksmith' is now tasting the sweets of power," the *Post-Dispatch* commented wryly. He

> is the Ward Warwick of St. Louis. He makes Constables, Aldermen, Judges, Legislators, Governors, etc., occasionally looks after slop contracts, city charters, *et cetera*. . . . We have never heard of him holding any office outside of ward committeeman, though his skill as an equine cobbler naturally causes the city horseshoeing contracts to gravitate in his direction.[1]

In the fall of 1882 Butler proposed to use his new supremacy for himself and his genteel allies by electing persons to office who could be counted on to serve the machine and the oligarchical interests behind it. The most important contest was to fill the seat of Congressman Thomas Allen who had died earlier in the year. In resisting these plans, the *Post-Dispatch* again challenged the combination of forces that had put an end to Joseph Pulitzer's political career in 1880.

In charge of the *Post-Dispatch* campaign was John A. Cockerill. Pulitzer had been ill during the summer—a forewarning of what long hours and unstinting expenditure of nervous energy was doing to his constitution—and his small son, Ralph, was in poor health, causing the Pulitzers to linger for weeks in eastern health resorts. In

---

[1] *Post-Dispatch,* Aug. 4, 1882, Sept. 11, 1882. See also, Zink, *City Bosses in United States,* p. 304.

the fall, after only a few days in St. Louis, the family left again, planning to be away all winter.[2] An experienced journalist, Samuel Williams—affectionately called "Colonel Sam"—was hired to help Cockerill with the editorial page.[3] More and more, therefore, the *Post-Dispatch* was left in the managing editor's capable hands. His brilliant pen was equal to the task of carrying on the paper's crusades, but his recklessness, ungoverned in Pulitzer's absence, was bound to cause trouble.

To fill Allen's place in the Congress the local oligarchs selected James O. Broadhead, a venerable member of the St. Louis bar, with the reputation of a prominent and public-spirited citizen.[4] But the *Post-Dispatch* also remembered that in 1873 this same distinguished citizen, while representing the city, had helped to arrange the Tri-partite Agreement by which the Gas-light Company had imposed outrageous rates on the municipality. And after this, Broadhead had conveniently switched sides, arguing the monopolists' case before the state supreme court when the city sought to cancel the franchise. Moreover, Broadhead now represented Jay Gould locally. In short, he typified the very interests in St. Louis against which the *Post-Dispatch* had long fought.

When reports first circulated that the oligarchs intended to nominate Broadhead in the September primary, the *Post-Dispatch* spoke out. As a "free and independent newspaper," it took the liberty of telling the politicians "a few plain truths without charge." The

---

[2] *Spectator*, Oct. 7, 1882; *Post-Dispatch*, Sept. 19, 1882, Oct. 14, 1882; Reynolds, "Joseph Pulitzer," p. 105.

[3] Williams was a veteran editorial writer, having served on Watterson's Louisville *Courier-Journal*, the *Times* in Kansas City, and the St. Louis *Republican*. On the *Post-Dispatch* he was to become editor of the editorial page in the nineties and one of Pulitzer's trusted lieutenants. An interesting story about Williams, printed in several St. Louis papers, had it that he had been a friend of Ulysses S. Grant during the latter's "hardscrabble" days in St. Louis, and that in 1861 in Springfield, Illinois, when a regiment of volunteers was seeking a commander, Williams suggested his old friend. *Life*, July 28, 1894, March 2, 1895; *American Journalist*, Jan. 1883; *The Journalist*, Oct. 30, 1886; *The Fourth Estate*, April 11, 1895; *Post-Dispatch*, Oct. 14, 1882; *Gould's St. Louis Directory*, 1873, p. 916; 1883, p. 1,173; Donald Padman: *A Sketch of Mr. Padman's Life* (St. Louis [1920]), p. 1.

[4] Broadhead, an eminent lawyer, was chosen the first president of the American Bar Association. Active as a Democrat, he was Cleveland's Minister to Switzerland in the 1890s. Broadhead had been a staunch Unionist during the Civil War, a follower of Frank Blair. In the 1870s he had played an important role in both the Missouri Constitutional Convention and the adoption of the St. Louis City Charter. *Reedy's Mirror*, Nov. 25, 1894; *Life*, Oct. 20, 1894; Memorandum, April 7, 1893, James O. Broadhead Collection; Barclay, *Movement for Municipal Home Rule in St. Louis*, pp. 75-76, 85-87, 101-10; Floyd C. Shoemaker, "James Overton Broadhead," *Dictionary of American Biography* (New York, 1929), III, 58-59.

Ninth Congressional District was Democratic, but only by a small margin, and

> no man can be elected who does not receive the entire party vote. A considerable portion of this vote is really independent. Even a blind man can see that the spirit of independence has grown in this city. There are thousands of voters in both parties who will bolt and scratch and vote as they please.

A candidate must be chosen, the paper added, who could "get the vote of merchants and independents," and Colonel Broadhead could not do this. So, "why not nominate a man who does not seek the place, [one] . . . more useful to the business interests of this city than any person yet named." [5]

Such comment, though forthright, was good tempered. But by early fall Cockerill's barbs began to sink deeper. A refusal by the candidate to appear before a meeting of Union veterans brought sneering remarks from the paper:

> It is observed that the KNAPPS [publishers of the *Republican*] permit Col. JAMES O. BROADHEAD to speak his views on . . . Prohibition, but they compelled him to place his hand over his mouth . . . when he was invited to pay a tribute to the memory of FRANK BLAIR—the man who helped pin Missouri to the Union.[6]

It took to referring to Broadhead as being "in the hands of ED. BUTLER," who "has the machinery and the facilities at his command to confer the Democratic nomination on the Colonel." [7] And when Broadhead's law partner, a fiery Southerner named Alonzo Slayback, planned a political rally, the *Post-Dispatch* lampooned his efforts:

> This is very kind on the part of the junior partner of the legal firm of "GRIMSHAW, GRABSHAW & BAGSHAW." Of course copies of this circular [announcing the meeting] have been placed in the hands of ED. BUTLER and Mr. RICHARD POWERS, the accomplished young ballot-box ravisher.

It added that John M. Glover, a young politician whom the paper was rather unenthusiastically supporting against Broadhead, was seeking votes among the working classes. "Mr. BROADHEAD is a pampered professional man, a slave to soulless monopolies and glut-

[5] *Post-Dispatch,* June 17, 1882. St. Louis was now divided into two congressional districts, the Eighth and Ninth.
[6] *Ibid.,* Sept. 7, 1882.
[7] *Ibid.,* Sept. 11, 1882.

tonous corporations and he does not attend a meeting of laboring men." [8]

These needling jabs suddenly changed a week before the primary, when, under such heads as A BROADHEAD BROADSIDE and A TOOL'S RECORD, the *Post-Dispatch* went all out to defeat the adversary. Sub-heads detailed the charges: "The Record of a Political and Legal Weather-Cock," "A Man Who Has Been 'Everything by Little and Nothing Long,'" "Vacillation, Duplicity, Selfishness and Uncertainty Typified," "The Story of Double Fees and Double Dealing in Politics." [9]

Declaring that he "has the cowardice rather than the courage of his convictions," the paper charged that Broadhead's Tripartite Agreement had cost the taxpayers three million dollars. It remarked that his propensity for accepting fees from both litigants in the gas dispute was "about as honorable as breaking into a man's house and appropriating his valuables." [10] As the candidate of such corporate interests as Jay Gould, "James O. Weakhead," if sent to Congress, "would be likely to serve his dangerous employer[s] with a zeal which would bring no good to the State of Missouri." [11]

Although the violence of the *Post-Dispatch* attack doubtless reduced Broadhead's vote, he squeaked through to victory in the primary.[12] The margin was provided, the paper charged, by the Village Blacksmith, "who calls out the saloon politicians, the primary ballot-box stuffers and the . . . 'strikers,'"—the pressure tactics of the monopolists. The paper exposed a number of instances where the machine swelled vote totals beyond registration figures; "it is a well known fact that . . . orders were issued through the M[issouri] P[acific] road here that their men should all support BROADHEAD. They were sent to the polls with BROADHEAD tickets." [13]

Far from quieting the *Post-Dispatch,* the primary victory only caused it to redouble its attacks. It declared that if the Republicans could "unite on a man of unimpeachable character . . . who has the confidence of the general business classes and respect of all, he will beat BROADHEAD" in the general election. Furthermore, the paper announced:

We pledge him the support of the POST-DISPATCH and all Independent Democratic voters who are absolved from support-

8 *Ibid.,* Sept. 20, 1882.
9 *Ibid.,* Sept. 26, 1882, Sept. 27, 1882.
10 *Ibid.,* Sept. 26, 1882.
11 *Ibid.*
12 *Ibid.,* Oct. 2, 1882.
13 *Ibid.,* Oct. 2, 1882, Oct. 4, 1882, Oct. 7, 1882.

ing a nominee forced upon them by legislative chicanery, machine bummerism, police interference and all the methods which belong to the ballot-stuffing saloon politicians.[14]

The violence of the paper's attacks caused bitter resentment, and feelings began to run high. Alonzo Slayback, Broadhead's hot-tempered associate, was heard to accuse the *Post-Dispatch* of being "a blackmailing sheet," and the next afternoon John Cockerill replied by printing an insulting year-old "card" from John Glover, the recently defeated candidate, who had had trouble with Slayback concerning a lawsuit. Glover accused Slayback of being a "coward." When the card was first received months before, Pulitzer, knowing well that it might cause trouble, refused to print it. But the managing editor was not so cautious.[15]

The four o'clock edition containing the card had been on the street less than an hour when Henry Moore, seated at his desk in the city room on the second floor of the *Post-Dispatch* building, glanced up to see a pale-faced Slayback, followed closely by another lawyer, William Clopton, who had been involved in a "cowhiding" himself a few days before, throw open the door to Cockerill's private office and enter it with a rush. What happened during the next few seconds is unclear, but it is known that the enraged attorney advanced upon Cockerill, who arose from his desk and seized a revolver. A shot rang out and Slayback staggered forward with blood gushing from his mouth. In a few moments he was dead.[16]

The room quickly filled with shocked reporters and outsiders who dashed upstairs from the street. Cockerill, aware of the gravity of the situation, but calm, left his office and went to the Lindell Hotel, where he changed his blood-spattered garments. At about eight

14 *Ibid.*, Oct. 3, 1882.
15 *Ibid.*
16 There are many contradictory versions of this dramatic tragedy. The only witnesses were Clopton and two *Post-Dispatch* colleagues of Cockerill. Their stories differed. John McGuffin, the business manager, swore that Slayback advanced upon the editor with a leveled pistol, but Clopton declared he was unarmed. One sinister account, published years later, has it that after Slayback was dead a gun was placed on his body by Cockerill's friends to give color to the plea of self-defense. Local newspapers quickly took sides. In general, the *Globe-Democrat, Spectator,* and *Criterion* were friendly to Cockerill, the *Republican* and *Chronicle* bitterly hostile. See *Globe-Democrat,* Oct. 14, 1882, Oct. 18, 1882; *Chronicle,* Oct. 14, 1882; *Spectator,* Oct. 21, 1882; *Criterion,* Oct. 21, 1882; and *Missouri Republican,* Oct. 14, 1882. See also, *Post-Dispatch,* Oct. 2, 1882, Oct. 14, 1882, Oct. 16, 1882, Oct. 17, 1882. The latter two citations are reports of the testimony before a coroner's jury. (Kelsoe, *St. Louis Reference Record* [St. Louis (1927)], 148-49). Writers still disagree about this affair, as two recent books show: Homer W. King, *Pulitzer's Prize Editor,* ch. 9, is favorable to Cockerill, while Putzel, *Man in the Mirror,* pp. 28-29, is unfavorable.

o'clock he gave himself up to the police at the Four Courts and was lodged in a cell where a number of boon companions soon appeared. To one the popular editor remarked, "Too bad, but it couldn't be helped." [17]

Meanwhile, attracted by the shot and the rapidly spreading rumors, a large crowd milled around the *Post-Dispatch*. Most were simply curious, but as time passed, hints of an ugly mood cropped up as friends of the deceased and assorted enemies of the paper began to mutter threats of vengeance. The mob dispersed with no untoward incident, but next morning the *Republican* vented its long-standing hatred for the *Post-Dispatch* in a vindictive story which one of its editors admitted later was deliberately designed to cause trouble.[18] The headlines read: ALONZO W. SLAYBACK "Shot and Killed by John A. Cockerill," "Singled out by the 'Post-Dispatch' as a Victim of Its Venom." "He Visits the Sanctum of That Paper to Vindicate His Manhood" "And Finds the Editor With a Revolver Ready at Hand." "Great Excitement throughout the City." "Fruits of Aggressive and Sensational Journalism of the 'Post-Dispatch School.' " [19] The killing also received wide publicity throughout the nation, stirring a vigorous debate upon the characteristics of sensational journalism. *Harper's Weekly* decried the new style in these words:

> The killing of "Colonel" Slayback by "Colonel" Cockerill . . . is a direct result of personal journalism. It must be owned that there is a desire in men to hear ill of their neighbors, and it is this "long-felt want" that personal journalism undertakes to supply. A newspaper publisher was heard not long ago to say: "If I could prove that somebody had stolen a million dollars, I could double my circulation.". . . A newspaper skillfully conducted for the purpose of skillfully goading private persons or public officers to fury will not lack an audience, and so long as it does not lack an audience, newspapers conducted upon that "theory of journalism" will continue to be published.
>
> There is risk in this. . . . It is the risk that the worm may turn, that the bull may gore. "Colonel" Slayback turned, and if he

---

[17] Thomas, *Print of My Remembrance*, pp. 135-37.

[18] Kelsoe, pp. 148-49.

[19] *Republican*, Oct. 14, 1882; *Spectator*, Oct. 28, 1882. There was also genuine sorrow among a host of friends of the dead man. Slayback was a convivial man-about-town, kind hearted and public spirited, as well as an excellent lawyer and staunch Democrat. A week after his death a benefit was staged for the bereaved family by the Merchants' Exchange. Hundreds attended. Early the next year a volume of Slayback's poems was published as a memorial. See Alonzo W. Slayback, *A Memorial Volume* (St. Louis, 1883). *Post-Dispatch*, Oct. 19, 1882; *Spectator*, Oct. 21, 1882, Oct. 28, 1882.

had shot "Colonel" Cockerill, there would have been a poetic justice in the transaction.[20]

The Kansas City *Star,* recently founded by William Rockhill Nelson, a young editor of the new journalism, sharply disagreed. "In many quarters the *Post-Dispatch* is held up as a frightening example of journalistic depravity," it said in a passionate defense of the St. Louis paper. "In our opinion there is very little occasion for these animadversions upon 'personal journalism' in general, or upon the *Post-Dispatch* in particular.

> The fact is [it continued] that what most of those who have moralized upon the Slayback-Cockerill tragedy choose to style "personal journalism" is the hope and protection of the country to-day. Every bribe-taking official, every public plunderer, every greedy monopolist—in short every rascal in the land—deprecates "personal journalism." . . . The fact is that a newspaper which fearlessly attacks wrong and corruption, whether high or low, which does not spare . . . wrong-doers, whatever their wealth, social position or political promises, is sure to arouse strong enmities. . . . Nevertheless, such journals invariably thrive because they serve the great public faithfully. . . . Such a journal is a great power for good, not only because of its positive achievements in exposing rascals and bringing them to punishment, but also because of the restraining influence which it exerts upon those who fear its lash. Such a force has the *Post-Dispatch* been in St. Louis. It has antagonized all the evil elements in the city, and has not hesitated to attack wrong, however securely entrenched in power and place. . . . There isn't a rogue in St. Louis who does not hate the *Post-Dispatch,* and all the rascally elements would have been delighted to have seen its building razed to the ground and its editor lynched after the recent tragedy. But this was not to be. A powerful public journal cannot be wiped out in this manner by a howling mob, even when it is led by so-called "prominent citizens." [21]

---

[20] *Harper's Weekly,* XXVI (Nov. 4, 1882).

[21] Reprinted in the *Post-Dispatch,* Nov. 4, 1882. For a life of Nelson, who was also important in the development of modern journalism, see Icie F. Johnson, *William Rockhill Nelson and the Kansas City Star* (Kansas City, 1935). See also, Mott, *American Journalism,* pp. 468-73. A typical reaction in a St. Louis paper was the following: "While we admire the progressive and fearless spirit of the *Post-Dispatch* we feel that it has been too aggressive and bitter in some respects, but that it has accomplished much for morality in this city is not to be denied and this is a virtue of sufficient magnitude to counterbalance many of its other faults." *Criterion,* Oct. 21, 1882.

Whatever the rights and wrongs of its style of journalism, the *Post-Dispatch* was unnerved by the catastrophe. Informed of the affair in New York, Pulitzer hurried to St. Louis, declaring he intended to stand by his editor. It was part of Pulitzer's extraordinary success that he always came to the defense of his subordinates in times of stress. He arrived in the city two days after the shooting, went directly to the Four Courts to reassure Cockerill, and then to the *Post-Dispatch* office where he wrote the following statement:

Mr. JOHN A. COCKERILL is in the hands of the law and his friends ask nothing for him but a fair trial and a public judgment upon the legal evidence. They do not propose to plead his cause in the newspapers or reply to publications made to arouse a murderous prejudice against him.[22]

And two days later he took full responsibility for the entire course of the *Post-Dispatch* during his absence:

The charge of blackmail is the worst that can be preferred against any honest paper or editor. If Mr. Cockerill had remained silent under it, he would, by his silence, have confessed its truth. . . . The publication of the Glover card under the circumstances was purely in self-defense, justified, invited, made inevitable by Col. Slayback's own provocation.

Mr Pulitzer is willing to go further. If Mr. Cockerill had allowed the public stigma and brand of blackmailing to go unresented he would have been unfit for his position, and would have ceased to be managing editor of the paper.[23]

Seven weeks later, after considering the evidence and finding that Slayback had been armed when he entered Cockerill's office, a grand jury refused to return an indictment.[24] But the enemies of the paper were not satisfied. The *Republican* goaded the local bar association into passing a resolution condemning the *Post-Dispatch*, constantly harassed the grand jury's proceedings and, when it failed to indict Cockerill, persuaded Mrs. Slayback to bring suit against him for damages, alleging that he had unlawfully deprived her of her husband. "I have been pursued with almost inhuman malignancy by the proprietors of the St. Louis *Republican* and such persons as they have

---

[22] *Post-Dispatch*, Oct. 16, 1882; Seitz, *Joseph Pulitzer*, pp. 110-12.

[23] *Post-Dispatch*, Oct. 18, 1882.

[24] *Ibid.*, Oct. 17, 1882, Dec. 5, 1882; *Spectator*, Dec. 2, 1882. The testimony proving that Slayback had been armed prompted the *Globe-Democrat* to remark that "this was the one revelation necessary to place Mr. Cockerill on the right side. Lawyers conceded almost to a man, that the discovery closed the case. It was a matter of clear self-defense." *Globe-Democrat*, Oct. 18, 1882.

been able to incite and control," Cockerill complained. "These men have a deep-seated business hostility against the POST-DISPATCH— a hostility which they were reasonably careful to conceal until they believed that I had been forced into a position . . . from which I would not be able to extricate myself." [25] By attacking Cockerill, the *Republican* succeeded in destroying his usefulness to the *Post-Dispatch*. He returned to his post after several weeks, but his influence in St. Louis was compromised.[26]

In the circumstances, Pulitzer found it necessary to reorganize his demoralized staff. He appointed Henry Moore temporary managing editor during Cockerill's absence and he, himself, took over the editorial page.[27] But even before the Slayback shooting St. Louis had begun to pall upon Pulitzer, and in the situation in which he now found himself he was almost as uncomfortable as Cockerill. Indeed, for the Pulitzers the atmosphere in what was, after all, a smallish community, had gradually become less and less bearable. The oligarchs—the socially elite—had snubbed Mrs. Pulitzer despite her impeccable Southern pedigree because of the policies of her husband's paper; as for Pulitzer, among "the men who counted for much in St. Louis . . . the most pronounced feeling concerning him was one of enmity." [28] Added to this was continued anxiety over his asthmatic child, whose condition required wintering in South Carolina.[29] Pulitzer, therefore, was anxious to move east as soon as possible.

[25] *Post-Dispatch*, Dec. 7, 1882; *Spectator*, Nov. 11, 1882, Dec. 2, 1882, Dec. 16, 1882, Feb. 24, 1883. Even a year later, when Cockerill was about to leave St. Louis forever and the local Elks Club elected him honorary president, the *Republican*, still vindictively pursuing him, carried the story with the remark: "For President, Colonel Slayback's slayer." *Ibid.*, Nov. 10, 1883.

[26] Pulitzer, who had been Slayback's friend, felt a sense of responsibility for the bereaved family. Some years later, when Slayback's eldest daughter, Suzanne, had fallen on evil days, she was hired to work in the society department of the paper, where she remained for many years. Interview with Richard J. Collins, March 20, 1951. Orrick Johns, *Time of Our Lives*, p. 60.

[27] *American Journalist*, Oct. 15, 1883.

[28] Frank R. O'Neil to Florence D. White, Dec. 4, 1903, Pulitzer Papers (CU); *Reedy's Mirror*, Nov. 4, 1894. In a study of Pulitzer, one authority remarks: "The few years that Pulitzer lived in St. Louis after his marriage and the purchase of the *Post-Dispatch* seemed the happiest of his life." (Reynolds, "Joseph Pulitzer," p. 102.) This is no doubt true, especially if one remembers his extremely unhappy life following his blindness in 1887. But by 1882 frustrations were building up. Illnesses, social ostracism for his wife and himself, and perhaps a growing feeling that he had gone as far as he could in St. Louis, began to plague him, producing that restlessness that was so characteristic.

[29] *Spectator*, Oct. 7, 1882, Jan. 6, 1883. Pulitzer was described by a close St. Louis friend of those years as a man of "tender feelings" and of "well grounded affection" towards his family. Charles Gibson to Joseph Pulitzer, May 14, 1883, Pulitzer Papers (CU).

Most of all, the Slayback shooting had affected the circulation of the *Post-Dispatch*. It lost 1,300 subscribers in the six weeks following the killing, and Pulitzer realized he needed an editor who would command the respect of the community.[30] For a solution to these perplexing problems he turned to his old associate, John A. Dillon, whose social position was unassailable.[31] During the three years since he had given up his partnership in the *Post-Dispatch*, Dillon had reverted to the leisurely habits of earlier days. At first he had gone back to the *Globe-Democrat*, where he wrote occasional pieces on literary and cultural subjects—always his main interest—but in 1881 he abandoned journalism to accompany his brother-in-law, James B. Eads, to Mexico City, where the latter was seeking permission to build a ship railway across the Isthmus of Tehuantepec.[32] The life was pleasant, and after a sojourn in England with Eads, Dillon went to Mexico as secretary of the American legation there. But for financial and family reasons, in the fall of 1882 he came back to St. Louis and assumed the editorship of the weekly *Spectator*.[33]

Dillon quickly accepted Pulitzer's proposal that he take charge of the editorial page of the *Post-Dispatch*. The *Spectator's* salary was small for one with nine children, and Dillon apparently was promised that he would not have the care of the business end of the paper—a responsibility which was always repugnant to him.[34] For Pulitzer, too, Dillon's return was eminently satisfactory. The two had great confidence in each other—despite the termination of their partnership in 1879—and when an outstate journal remarked that Dillon was "a forcible writer and fearless, a first-class newspaper man," Pulitzer called it "a merited tribute."[35] Almost immediately, Pulitzer left for New York and his family. In a sense, he was abandoning St. Louis.[36]

---

30 Memorandum [1906], Pulitzer Papers (CU). Possibly, too, Pulitzer feared a loss in advertising.

31 *Post-Dispatch*, March 19, 1881. Dillon belonged to the ultra-exclusive Home Circle and Imperial Clubs, whose members included the most prominent families in St. Louis.

32 *Spectator*, Nov. 6, 1880, March 26, 1881, April 2, 1881; Dorsey, *Road to the Sea*, pp. 247-48.

33 *Post-Dispatch*, Aug. 7, 1882, Oct. 12, 1882; *Spectator*, Aug. 12, 1882; interview with Gertrude McDonald, Feb. 5, 1951.

34 Family tradition has it that Dillon was exempted from worry over the business side of the paper. Interview with Gertrude McDonald, Feb. 5, 1951. It is evident from Dillon's correspondence preserved in the Pulitzer Papers that he did become, as editor in chief of the *Post-Dispatch* between 1883 and 1891, involved in the business side of the paper. He found it distasteful. Oddly enough, in 1891 Pulitzer called Dillon to the New York *World* as business manager; the experiment was not a success.

35 *Post-Dispatch*, Nov. 4, 1882.

36 *Spectator*, Nov. 11, 1882.

Under the gentlemanly Dillon the *Post-Dispatch* proceeded cautiously at first, no doubt on Pulitzer's orders. The sensational news policy was muted and on the editorial page the new editor's restrained and urbane prose replaced Cockerill's free-swinging style. There were no crusades and, except for one vigorous editorial on the eve of the general election, there were no further attacks on Broadhead, who won an extremely close contest.[37] The paper's circulation continued to decline in November and December, but in January the tide slowly turned and by March readership was growing again. The crisis was passed.[38]

Dillon's editorials were quite different from those of his predecessors. Under him, the *Post-Dispatch* went in for speculative pieces, like one on THE SCARCITY OF GREAT MEN and another dealing with the place of women in modern society. In some ways Dillon was more liberal-minded than Pulitzer, who was sometimes inclined to be conventional. Characteristic of the new editor's style and views was the following paragraph:

That very large number of well-meaning but mistaken people who are fond of asserting the intellectual superiority of the male sex and the corresponding inferiority of women will have a hard time accounting for the fact that at the commencement of Washington University this week, the highest honors were won by a young lady, Miss JENNIE LIPPMAN. . . . One incident of this kind is worth more than a book full of sermons from MORGAN DIX and other reverend and unreverend gentlemen who think that woman's place is in the background.[39]

Dillon had a better sense of history and a more philosophical approach to public questions than the practical Pulitzer; his humor was of a restrained type, in contrast with Cockerill's spontaneity. But in his dignified way he was quite as effective as they, and by the early spring of 1883, when the *Post-Dispatch* recovered its vigor, Dillon's editorial campaigns were as hard-hitting as those of his predecessors. His general outlook did not differ from Pulitzer's, as the following editorial in 1883 clearly shows. Declaring that the *Post-Dispatch* would support the Democratic Party only if it were "truly democratic," he laid down the views of the paper once more:

All that is needed is to be truly democratic; to limit the functions of government to its proper sphere; to enforce rigid economy in

---

[37] *Post-Dispatch*, Nov. 6, 1882, March 20, 1883.

[38] Memorandum [1906], Pulitzer Papers (CU). The December low point was 20,000, which was a decline from 22,300 at the end of September. In January the paper regained 500 readers and by March circulation again was at 22,000.

[39] *Post-Dispatch*, June 16, 1883.

every expenditure; to maintain the highest efficiency in every department; to hold party leaders and officers strictly responsible for the political and official trusts they hold; to abolish useless and vexatious taxation; to give the people to understand that no attempt will be made to interfere with their personal and private rights or opinions; and above all things, to make it clearly understood that the interests of the great body of the people are at all times and under all circumstances to prevail over the demands of monopolies or corporations.[40]

Dillon renewed a number of crusades which the *Post-Dispatch* had been carrying on, such as those against the bridge monopolists and the horse-car and gas company corporations, and he inaugurated the campaigns for the exposition hall and high license. But perhaps the most spectacular crusade—a combination exposure and editorial campaign conducted by Dillon and Henry Moore together—was one revealing for the first time the wholesale boodling taking place in the municipal assembly. The campaign accomplished nothing then, but the *Post-Dispatch* kept at it from time to time through the years and in 1901 a renewed crusade would make nationwide names for Joseph Folk, St. Louis's famous circuit attorney, and Lincoln Steffens, the muckraker.[41]

By the spring of 1883 Ed Butler, who had been elected to the state central committee and was more firmly entrenched than ever in St. Louis, forged such an impregnable combine in the Municipal Assembly that the great corporations who had raised him up were having to pay tribute to him.[42] He was becoming a Frankenstein's monster. This development was first exposed by the *Post-Dispatch* in a column length story headed: A DELEGATE'S DIVVY. It purported to be based on an interview with an unnamed assemblyman who had been defeated in the last election. The ex-delegate, a member of the lower house of the assembly, revealed how an organized "gang" of "the boys" regularly extracted bribes from corporations seeking franchises from the city, citing several instances. Although it cost a candidate for the House of Delegates a "fee" of three hundred dollars to run for office —his first year's salary—once a man took his seat he stood to make

---

[40] *Ibid.*, July 26, 1883.

[41] See James W. Markham, *Bovard of the Post-Dispatch* (Baton Rouge, 1954), chs. 1, 3; Wetmore, *Battle Against Bribery;* Wetmore and Steffens, "Tweed Days in St. Louis," *McClure's Magazine,* XIX (Oct. 1902), 577-87; Lincoln Steffens, *The Autobiography of Lincoln Steffens* (New York, 1931), pp. 365-73; Lincoln Steffens, *The Shame of the Cities* (New York, 1904), ch. 2; Orrick Johns, *Time of Our Lives*, pp. 145-56; Geiger, *Joseph W. Folk*, chs. 3-4.

[42] *Post-Dispatch,* Jan. 27, 1883.

many times that figure. When an important franchise came before the House, the informant continued, there were "bushels" of bribe money floating about. The average "take" of a delegate in the group was about $2,000 per annum, he said, while councilmen often pocketed $6,000. He listed a number of ways by which franchise-seekers or holders were "bled." If a company should prove balky by protesting the amount of a bribe, "the boys" would "buck"—refuse to pass the bill—until the proper amount was forthcoming. On other occasions, when business was light, "bunkum bills" would be introduced. These were proposals not really intended for passage, but which were for the purpose of frightening franchise holders into passing out boodle to insure their defeat. The corporations usually "came tumbling around to 'see' . . . influential men. . . . We buck, get the dust and the bill is killed." By 1883, no franchise, no claim, no favor, however small, could get through the assembly without a payment of some kind, the politician concluded. Even the closing of an alley cost fifty to a hundred dollars in bribe money.[43]

The exposure produced a sensation, and public reaction became loud when succeeding revelations added details. TRICKS OF THE TRADE, A SNUG SUM, and POLITICAL PLUNDER, all purporting to be based on interviews with the same disgruntled politician, brought out more and more. The *Post-Dispatch* followed them up with investigations of its own, discovering that a Councilman Rowse had made a killing by selling a piece of property for $13,000 to the Union Depot Company as a payoff by the corporation in return for a franchise. A final story exposed how ward bosses like Ed Butler, John Carroll, and Dan Kerwin systematically charged "fees" of hundreds of dollars to permit candidates to run for office or obtain municipal employment. "If de aspirant fur office or fur a $600-a-year job is got nothin' he gets nothin'," one politician admitted. "Fees" often ran as high as $1,500 to $2,000 for a councilman's seat.[44]

"The people of St. Louis would do well to keep a close eye on the bills that are brought up in the Municipal Assembly," the *Post-Dispatch* warned, and it demanded a grand jury investigation, declaring that "leading citizens of every political creed heartily indorse the crusade which the POST-DISPATCH has inaugurated." [45] The grand jury which met in May was instructed to look into the paper's charges of profligate boodling, but no one would talk and the matter had to

<hr />

[43] *Ibid.*, April 4, 1883.
[44] *Ibid.*, April 5, 6, 7, 9, 10, 1883.
[45] *Ibid.*, April 6, 1883, April 9, 1883.

be dropped.[46] The *Post-Dispatch,* however, immensely enhanced its reputation as a crusading journal. No other paper touched the issue.

The *Post-Dispatch* once more was on the high road of prosperity. By June circulation reached 23,000 daily and was still rising, and Business Manager McGuffin was reporting record profits from advertising.[47] But Joseph Pulitzer was not in St. Louis. The truth was, in addition to his personal troubles, he had outgrown St. Louis; it could no longer contain his driving ambition. Pulitzer had long dreamed of publishing a newspaper in New York. After all, he remarked in another connection, "I want to speak to a nation." As far back as 1876, when he was Washington correspondent for the *Sun,* he had approached Dana with the proposition of publishing a German edition of the *Sun.*[48] And early in 1882 he tried to persuade his old friend, Daniel Houser of the *Globe-Democrat,* to join him in establishing a New York paper. Houser demurred, protesting that in good conscience he could not print a Democratic journal in New York and a Republican one in St. Louis.[49] There had been other gestures from time to time, indicating clearly that Pulitzer never had any intention of making St. Louis his permanent home.[50]

At last, in 1883, his opportunity came. The New York *World,* the most prominent Democratic journal in the metropolis, was for sale. It had fallen on evil times in the seventies and about 1879 had been acquired by Jay Gould.[51] Gould, too, failed to make it pay and now desired to get rid of it. Quite possibly one reason Pulitzer hurried east after hiring Dillon was to launch negotiations for the purchase of the *World.* Certainly by January there was considerable competition for it. The *Post-Dispatch* remarked, perhaps with disgust, that "it is a cold day when there is not a new rumor about the disposition to be made of the . . . mummified corpse of the once bright and lively New York *World.*" [52] The paper understood that John R. McLean of the Cincinnati *Enquirer* had the inside track. But by April the *Enquirer* itself remarked—somewhat enigmatically—that "as Joseph has more stamps than the rest [of us]—I might say the only one with stamps—I suspect he will get it ultimately." [53] Even so, despite the few rumors which escaped now and then, the news that Pulitzer had, indeed, bought the *World* on May 10, 1883, burst like a

---

46 *Ibid.,* May 7, 1883.

47 Memorandum [1906], Pulitzer Papers (CU); *Spectator,* May 26, 1883.

48 *Post-Dispatch,* May 11, 1883; Reynolds, pp. 103-104.

49 John Norris to Joseph Pulitzer, March 10, 1900, Pulitzer Papers (CU).

50 Reynolds, pp. 126-27.

51 Seitz, pp. 126-27.

52 *Post-Dispatch,* Jan. 25, 1883.

53 Reprinted in *Post-Dispatch,* April 11, 1883.

bombshell on St. Louis.[54] ALL THE WORLD, the *Post-Dispatch* head-lined the news from New York. In high glee it added the next day that "it is Mr. PULITZER'S intention to infuse into the *World* some of that vim, energy, dash and sincerity of purpose which alone can carry a newspaper to popular success in this land. . . ." The same issue reprinted Pulitzer's *World* salutatory, which must have sounded familiar to many St. Louisans:

> There is room in this great and growing city [of New York] for a journal that is not only cheap but bright, not only bright but large, not only large but truly democratic—dedicated to the cause of the people rather than that of purse-potentates—devoted more to the news of the New than the Old World—that will expose all fraud and sham, fight all public evils and abuses—that will serve and battle for the people with earnest sincerity.[55]

And a few days later the *Post-Dispatch* listed the *World's* platform, propositions which were, in a real sense, forged in St. Louis. They were the platform of a reforming middle class newspaper seeking to protect city dwellers in their rights to equal opportunity and clean government. The *World,* said the *Post-Dispatch,* called for taxes upon inheritances and large incomes, a tax on monopolies and privileged corporations, a tariff for revenue only, reform of the civil service, and punishment of corrupt office-holders, vote-buyers, and employers who coerced their employees in elections.[56]

The *Post-Dispatch* also carried an important announcement:

> It may be said . . . that this departure will in no way affect the POST-DISPATCH. Mr. PULITZER will remain its pro-

---

[54] Negotiations took longer than anticipated, apparently, because Gould hoped to unload the *World's* dilapidated building on Pulitzer, who did not want it. In fact, the snag was so serious that possibly negotiations were broken off in April, for Pulitzer remarked to a reporter that the final arrangements of the sale happened "almost unexpectedly." (*Ibid.,* May 11, 1883.) This no doubt is the origin of the accepted account that Pulitzer just happened to be going through New York on the way to Europe for his health when he heard the *World* was for sale and purchased it on the spot. Seitz, p. 114; Barrett, *Joseph Pulitzer*, pp. 59-60; George S. Johns, *Joseph Pulitzer*, p. 92. It was true that Pulitzer had planned to take a six-month sojourn in Europe; and the threat of this trip might well have made Gould come around to Pulitzer's terms that he would lease the *World* building from Gould, not buy it. Indeed, asked why he had not purchased the *World* earlier, Pulitzer remarked, "Chiefly because Mr. Gould insisted on selling me the building . . . at about $200,000. I was not in real estate speculation and did not want it, so I have least [sic] it at a . . . fair interest . . . for ten years." (*Post-Dispatch*, May 11, 1883.) Actually, the negotiations for the sale were substantially concluded on April 28, almost two weeks before Pulitzer took over the paper. See Reynolds, pp. 106-107.

[55] *Post-Dispatch*, May 11, 1883.

[56] *Ibid.*, May 22, 1883.

prietor and director, and the paper will continue to be a faithful and untiring chronicler of events, expanding with its own force and growing with its surroundings.[57]

Reaction to Pulitzer's invasion of New York ranged from enthusiasm to resentment. The *Globe-Democrat*, long Pulitzer's friendly rival, thoroughly approved and wished him well.[58] The Kansas City *Star* voiced the attitude of many a Western journal:

> There is scarcely a man, west of the Allegheny mountains who does not wish Mr. Pulitzer success . . . and it may be said . . . that there is not one who doubts that he will carry the "Western method" into the *World* office. His paper will be a news-paper. . . . It will no longer be the organ of dudes and dudines of Fifth and Madison avenues . . . it will cease to devote its space to the coaching trips of DeLancey Kane and the postings of the Oscar Wildes. It will devote itself to the news. . . .[59]

But the *Missouri Republican,* Pulitzer's old enemy, was bitterly resentful. Wishing it were not so, it refused to print the original report of Pulitzer's purchase. But later, when the *World* began to trumpet Grover Cleveland for the Presidency in 1884, the *Republican* could not contain its wrath:

> Occasionally some mountain of Cheek—some Himalaya of assurance—will spring up in the pathway of ordinary men to make them stare and wonder. Such an altitudinous peak of effrontery has erected itself athwart the public gaze in the person of the editor of the New York *World.*
>
> To people here in St. Louis the attitude of Mr. Pulitzer posing as the conductor of a democratic organ, and having himself spoken of . . . as the framer of national democratic platforms is —well, amusing. . . . From the time of Garfield's election to his getting into the *World* newspaper his every expression in regard to the Democracy showed he despised it.[60]

The *Post-Dispatch's* reply was that the *Republican,* like all party organs, was a "political strumpet"; it could not comprehend the course of a paper conducted on principles.[61]

In part, at least, the prosperity of the *Post-Dispatch* enabled Pulitzer to buy the *World* and move to the center of journalism.

---

[57] *Ibid.,* May 11, 1883.

[58] *Globe-Democrat,* May 11, 1883.

[59] Reprinted in the *Post-Dispatch,* May 21, 1883.

[60] *Republican,* June 25, 1883.

[61] *Post-Dispatch,* June 25, 1883, June 30, 1883.

Profits from his St. Louis paper were used to pay the first installment on the purchase price.[62] But this by no means exhausted the contribution of the *Post-Dispatch* to the New York venture. Two days after he started to publish the *World,* Pulitzer sent for John Cockerill, who, more than anyone else, had helped him make the *Post-Dispatch* a success. In fact, for the rest of the summer and on into the fall Cockerill and Dillon shuttled between St. Louis and New York before, late in November, Cockerill was permanently installed as the *World's* managing editor.[63] About the same time, John McGuffin, the *Post-Dispatch* business manager, was named publisher of the *World.*[64] Thus, two-thirds of the energetic, original-minded team Pulitzer had assembled in 1879 were transplanted to New York. The proprietor did not stop with editors; a score of reporters, then and later, were attracted to the *World* from all the St. Louis papers.[65] The key man, however, was Cockerill. On the metropolitan stage this magnetic and brilliant editor acquired the reputation of being "unquestionably the best news editor in the country," and some were inclined to believe he was even more indispensable to the success of the *World* than Pulitzer himself.[66] One man stated positively that Pulitzer would

[62] Pulitzer wrote St. Clair McKelway, publisher of the Brooklyn *Eagle,* a number of years later that the "prosperity" of the *Post-Dispatch* "enabled me to pay the necessary purchase money for the *World.*" (Seitz, p. 133.) This is the standard version, which fits well with Pulitzer's habits. However, the day following his inaugural issue of the *World* Pulitzer told a reporter: "I needed to have ready money, and I got it in St. Louis among my friends and business connections there. I own the whole stock of the *World,* however." *Post-Dispatch,* May 11, 1883.

[63] *Spectator,* May 12, 1883, June 14, 1883, Aug. 18, 1883, Sept. 8, 1883, Nov. 10, 1883, Jan. 5, 1884; *American Journalist,* Nov., 1883.

[64] "Publisher" was another title for business manager. *American Journalist,* Oct., 1883.

[65] Stevens, "New Journalism in Missouri," *Missouri Historical Review,* XVII (April 1923), 327. John Reavis, on the first staff of the *Post-Dispatch* and later a founder of the *Spectator,* was the most important reporter to go to the *World.* He became Pulitzer's first London correspondent. He is also credited with originating the famous *World* campaign to raise money by popular subscription for the base of the Statue of Liberty on Bedloe's Island. McDougall, *This is the Life!,* p. 167; *Post-Dispatch,* July 29, 1884.

[66] *Journalist,* May 8, 1886. An obituary published in 1897 was characteristic. It declared that the *World's* success was "almost universally ascribed to Col. Cockerill. A Western man, his Western methods rattled the dry bones in Park Row." *(Ibid.,* Oct. 2, 1897). St. Louis newspapermen had an equally high opinion of Cockerill. One remarked that "in organizing all the essential detail of modern daily journalism, Cockerill has no superior in the country," and another commented that it was due principally to the acquisition of Cockerill as managing editor in 1879 that the *Post-Dispatch* enjoyed "extraordinary success." *(Spectator,* May 26, 1883; *American Journalist,* Oct. 1883.) Pulitzer was aware of these opinions held by the members of the working press, and it nettled him. It was a factor in the rupture which eventually took place in their association. *Journalist,* Oct. 2, 1897.

never have dared to invade New York if his aggressive and handsome assistant had not consented to come with him.[67]

These developments necessitated a drastic reorganization of the *Post-Dispatch*. As soon as he decided to keep Cockerill in New York, Pulitzer designated John Dillon his editor-in-chief in St. Louis, endowing him with supervisory responsibilites over the entire establishment, but with his major duty the editorial page.[68] Henry Moore, "the best news gatherer in St. Louis," was made managing editor, his duties being confined to the news department, and John Magner, an irascible but able reporter, was elevated to the city editorship.[69] In the counting room Ignatz Kappner, the courtly and elderly cashier, replaced McGuffin as business manager.[70] Billy Steigers, however, continued to have a free hand with advertising.

This new team, although it was not entirely harmonious, was destined to guide the *Post-Dispatch* for the next half-dozen years; under it the paper continued to maintain its remarkable progress. Circulation boomed. By December 1883 it had reached 27,000 per day, and by January 1, 1888 the *Post-Dispatch* achieved a volume of 30,000 copies.[71] Most significant, although it did not finally overtake the mighty *Globe-Democrat* in total readership for many years, by December 1884 the *Post-Dispatch* enjoyed the largest local circulation of any paper.[72] Partly because evening journalism was coming into its own, partly because the sensational news the *Post-Dispatch* carried appealed to urban readers, and perhaps most of all because it expressed the average city man's outlook on affairs of the day, Pulitzer's newspaper became the most widely read journal in St. Louis.

---

[67] This, no doubt, is an exaggeration, but it was typical of the extravagant admiration in which Cockerill was held by newspapermen. One man who had worked under him in St. Louis exclaimed: "If Col. Cockerill was a statesman, I think James G. Blaine would not be the only magnetic statesman. I never knew a man who could win people so easily to him as can Col. Cockerill." (*Journalist*, March 3, 1888.) So popular was he that five times straight he was elected president of the New York Press Club. *Fourth Estate*, April 16, 1896.

[68] Dillon left the news and business departments largely to themselves. Interview with Richard J. Collins, March 20, 1951. Collins came to the paper in 1887 when Dillon was editor-in-chief. Dillon did not receive the formal title until 1884 or 1885. *Gould's St. Louis Directory*, 1884, p. 311; 1885, p. 323; *Spectator*, July 14, 1883; *Journalist*, Dec. 5, 1885, July 14, 1888.

[69] *Gould's St. Louis Directory*, 1884, pp. 730, 799; *American Journalist*, Oct. 1883; *Spectator*, Feb. 17, 1883. See characterization of Magner in Thomas, pp. 203-04.

[70] *Gould's St. Louis Directory*, 1884, p. 591; 1885, p. 618; *American Journalist*, Dec. 1883; interview with Harry Duhring, Nov. 1, 1950. Duhring went to work for the *Post-Dispatch* business department in 1888.

[71] Memorandum [1906], Pulitzer Papers (CU). The paper claimed publicly a circulation of 30,000 in 1884, but records in the Pulitzer Papers make no such claim this early.

[72] *Journalist*, April 5, 1884.

Financially, too, the *Post-Dispatch* continued to be extremely profitable—though it trailed the *Globe-Democrat*. In 1883 it earned $120,000, the highest profits yet attained, and it remained at or near this figure for most of the decade.[73] This prompted Pulitzer to exclaim to a balky lieutenant years later that in 1885 his St. Louis property brought him $100,000, although there was "no proprietor or compet[ent] manager" on the scene, "only a *good* editor." [74]

After he bought the *World* Pulitzer rarely returned to St. Louis, and his visits were brief. He set the pattern in July 1883, a few weeks after the purchase of the New York paper, when he appeared in the city for a single day. "He was so well pleased with the prosperity of the *Post-Dispatch* that he did not think it necessary to give it much of his personal attention." [75] Yet he was always proud of the paper where he forged the style of journalism which, in New York, was to make him famous as the man who did more "toward setting the pattern of modern journalism than anyone else." [76] Sometimes in a fit of frustration in later years he thought of selling the *Post-Dispatch*— in 1885 he dickered with George Fishback, a St. Louis journalist— but in the end he could never bring himself to part with it.[77] And soon after he left he ordered Dillon to run on the masthead: "ST. LOUIS POST-DISPATCH. Published by the Post-Dispatch Publishing Co. Joseph Pulitzer, President."

Equally proud of its publisher, on May 31, 1883, the *Post-Dispatch* boasted:

> Under its new management the New York *World* has in two weeks increased its circulation more than thirty-five per cent.

---

[73] *Missouri Press Association, Annual Proceedings*, 1884, p. 52; *Journalist*, Dec. 13, 1884. The *Globe-Democrat* made $150,000 the same year.

[74] Joseph Pulitzer to ? [1905], Pulitzer Papers (CU). In 1886 the *Post-Dispatch* earned $85,000 and the *World* $500,000, prompting one of the Rothschilds to observe that "if Joseph Pulitzer had chosen to be a banker, he would have been one of the world's greatest." (*Editor & Publisher, A Journal for Newspaper Makers*, LXXVII [Aug. 22, 1944].) Willard Bleyer remarked: "During a little less than half a century, since the time when Pulitzer reached Boston, a penniless immigrant, he had amassed a fortune which, according to the final appraisal [in 1911], amounted to more than $18,650,000. This was unquestionably the largest fortune ever made in America through the editing and publishing of newspapers." Bleyer, *Main Currents in History of American Journalism*, p. 351.

[75] *Spectator*, Aug. 4, 1883. Despite outward appearances, this was far from the case. Although he failed to come to St. Louis very often Pulitzer maintained close touch with the *Post-Dispatch* through a flood of weekly reports sent to him by his editors and managers in St. Louis. See *Pulitzer Papers* deposited at Columbia University and the Library of Congress.

[76] Mott, p. 430.

[77] Charles Gibson to Joseph Pulitzer, Jan. 2, 1885, May 21, 1885, Oct. 11, 1885, Nov. 1, 1885; George W. Fishback to Joseph Pulitzer, Nov. 2, 1885, Pulitzer Papers (CU). Fishback was a prominent newspaperman in St. Louis at the time. See Hart, *History of St. Louis Globe-Democrat*, ch. 9 *passim*.

It has long been the settled belief of this office that a New York edition of the POST-DISPATCH would take Gotham by storm . . . and soon spread its beaming influence over the entire Union.[78]

Perhaps the highest—if somewhat grudging—praise of all came from two of Pulitzer's old rivals in St. Louis. In 1907, at an anniversary dinner, Charles W. Knapp, publisher of the St. Louis *Republic,* as the old *Republican* was renamed, declared that Pulitzer combined the traits of a superb businessman with the "intellectual grasp . . . [of] a powerful editor." [79] And in 1917, a member of the city's oligarchy which the *Post-Dispatch* had fought for so long admitted to a friend that Joseph Pulitzer was "the most successful newspaper man America has ever seen." [80]

In just four and a half years Pulitzer created a newspaper whose sensational and entertaining style attracted to it a mass city readership. Adapting, developing, and exploiting ideas and trends already evident in the "new journalism," his *Post-Dispatch* became an astounding business success almost overnight. The greatest significance of the *Post-Dispatch,* however, was that once Pulitzer turned his attention exclusively to journalism, it mobilized the middle class elements of St. Louis into a dynamic movement of reform. As it turned out, the struggle was long and bitter, as the allied forces of political corruption and economic privilege were strongly entrenched, but "the red thread of continuous policy" which became such a striking characteristic of *Post-Dispatch* journalism after 1880 guaranteed a constant campaign in the future until, in the first decade of the next century success began to crown its efforts. The age of progressivism in St. Louis and Missouri, which eradicated Butlerism and tamed the monopolies, had its roots in the late 1870s and early 1880s when the tough little *Post-Dispatch* began publication.

---

[78] *Post-Dispatch*, May 31, 1883.
[79] *Anniversary Dinner, Post-Dispatch*, May 10, 1907.
[80] John F. Lee to David R. Francis, Oct. 15, 1917, David R. Francis Papers.

Bibliography

Unpublished Collections, Private Papers, and Documents

James O. Broadhead Papers, Missouri Historical Society, St. Louis, Mo.
William Vincent Byars Papers, Missouri Historical Society, St. Louis, Mo.
Thomas T. Crittenden Papers, Missouri Historical Society, St. Louis, Mo.
David Rowland Francis Papers, Missouri Historical Society, St. Louis, Mo.
Albert G. Lincoln, Diary, St. Louis *Post-Dispatch.*
Miscellaneous Newspaper Collection, Missouri Historical Society, St. Louis, Mo.
Missouri Press Association: Annual Proceedings, 1884. St. Louis, Mo.
Joseph Pulitzer Papers, Columbia University, New York.
Joseph Pulitzer Papers, Library of Congress, Washington, D.C.
Collins Thompson Papers, Private Collection, St. Louis, Mo.

Newspapers

St. Louis *Evening Chronicle,* 1880-83.
St. Louis *Evening Dispatch,* 1864-78.
St. Louis *Evening Post,* 1878.
St. Louis *Globe-Democrat,* 1878-83.
Missouri Republican (St. Louis, Mo.), 1878-83.
St. Louis *Post-Dispatch,* 1878-83 and subsequent issues.
St. Louis *Times,* April 15, 1908.

Periodicals

The American Journalist: A Magazine for Professional Writers. St. Louis, 1883-84.
The Billiard Reporter. Chicago, June 1928.
Bulletin of the Missouri Historical Society. St. Louis, 1944—
The Criterion. St. Louis, 1882-83, 1896-97.
Editor & Publisher: A Journal for Newspaper Makers. New York, 1901-12.
The Fourth Estate: A Newspaper for the Makers of Newspapers. New York, 1894-1900.
Harper's New Monthly Magazine. New York, 1884, 1888.

Harper's Weekly: A Journal of Civilization. New York, XXVI (Nov. 4, 1882).

The Harvard Graduates Magazine. Boston, XI (1902-1903).

Holiday Magazine. New York, VIII (Oct. 1950).

The Hornet. St. Louis, 1880-83.

Inland Printer. Chicago, II (1884).

The Journalist. New York, 1884-1900.

Leslie's Monthly Magazine. New York, 1904.

The Life. St. Louis, 1889-90, 1892-96.

McClure's Magazine. New York, XIX (May-Oct. 1902).

Missouri Historical Review. Columbia, Mo., 1902–

National Editorial Journalist. Indianapolis, 1888.

New England Magazine: An Illustrated Monthly (New Series). Boston, V (1892).

P-D Notebook. St. Louis, 1948-56 (monthly publication of Pulitzer Publishing Company).

Page One. St. Louis, 1948 (St. Louis Chapter, *American Newspaper Guild,* annual pamphlet).

Pearson's Magazine. New York, XXI (1909).

Printers' Ink: A Journal for Advertisers. New York, 1891.

Reedy's Mirror. St. Louis, 1894-1910.

The Spectator. St. Louis, 1880-92.

The Typographical Journal. Indianapolis, 1896-1911.

Union Printer. New York, 1884-98. (Sometimes called *The Boycotter.*)

The Whip. St. Louis, 1885-97.

Unpublished Works

Brown, Dorothy Grace. "Early St. Louis Newspapers, 1808-1850." Unpub. M.A. diss. (Washington University, 1931).

Clevenger, Homer. "Agrarian Politics in Missouri, 1880-1896." Unpublished Ph.D. dissertation, University of Missouri, Columbia, Mo., 1940.

Reynolds, William Robinson. "Joseph Pulitzer." Unpublished Ph.D. dissertation, Columbia University, 1950.

Soraghan, Catherine Virginia. "The History of St. Louis, 1865-1876." Unpublished M.A. dissertation, Washington University, St. Louis, 1936.

Stevens, Walter B. MS biography of David R. Francis.

General Reference Works

N. W. Ayer & Sons American Newspaper Annual and Directory. Philadelphia, 1880-1909.

Bowie, Robert R., ed. *Government Regulation of Business: Cases from the National Reporter System.* Brooklyn, 1949.

Gould's St. Louis Directory. Gould Directory Company. St. Louis, 1870-1883.

Hyde, William and Howard L. Conard. *Encyclopedia of the History of St. Louis.* 4 vols. New York, 1899.

Johnson, Allen and Dumas Malone, eds. *Dictionary of American Biography.* 21 vols. New York, 1928-1937.

Barclay, Thomas S., "Emil Preetorius," XV, 185.

Dilliard, Irving. "Erastus Wells," XIX, 638-39.

Dilliard, Irving. "John Scullin," XVI, 527.

Lee, John M. "John A. Cockerill," IV, 256.

Shoemaker, Floyd C. "James Overton Broadhead," III, 58-59.

Villard, Oswald Garrison. "Joseph Pulitzer," XV, 260-63.

Williams, Walter. "George Knapp," X, 448-49.

Williams, Walter. "Joseph McCullagh," XII, 5.

Kelsoe, William A. *St. Louis Reference Record.* St. Louis [1927].

Pettingill's Newspaper Directory and Advertisers' Hand-Book for 1878. New York, 1878.

Who Was Who in America, 1897-1942. Chicago, 1942.

Books

Allen, Robert S., ed. *Our Fair City.* New York, 1947.

Amory, Cleveland. *The Last Resorts.* New York, 1948.

Archer, Addison. *American Journalism from the Practical Side.* New York, 1897.

Barclay, Thomas S. *The Liberal Republican Movement in Missouri, 1865-1871.* Columbia, Mo., 1926.

————. *The Movement for Municipal Home Rule in St. Louis.* University of Missouri Studies, XVIII, No. 3. Columbia, Mo., 1943.

Barnard, Harry. *Rutherford B. Hayes and His America.* Indianapolis, 1954.

Barrett, Don C. *The Greenbacks and Resumption of Specie Payments, 1862-1879.* Harvard Economic Studies, XXXVI. Cambridge, Mass., 1931.

Barrett, James Wyman. *Joseph Pulitzer and His World.* New York, 1941.

Bartow, Edith Merwin. *News and These United States.* New York, 1952.

Baumhoff, Richard G. *The Dammed Missouri Valley.* New York, 1951.

Belcher, Wyatt Winton. *The Economic Rivalry Between Chicago and St. Louis, 1850-1880.* New York, 1947.

Bent, Silas. *Newspaper Crusaders.* New York, 1939.

Binkley, Wilfred E. *American Political Parties: Their Natural History.* New York, 1947.

Bisland, Elizabeth. *The Life and Letters of Lafcadio Hearn.* 2 vols. New York, 1906.

Bleyer, Willard Grosvenor. *Main Currents in the History of American Journalism.* Boston, 1927.

Bogart, Ernest L. and Charles M. Thompson. *The Industrial State, 1870-1893. The Centennial History of Illinois,* IV. Springfield, Ill., 1920.

Brann, William Cowper. *The Complete Works of Brann the Iconoclast.* 12 vols. New York, 1898.

Breihan, Carl W. *The Complete and Authentic Life of Jesse James.* New York, n.d.

Bryce, James. *The American Commonwealth.* 2 vols. Third edition, New York, 1901.

Buck, Solon J. *The Agrarian Crusade. The Chronicles of America Series,* XLV. New Haven, 1920.

———. *The Granger Movement: A Study of Agricultural Organization and Its Political, Economic and Social Manifestations, 1870-1880. Harvard Historical Studies,* XIX. Cambridge, Mass., 1913.

Byars, William Vincent. *An American Commoner: The Life and Times of Richard Parks Bland.* Columbia, Mo., 1900.

Chapin, Charles. *Charles Chapin's Story: Written in Sing Sing Prison.* New York, 1920.

Clancy, Herbert J. *The Presidential Election of 1880.* Jesuit Studies, IX. Loyola University, Chicago, 1958.

Clemens, Samuel (Mark Twain). *Life on the Mississippi.* Harper and Brothers edition. New York, 1917.

Cochran, Negley D. *E. W. Scripps.* New York, 1933.

Coolidge, Louis A. *Ulysses S. Grant.* Boston, 1917.

Cox, James. *Old and New St. Louis.* St. Louis, 1894.

———, ed. *Notable St. Louisans in 1900.* St. Louis, 1902.

Crittenden, H. H. *The Crittenden Memoirs.* New York, 1936.

Croy, Homer. *Country Cured.* New York, 1943.

———. *Jesse James Was My Neighbor.* New York, 1949.

Culmer, F. A. *A New History of Missouri.* Mexico, Mo., 1938.

Destler, Chester McArthur. *American Radicalism, 1865-1901: Essays and Documents.* Connecticut College Monographs, III. New London, 1946.

Dorsey, Florence. *The Road to the Sea: The Story of James B. Eads and the Mississippi River.* New York, 1947.

Dreiser, Theodore. *A Book About Myself.* New York, 1926.

Dyer, David P. *Autobiography and Reminiscences.* St. Louis, 1922.

Eckenrode, H. J. *Rutherford B. Hayes: Statesman of Reunion (American Political Leaders).* New York, 1930.

Fine, Sidney. *Laissez Faire and the General-Welfare State: A Study of Conflict in American Thought. University of Michigan History and Political Science Series,* XXIX. Ann Arbor, 1956.

Fish, Carl Russell. *The Rise of the Common Man (A History of American Life,* VI). Arthur M. Schlesinger and Dixon Ryan Fox, eds. New York, 1927.

Fuess, Claude. *Carl Schurz: Reformer (American Political Leaders).* New York, 1932.

Gardner, Gilson. *Lusty Scripps: The Life of E. W. Scripps, 1854-1926.* New York, 1932.

Garwood, Darrell. *Crossroads of America: The Story of Kansas City.* New York, 1948.

Geiger, Louis. *Joseph W. Folk of Missouri* (University of Missouri Studies, XXV, No. 2). Columbia, Mo., 1953.

Goldman, Eric F. *Rendezvous with Destiny.* New York, 1952.

Green, Constance McLaughlin. *American Cities in the Growth of the Nation.* Harper Colophon edition, New York, 1965.

Grodinsky, Julius. *Jay Gould: His Business Career, 1867-1892.* Philadelphia, 1957.

Hart, Jim Allee. *A History of the St. Louis Globe-Democrat.* Columbia, Mo., 1961.

Heaton, John L. *The Story of a Page.* New York, 1913.

Hofstadter, Richard. *The American Political Tradition and the Men Who Made It.* New York, 1948.

———. *The Age of Reform: From Bryan to F.D.R.* New York, 1955.

Hutton, Graham. *Midwest at Noon.* Chicago, 1946.

Ireland, Alleyne. *Joseph Pulitzer.* New York, 1914.

Jackson, William Rufus. *Missouri Democracy: A History of the Party and Its Representative Members—Past and Present.* Chicago, 1935.

Jennings, John J. *Theatrical and Circus Life; Or, Secrets of the Stage, Green-Room and Sawdust Arena.* St. Louis, 1883.

———. *The Widow Magoogin.* New York, 1900.

Johns, George S. *Joseph Pulitzer: His Early Life in St. Louis and His Founding and Conduct of the Post-Dispatch up to 1883.* Reprinted from the *Missouri Historical Review*, 1931-32. St. Louis, 1932.

Johns, Orrick. *Time of Our Lives: The Story of My Father and Myself*. New York, 1937.

Johnson, Mrs. Charles P. *Notable Women of St. Louis: 1914*. St. Louis, 1914.

Johnson, Icie F. *William Rockhill Nelson and the Kansas City Star*. Kansas City, 1935.

Jones, J. Elbert. *A Review of Famous Crimes Solved by St. Louis Policemen*. St. Louis [1916].

Jones, Robert W. *Journalism in the United States*. New York, 1947.

Josephson, Matthew. *The Politicos, 1865-1896*. New York, 1938.

———. *The Robber Barons, 1861-1901*. New York, 1934.

Juergens, George. *Joseph Pulitzer and the New York World*. Princeton, 1966.

Kargau, E. D. *Mercantile, Industrial and Professional St. Louis*. St. Louis, n.d.

King, Homer W. *Pulitzer's Prize Editor: A Biography of John A. Cockerill, 1845-1896*. Durham, N.C., 1965.

Kirschten, Ernest. *Catfish and Crystal*. New York, 1960.

Koenigsberg, M. *King News*. Philadelphia, 1941.

Land, John E. *St. Louis: Her Trade, Commerce and Industries, 1882-3*. St. Louis, 1883.

Lasch, Christopher. *The New Radicalism in America, 1889-1963: The Intellectual as a Social Type*. New York, 1965.

Lee, Alfred McClung. *The Daily Newspaper in America: The Evolution of a Social Instrument*. New York, 1937.

Lieb, Frederick G. *The St. Louis Cardinals: The Story of a Great Baseball Club*. New York, 1944.

Lingley, Charles Ramsdell. *Since the Civil War*. New York, 1926.

Love, Robertus. *The Rise and Fall of Jesse James*. New York, 1926.

McCabe, Charles R., ed. *Damned Old Crank*. New York, 1951.

McCloskey, Robert Green. *American Conservatism in the Age of Enterprise*. Cambridge, Mass., 1951.

McDonald, Gen. John. *Secrets of the Great Whiskey Ring, and Eighteen Months in the Penitentiary*. St. Louis, 1880.

McDougall, Walt. *This is the Life!* New York, 1926.

McKelvey, Blake. *The Urbanization of America, 1860-1915*. New Brunswick, N.J., 1963.

McRae, Milton A. *Forty Years in Newspaperdom*. New York, 1924.

McReynolds, Edwin C. *Missouri: A History of the Crossroads State*. Norman, Okla., 1962.

Mann, Arthur. *Yankee Reformers in the Urban Age.* Cambridge, Mass., 1954.

Markham, James. W. *Bovard of the Post-Dispatch.* Baton Rouge, 1954.

Masterson, V. V. *The Katy Railroad and the Last Frontier.* Norman, Okla., 1952.

Meriwether, Lee. *My Yesteryears: An Autobiography.* Webster Groves, Mo., 1942.

Merrill, Horace Samuel. *Bourbon Democracy of the Middle West, 1865-1896.* Baton Rouge, 1953.

Mitchell, Stewart. *Horatio Seymour.* Cambridge, Mass., 1938.

Moody, John. *The Railroad Builders.* New Haven, 1919.

Morison, Samuel Eliot. *Three Centuries of Harvard.* Cambridge, Mass., 1946.

Mott, Frank Luther. *American Journalism: A History, 1690-1960.* Third edition, New York, 1962.

Nevins, Allan. *Grover Cleveland: A Study in Courage (American Political Leaders).* New York, 1933.

———. *The War for the Union (I, The Improvised War, 1861-1862).* 2 vols. New York, 1959.

O'Brien, Frank M. *The Story of the Sun.* New York, 1928.

Payne, George Henry. *History of Journalism in the United States.* New York, 1920.

Peterson, Norma L. *Freedom and Franchise: The Political Career of B. Gratz Brown.* Columbia, Mo., 1965.

Putzel, Max. *The Man in the Mirror: William Marion Reedy and His Magazine.* Cambridge, Mass., 1963.

Randall, James G. *The Civil War and Reconstruction.* Boston, 1937.

Reavis, Logan U. *St. Louis: The Future Great City of the World and Its Impending Triumph.* St. Louis, 1881.

Reedy, William Marion. *The Makers of St. Louis.* St. Louis, 1906.

Rhodes, James Ford. *History of the United States from the Compromise of 1850.* 8 vols. New York, 1899-1914.

Riegel, Robert. *The Story of the Western Railroads.* New York, 1926.

Rosewater, Victor. *History of Co-operative News-gathering in the United States.* New York, 1930.

Ross, E. D. *The Liberal Republican Movement.* New York, 1910.

Rossiter, Clinton. *Conservatism in America.* New York, 1955.

Scharf, J. Thomas. *History of St. Louis City and County.* 2 vols. Philadelphia, 1883.

Schlesinger, Arthur Meier. *Paths to the Present.* New York, 1949.

————. *The Rise of the City, 1878-1898 (A History of American Life,* Arthur M. Schlesinger and Dixon Ryan Fox, eds. X). New York, 1933.

Seitz, Don C. *Joseph Pulitzer: His Life and Letters.* New York, 1924.

Shoemaker, Floyd C. *Missouri and Missourians.* 5 vols. Chicago, 1943.

————. *Missouri: Mother of the West.* Chicago, 1930.

Slayback, Alonzo W. *A Memorial Volume.* St. Louis, 1883.

Snider, Denton, J. *The St. Louis Movement in Philosophy, Literature, Education, Psychology, with Chapters of Autobiography.* St. Louis, 1920.

Steffens, Lincoln. *The Autobiography of Lincoln Steffens.* New York, 1931.

————. *The Shame of the Cities.* New York, 1904.

Stevens, Walter B. *St. Louis: The Fourth City.* 3 vols. St. Louis, 1909.

Stevenson, Elizabeth. *Lafcadio Hearn.* New York, 1961.

Stone, Melville. *Fifty Years a Journalist.* New York, 1923.

Taft, William H. *Missouri Newspapers.* Columbia, Mo., 1964.

Tansill, Charles Callan. *The Congressional Career of Thomas Francis Bayard, 1869-1885.* Washington, D.C., 1946.

Tarbell, Ida M. *The Nationalizing of Business (A History of American Life,* IX). Arthur M. Schlesinger and Dixon Ryan Fox, eds. New York, 1936.

Thomas, Augustus. *The Print of My Remembrance.* New York, 1922.

Unger, Irwin. *The Greenback Era: A Social and Political History of American Finance, 1865-1879.* Princeton, 1964.

Van Deusen, Glyndon C. *Horace Greeley: Nineteenth Century Crusader.* Philadelphia, 1953.

Wade, Richard C. *The Urban Frontier: The Rise of Western Cities, 1790-1830.* Harvard Historical Monographs, XLI. Cambridge, Mass., 1959.

Weisberger, Bernard A. *Reporters for the Union.* Boston, 1953.

Wetmore, Claude. *The Battle Against Bribery.* St. Louis, 1904.

Williams, Sara Lockwood. *Twenty Years of Journalism: A History of the School of Journalism of the University of Missouri, Columbia, Missouri, U.S.A.* Columbia, Mo., 1929.

Williams, Walter. *The State of Missouri: An Autobiography.* Columbia, Mo., 1904.

———— and Floyd C. Shoemaker. *Missouri: Mother of the West.* 2 vols. Chicago, 1930.

Wittke, Carl. *The German-Language Press in America.* Lexington, Ky., 1957.

———. *We Who Built America.* New York, 1939.

Woodward, C. M. *A History of the St. Louis Bridge.* St. Louis, 1881.

Yeakle, M. M. Sr. *The City of St. Louis of To-day: Its Progress and Prospects.* St. Louis, 1889.

Zink, Harold. *City Bosses in the United States: A Study of Twenty Municipal Bosses.* Durham, N.C., 1930.

Articles

Anon. "History of Woman Suffrage in Missouri," *Missouri Historical Review,* XIV (Jan. 1920), 294-95.

Barclay, Thomas S. "The Liberal Republican Movement in Missouri," *Missouri Historical Review,* XX (Oct. 1925), 3-78; XXI (Jan. 1926), 232-62; (April 1926), 406-37; (July 1926), 515-63; (Oct. 1926), 59-108.

Barnett, George E. "The Printers: A Study in American Trade Unionism," *American Economic Association Quarterly,* October 1909.

Basso, Hamilton. "St. Louis," *Holiday Magazine,* VIII (Oct. 1950), 34-49, 72-76.

Beuttenmuller, Doris Rose Henle. "The Granite City Steel Company: History of an American Enterprise," *Bulletin of the Missouri Historical Society,* X (Jan. 1954), 135-55, 199-282.

Bishop, W. H. "St. Louis," *Harper's New Monthly Magazine,* LXVIII (March 1884), 497-517.

Brann, William Cowper. "Behind the Scenes in St. Louis," *The Complete Works of Brann the Iconoclast,* X, 205-14.

Byars, William Vincent. "A Century of Journalism in Missouri," *Missouri Historical Review,* XV (Oct. 1920), 53-73.

Clevenger, Homer. "The Farmers' Alliance in Missouri," *Missouri Historical Review,* XXXIX (Oct. 1944), 24-44.

———. "Railroads in Missouri Politics, 1875-1887," *Missouri Historical Review,* XLIII (April 1949), 220-236.

Creelman, James. "Joseph Pulitzer—Master Journalist," *Pearson's Magazine,* XXI (March 1909), 229-56.

Crisler, Robert M. "Missouri's 'Little Dixie,'" *Missouri Historical Review,* XLII (Jan. 1948), 130-39.

De Menil, Alexander N. "A Century of Missouri Literature," *Missouri Historical Review,* XV (Oct. 1920), 74-125.

Edmundson, Charles. "Pulitzer's Prime Minister," *Page One* (St. Louis, 1948), pp. 25-26.

Hart, Jim A. "The Missouri Democrat, 1852-1860," *Missouri Historical Review,* LV (Jan. 1961), 127-41.

"History of Woman Suffrage in Missouri," *Missouri Historical Review,* XIV (Apr. 1920), 281-384.

Kelsoe, William A. "Missourians Abroad, No. 10: Florence D. White," *Missouri Historical Review*, XVI (Jan. 1922), 247-52.

Hurd, Carlos. "St. Louis: Boundary Bound," *Our Fair City*. Robert S. Allen, ed. New York, 1947.

Hyde, William. "Newspapers and Newspaper People of Three Decades," *Missouri Historical Society Collection*, I, No. 12, 1896.

Irwin, Will. "The American Newspaper, Part III," *Collier's Magazine*, XLVI (Feb. 18, 1911 , 14-17, 24, 27.

Leach, J. A. "Public Opinion and the Inflation Movement in Missouri, 1875-1879," *Missouri Historical Review*, XXIV (April 1930), 379-413; (July 1930), 568-85; XXV (Oct. 1930), 116-46.

McAuliffe, Joseph J. "From Blacksmith to Boss," *Leslie's Monthly Magazine*, LVIII (Oct. 1904), 635-39.

McClure, C. H. "A Century of Missouri Politics," *Missouri Historical Review*, XV (Jan. 1921), 315-36.

Meriwether, Lee. "A Century of Labor in Missouri," *Missouri Historical Review*, XV (Oct. 1920), 163-75.

Munford, F. B. "A Century of Missouri Agriculture," *Missouri Historical Review*, XV (Jan. 1921), 277-97.

Rammelkamp, Julian S. "St Louis in the Early 'Eighties," *Bulletin of the Missouri Historical Society*, XIX (July 1963), 328-39.

Riegel, Robert E. "The Missouri Pacific Railroad to 1879," *Missouri Historical Review*, XVIII (Oct. 1923), 3-26.

———. "The Missouri Pacific, 1879-1900," *Missouri Historical Review*, XVIII (Jan. 1924), 173-96.

Settle, William A., Jr. "The James Boys and Missouri Politics," *Missouri Historical Review*, XXXVI (July 1942), 412-29.

Seymour, Harold. "St. Louis and the Union Baseball War," *Missouri Historical Review*, LI (April 1957), 257-69.

Stark, Louis. "The Press and Labor News," *The Press in the Contemporary Scene. The Annals of the American Academy of Political and Social Science*, CCXIX. Philadelphia, 1942.

Steffens, Lincoln. "Enemies of the Republic: The Political Leaders Who Are Selling Out the State of Missouri, and the Leading Business Men Who Are Buying It—Business as Treason—Corruption as Revolution," *McClure's Magazine*, XXII (April 1904), 587-99.

Stevens, Walter B. "Joseph B. McCullagh," *Missouri Historical Review*, XXV (Oct. 1930), 3-9; (Jan. 1931), 245-53; (April 1931), 425-31; (July 1931), 576-84; XXVI (Oct. 1931), 40-53; (Jan. 1932), 153-62; (April 1932), 256-66; (July 1932), 375-86; XXVII (Oct. 1932), 50-62; (Jan. 1933), 151-56; (April 1933), 257-61; (July 1933), 337-43; XXVIII (Oct. 1933), 38-42; (Jan. 1934), 125-29; (April 1934), 206-10.

———. "The New Journalism in Missouri," *Missouri Historical Review*, XVII (April 1923), 321-30; (July 1923), 470-78; XVIII (Oct. 1923), 55-63; (Jan. 1924), 197-211; (April 1924), 404-14; (July 1924), 553-61; XIX (Oct. 1924), 105-13; (Jan. 1925), 325-37; (April 1925), 427-37; (July 1925), 675-88.

———. "The Tragedy of the St. Louis Republic," *Missouri Historical Review*, XXII (Jan. 1928), 139-49.

"The Summer Beer Gardens of St. Louis," *Bulletin of the Missouri Historical Society*, IX (July 1953), 391-95.

Wallace, Agnes. "The Wiggins Ferry Monopoly," *Missouri Historical Review*, XLII (Oct. 1947), 1-19.

Warner, Charles Dudley. "Studies of the Great West, VIII—St. Louis and Kansas City," *Harper's New Monthly Magazine*, LXXVII (Oct. 1888), 748-62.

Wetmore, Claude M. and Lincoln Steffens. "Tweed Days in St. Louis," *McClure's Magazine*, XIX (Oct. 1902), 577-86.

White, Z. L. "Western Journalism," *Harper's New Monthly Magazine*, LXXVII (Oct. 1888), 678-99.

Wilson, Harry. "McCullagh of the Globe-Democrat," *Page One* (St. Louis, 1948), pp. 9, 24.

Woodward, C. M. "The City of St. Louis," *New England Magazine: An Illustrated Monthly*, V (New Series), Jan. 1892, 602-604.

Pamphlets, Brochures, and Addresses

Birthday Anniversary Dinner, Given by Joseph Pulitzer, April 10, 1907. St. Louis, 1907.

Bradley, Richard T. and David Leubrie. *The Illustrated Guide to the Exposition and Great Fair [of] St. Louis.* St. Louis, 1878.

Padman, Donald: A Sketch of Mr. Padman's Life. St. Louis [1920].

Ross, Charles G. and Carlos F. Hurd. *The Story of the St. Louis Post-Dispatch.* St. Louis, 1940.

St. Louis Through a Camera. St. Louis, 1899.

Two Anniversaries: The World, 1883-1903; The St. Louis Post-Dispatch, 1878-1903. New York, 1903.

The World, Its History and Its New Home. New York, 1890.

Interviews

Behymer, Frank A. Numerous interviews. Reporter on *Post-Dispatch* beginning in 1888.

Collins, Richard J. March 20, 1951. Reporter on *Post-Dispatch* beginning in 1887.

Dietrich, Byron J. Numerous interviews. In advertising dept. of *Post-Dispatch* since 1909.

Duhring, Harry. Nov. 1, 1950, Dec. 29, 1950. Beginning in 1888, in advertising department of *Post-Dispatch.*

Lincoln, Albert G. Dec. 15, 1949. From 1895, circulation manager of *Post-Dispatch.*

McAuliffe, Daniel J. W. Jan. 17, 1951. Managing editor of St. Louis *Republic,* 1900-20.

McDonald, Gertrude. Jan. 16, 1951, Feb. 5, 1951. Granddaughter of John A. Dillon.

Peers, Mary E. Dec. 8, 1950. Employee of *Post-Dispatch,* beginning in 1894.

Saportas, Frances Cabanne. March 10, 1951. Early society editor of *Post-Dispatch.*

Wray, J. Edward. Jan. 17, 1951. Sports editor of *Post-Dispatch* for 50 years.

Private Letters

Beadel, Mrs. H. L. Feb. 9, 1951. Daughter of John A. Dillon.

Behymer, Frank A. Numerous letters.

Burke, Harry. Nov. 12, 1953. Veteran reporter, St. Louis *Globe-Democrat.*

Jones, R. Bruce. Feb. 8, 1954. N. W. Ayer & Sons officer.

McAuliffe, Daniel J. W. Oct. 9, 1950, Oct. 23, 1950, Nov. 10, 1953.

Saportas, Frances Cabanne. April 2, 1951.

Index

Abbott, Emma, 98
Adams, Charles Francis, 9n
advertising, 38, 42, 60-61, 76n, 88, 106-108, 164, 202-204, 203n; legal, 1, 12, 42, 203; personals, 107, 107n; rates, 203, 203n; real estate, 202; "telephone offices," 204; wants, 68-69, 69n, 107, 107n, 203-204
afternoon journalism, 37-38, 61
agrarians, 100, 141-47, 151, 213, 223-24, 229-34, 236
Alexandria: British bombardment of, 178
Allen, Gerard B., 52
Allen, Thomas, 45-47, 60, 154-55, 219-20, 284
Allison, W. L., 40
Allison, William B., 129
Alton, Ill., 279
American Association, 181
American Journalist, 195, 195n
American Social Science Association, 68n
Americans of Gentle Birth and Their Ancestry, 194
Anzeiger des Westens, 71
Appleton Book Co., 264
Armory Hall Democrats, 159-61, 238
Arnold, Simon J., 3
Arthur, Chester A., 124-25, 212
assessments, 55n, 242
Atlanta *Constitution*, 190
Atlantic & Pacific RR., 48

Babcock, Orville E., 135, 135n
Baltimore, 195n, 237, 266n
Baltimore *Gazette*, 91; *Herald*, 90n; *News*, 90n
barges, 24, 224, 280
Barrett, James Wyman, 62n
baseball news, 180-81
Bashaw, T. P., 228
Bayard, Thomas F., 130-31
Beadel, Mrs. H. L., 14n
Beecher, Henry Ward, 191
beer gardens, 24, 25, 259
Belleville, Ill., 96, 201
Bennett, James Gordon, Sr., 98n
Bennett, James Gordon, Jr., 66, 100
Bessemer furnaces, 25n
Bigney, Frank, 97n, 171
Blaine, James G., 115, 119, 122, 123-24, 301
Blair, Frank, Jr., 39, 285n, 286

Bland, Richard P., 44, 128-29
Bland-Allison Act, 129
Bleyer, Willard, 302n
Blong, Andrew, 159
"Bloody Island," 28
"bloody shirt," 116, 119-20, 148
Bly, Nellie, 104n
Board of Equalization, 30, 145, 230, 230n
"bob-tail" cars, 271-72
Boland, Morgan, 214, 251
boodling: in St. Louis, 58, 268n, 295-97
Boston, 195n
Bothwell, Sam, 90
Bourbons, 80, 125, 142-43, 145, 228, 230, 231. See also oligarchy
Bowman, Frank J., 111-12
boxing news, 180
branch system, 105, 201
brewing industry: in St. Louis, 25
Brickenor, William A., 67n
Bridge, Eads, 14, 21, 26, 29, 226n; monopoly, 277-78, 277n, 295; and *Republican*, 33
Broadhead, James O., 81, 160, 285n, 285-88, 294
Brooklyn, 158n
Brooklyn *Eagle*, 300n
Brooks, John A., 221
Brown, Anthony, 12
Brown, B. Gratz, 8, 9, 9n, 33
Brown, Joseph, 48
Brown Stockings, 181
buildings: *Evening Post*, 19; *Dispatch*, 12; *Post and Dispatch*, 62-63; *Post-Dispatch*, 63, 204-205, 205n; fire damage to, Post-Dispatch building, 108
Bureau of Labor Statistics, *see* Labor Statistics
Burnes, James, 227
businessmen: and Democratic Party, 125
businessmen's revolt, 143-44, 213, 223, 238
Butler, Edward, 152-55, 156, 158-59, 160, 161n, 162, 216, 223, 233n, 250-51n, 251, 256-57n, 260, 284, 286, 295, 296. See also Dark Lantern
Byars, William V., 128n

"cabbage wards," 158, 158n, 160-61
cable car line, 274, 274n
California, 58, 230
Cameron, Don, 122

INDEX

Edison, Thomas, 267
editions, 87, 95-97
Edwards, John N., 177-78
Edwardsville, Ill., 201
Egypt, 178-79
election of 1880: in St. Louis, 149n, 155; in Missouri, 149n, 150; national, 137-38
election of 1881: in St. Louis, 162
election of 1882: in St. Louis, 287, 294; in Missouri, 227; national, 209
electoral commission of 1877, 11, 129
electricity: in St. Louis, 267-68
elevated railroad, 274-76
Eliot, Charles W., 212
Elks Club, 292n
Ernst, John, 159
Evening Chronicle, 105n, 109-11, 184, 196n, 199, 200, 288n
Evening Dispatch: history of, 1-2, 38-40; auction of, 1-4; combined with *Post*, 19; circulation, 12; debts, 111-12; advertising, 203
Evening Post: founding of, 15-17; and *Globe-Democrat*, 15; and wire franchise, 2n; no press, 15; circulation, 15; editorial policy, 16; anti-gambling crusade, 17, 53; combined with *Dispatch*, 18; importance to Joseph Pulitzer, 19n; first of New Journalism in afternoon in St. Louis, 38; staff, 65; features, 73, 96
Evening Star, 13, 18, 19, 62, 86, 86n
Ewing, William L., 161n, 161-62, 167n, 267, 284
exchange page, 182n
Exposition building, 260-61, 295
extras, 87

factory and mine inspections, 235-36
"Farmers' Club," 228, 228n, 229, 230, 233
farm implement industry: in St. Louis, 25
farm revolt: in Missouri, 30-31, 44, 127, 142-43, 213, 223, 226, 228-34
Farmington, Mo. *Times,* 63
Faust, Tony, 268
features: in *Post-Dispatch,* 73-74, 87, 96-97, 182-90
"fellow servant" rule, 234n, 236, 236n
Ferguson, Mo., 201
Field, Eugene, 36
Filley, Chauncey I., 3, 16, 36, 123, 137n, 149, 150-51, 227n
finances: of *Post-Dispatch,* 61-62, 106-107, 202, 205-206, 302
fire department, 245-47, 246n

Fishback, George, 302
Folk, Joseph W., 257n, 295
Ford, Bob, 176
Forest Park, 23, 273, 275
format: of *Post-Dispatch,* 68-69, 108
Four Courts, 22, 67, 85, 99, 253, 289, 291
Foy, Peter, 39
Fraley, Moses, 242
France, William C., 74
Francis, David R., 218n
Frank Leslie's magazine, 175
fraternal clubs, 97
freight bureau, 279-80
Fremont, John C., 39
"Frenchtown," 21
fund raising, 100-104, 103n

Galvin, James ("Red"), 13, 13n, 68n
gambling: in St. Louis, 55-56, 58, 163-64, 214-16, 250-56, 250-51n, 256-57n
Garfield, James A., 123-24, 133, 138, 138n, 169, 173-75, 173n, 179, 200
gas rates, 48 266n
Germans: in St. Louis, 23
gerrymander: by Democrats, 218-19
Gettysburg, 134, 137
Gilmore, Patrick S., 261n
Gleason Case, 171
Globe-Democrat, 4, 14, 15, 17, 18, 19n, 37, 61, 65, 69, 87, 88, 90, 96, 99, 99n, 104-106, 157, 166n, 176n, 182, 192, 193, 193n, 195, 293, 297, 299; advertising in, 69, 107n, 203, 203n; and "bloody shirt," 119; and circulation, 37, 202; editorial policy, 36-37; and elevated railways, 275, 275n; and *Evening Post*, 15, 38; founded, 35; and gambling, 53, 74, 215, 250-51, 253, 255, 256; and [St. Louis] Gas-light Co., 51; and greenbacks, 146; leading St. Louis paper, 35n, 301-302; and monopoly, 266, 269n; and news policy, 36; and *Post and Dispatch*, 19, 28n, 42; and *Post-Dispatch*, 108; and press, 204n; and printers, 198; and reforms, 239n; wages of reporters on, 195n; and *Missouri Republican*, 37; and Slayback shooting, 288, 291n; and Union Depot Co., 283n
Glover, John M., 286
Glover, Samuel, 45-47, 286, 288
gossip column, 188-90, 189n
"Gossip on the Streets," 189
Gould, Jay, 99, 224-25, 225n, 226-28, 236, 276, 277, 277n, 280, 285, 287, 297, 298n

grain inspection: in Illinois, 231n; in Missouri, 228, 231-33
grain trade: in St. Louis, 22, 24, 58, 143, 231-34
Gramercy Park, 170
Granger movement, 10, 27, 30-31, 127, 142-43, 213, 228n, 231, 232n, 234
Grant, Ulysses S,. 99, 114-15, 117, 122-24, 133-35, 135n, 285n
Great Britain, 178
"Great Illusion," 25, 57-59, 237
Greeley, Horace, 9, 98n
Greenback movement, 31, 40, 44, 127-28, 127n, 128n, 143, 146-47, 146n, 150, 213, 227, 227n, 228n
Guiteau, Charles J., 175

Halstead, Murat, 112
Hamburg, 4
Hamilton, Ohio *True Telegram*, 91
Hancock, Winfield S., 133-34, 137-38, 139n
Hannibal & St. Joseph RR., 147, 224
Hardy, James, 156
Harper's Weekly, 134, 289
Harris, Charles, 68n
Harris, Joel Chandler, 189, 190
Harris, Thomas D., 68n, 86
Harris, William T., 264
Harrison, Edwin, 189
Harvard Annex, 14n
Harvard College, 13, 14n, 212
Haseltine, Nellie, 169-70
Hayes, Rutherford B., 67n, 115-116, 122, 125, 130
Hearn, Lafcadio, 91
"Herdic" coaches, 274, 274n
"high license," 257-59, 258n
high school, 263n
Hobbs, William, 193
Hoblitzelle, Clarence, 218, 218n
Hockaday, John A., 147
Hoe, Richard Co., 204
Home Circle Club, 172, 293n
Hong Kong, 122
Hornet, The, 90n, 162, 252n, 254, 255n, 277n
House of Delegates (St. Louis), 242, 244, 258-59, 259n, 268n, 272, 295
Houser, Daniel M., 4, 18n, 34, 37, 157, 157n, 297
Howard, Frankie, 253
Huber, William, 159
Hutchins, Stilson, 39-40, 91
Hyde, William, 2, 33, 46, 228

Illinois, 26, 60, 85, 101, 201, 226, 231, 258n, 276, 279

Illinois-St. Louis Bridge Co., 14, 155
Illinois Town, 28
illustrations, 98-100, 98n, 99n, 173-75, 177, 179, 180, 255
Imperial Club, 172, 293n
"In the Corridors," 189n
income tax, 211, 211n
Indiana, 26, 87, 135, 137n, 209, 279
Indianapolis, 135
Independence, Mo., 177
insurance companies: in St. Louis, 76-78
Iowa, 60, 87, 128, 220n
Ireland, 99, 100
Iron Mountain RR., 45, 154, 224
Irish: in St. Louis, 22
Irish Relief Fund, 100

James, Frank, 30, 176, 178
James, Jesse, 30, 176-178
Jefferson City, 7, 67, 80, 141, 145, 193, 213, 228, 229, 233, 258, 265
Jefferson City *Tribune*, 229n
"Jenkins," 56, 56n
Jennings, John J., 51, 65, 65n, 73n, 90, 172, 189-90, 190n, 195n
Jockey Club, 87
Johns, George S., 5n, 193, 193n, 251n
Johnson Act, 252-53, 252n, 255
Johnson, Charles P., 5, 5n, 39, 251-52, 253, 255n
Journal of Agriculture, 129n
journalism, afternoon, 37-38, 61, 195n; penny, 110; personal, 45; political, 32-33; "stunt," 104
Juergens, George, 109n
Julian, George, 114n

Kansas, 58, 60, 223; temperance movement in, 220n
Kansas City, 29, 176, 234, 236
Kansas City *Star*, 290, 299; *Times*, 12, 230, 285n
Kansas, Texas & Pacific RR., 224
Kappner, Ignatz, 90n, 106, 197, 301
Kelley, George, 182
Kelley, James, 182n
Kennard, Samuel, 261
Kennett, Ferdinand, 248, 253
Kentucky, 279
"Kerry Patch," 22, 65, 187, 247
Kerwin, Daniel, 159, 160, 216, 260, 296
Kirkwood, Me., 201
Knapp, Charles W., 67n, 303
Knapp, George, 32, 32n
Knapp, John, 32
Koenigsberg, M., 34n